A

MYTHOLOGICAL,

ETYMOLOGICAL,

AND

HISTORICAL

DICTIONARY;

EXTRACTED FROM THE

ANALYSIS

OF

ANCIENT MYTHOLOGY.

By WILLIAM HOLWELL, B.D.

VICAR OF THORNBURY, GLOUCESTERSHIRE,

AND

PREBENDARY OF EXETER.

LONDON:

PRINTED FOR C. DILLY, IN THE POULTRY.

M.DCC.XCIII.

TO

Sir GEORGE BAKER, Bart.

F.R.S. F.A.S.

PRESIDENT

OF THE ROYAL COLLEGE OF PHYSICIANS,

AND

PHYSICIAN IN ORDINARY

TO THEIR MAJESTIES;

THE FOLLOWING COMPILEMENT

IS,

WITH ALL RESPECT AND REGARD,

DEDICATED,

BY HIS MOST OBEDIENT

AND OBLIGED SERVANT,

WILLIAM HOLWELL.

[v]

PREFACE.

---

*T*HE ANALYSIS OF ANCIENT MYTHOLOGY *in three Volumes Quarto, by* JACOB BRYANT, Efq; *is a work of the deepeft erudition, and moft juftly held in the higheft eftimation by the learned. It is alfo a work of Price, and therefore not eafily obtained by many, however defirous they may be of gaining further infight into Sacred and Profane hiftory, &c. For which reafon it was thought, that a Compendium of the above work (together with fome extracts from a treatife by the fame learned Gentleman, intitled,* Obfervations upon the ancient hiftory of EGYPT) *would not be unacceptable. Moreover it was apprehended, that the better way to execute this defign would be by throwing fuch Compendium into the form of a Dictionary, as thereby the feveral Articles would be more readily found and confulted; paffages which*

A   *occur*

occur upon the fame fubject in different places of the three Volumes, would be better feen and comprehended. An Index is fubjoined, which though unufual, was judged to be neceffary; there being many Terms of importance, which could not properly make diftinct articles of themfelves: and many, which although they do, yet occurring in other places, give further infight into the fubject.

The Compiler flatters himfelf that the following fheets will be of fome fervice to the young beginner, as a kind of Initiatory Compendium: to the more learned and informed they are fubmitted only as fhort references to the Original Work. Some repetitions muft neceffarily occur; fhould there be any unneceffary ones, let fuch be imputed to the Compiler's inattention; for which he begs the Reader's pardon.

That the common Pantheons, Theogonies, &c. are filled with the greateft inconfiftencies, and abfurdities, not to add indecencies, every one muft be fenfible: alfo, how very difficult it is to eradicate opinions imbibed in the early part of life. Of this Mr. B. *very juftly complains, and laments that fo many learned men, fuch as* Cumberland, Ufher, Pearfon, Petavius, Scaliger, *with many others, and among the foremoft the great* Newton, *could not entirely diveft themfelves of their prejudices.*

We

We are, *says he* (*Vol. I. p.* 453.) fo imbued in our childhood with notions of Mars, Hercules, and the reft of the celeftial outlaws, that we fcarce ever can lay them afide. We abfolutely argue upon Pagan principles: and though we cannot believe the fables, which have been tranfmitted to us; yet we forget ourfelves continually; and make inferences from them, as if they were real. In fhort, till we recollect ourfelves, we are Semipagans. It gives one pain to fee men of learning, and principle, debating which was the Jupiter who lay with Semele; and whether it was the fame, that outwitted Amphitrion. This is not, fays a critic, the Hermes who cut off Argus's Head; but one of later date who turned Battus into a ftone. I fancy, fays another, this was done, when Iö was turned into a Cow, &c. Were it not invidious, I could fubjoin names to every article, which I have alledged; and produce numberlefs inftances to the fame purpofe.

The defign of Mr. BRYANT *in the* ANALYSIS *will be beft known from his own words. Preface to Vol. I. p. vi.* It has been obferved by many of the learned, that fome particular family betook themfelves very early to different parts of the world; in all which they introduced their rites, and religion, together with the cuftoms of

their

their country. They reprefent them as very knowing and enterprizing; and with good reafon. They were the firft who ventured upon the feas, and undertook long voyages. They fhewed their fuperiority and addrefs in the numberlefs expeditions, which they made, and the difficulties, which they furmounted. Many have thought that they were colonies from Egypt, or from Phenicia; having a regard only to the fettlements made in the weft. But colonies of the fame people are to be found in the moft extreme parts of the eaft: where we may obferve the fame rites and ceremonies, and the fame traditional hiftories, as are to be met with in their other fettlements. The country called Phenicia could not have fufficed for the effecting all, that is attributed to thefe mighty adventurers.——— They were the defcendants of Chus: and called **Cuthites,** and Cufeans. They ftood their ground at the general migration of families: but were at laft fcattered over the face of the earth. They were the firft apoftates from the truth; yet great in worldly wifdom. They introduced, wherever they came, many ufeful arts; and were looked up to, as a fuperior order of beings: hence they were ftiled Heroes, Dæmons, Heliadæ, Macarians. They were joined in their expeditions by other nations; efpecially by the collateral branches of their family, the Mizraim, Caphtorim,

Caphtorim, and the fons of Canaan. Thefe were all of the line of Ham, who was held by his pofterity in the higheft veneration. They called him Amon: and having in procefs of time raifed him to a divinity, they worfhiped him as the Sun; and from this worfhip they were ftiled Amonians.——They were a people, who carefully preferved memorials of their an-ceftors; and of thofe great events, which had preceded their difperfion. Thefe were defcribed in hieroglyphics upon pillars and obelifks: and when they arrived at the knowledge of letters, the fame accounts were religioufly maintained in their facred archives, and popular records. *v. Eufeb. Præp. Evang. l. 1. c. 9. p. 32.*

Upon enquiry we fhall find, that the Deluge was the grand epocha of every ancient kingdom. It is to be obferved, that when colonies made any where a fettlement, they ingrafted their antecedent hiftory upon the fubfequent events of the place. And as in thofe days thefe could carry up the genealogy of their princes to the very fource of all; it will be found, under whatever title he may come, that the firft king in every country was Noah. For as he was mentioned firft in the genealogy of their princes, he was in after-times looked upon as a real monarch: and reprefented as a great traveller, a

A 3

mighty

mighty conqueror, and fovereign of the whole earth. This circumftance will appear even in the annals of the Egyptians; and though their chronology has been fuppofed to have reached beyond that of any nation, yet it coincides very happily with the accounts given by Mofes.

I fhall endeavour to compare facred hiftory with profane, and prove the general affent of mankind to the wonderful events recorded. My purpofe is not to lay fcience in ruins; but inftead of defolating to build up, and rectify what time has impaired: to diveft mythology of every foreign and unmeaning ornament; and to difplay the truth in its native fimplicity: to fhew, that all the rites and myfteries of the Gentiles were only fo many memorials of their principal anceftors; and of the great occurren-cies, to which they had been witneffes. Among thefe memorials the chief were the ruin of mankind by a flood; and the renewal of the world in one family. They had fymbolical reprefentations, by which thefe occurrencies were commemorated: and the ancient hymns in their temples were to the fame purpofe. They all related to the hiftory of the firft ages; and to the fame events, which are recorded by Mofes.—

As

As the Amonians betook themſelves to regions widely ſeparated; we ſhall find in every
place, where they ſettled, the ſame worſhip and
ceremonies, and the ſame hiſtory of their anceſtors. There will alſo appear a great ſimili-
tude in the names of their cities and temples:
ſo that we may be aſſured, that the whole was
the operation of one and the ſame people.—

It appears to me, as far as my reading can
afford me light, that moſt ancient names, not
only of places, but of perſons, have a manifeſt
analogy. There is likewiſe a great correſpondence to be obſerved in terms; and in the titles,
which were of old beſtowed on magiſtrates and
rulers. The ſame obſervation may be extended
even to plants, and minerals, as well as to animals; eſpecially to thoſe, which were eſteemed
at all ſacred. Their names ſeem to be com-
poſed of the ſame, or ſimilar elements; and bear
a manifeſt relation to the religion in uſe among
the Amonians, and to the deity, which they
adored. This deity was the Sun : and moſt of
the ancient names will be found to be an aſſemblage of titles beſtowed upon that luminary.
Thence there will appear a manifeſt correſpondence between them.—

If

If it should be asked; How is it possible that the descendants of one branch only should extend themselves so widely, and perform such mighty works, as are attributed to them? the answer given is, That the sons of Chus were an ingenious and knowing people; and at the same time very prolific. They combined with others of the sons of Ham, and were enabled very early to carry on an extensive commerce, and to found many colonies; so that they are to be traced in the most remote parts of the earth.—We are informed by Moses (*Gen. x.*) when he enumerates the principal persons, by whom the earth was peopled, that Ham had thirty and one immediate descendants, all of them heads of families, when Shem had but twenty six; and fourteen only are attributed to Japhet.—Note: on account of the comparative smallness to be observed in the line of Japhet, that encouraging prophecy was given, that Japhet should be enlarged. *God shall enlarge Japhet.* This, within these few centuries, has been wonderfully completed. Vol. III. p. 175.

Towards the close of the third volume (p. 595.) Mr. BRYANT *has introduced two prayers taken from the Zend-Avesta (the former from vol. 3. p. 17. the latter from vol. 2. p. 424.) As they*

are

*are extremely curious, it is prefumed that the Reader
will not be difpleafed to fee them here alfo inferted.*

The Flood was looked upon as a great bleffing; for from thence proceeded the plenty,
with which the prefent world is bleft. There
feems to have been a notion, which of old prevailed greatly, that the Antediluvian world was
under a curfe, and the earth very barren. Hence
the ancient Mythologifts refer the commencement of all plenty, as well as of happinefs in
life, to the æra of the Deluge. And as the
means by which mankind, and the fruits of the
earth were preferved, had been of old defcribed
in hieroglyphics; people in time began to lofe
fight of the purport; and miftake the fubftitute
for the original. Hence inftead of the man of
the earth, and the great hufbandman, they payed
their veneration to the fymbolical ox: and all
that had been tranfmitted concerning the lunar
machine, they referred to the moon in the heavens. This we learn from the prayers of the
Brahmins and the Parfees; in which may be
difcovered the traces of fome wonderful
truths.

NEAESCH

NEAESCH de la LUNE.

A PRAYER of the PARSEES.

Je prie Ormuſd, je prie * Amſchaſpands, je prie la Lune, qui garde la ſemence du Taureau; je prie en regardant en haut, je prie en regardant en bas.—Que la Lune me ſoit favorable, elle, qui conſerve la ſemence du Taureau : qui a été créé unique, et dont ſont venus des animaux de beaucoup d'eſpeces: je lui fais izeſchné, et néaeſch, &c. Je prie Ormuſd, je prie Am-ſchaſpands, je prie la Lune, qui garde la ſemence du Taureau, &c. Comme la Lune croît, elle décroît auſſi: pendant quinze jours elle croît; pendant quinze jours elle decroît. Lorſqu'elle croît, il faut la prier; lorſqu'elle decroît, il faut la prier: mais ſur-tout, quand elle croît, on doit la prier. Lune, qui augmentes, et diminues, toi Lune, qui gardes la ſemence du Taureau, qui es ſainte, pure, et grande, je te fais izeſchné.

Je regarde en haut cette Lune: j'honore cette Lune, qui eſt élevée: je regarde en haut la lumiere de la Lune : j'honore le lumiere de la Lune, qui eſt élevée.

* *Les ſept premieres Eſprits céleſtes.*

Lorſque

Lorſque la lumiere de la Lune répand la chaleur, elle fait croitre les arbres de couleur d'or; elle multiplie la verdure ſur la terre avec la nouvelle Lune, avec la pleine Lune viennent toutes les productions.

Je fais izeſchné à la nouvelle Lune, ſainte, pure et grande; je fais izeſchné à la pleine Lune, ſainte, pure et grande.

Je fais izeſchné à la Lune, qui fait tout naitre, qui eſt ſainte, pure et grande; j'invoque la Lune, qui garde la ſemence du Taureau, &c.

A PRAYER

Of the ſame nature to the ſacred BULL.

ADRESSEZ votre priere au Taureau excellent: adreſſez votre priere au Taureau pur: adreſſez votre priere à ces principes de tout bien: adreſſez votre priere à la pluie, ſource d'abondance: adreſſez votre priere au Taureau devenu pur, célefte, ſaint, qui n'as pas été engendré; qui eſt ſaint.

Lorſque

Lorſque Djé ravage le monde, lorſque l'impur Aſchmogh affoiblit l'homme, qui lui eſt dévoué, l'eau ſe répand en haut : elle coule en bas en abondance : cette eau ſe réſout en mille, en dix mille pluies. Je vous le dis, ô pur Zoroaſtre, que l'envie, que la mort ſoit ſur la terre : l'eau frappe l'envie, qui eſt ſur la terre : elle frappe la mort, qui eſt ſur la terre. Que le Dew Djé ſe multiplie; ſi c'eſt au lever du ſoleil, qu'il déſole le monde, la pluie remet tout dans l'ordre, lorſque le jour eſt pur.—Si c'eſt la nuit, que Dje déſole le monde, la pluie rétablit tout au (gâh) Oſchen. Elle tombe en abondance : alors l'eau ſe renouvelle, la terre ſe renouvelle; les arbres ſe renouvellent, la ſanté ſe renouvelle; ce qui donne la ſanté, ſe renouvelle.

Lorſque l'eau ſe répand dans le fleuve Voorokeſché, il s'en éleve (une partie, qui tombant en pluie) mêle les grains avec la terre, et la terre avec les grains. L'eau, qui s'éleve, eſt la voie de l'abondance : les grains donnés d'Ormuſd naiſſent, et ſe multiplient. Le Soleil, comme un courſier vigour-ouz, s'elance avec majeſté du haut de l'effrayant *Albordj*, et donne la lumiere au monde. De cette montagne, qu'il poſſede, montagne donnée d'Ormuſd, il domine ſur le monde; qui eſt la voie aux deux deſtins, ſur les grains donnés en abondance,

abondance, et fur l'eau. Soit qu'auparavant vous ayez fait le mal, ou qu'auparavant vous ayez lû la parole excellente, je fais naître pour vous tout en abondance; moi, qui vous lave alors avec l'eau.—Par l'eau je purifie mille chofes, que je vous ai données, &c.

Lorfquè l'eau fe répand dans le fleuve Voo-rokefché, il s'en éleve une partie, qui tombant en pluie, mêle les grains avec la terre, et la terre avec les grains. L'eau, qui s'eleve, eft la voie de l'abondance. Tout croît, tout fe multiplie fur la terre donnée d'Ormufd. La Lune, dé-pofitaire de la femence du Taureau, s'elance avec majefté du haut de l'effrayant *Albordj*, et donne la lumiere au monde. De cette montagne, qu'elle poffede, montagne donnée d'Ormufd, elle domine fur le monde, qui eft la voie aux deux deftins, fur les grains donnés en abondance, et fur l'eau, &c. &c.

(P. 475.) Lorfque l'eau fe répand dans le fleuve Voorokefché, &c.—Ce cruel Djé, maître de magie, s' éleve avec empire; il veut exercer fa violence; mais la pluie éloigne Afcheré; éloigne Eghoüere, elle éloigne Eghranm, &c. elle éloigne l'envie, elle éloigne la mort.—Elle
éloigne

éloigne la * Couleuvre ; elle éloigne le men-
fonge ; elle éloigne la méchanceté, la corruption,
et l'impureté, qu' Ahriman a produites dans les
corps des hommes.

We may perceive, that the Moon, and the
facred Steer, were two principal emblems in the
Pagan world. And though the mythology of
the more eaftern countries has hitherto appeared
obfcure, and even unintelligible : yet by the
light, which we have obtained from the writings
of Greece, it is now rendered fufficiently plain :
fo that the main purport may be eafily underftood. It is to be obferved alfo (fee the quo-
tations, p. 588, &c. of Vol. III.) that there were
two perfons alluded to under the fame character,
called in the Zend-Avefta l'Homme Taureau :
both of whom were looked upon as the authors
of the human race. It is probable, that the
like was intended in the Apis and Mneuis of
Egypt : and that in thefe characteriftics, there
was originally a twofold reference. By the for-

* *In another part of the Zend-Avefta mention is made of this
Serpent. Ormufd, le jufte Juge, dit à Nériöfengh.—Après
avoir fait ce lieu pur, dont l' éclat fe montroit au loin, je marchois
dans ma grandeur ; alors la Couleuvre m' apperçut : alors cette
Couleuvre, cette Abriman, plain de mort, produifit abondamment
contre moi, neuf, neuf fois neuf, neuf cens, neuf mille, quatre-
vingt-dix mille envies. Vendidad Sadi. vol. ii. p. 429.*

mer

mer was perhaps fignified our great Progenitor, from whom all mankind has been derived; by the other was denoted the Patriarch in whom the world was renewed.

The Compiler is fenfible, that feveral learned perfons differ from Mr. BRYANT *as to fome of his Pofitions and Etymologies. All however, who have a real regard for the Sacred Writings, and the Truths therein contained, muft furely feel themfelves highly endebted to Him: as he omits no opportunity of elucidating thofe Writings, and of confirming their Authenticity.*

I cannot conclude, without returning my fincere thanks to Sir GEORGE BAKER *for the honour he has done me, by allowing me to fubmit the following Compliment to Public View under the Protection of his Name.*

A MYTHO-

A

MYTHOLOGICAL, &c.

DICTIONARY.

A.

A B,

SIGNIFIES a Father, fimilar to אב of the
Hebrews. It is often found in compofition,
as in Ab-ël, Ab-on, Ab-or. I. 12. Although it
generally fignifies a Father, yet it fometimes means
a Serpent, and is indifferently pronounced Ab,
Aub, Ob. I. 477. Ab and Adir, means the
Serpent deity Addir, the fame as Adorus. I. 49.
Abaddir, which fhould be expreffed Abadir,
and feems to be a variation of Ob-Adur, fignifies
the Serpent god *Orus*. Saturn was fuppofed to
have fwallowed a ftone, called Ab-Adur, from
the deity reprefented by it. I. 476.

ABADON, or ABADDON,

Signifies the Sun, the fame with Apollo. I. 18.
Apocal. c. 9. v. 11.—c. 20. v. 2. It alfo fignifies
Serpens Dominus, vel *Serpens Dominus Sol.* I. 477.

ABDERUS,

The founder of Abdera, is fuppofed to have fallen a victim to horfes. II. 38. Abdera, fignifies the place of Abdir, a contraction of Abadir, the Serpent deity Ad-ur, or Adorus. I. 34.

AB-EL-EON,

Pater Summus Sol, or *Pater Deus Sol*. Voffius. with reafon thinks that the Abelion of the eaft was the Apollo of Greece and Rome. Apollo was anciently Apello, as Homo, Hemo, &c. I. 17. Voff. de Idol. v. 1. l. 2. c. 17. p. 391.

ABIS,

The Egyptian Crane, for its great fervices, was held in high honour, being facred to the god of light: the Greeks expreffed it Ibis. It was alfo called Keren; by the Greeks Γερανος, the noble bird, being moft honoured of any. It was a title of the Sun himfelf. I. 47.

ABOR, ABORUS, ABORRAS,

Compounded from Or or Ur, a title often given to Chus by his defcendants. I. 13. The Sun was called Abor, the parent of light. I. 105.

ABYLA,

From Ab-El, *Parens Sol*.

ACH,

Was a term of honour among the Babylonians, and the reft of the progeny of Chus; and occurs continually in the names of men and places, which have any connection with their hiftory. v. Uch.

AC-CAPH-EL.

i. e. The right noble, or facred rock of the Sun; hence the Greek Ακεφαλοι, όι εν· ςηθεσιν οφθαλμους εχοντες. Herodot. v. Cunocephali.

ACHAD,

ACHAD, ACHON,

Were names of the deity, the Sun, and many
cities and countries were hence denominated.
Achad was one of the firſt cities in the world,
Gen. x. 10. The city Niſibis was named Achad
and Achar. Geogr. Hebr. Ext. Michaelis, p. 227.
Acon, in Palæſtine, is ſaid to have been ſo named
in honour of Hercules, the chief deity in thoſe
parts. I. 83. Cadmus, the ſame as Ham, is a
compound of Achad-Ham, rendered by the Greeks
Acadamus and Academus, and contracted Cadmus,
from whom the Academia at Athens was undoubtedly denominated. II. 157.

ACHAMIN,

So was ſtiled the great founder of the Perſic
monarchy, rendered by the Greeks Αχαιμενης,
Achæmenes: all his family afterwards had the
title of Αχαιμενιοι and Αχαιμενιδαι. They all of
them univerſally eſteemed themſelves the children
of the Sun; though they were likewiſe ſo called
from their worſhip, *ſolis cultores*; but the title was
generally more limited, and confined to the royal
race of the Perſians, who were looked upon as the
offspring of the Sun. I. 84. Plato (in Alcibiad.)
truly ſays that the Heraclidæ in Greece, and the
Achæmenidæ among the Perſians were of the ſame
ſtock. II. 67.

ACHERON,

A river in Egypt; the Charonian branch of the
Nile. There was a river of the ſame name in
Epirus, and a lake, Acheruſia; for a colony from
Egypt ſettled here, and the ſtream was of as foul a
nature as that near Memphis. There was alſo one
of the ſame name in Elis and in Pontus, and the
ſame rites were obſerved in honour of the Θεος μυιαγρος, that were practiſed in Cyrene. I. 108.

B 2   Acheronian

Acheronian and Acherufian plain; fo was called the region of the Catacombs; and likewife the Elyfian; and the ftream which ran by it, had the name of Acheron. They are often alluded to by Homer, and other poets, when they treat of the region of departed fouls. The Amonians conferred thefe names upon other places, where they fettled, in different parts of the world. I. 439. 504. This river, like Cocutus, was looked upon as a melancholy ftream; ΑχερονΊα πολυστονον, Theoc. Id. 17. A temple of the fun called Achor-on, gave name to the river, on whofe banks it ftood. II. 24. Acheron, Ops, Helle, Gerys (Ceres, *Varro*) Terra, Demeter, are by Hefychius V. Αχειρω, faid to be the fame. II. 38.

ACHOR, ACHUR.

Under thefe titles the Sun was worfhiped by the Ethiopians or Cuthites, as well as by the Egyptians; and they efteemed him the Θεος απομυιος. Hence we may infer that their country was at firft called Acurana, a compound of Achur-Ain, i. e. the great fountain of light. I. 81. v. Curene. Achor, compounded with Ων, On, another name of the Sun, formed Acharon, the true name of the city in Palæftine, called in our Bible *Ekron*, 1 Sam. c. 6. v. 15. but by the LXX. Αχκαρων. It was denominated from Achor, the god of Flies, worfhiped alfo under the name of Baal-zebub with the fame attribute. I. 83.

ACHOREZ,

Is a compound of Ach-Ares, *magnus Sol*, equivalent to Achorus, another name of the fame deity, and affumed as a title by fome of the Egyptian kings; this latter was expreffed Achor, Achoris, *Ochuras*, *Uchoreus*, which are all the fame name diverfified in different ages, and by different writers. I. 77.
v. Uch.

v. Uch. Acherez, Achencherez, names of two very ancient Egyptian kings. Ib.

ACHILLES.

The Shield of Achilles in Homer seems to have been copied from some Pharos, which the Poet had seen in Egypt: for he is continually alluding to the customs, as well as to the history, of that kingdom. And it is evident, that what he describes on the central part of the shield, is a map of the earth, and of the celestial appearances.

Ἐν μεν Γαιαν ἰ]ευξ', εν δ' Ουρανον, εν δε Θαλασσαν.
Ἐν δ' ἰ]ιθει ΠΟΤΑΜΟΙΟ μεγα σθενος ΩΚΕΑΝΟΙΟ.

I. 393. v. Maps.

ACMON,

So was called the chief Cyclopian deity, and under this title was worshiped in Phrygia, where was a city and district called Acmonia. There was a sacred grove upon the Thermodon called Acmonium, which was held in great repute. He was looked upon by some as the offspring of Heaven; by others worshiped as Ouranus, and Cœlus, the Heaven itself. Acmonides is supposed to have been his son; but this word seems not to be a patronymic, but an Amonian compound Acmon-Ades, Acmon the god of light, the same as Cœlus, Cronus and Osiris. Acmon and Acmonides were the same person. He seems to have been worshiped of old at Tiryns, that ancient city of Greece, whose towers were said to have been built by the Cyclopians. He is represented by Callimachus H. in Dian. v. 146, as the θεος προπυλαιος, or guardian deity of the place:

. . . . . τοιος γαρ αει Τιρυνθιος Αχμων
Ἐσ]ηχε προ πυλεων . . . .

here Αχμων is not an adjective (*indefessus*) but the same god, that was afterwards called Hercules, and

particularly

particularly ſtiled Tirynthius, to whom the poet
here alludes under a more ancient name.   I. 513.

Ac-Mon, *Nobilis Lunus,* ⎱
Ac, Ach, βασιλικος.   ⎰ II. 447. n.

ACRISIUS,

The father of Danae, is ſaid to have been buried
in the Acropolis at Argos.   The name is a meta-
theſis of Arciſius, or Arcaſius, by which is meant
the great Arkite, the perſon there worſhiped.
He was called Argus, Arcas, Arcaſius, and compounded Arcas-Ionas: theſe terms were changed
to Acriſius, and Acriſionæus; whence the people
in the Argive colonies were ſtiled Acriſionei Coloni.
II. 453.

AD,

Is a title, occurring very often in compoſition, as
in Ad-Or, Ad-On, hence Adorus, Adon, Adonis;
it is ſometimes found in compoſition with itſelf, as
Adad, and was then uſed for a ſupreme title, with
which both deities and gods were honoured.   The
Amonians generally formed their ſuperlative by
doubling the poſitive.

Ada was the feminine; by which title Plutarch
(Apopth. p. 180,) mentions a queen of Caria; a
ſacred title belonging to the chief Babyloniſh goddefs; Αδα, ηδονη· και υπο Βαϐυλωνιων η 'Ηρα. Heſych.
One of Eſau's wives was called Adah, daughter of
Elon the Hittite.   Gen. c. 36. v. 2.   Ad and Ada
ſignified *firſt*, more laxly, a Prince, or Ruler; therefore Adad anſwers to the Moſt High, or Moſt
Eminent.   I. 23.

ADAS,

Eſteemed the god of the infernal regions; expreſſed by the Ionians, &c. Ades and Hades, and
by other nations Ait and Atis.   I. 114.

Aᴅ-Eᴇs,

AD-EES, AD-IS,

Compounds, v. *Ees*, *Is*; hence the Hades of the
Greeks; and the Atis, Attis, of the Afiatics; names
of the fame deity, the Sun. Many places were
hence denominated; as a city in Africa; a river
Adefa, near Choma in Afia minor. Alfo one of
the chief cities in Syria. I. 26.

AD-HAM,

Or Adam contracted; Ham was often fo ftiled,
which has occafioned much miftake. There were
many places named Adam, Adama, Adamah, Ada-
mas, Adamana, which had no relation to the Protoplaft, but were by the Amonians denominated
from the head of their family. I. 25. Adam is
fometimes found reverfed, as in Amad, a Canaan-
itifh town; Hamad as well as Hamon in Galilee;
alfo Amida in Mefopotamia. Ib. n.

ADIONA,

A deity conftituted from the words Ad or Ada,
Ionah compounded. According to our method of
rendering the Hebrew term, it is called *Idione*; this
Idione or *Adione* was probably the *Dione*, Διωνη, of
the Greeks; the deity who was fometimes looked
upon as the mother of Venus; at other times the
goddefs herfelf, ftiled *Dione*, or *Venus Dionæa*; fhe
was faid to have been the mother of Niobe; and under
the name of Pleione, was efteemed the mother of
the Pleiades. This Idione is the fame deity as
occurs in St. Auguftine under the name of Adeona.
II. 315.

ADON,

Or Adonis, the true name of the river Eridanus.
I. 376.

ADONIS,

Under which title befides others, the Canaanites
worfhiped their chief deity the Sun. I. 371.

B 4   Or

Or Thamuz. He was the fame as Thamas and
Ofiris in Egypt. I. 372. His rites, and the la‑
mentations on his account at Sidon and Byblus,
were copies of the mourning for Ofiris, and repre‑
fented in the fame manner. II. 188.

ÆACEUM,

At Epidaurus; near it was a hill, reputed to
have been the tomb of the hero Phocus. This
Æaceum was an inclofure planted with olive trees
of great antiquity : and at a fmall degree above
the furface was an altar, facred to Æacus. To di‑
vulge the fecrets of this altar was an high profana‑
tion. Before this facred feptum was the fuppofed
tomb, confifting of a mound of raifed earth, fenced
round with a border of ftone work, and a large
rough ftone was placed upon the top of all. Thefe
in reality were high altars, with their facred τεμενη,
which had been erected for divine worfhip in the
moft early times. I. 466.

ÆETES,

Suppofed to be the name of a king of Colchis,
who is faid to have detained the famous Golden
Fleece, and to have impofed almoft impracticable
terms upon the Argonauts; which however being
performed by Jafon, and the Fleece obtained, the
king purfues them by fea, and precludes their re‑
treat by feizing the pafs at the Thracian Bofphorus.
But Strabo fays that Scepfius maintained, that Æetes
lived far in the eaft upon the ocean. (L. 1. p. 77,
80.) Mimnermus fpeaks of the city of Æetes as
lying in a region, where was the chamber of the
Sun, and the dawn of day, at the extremities of
the eaftern world. (Strabo, L. 1. p. 80.) II. 476.
Strabo takes notice (p. 77,) that there ftill remain‑
ed a city called Aia upon the Phafis; and the na‑
tives retained notions, that Æetes once reigned in
that country. Ib. 484.

ÆGEON,

ÆGEON.

The Nile being of old called Oc-Gehon, and having many branches, or arms, gave rise to the fable of the sea-monster Ægeon, whom Ovid (Metam. L. 2.) represents as supporting himself upon whales:

—— balænarumque prementem
Ægæona suis immania terga lacertis.
I. 392.

ÆNON,

From Ain-On, *Fons Solis*, near to Salem. (q. v.) I. 51. Mines were held sacred; and like fountains were denominated from Ænon and Hanes, those titles of the Sun. Ib. 90.

ÆON.

Nonnus, L. 41. v. 31, describes him as a prophet, who had renewed his youth, and been washed in the waters of justice; wherefore he took off the veil of equity, the bandage and covering, under which Beroe had been, before her delivery, confined.

Χερσι δε γηραλινσιν ες αρ]ι]οχου χροα κουρης
Σπαργανα, πεπλα δικης, ανεκουφισε συν]ροφος Αιων,
Μαν]ις επισσομενων, οτι γηραος αχθος αμειβων,
'Ως οφις αδρανεων φολιδων σπειρημα τιναξας,
Εμπαλιν η]βησει, λελουμενος οιδμασι Θεσμων.

Here the Patriarch is plainly figured under the type of Time growing young again. II. 362.

ÆTNA,

Very truly derived by Bochart from Aituna, *fornax*, as being a reservoir of molten matter. The hill and the city were by the natives called Inessus; which is a compound of Ain-Es, like Hanes in Egypt; and signifies a Fountain of Fire. It is called Ennesia by Diodorus; who says, that this

name

name was afterwards changed to Ætna. Strabo (l. 6.) expreſſes the name Inneſa, and informs us that the upper part of the mountain was ſo called. I. 194.

AGAMEDES,

And Trophonius his brother, were Cyclopians, q. v. and were famous for their great ſkill in architecture. I. 502.

AGAMEMNON,

And Menelaus, are ancient titles of the chief deity; the former is ſuppoſed to have been the ſame as Zeus, Æther, Cœlus. He ſeems to have been worſhiped under the ſymbol of a ſerpent with three heads: hence Homer thus deſcribes this hero, Ἰλ. Λ. 38.

Τῆς δ' ἐξ αργυρεος τελαμων ην, αυλαρ επ' αυλῳ
Κυανεος ελελιχλο δρακων· κεφαλαι δε οι ησαν
Τρεις αμφιϲλεφεες, ἰνος αυχενος εκπεφυυιαι. II. 169.

AGE GOLDEN.

. This age of the poets aroſe from a miſtake. What was termed Γενος Χρυϲιον and Χρυϲειον, ſhould have been expreſſed Χυϲιον and Χυϲειον, as it relates to the age of Chus, and to the denomination of his ſons. It is deſcribed as a period of great happineſs; and the perſons, to whom that happineſs is attributed, are celebrated as ſuperior to the common race of men: and upon that account, after their death, they were advanced to be deities. (See Heſiod. Ερ. και Ἡμ. L. 1. v. 109, &c.) The ancients had a high notion of this Golden, or Cuſean age; and always ſpeak of it with great deference, as a time of uncommon equity and happineſs. They indeed take into the account the æra of patriarchal government, when all the world was as yet one family, and under the mild rule of the head of mankind. Aratus ſays (v. 113.) that this was the ſeaſon, when

Aſtræa,

Aſtræa, or Juſtice, appeared perſonally in the world. And he laments, that thoſe excellent perſons, who then flouriſhed, ſhould be ſucceeded by a poſterity ſo degenerate and baſe. (v. 123.)

'Οιην Χρυσειοι Πατερες γενην ελιπονͿο
ΧειροͿερην ;———

By this we find, that not only a particular age, but perſons were ſtyled Χρυσιοι, or Golden. Thoſe who came into Greece, and built the temple at Olympia, are repreſented as Χρυσουν γενος, a Golden race: by which is certainly meant Cuſoan or Cuſean.

The Grecians by rendering what ſhould be Cuſean, Χρυσεον, Chruſean, have been led ſtill farther in characteriſing the times: and to this ſuppoſed Golden Age, which they have embelliſhed with many fictions, they have added an age of Silver, of Braſs, and of Iron.

The Chruſean age being ſubſtituted for the Cuſean, and being alſo ſtiled the æra of the Cuthim (כרם, ſignified Gold and Golden) was the cauſe of theſe after-diviſions being introduced; that each age might be diſtinguiſhed by ſome baſer metal. III. 163.

ΑΓΩΝ, ΑΕΘΛΟΣ, 'ΑΜΙΛΛΑ,

Were all Amonian terms, taken from the titles of the deity, in whoſe honour the games were inſtituted. II. 53.

AI, AIA,

Signifies a Diſtrict or Province; in Egypt often an Iſland; in other parts it was of much the ſame import as Αια among the Greeks, and betokened any region or country; hence ſo many places repreſented as plurals by the Greeks; Athenai, Thebai, Pherai, Patrai, Amyclai, &c. others in eia, as Eleia, Coroneia, Chæroneia. In others it was rendered ſhort, as Æthiopia, Scaria, Cœnia, Oropia, Ellopia,

Ellopia, &c. Sometimes it is found expreſſed by a ſingle letter, ſtill ſubjoined to the proper name Ætna, Arbela, Roma, Nuſa, &c. From hence, and many other inſtances it may be proved, that the Eaſtern people, as well as other nations, had the word in regimine often final: e. g. from Aſſur came Aſſyria; from Ind, India; Lud, Ludia, &c. in which the region is ſpecified by the termination: to ſay Lydia tellus, &c. would be redundant. In the name of Egypt this term preceded, the country being ſtiled Ai-Gupt, Αιγυπίος, the land of the Gupti, al. Cupti, and Copti. The Ionians changed this termination into ﮞ, as in Arene, Cyrene, Thebe, &c. I. 90.

Ai-Mon, a country (Theſſaly) in aftertimes rendered Aimonia. II. 501. v. Mon. Ισις αρχαια, Αιμορια αρχαια.

Ai-Tur. Hence Hetruria ſeems to have been compounded, and to have ſignified the land of Towers. I. 404.

Ai-Ete, Ai-Ata, was the region of Ait, the deity to whom it was ſacred; whence the king of Col-chis was called Aietes; Egypt had the ſame name, expreſſed by the Greeks Αἰλια. Aiete was the diſ-trict, Caiete (v. Cai) was the cave and temple in that diſtrict, where the deity was worſhiped. I. 20. 116. II. 17.

ΑΙΜΟΣ,

A word among the Greeks, of the ſame purport with Λυκος. I. 80.

AIN, AN, EN.

The ſame word differently pronounced, ſignifies a Fountain; it was prefixed to the names of many places, which were ſituated near fountains, and were denominated from them, e. g. Ænon, or the Fountain of the Sun. Here John baptized, John c. 3. v. 23. the name was given long before by the Canaanite.

Canaanite. Many places were ſtiled An-Ait, An-
Abor, Anabouria, Anathon, Anopus, Anorus.
Some of theſe were ſo called from their ſituation ;
others from the worſhip there eſtabliſhed. I. 51.

Wherever the Amonian religion (which dealt
largely in fountain worſhip) was propagated,
names of this ſort will occur; being originally
given from the mode of worſhip eſtabliſhed :
hence Anthedon, Anthemus, Ain-Shemeſh, and
the like. The iſland Ægina was called Oenone,
and Oenopia, probably from its worſhip. As
Divine wiſdom was ſometimes expreſſed Aith-Ain
or Αθηνα; ſo at other times the terms were reverſed,
and a deity conſtituted, called An-Ait. Temples
to this goddeſs occur in many places, where the
rites of fire were particularly obſerved. She was
not unknown to the ancient Canaanites. A temple
called Beth-Anath occurs, Joſhua, c. 1. 19, 38.
I. 52.

AIN-ADES,

The Fountain of Ades, or the Sun, changed to
Ναιαδις, Naiadæ. (q. v.) I. 278.

AIN-APTHA,

The Fountains of Aptha, the god of Fire. I. 278.

AINEIUS, AINESIUS,

Both from Hanes, the deity of Egypt, whoſe
rites may be traced in various places; in Thrace
were places named Aineas, Aineſia, from the ſame
original. I. 200.

AIN EL SHAM,

The Fountain of the Sun.

AIN-OMPHE,

i. e. *Fontes Oraculi.* Theſe terms, which denoted the fountain of the prophetic god, the Greeks
contracted

contracted into Νυμφη, a Nymph, and fuppofed fuch a perfon to be an inferior goddefs, who prefided over the waters. I. 276.

AIR,

Is a City; often expreffed Ar and Ara; hence Arachofia, Arachotus, Aracynthus, Arambis, Aramatha, (Ar-Ham-Aith) Argile, Arzella, Arthedon, cities or regions. I. 91.

AIT, AITH,

Were titles of Ham, or the Sun; terms of great confequence refpecting etymology, and continually occurring in Egyptian names of places, deities and men. Many ancient words in the Greek language were derived from them; e. g. Αιθαλοεν (κεκαυμενον) a compound of Aith-El, Αιθωνα (μελανα, πυρωδη) a compound of Aith-On; and others enumerated by Hefychius. The Sun's difk was ftiled Αιθοψ. Ἱππευων ἑλιχηδον ὁλον πολον Αιθοπι Δισκω. Nonnus. L. 40. v. 371. Ham, as the Sun, was ftiled Ait, and fo was Egypt, the land of Ham; rendered by the Greeks Αιλια; it was alfo called Αιθιοπια, Αερια and Πολαμια. One of the moft ancient names of the Nile was Αιλος.

Ait relates alfo to Fire, Light, Heat, and to the confequences of Heat. As the Heart is to the body, what the Sun is to the world, the fource of heat and life, fo it was called Ηθ Ionice, which the Dorians with more propriety would have called Ath. I. 18.

As Egypt was called Ait and Ai-Ait, by the Greeks expreffed Αιλια, fo, in confequence, the natives were called Αιλιοι and Αιλαι, which was interpreted Eagles. Hence we are told by Plutarch, that fome Eagles or Swans came from the remote parts of the earth, and fettled at Delphi. By thefe birds were undoubtedly meant colonies from Egypt and Canaan. I. 378. Which former was Ai-Gupt alfo; *Gupt,* a Vulture; an Eagle and Vulture being

among

among the Infignia of that country. I. 426. And as Ait fignified among the Egyptians the Heart, this over burning coals was an emblem of Egypt. Ib.

AITHYIA,

A bird fo called, probably a fpecies of Seacoot. It was held very facred, as feveral perfonages were fo called, or had it in the compofition of their names; e. g. Minerva, Orithyia, Idithyia, Ilythyia. II. 454.

AL

Or El, is to this day an Arabian prefix. The Sun is there called Al-Achor (or Alachar). It is in compofition fo like to Hλ, the name of Ἡλιος, the Sun, that it is not always eafy to diftinguifh one from the other. I. 118.

AL-AS,

Amonian terms; hence Gr. Ἁλος, Ἁλας, Ἁλς. And from the fame terms reverfed (As-El) were formed, Lat. Sol, Sal, Salum. I. 30.

ALBA,

Near mount Albanus (denominated Al-Ban from its fountains and baths) was anciently Alban; for the Romans dropped the final n; fo Cuma was Cuman, Pifa Pifan. I. 201.

ALBANI,

Places fo called feem to have had the name from Al-Laban, the Moon, the object of worfhip, contracted to Alban, and rendered with a termination Albanus. There feems no doubt, but that the Arkite idolatry prevailed in moft of thefe places. Ἱερον Μηνος Αρχαιου εν τοις Αλβανοις. Stra. l. 12. Upon mount Albanus in Latium a facred fhip was reverenced; which Dion. Caf. l. 39. calls the fhip

of

of Juno, or Jonah. From hence we may infer, that it was a copy of the ſhip of Iſis, called Baris; that memorial of the Ark in Egypt. II. 446.

ALECTOR.

The ancients divided the night into different watches; the laſt of which was called cock-crow: wherefore they kept a cock in their Tirit, or towers, to give notice of the dawn. Hence this bird was ſacred to the Sun, and named Αλικlωρ; which ſeems to be a compound out of the titles of that deity, and of the tower ſet apart for his ſervice: for theſe towers were temples. I. 406.

ALESA,

A city and fountain in Sicily. The fountain was of a wonderful nature. I. 32. n. A city in Epirus called alſo Eliſſa, and Laſa: hard by were the Aleſian plains, ſimilar to the Elyſian in Egypt; in theſe was produced a great quantity of foſſil ſalt.

There was Aleſia in Arcadia, and a mountain Aleſium, with a temple upon it; here an ancient perſonage, Æputus, was ſaid to be ſuffocated with ſalt water. There was a tradition, that anciently there had been an eruption of ſalt water in the temple. I. 31. There was in Gaul, an Aleſia, ſaid to be founded by Hercules, of which there are traditions to this day. II. 75.

ALEXANDER,

Upon his expedition to the temple of Ammon, is ſaid to have been conducted by two crows. (Strabo. L. 17.) Curtius ſays (l. 4. c. 7.) that a good number went out to meet him. Theſe were undoubtedly the prieſts of the place, who, from their complexion, were called Crows or Ravens. II. 291.

ΑΛΑΛΑ,

An idolatrous invocation, originally made to the god of war, which Mahomet changed to Allah. It was not unknown to the Greeks. Plut. de Amor. Frat. makes the deity feminine, Κλῦθ' Ἀλαλα, πολεμόυ θυγαῖερ. Hence Ἀλαλαζεις, επινικιως ηχει,—Ἀλαλαγμος, επινικιος ὑμνος,—Ἐλελευ, επιφωνημα πολεμικον, Hefych. It is probably the fame as הֵילֵל in Ifaiah, xiv. 12. I. 15.

ALMON,

A city fo named, by which was meant a city of the Deus Lunus. There were feveral of this name. It was alfo called Minua, q. v.

There was a river Almon near Rome, which was held very facred. In the waters of this ftream they ufed annually with great reverence to lave the image of Cybele, the mother of the gods. Ovid. Faft. L. 4. v. 337.

Eft locus in Tiberim, quo lubricus influit *Almon*,
  Et nomen magno perdit in amne minor.
Illic purpureâ canus cum vefte facerdos
  Almonis dominam facraque lavit aquâ.

The ceremony feems to have been accompanied with lamentations, like the rites of Ifis in Egypt. People of confequence were ufually called by fome title of the deity: accordingly Virgil, to give an air of authenticity to his poem, often confers fome of the antient provincial names upon his heroes; among others he introduces this, which he gives to the fon of Tyrrhius, an Hetrurian. Æn. L. 7. v. 531.

Hic juvenis primam ante aciem ftridente fagittâ,
Natorum Tyrrhi fuerat qui maximus *Almon*
Sternitur.——

It was properly a facred title. II. 448.

C

ALORUS,

The firſt king of Chaldæa, meaning Nimrod. I. 9. This word and Elorus, were names both of perſons and places. 14. Nimrod by Abydenus and Apollodorus is called Alorus, which was often rendered with the Amonian prefix Pelorus. 413.

AL-OURAH,

The cat. From whence the Greeks formed Αλουρος. I. 333. v. Egyptians.

ALPHI.

An Oracle was ſo termed by the Amonians; and Alpha, the voice of God. The ſacred animals Apis and Mneuis were ſtiled Alphi and Alpha; which name was current among the Tyrians and Sidonians. Hence Plutarch (Sympoſ. L. 9. c. 3.) ſpeaking of the letter *Alpha*, ſays, Φοινικας ουʰω καλειν τον Βουν. Alpha was therefore both an Oracle and an Oracular Animal: the Græcians took it in the latter acceptation; and inſtead of ſaying that the Cadmians acted in obedience to an oracle, they gave out that Cadmus followed a Cow. II. 161. In a ſecondary ſenſe it ſignified a Leader. As it was a leading letter in the Alphabet, it was conferred as a title upon any perſon who took the lead, and ſtood foremoſt upon any emergency. Ib. n.

Al-Ompha; hence came Lympha. This differed from Aqua, or common water, as being of a ſacred and prophetic nature. The ancients thought that all mad perſons were gifted with divination; and they were, in conſequence of it, ſtiled Lymphati. I. 280.

Alphi is in acceptation the ſame as Amphi. Ham being by his poſterity eſteemed the Sun or El; and likewiſe Or, the ſame as Orus, his oracles were in conſequence ſtiled not only Amphi, and Omphi, but Alphi, Elphi, Orphi, Urphi. I. 244.

Alphira

Alphira was an ancient city in Elis; in which province was a grove of Artemis Alpheionia, and the whole was watered by the sacred river Alpheus. All thefe are derived from El, the prophetic deity, the Sun, and more immediately from his oracle Alphi. The Greeks deduced every place from fome perfonage, and accordingly makes Alpheus one of thofe who derived their race from the Sun. He is faid to be one of the twelve principal and moft ancient deities, called Συμϐωμοι.. I. 243. v. Schol. Pindar. Olymp. Ode 5.

Alphita, Sacred cakes, purchafed at the oracu-lar temple of Alphi. I. 296.

AMAZONIANS,

Were a very ancient people, who worfhiped their provincial deity under the character of a fe-male, and by the titles of Artemis, Oupis, Hippa. They firft built a temple at Ephefus; and accord-ing to Callimachus (H. in Dian.) the image of the goddefs was formed of the ftump of a beech tree :

Σοι και Αμαζονιδις πολεμου επιθυμηθειραι
Εx κολι παρραλιη Εφισου ϐρϵΙας ιδρυσαιΊο
Φηγω υπο πρεμνω, τελεσεν δε τοι ιερον Ιππω·
ΑυΊαι δ', Ουπι ανασσα, πϵρι πρυλιν ωρχησανΊε.

It is obfervable, that the Chinefe, as well as the people of Japan, ftill retain fomething of this cuftom. When they meet with an uncouth root or fpray of a tree, they humour the extravagance; and by the addition of a face give it the look of a Jofs or Bonzee, juft as fancy directs them. I. 272.

The Amazonians worfhiped Acmon, and there was a facred grove called Acmonium upon the Thermodon, which was held in great repute. Here Mars was fuppofed to have married Harmo-nia, the mother of the Amazonians. I. 513.

    They

They are said to have been called Aorpata, or, as in Herodotus. L. iv. c. 110. Oiorpata, which he interprets Ανδροκτονοι, for they sacrificed all strangers, whom fortune brought upon their coast; so that the whole Euxine Sea, upon which they lived, was rendered infamous from their cruelty. There were several nations under the title of Aorpata; but all of one family; all colonies from Egypt. I. 44.

The whole of their strange story has been owing to a wrong etymology. The Greeks, who would fain deduce every thing from their own language, imagined, that by the term Amazon was signified a person without a breast. (Αμαζων from α and μαζος.) This person they inferred to be a female: and in consequence of it, as the Amazons were a powerful people, they formed a notion, that they were a community of women, who subsisted by themselves; and every absurdity, with which this history is attended, took its rise from the misconception above. They did not consider, that there were many nations of Amazons widely separated from each other; nor did they know, that they were theirselves of Amazonian race. There may be found however some few, who saw the improbability of the story, and treated it with suitabl contempt. Palæphatus, a man of sound sense gave it no credit: and Strabo says, that the whol is a monstrous and absurd detail, without the leat shew of probability. (τερατωδη τ' οντα, και πιστεως πορρω L. 11. p. 770.)

Amazonians were settled in Africa; in mour Caucasus; near the Palus Mæotis; in India, an Ethiopia: they once possessed all Ionia; and ai said to have been at Samos, and in Italy. Eve the Athenians and Bœotians; the Colchians an Iberians; the Cimmerians and Mæotæ; the A lantians in Mauritania were of the same famil
The

They were in general Cuthite colonies from Egypt and Syria: and as they worshiped the Sun, they were called Azones, Amazones, Alazones; which are names of the same purport; and have equally a reference to the natural object of worship.

As this people had different titles in the countries where they settled; and often in the same region; their history by these means has been confounded. They were called not only Amazonians, but Syri, Assyrii, Chaldæi, Mauri, Chalybes, &c. They were the same as the Iönim; and in consequence of it, they are said to have founded the chief and most ancient cities in Ionia, and its neighbourhood. The devices upon their coins witnefs their original, which is often an Amazon; at other times a Rhea, or Cybele, crowned with a tower, to denote the religion of the place.

The Amazons were Arkites, who came from Egypt; and worshiped the Sun, and Selene, the chief deities of the country, from whence they came. It is well known, that the Egyptians admitted the sistrum among their military instruments of music; and made use of it, when they went to war. The same practice prevailed among the Amazons, who worshiped the Isis of Egypt, and made use of her sistrum, when they engaged in battle.

The Amazonians of Colchis and Armenia were not far removed from the Minyæ near mount Ararat: and were undoubtedly of the same family. They were Arkites, as we may learn from the people of Pontic Theba: and followed the rites of the Ark, under the name of Meen, Baris, and Iöna. Hence it is, that they have ever been reprefented with lunar shields. Many have thought, that they were of a lunar shape: but this is a mistake, for most of the Asiatic coins reprefent them otherwife. The lunette, was a device taken from their wor-

C 3   ship.

ſhip. It was the national enſign, which was painted upon their ſhields: whence it is ſaid of them, Virg. Æn. L. xi. v. 660.

—— pictis bellantur Amazones armis;

—— magnoque ululante tumultu
Fœminea exſultant lunatis agmina peltis.

And Lib. 1. v. 490.

Ducit Amazonidum lunatis agmina peltis
Penthiſelea furens———

The Amazonian ſhield approached nearly to the ſhape of a leaf, as did the ſhields of the Gothic na- tions. Pliny (N. H. L. 12. c. 5.) ſays of the Indian fig; upon theſe ſhields they had more lunettes than one: and from them the cuſtom was derived to the Turks, and other Tartar nations.

It is mentioned by Apollonius Rhodius, that, when Orpheus played upon the lyre, the trees of Pieria came down from the hills to the Thracian coaſt, and ranged themſelves in due order at Zona. As the Amazons worſhiped the Sun, whom they ſtyled Zon, there were in conſequence of it many places, which they occupied, called Zona. There was one in Thrace, near the Hebrus; another in Africa; and another in Cappadocia: this laſt led the Greeks into a ſtrange miſtake. For when, in their legendary hiſtories, they ſuppoſe Hercules to march to Zona, and to take it; they miſconſtrue the name, and imagine, that it was ζωνη, *a bandage*. Hence, inſtead of a city, they uniformly render it ζωνη, and make the grounds of the Amazonian war to have been a woman's girdle.

The Cadmians were certainly Amazonians; but their ancient name by length of time was effaced.

One of the moſt extraordinary circumſtances in the hiſtory of the Amazons is their invaſion of
Attica,

3

Attica. They are reprefented as women; and were fuppofed to have fought always on horfeback. Yet it is certain, that the ufe of cavalry in war was not known in Greece till long after this æra: and, if we may credit Homer, the Afiatic nations at the fiege of Troy were equally unacquainted with this advantage. The hiftory given of this invafion is circumftantial, yet abounds with inconfiftencies; and is by no writer uniformly related. The credulity of the ancients was wonderful about one of the moft improbable ftories, that was ever feigned. Strabo had the fenfe to give it up: and Plutarch, after all the evidence collected, and a vifible prepoffeffion in favour of the legend; nay, after a full affent given, is obliged in a manner to forego it, and to allow it to be a forgery: περιφανως εοικε μυθῳ και πλασμαλι. in Thefeo. p. 13.

This, in fhort, feems to be certain, that what has been reprefented as a warlike expedition, was merely the fettling of a colony: and thefe, who had the conduct of it, were Amazonians, who have been reprefented as women. And fo far is probable, that there were women among them, who officiated at the religious ceremonies, which were inftituted. The Scholiaft upon Theocritus (Idyl. 13. v. 25.) gives a fhort but curious account of the firft Amazonian priefteffes. Καλλιμαχος φησι, τας βασιλισσης των Αμαζονων ησαν θυγαλερες· αι Πελειαδες προσηγορευθησαν. πρωλαι δε αυλαι χορεαν και παννυχιδα συνιςησανΊο. The Peleïades, or Doves, were the female branch of the Ïonim, by whom idolatry was firft introduced. (Eufeb. Chron. p. 13.) And as they were at the fame time Amazonians, it proves, that they were all the fame people, under different denominations, (Titanians, Atlantians, Ïonim, Amazonians, &c.) who came chiefly from Egypt, and were widely fcattered over the face of the earth. III. 457.

AM-EES-AIN,

Rendered Amifene. I. 53.

ΑΜΕΙΛΙΚΤΟΣ.

Βασιλευς Κρονος ὑπος]αίης ες]ι—της αμειλικίου Τριαδος, Proclus in Plat. Timæum. L. v. c. 10. What some ufed by miftake to render μηλιχος and μηλιχιος, he has expreffed Αμηλικίος. This is a Græcian word formed from the ancient terms Melech and Melechat, to which it had no relation. II. 278.

AM-ON,

The Egyptian compound for Ham, h. Αμων and Αμμων; he was the Zeus of Greece. I. 3.

AMMON,

Temple of in Lybia, faid to have been built by a Shepherd. II. 183. His priefts ufed at particular feafons to carry in proceffion a boat, in which was an oracular fhrine, held in great veneration. II. 218.

Amanus and Omanus; fo the Greeks expreffed Αμων. I. 3.

AMMONITES,

Were a mixed race, being both of Egyptian and Ethiopic original; Αιγυπ]ιων και Αιθιοπων αποικοι. (Herod. L. 2. c. 42.) I. 251. n.

AMONIANS,

A wonderful people. They were the defcendants of Chus, and called Cuthites, and Cufeans. They ftood their ground at the general migration of families, but were at laft fcattered over the face of the earth. They were the firft apoftates from the truth, yet great in worldly wifdom. They introduced, wherever they came, many ufeful arts; and were looked up to as a fuperior order of beings; hence they were ftiled Heroes, Dæmons, Heliadæ, Macarians. They were joined in their expeditions by

by other nations, especially by the collateral branches of their family, the Mizraim, Capthorim, and the sons of Canaan. These were all of the line of Ham, who was held by his posterity in the highest veneration. They called him Amon; and having in process of time raised him to a divinity, they worshiped him as the Sun; and from this worship they were called Amonians. Pref. vi. One of their most ancient deities was named Meed or Meet, Μηλις, by which was signified Divine Wisdom. II. 27. They introduced some history of the Deluge wherever they came. Ib. 213. All the Amonian families affected to be called Heliadæ, or the offspring of the Sun: and under this title they alluded to their great Ancestor, the Father of all; as by Osiris they generally meant Ham. Ib. 61. They esteemed no places so sacred, as those, where there were fiery eruptions, uncommon steams, and sulphureous exhalations: and they were determined in the situation both of their cities and temples by these strange phænomena. L. 30. They held all streams and cavities of the earth sacred. 89. They dealt largely in Fountain worship; that is, in the adoration of subordinate dæmons, which they supposed to be emanations and derivatives from their chief deity. They called them Zones, Intelligences, Fountains, &c. 52. n. They esteemed every emanation of light, a Fountain, and called it *Ain*, (q. v.) 404. Wherever they founded any places of worship, and introduced their rites, there was generally some story of a serpent. 49. Wherever they came, they founded cities in honour of Noah; hence places called Nusa (from Nusus and Nus, Nous and Noufis, eastern names for Noah) will often occur. II. 209. They settled upon the Tiber. I. 53. Those of them who settled at Rhodes, stiled themselves Ἡλιαδαι, the Solar race; and those who settled upon the Padus, did the same. 85. They who travelled
westward

weftward carried the worſhip and rites of Camulus
with them. 103. Some of this race were the firſt
who paſſed the Alps. 212. They introduced the
worſhip of Ham into Phrygia and Aſia Minor, 273.
They ſettled in Thrace, under the name of Adonians, and founded the city Adonis, called (Ionice)
Edonis, 377. And in this country are to be found
many plain traces of their original hiſtory. II. 339.
Thrace ſeems once to have been the ſeat of Science,
from whence the Athenians acknowledge to have
borrowed largely. I. 508.

When they ſettled in Greece, they raiſed many
Tupha or Tapha in different parts; which were
denominated from ſome title of the deity to whoſe
honour they were erected. 451. They occupied
all the upper part of the Adriatic gulph. II. 441.
Among the many tribes which went abroad from
them, were to be found people who were ſtiled
Anakim. I. 494.

Wherever they ſettled, they were celebrated for
their ſuperiority in ſcience, and particularly for
their ſkill in architecture. They were doubtleſs
ſome of thoſe who were ſtiled Cyclopians, as the
people under this appellation were far the moſt
eminent in this way. 502. It was uſual with the
Egyptians and other Amonians, to deſcribe upon
the architrave of their temples ſome emblem of the
deity, who there preſided. This was often an
Eagle, or Vulture; a Wolf, or a Lion; an Heart or
an Eye; this laſt was intended to ſignify the ſuper-
intendence of Providence, from whom nothing was
hid. 510. There once exiſted a wonderful reſemblance in the rites, cuſtoms, and terms of worſhip, among nations widely ſeparated (in Britain,
Ireland, China, Japan, and the new diſcovered
countries); this was owing to one great family, who
ſpread themſelves almoſt univerſally. Their colonies went abroad under the ſanction and direction

of

of their Priests; and carried with them both the rites and records of their country. 281.

All the Amonian deities, as well as their princes, were called Shepherds; and those, who came originally from Chaldea, were ftiled the children of Ur, or Urius. 445.

Their colonies, though varioufly denominated, and fettled in parts very remote from each other, had once a great and general refemblance; and which lafted for ages.

They were famous at the woof; and carried the art of weaving to a great degree of excellence. This art was firft practifed at Arach in Babylonia. Nor was it only the original texture, which was found out by people of this family; the dying, and alfo imprinting thefe commodities with a variety of colours and figures, muft alfo be attributed to them. That wonderful art of managing filk, and likewife of working up cotton, was undoubtedly found out by the Indo-Cuthites (P. Mela. L. 3. c. 7. Strabo. L. 15. p. 1044.) and from them it was carried to the Seres. To them alfo is attributed the moft rational and amufing game, called Chefs: and the names of the feveral pieces prove, that we received it from them. We are alfo indebted to them for the ufe of thofe cyphers, or figures, commonly termed Arabian: an invention of the greateft confequence. They are faid to have written letters εν σινδοσι, (Strabo. ibid.) but whether by this was meant really linen; or whether we are to underftand a kind of paper manufactured from it, is uncertain. Probably it was a compofition from macerated filk: for paper of this kind was of old in ufe among them.

Thofe who cultivated the grape brought it in many parts to the higheft degree of perfection. The Mareotic wine is well known. (Gratii Cuneget. v. 312.) All the Ionian coaft about Gaza

in

in Palæftine was famous for this commodity: as was the region about Sarepta, at the foot of Libanus. The wine of Chalybon in Syria was of the higheft repute. Cyprus, Crete, Cos, Chios, and Lefbos, called Æthiope, were famous on the fame account. There was alfo fine wine very early in Sicily about Tauromenium, in the country of the Læftrygons and Cyclopians. (Hom. Od. I. 357.) In Thrace were the Maronian wines upon mount Ifmarus. But no place was in more repute than Campania, where were the Formian and Falernian grapes. Some of very noble growth were in Iberia and Mauritania. (Strabo, L. 17. p. 1182.) There was wine among the Indic Ethiopians, particularly in the country of the Oxydracæ, who were fuppofed to be the defcendents of Bacchus. They had alfo a ftrong drink made of rice. (Id. L. 15. p. 1035.) The people of Lufitania and Bœtica made a fermented liquor called Zuth; the knowledge of which was borrowed from Egypt. Hefychius calls it wine, made from barley. (Strabo. L. 3. p. 233.)

The knowledge of this people was very great, and defervedly celebrated. Hence Antiphanes (ap. Athenæum. L. 6. p. 226.) tells us, σοφοι δη' ασιν οι Σκυθαι σφοδρα. By this is meant, that all of the Cuthite family were renowned for their wifdom. The natives of Colchis and Pontus were much fkilled in fimples. Their country abounded with medicinal herbs, of which they made ufe both to good and to bad purpofes. In the fable of Medea we may read the character of the people. Iberia in the vicinity of Colchis was noted for its falutary and noxious plants. Strabo (L. 11. p. 763.) fays, that the Soanes were fkilled in poifons, and that their arrows were tinged with a deadly juice. (fee alfo Plutarch. Sympof. L. 5. c. 7.)

Mount Caucafus, mount Pangæus in Thrace, the Circean promontory in Italy, mount Pelion in Theffaly,

Theffaly, were famous for uncommon plants. Circe and Calypfo are like Medea, reprefented as very experienced in pharmacy, and fimples. Under thefe characters we have the hiftory of Cuthite priefteffes, whofe charms and incantations were thought to have a wonderful influence.

From the knowledge of this people in herbs, we may juftly infer a great excellence in phyfic. Egypt, the nurfe of arts, was much celebrated for botany, (Hom. Od. δ. v. 229.) To the Titanians was attributed the invention of chemiftry. Χημια Γιγανlων ιυρημα. (Syncellus, p. 14.) The Pæonians of Thrace (upon the Hebrus) were fo knowing in pharmacy, that the art was diftinguifhed by an epithet taken from their name.

The Pierians were famed for poetry and mufic. In latter times we find people in thefe parts, who difplayed no fmall fhew of genius ; and were much addicted to letters. (Tacit. Annal. L. 2. c. 64. Ovid. de Ponto. L. 2. El. 9. v. 65.) The Hyperboreans feem to have been equally celebrated. The mufic of the Egyptians and Canaanites was very affecting. The Marianduni, an Amazonian tribe, were noted for the moft melancholy airs. (Dionys. v. 788. et Schol.) The Iberians of Bœtica delighted in a kind of dirges, and funereal mufic. (Philoftrat. in vita Apollon. p. 211.) The ancients fpcak of the Dorian and the Phrygian meafures as more animated and manly. Thofe of Lefbos and Æolia were particularly fweet and pleafing; nor was it only harmony, which they efteemed a requifite in their hymns ; they were made the repofitaries of all knowledge, and contained an hiftory of their anceftors, and of their deities, and the annals of paft ages.

In fhort; wherever this great family fettled, they always fhewed themfelves fuperior in fcience: and though they degenerated by degrees, and were oftentimes overpowered by a barbarous enemy,

which

which reduced them to a ftate of obfcurity; yet
fome traces of their original fuperiority were in
moft places to be found. Thus the Turditani, one
of the Iberian nations upon the great weftern ocean,
are to the laft reprefented as a moft intelligent
people. Σοφωῖαῖοι δ' ἐξῖαζονῖαι των Ιϐηρων ὀυῖοι, και γραμ-
μαῖκη χρωνῖαι, και της παλαιας μνημης ἐχουσι συγγραμ-
μαῖα, και ποιημαῖα, και νομους ἐμμεῖρους ἐξακισχιλιων ἰῶν,
ὡς φασι. Strabo. L. 3. p. 204. We muft lament
that the Romans have not tranfmitted to us the
leaft fample of thefe valuable remains.

In Tatianus Affyrius (c. 1. p. 243.) and more
efpecially in Clemens of Alexandria (L. 1. p. 364.)
we have an account of thofe perfons, who were
fuppofed to have bleffed the world with fome invention : and upon examination almoft all of them
will be found to have been of Cuthite original.
III. 509.

AMORA,

Cakes made in honour of Ham-Orus. I. 297.

AMPEL.

This term is a title, the fame as Omphel, and
relates to the oracular deity of the pagan world;
under which charaćter Ham was principally alluded
to. As the Vine was efteemed facred both to Dionufus, and Bacchus, and had the name of Ampel,
which the Greeks rendered Αμπελος; and as it was
their cuftom out of every title to form a new perfonage, fo they have fuppofed Ampelus to have been
a youth of great beauty, and one whom Bacchus
particularly favoured. Wherever the Amonians
fettled this name occurs. Many cities, promontories, mountains, barren crags, rocks of the fea,
ftrands and fhores, ill fuited to the cultivation of
the Vine, were denominated from it, becaufe here
were altars and pillars to this oracular deity. The
name therefore could have no relation to the Greek
word,

word, fignifying the Vine, but they were fo called
from the deity to which they were facred. We
meet with Ampelus, Ampeloëffa, a nation in Lybia
called Ampeliotæ; Ampelona, Ampelufia, &c.

Ampelus and Omphalus were the fame term
originally, however varied afterwards, and differently appropriated. They are each a compound
from Omphe; and relate to the oracular deity.
L 273.

AMPHI.

This term originally related to oracular revela-
tion. It is always found annexed to the names of
perfons famous on that account; e. g.

Amphiaraus, (He was worfhiped by the Oropians, and his temple was built in imitation, or in
memory, of one called Cnopia at Thebes.)

Amphilochus, (He was the god of light and
prophecy. I. 253. n.)

Amphimachus; perfons reprefented as under
particular divine influence, and interpreters of the
will of the gods.

Amphion, though degraded to a harper, was
Amphi-On, the oracle of Apollo, the Sun.

Ampucides, Αμπυκιδης, (fo was Mopfus ftiled).
This is not a patronymic, but a title of the oracular
deity.

Ampycus, faid to be the father of Mopfus; but
he was the fame with Apollo.

But thefe fuppofed prophets were deities, to
whom temples were confecrated under thefe names;
or rather, they were all titles, which related to one
god, the Sun.

Amphictuons were originally prophetic perfonages, who attended at Delphi.

Amphira, fo is Minerva ftiled by Lycophron; it
is a compound of Amphi-Ur; the divine influence,
or oracle of Orus.

Amphiffa,

Amphiffa, a city in Phocis, famous for the oracle of an unknown goddefs, the daughter of Macaria.

Amphryfus, in Bœotia, much famed for the influence of Apollo.

Amphimallus, in Crete, well known for its oracle.

Amphiclea, in Phocis; here was a fhrine of Dionufus, which was oracular.

Amphipolis (called of old Oropus. II. 165.) I. 252. &c.

Amphi-Tirit is merely an oracular tower, whom the poets have changed into Amphitrite, and made the wife of Neptune. I. 405.

ΑμφιμανΊορα, facred cakes, fo called from an oracular temple ftiled Mentor, and Mantor (q. v.) I. 440.

Amphi, Αμφι. I imagine that the facred oracular influence under this term is often alluded to in the exordia of poets, efpecially by the writers of Dithyrambic meafure, when they addrefs Apollo. Taken in its ufual fenfe for *circum*, it has no meaning; and there is otherwife no accounting for its being chofen above all others in the language to begin hymns of praife to that deity, who was the principal god of prophecy. We have one inftance in the Nubes of Ariftoph. v. 595.

Αμφι μοι αυΊε αναξ,
Δηλιε, Κυνθιαν εχων
'ΤψικεραΊα πΊραν.

Apollo was fo frequently called Αμφι αναξ, that it was in a manner looked upon as a neceffary proœmium. In the fhort hymns afcribed to Homer, this term is induftrioufly retained; it was a term of long ftanding; the fenfe of which was no longer underftood, yet the found was retained by the Greeks, and ufed for a cuftomary exclamation. I. 255.

AMPHIPRUMNAIS,

A kind of veffel copied by the Greeks from one at Thebes in Egypt; the extremities were fashioned nearly alike; no diftinction of head or ftern. Danaus (q. v.) is faid to have croffed the fea from Egypt to Argos in a fhip of this form. There was fomething efteemed facred and falutary in this kind of veffels. Αμφιπρυμνα, τα επι σωΊηρια πεμπομενα πλοια. Hefych. This Navis biprora was not a veffel commonly made ufe of to crofs the feas; it was a copy of the facred fhip of Ifis. II. 226. 248.

AMUMONE.

There was a place in Argos named Triaina where the waters of Amumone arofe; this word is a variation from Amim-On, *the waters of the Sun.* The ftream rofe clofe to the place, whofe true name was undoubtedly Tor-Ain from its vicinity to the fountain. I. 409.

AMYCLÆ,

A city in Italy, of Spartan original; it was faid to have fwarmed of old with ferpents. I. 485.

AMYCUS,

A king of Bithynia, is reprefented as of a gigantic fize, and a great proficient with the cæftus. (Paufan. L. 1.) He was in confequence of it the terror of all ftrangers who came upon the coaft. II. 45.

AN-AIT,

Fountain of the Sun. In Armenia, near Comana and Camifene, was the temple of Anait; it was a Perfic and Babylonifh deity, as well as an Armenian, which was honoured with Puratheia, where the rites of fire were particularly kept up. The city was called Zela, and clofe behind was a nitrous lake.

D   Anait,

Anait fignifies alfo a Fountain of Fire, under which name a female deity was worfhiped. Where-ever a temple is mentioned dedicated to her wor-fhip, there will be generally found fome hot ftreams either of water or bitumen; or elfe falt and nitrous pools. I. 30.

ANAC,

A title of high antiquity, originally appropriated to perfons of great ftrength and ftature : fuch were called in the plural Anakim. Some of the deities of Greece were ftiled Αναχ]ες, (fo efpecially were Caftor and Pollux, I. 407. 442.) and their temples Αναχ]ορια. I. 72.

The Cadmians were ftiled Αναχις and Αναχ]ες, and the temples of their gods Αναχ]ορια; thefe terms were imported from the Anakim of Egypt and Canaan, though ultimately from Babylonia. II. 180.

Αναχεια, fo was ftiled the feftival at Athens of Caftor and Pollux. Αναχειον, fo was ftiled the temple of Caftor and Pollux in Laconia. I. 407.

Anaco, Anachus. Hence feem to come the ab-breviations, Necho, Nacho, Necus, Negus, which in the Egyptian and Ethiopic languages fignified a *king*. It was fometimes expreffed Nachi, and Nacchi. The buildings reprefented at Perfepolis are faid to be the work of Nacki Ruftan; which fignifies the lord or prince Ruftan. Satanaki feems to be Satan-Anac, Διαβολος βασιλευς. I. 73.

ANAXAGORAS,

The Scholiaft upon Pindar writes thus; (Olymp. Ode I.) Περι δε του Ηλιου οι φυσιχοι φασιν, ως Λιθος χαλει]αι ο Ηλιος, και Αναξαγορου γενομενον Ευριπιδην μαθη-την, Πε]ρον ειρηχεναι τον Ηλιον δια των προχειμενων.

Ο γαρ Μαχαριος, χ' ουκ ονειδιζω τυχας,
Διος πεφυκως, ως λεγουσι, Ταν]αλος,
Κορυφης υπερ]ελλον]α δειμαινων ΠΕΤΡΟΝ,
Αερι πο]α]αι, και τινει ταυ]ην διχην.

, Hence

Hence we may difcover whence the ftrange notion
arofe about the famous Anaxagoras of Clazomenæ;
who is faid to have prophefied, that a ftone would
fall from the fun. All that he averred may be feen
in the Scholiaft, which amounts only to this, that
Petros was a name of the Sun; a word of Egyptian
original, derived from Petor, the fame as Ham, the
Iämus of the ancient Greeks. This Petros fome
of his countrymen underftood in a different fenfe;
and gave out, that he had foretold a ftone fhould
drop from the Sun. I. 290. This philofopher, or
his followers, mifled by found, fuppofed that
Zéuth, or Prometheus, was by interpretation Νοος,
mens. They are guilty of a great miftake. For
what they called Νοος or Νους in a philofophical fenfe,
was the eternal Mind; what they appropriate to a
perfon, was a term of a different purport. It was
in fhort a proper name. II. 273.

ANCIENTS.

It was a common miftake of them to transfer to
one perfon, what belonged to a people. II. 304.

The ancients were in general materialifts, and
thought the world eternal. But the mundane
fyftem, or at leaft the hiftory of the world, they
fuppofed to commence from the Deluge. Ib. 371.
They formed perfonages out of places, and made
the natives the children of thofe perfonages.
Ib. 527.

All their ideas about the infernal regions, and
the torments of hell, were taken from the temples
in each country, and from the rites and inquifition
practifed in them. I. 502.

ANDROMEDA.

Virgins are often defcribed as expofed to dragons
and fea-monfters. This relates to women, who
were immured in towers by the fea-fide. The au-

thor

thor of the Chronicon Pafchale fuppofes, that Andromeda, whom the poets defcribe as chained to a
rock, and expofed to a fea-monfter, was in reality
confined in a temple of Neptune, a kind of Petra.
I. 433.

ANELON,

A river; a compound of An-El-On, *Fons dei
Solis:* it was alfo called Halejus. I. 206.

ANIMAL

Every, among the Egyptians, which was in any
degree appropriated to a deity, was called by fome
facred title. II. 66.

ANOPIANS,

Afopians, Elopians, Europians, Inopians, Oropians, other names of the Cyclopians, and relate
to the worfhip of the Pytho Ops, or Opis. I. 508.

ANTEDILUVIAN.

Sifuthros (Eufeb. Chron. p. 8.) i. e. Noah, is
faid to have appeared twice, and to have difcourfed much with mankind; but would not eat with
them. This, I imagine, was in his Antediluvian
ftate; when there is reafon to think, that men in
general fed upon raw flefh; nay, eat it crude, while
the life was in it. This we may infer from that
pofitive injunction, given by God to Noah, after
the Deluge, Gen. ix. 3, 4. *Every moving thing
that liveth fhall be meat for you—but flefh with the
life thereof, which is the blood thereof, fhall you not
eat.* Such a cuftom had certainly prevailed: and
a commemoration of it was kept up among the
Gentiles, in all the rites and myfteries of Dionufus
and Bacchus. Hence the latter was called ωμοφα-
γος, ωμησης.—Vivum laniant dentibus taurum. Jul.
Firmicus of the rites of Crete. III. 110.

ANTIOCHÆA.

This city was firft called Iöna, built by fome of the Iönim, who fettled upon the Orontes. II. 507.

AOR-PATA,

The fame as Petah Or, the Priefts of Orus, or in a more lax fenfe, the votaries of that god. v. Amazonians; Petah.

APÆSANTUS,

A mountain in Argolis, faid to be denominated from *Apæfantus* a fhepherd. II. 185.

APAMEA,

Απαμεια, ἡ λεγομενη Κιβωτος. Strabo. l. 12. The ancient name was Cibotus, undoubtedly in memory of the Ark, and of the hiftory with which it is connected. The people here had preferved more particular and authentic traditions concerning the flood, and the prefervation of mankind through Noah, than are to be met with elfewhere. II. 230. [v. Octav. Falconerii Differt. de Numm. Apameenfi; and Mr. Bryant's Differt. on the fame fubject.]

APE

The, was facred to the god Apis, and was rendered by the Greeks Capis and Ceipis. I. 335.

APHA, APHTHA,

Amonian terms for Fire, and the god of fire; by different authors expreffed Apthas, Thas, Tha. However the Greeks and Romans may have appropriated the term (Cic. de N. D. l. 3. c. 22.) it was properly a title of Amon; at the fame time it related to fire; and every place, in the compofition of whofe name it is found, will have a reference to that element, or to its worfhip. e. g.

Aphytis, a place in Thrace, where the Amonians settled very early; and where was an oracular temple of Amon.

Aphace, a city; also a temple (where was an oracle) of that name in mount Libanus, sacred to Venus Aphacitis, and denominated from fire.

Apha, Aphæa, were names not only of Vulcan, but of Diana also; and in Crete Dictynna had the same name.

Castor and Pollux were stiled Αφίηριοι. Mars Aphæus, was worshiped in Arcadia. Apollo was also called Αφηΐωρ, which was expressed by the ancient Dorians Apha-Tor, a fire tower or Prutaneum, the same which the Latins called of old Pur-Tor.

Aphetæ were originally priests of fire.

Απαΐυρια is compounded of Apatour, a fire tower. I. 59.

Ain-Aptha, the Fountains of Aptha, the god of fire; which by the Greeks was rendered Naptha, a name given to Bitumen. I. 278. Apha-Astus, rendered by the Ionian Greeks Hephæstus, I. 63.

APIA.

The whole region of the Peloponnesus was of old so stiled, undoubtedly from Apis of Egypt; from which also came the terms Appa, Appas, and Apia, among the Greeks; which last is equivalent to *Patria* among the Romans. Among the Scythæ the name of the earth itself was *Apia*, the feminine of Apis. The word therefore could not signify *remote*. Hence Homer, who adheres to ancient words, when he speaks of Nestor (Iλ. A. 270.) that he went τηλοθεν εξ απιης γαιης, must mean either that he went far away *e patria terra*, from his own country; or else at a distance from the region of Apis;

Apis; for it is fcarcely fenfe to fay *longe a longinqua terra*. II. 420.

APIS,

Phoroneus, Inachus, Zeuth, Deucalion, Prometheus, were all one perfon; and with that perfon commenced the Gentile hiftory not of Greece only, but of the world. II. 268. At Memphis they worfhiped the facred Bull Apis; as they did at Heliopolis the Bull Mnevis or Mneuis. Apis and Mneuis were both reprefentations of the fame ancient perfonage, fc. Noah. Ib. 418. Apis feems to have been an Egyptian name for a *father*; hence Appa, &c. v. fupra. He is faid to have come from Egypt, and to have fettled at Argos. Æfchylus in his Suppl. thus fpeaks of him :

Απις γαρ ελθων εκ περας Ναυπακλιας,
Ιατρομανλις, παις Απολλωνος, χθονα
Την δ᾽ εκκαθαιρει κνωδαλων ϛρολοφθορων. I. 485.

Apis is defcribed by Pliny (L. 8. c. 46.) as a deity. II. 423.

ΑΠΟΒΑΘΜΟΣ,

Near Nauplia in Argolis, was a fpot of ground, called the place of Defcent ; τουτου δ᾽ εχει αι χωριον αλλο Αποβαθμος (Paufan. L. 2.) fimilar to the place called Αποβατηριον upon mount Ararat, mentioned by Jofephus, (Antiq. L. 1. c. 3.) and undoubtedly named from the fame ancient hiftory. The tradition among the people of Argolis was, that the place was fo named, becaufe in this fpot Danaus made his firft defcent from the fhip, in which he came over. II. 269.

APOLLO,

Of Greece and Rome, the fame as the Abelion of the Eaft. The old Romans called him Apello. I. 17. He was alfo called Cunnius ; likewife

Craneus

Cranëus and Carnëus (expreſſed by the Romans in
lateř times Granus and Grannus) the ſame with
Cerenëus, the ſupreme deity, the lord of light. 47.
He was frequently called Αμφι Αναξ; alſo Επαξιος,
or the tutelary god of the coaſt; he was the ſame
as Ampycus. He was called Οικλιςης and Αρχηγεℓης,
from being the ſuppoſed founder of cities, which
were generally built in conſequence of ſome oracle.
282. Why he was repreſented by the Greeks as
gaping, ſee Cahen. By a miſtake of theirs he had
beſtowed upon him the epithet of Chruſaor. He had
the title of Phaeton given to him, as the god of
light. 369. He was the ſame with Bacchus and
Dionuſus, for each was the Sun. 308. He was
the ſame with Python, or the Sun. 464. And had
the title of Hippa. II. 31. He had the title of
Εχℓος, rendered more commonly by the Greeks
Ἑκαℓος

Αρℓεμις ιοχεαιρα, κασιγνηℓη Ἑκαℓοιο. ΙΛ. Τ. 71.

as if it came from ἱκας; whereas it was an Amonian
title by which Orus and Oſiris were called. 49. He
was the ſame as Orpheus, and Orus of Egypt. 136.
He was ſtiled Νομευς and Ποιμνιος, and was ſaid to
have been educated in Arabia. Indeed almoſt all
the principal perſons, whoſe names occur in the
mythology of Greece and Italy, are repreſented as
Shepherds. 182. The Greeks called Apollo himſelf Python, which is the ſame as Opis, Oupis, and
Oub. I. 49.

APOLLONIUS

Rhodius, a native of Egypt. He continually
alludes to the antiquities of that country. I. 143.

AQUÆ

Perſianæ, ſome ſalutary waters near Carthage.
They were ſo named from Perez, the Sun, to whom
they

they were facred. Indeed all falutary ftreams were confecrated to the Sun. II. 66. n.

Ager Pifanus, the etymology of this name is the fame as that of Hanes and Phanes (q. v.) only the terms are reverfed. It fignifies *Ignis fons*; it was a diftrict in the north of Italy; and the place was famous for its hot ftreams, which are called by Pliny Aquæ Pifanæ. I. 200.

AQUARIUS,

The watery fign; that great effufion of water, as it is depicted on the fphere, undoubtedly had reference to the Deluge. Some fay that Aquarius was Ganymede; others Deucalion. II. 234.

AR,

In Hofea, x. 14. does not fignify *a city*, but אור, the title of the deity; from whence was derived ἱερος of the Greeks. I. 100. n.

ARACHNAON,

The name of a remarkable temple, of great antiquity, in Argolis; fuppofed to have been built in the time of Inachus: clofe to it was an altar upon which they only made offerings when they wanted rain. In the mafculine *Arach-Naos*; it is literally the temple of Arech. II. 522. v. Erech.

ARBELA,

Was a place facred to Bel, called Arbel, אור בל of the Chaldeans. It is of the fame import with Gaugamela. There was a city of this name in Sicily; alfo in Galilee, fituated upon a vaft cavern.

Arbelus is by fome reprefented as the firft deified mortal. I. 99.

ARCA, ARCAS, ARGUS,

All fignified the Ark, and Archaia betokened any thing that had any relation to it. But as the
Ark

Ark and Deluge were of the higheft antiquity in the mythology of Greece; and every thing was deduced from that period; from hence Archaia came to fignify any thing very ancient, and Archa, Αρχα, the beginning. II. 384.

ARCADES, ARGAEI,

So were ftiled the people, who introduced the Arkite worſhip into Italy. II. 503.

ARCADIANS,

The ancient; were faid to be the offspring of Typhon; and by fome the children of Atlas; by which was meant, that they were people of the Typhonian, and Atlantian religion. I. 496.

In Arcadia and Elis, the moſt ancient rites were preferved. II. 29. They were undoubtedly an Amonian colony; fome of whom the Greeks called Parrhafians. 66. Their ancient name was Minyæ, interpreted Σεληνίlαι, Lunares. II. 200.

ΑΡΧΗΓΕΤΑΙ.

· The colonies of the Amonians, went abroad under the fanction and direction of their priefts ; and carried with them the rites and cuſtoms of their country. And as they went abroad under the influence and direction of their tutelary deities, thofe deities were ftiled 'Ηγεμονες and Αρχηγέlαι; and the colony was denominated from fome facred title of the god. I. 282.

ARCHEMAGORAS,

(expreffed by Paufanias Αιχμαγορας) by which is meant the father, or chief of the Magi. The Greeks made him a fon of Hercules. II. 77.

AREIMANIUS.

The name of the Evil principle, as Oromazus, was of the Good. II. 117.

AREN, ARENE,

One of the Amonian names for the Ark; and Bœotus is faid by Diodorus Siculus (L. 4.) to have been the fon of Neptune and Arne, which is a contraction of Arene. II. 328.

Αρηνη——Εσ]ι δε τις πολαμος Μινυηιος ας αλα ϭαλλων, Εγγυθεν Αρηνης. Hom. Ιλ, Λ. 387.

The city Arena is literally the city of the Ark. It feems to have been fituated upon a facred hill called Sama-Con, near the grove and temple of Iöna : in all which names we may fee a reference to the fame rites and hiftory. II. 512.

AREZ.

According to Suidas, he was the fame as Theuth, ftiled by the Arabians Theus-Arez, and fo worfhiped at Petra. I. 12. It was one name of the Sun ; and the Lion, which was an emblem of the Sun, had the fame denomination. 511.

ΑΡΗΣ ἹΠΠΙΟΣ,

Mars the horfeman; fo called through ignorance by the Greeks. II, 28.

ARGAIUS

Mons, may be derived from Har, a mountain; or from Aur, fire. We may fuppofe Ar-Gaius to fignify *Mons cavus*; or rather *Ignis cavitas*, five *Vulcani domus*; a name given from its being hollow, and at the fame time a refervoir of fiery matter. I, 207. v. Patinæ Numifm. Imp. p. 180.

ARGO,

That facred fhip, which was faid to have been framed by divine wifdom, and which is to be found in the Chaldaic and Egyptian fpheres, was

no

no other than the ark. II. 236. However the Græcians may have taken the hiftory to themfelves, it is plain that the Argo was the facred fhip of Ofiris, and confequently was the Ark. 519. It was the fame as the fhip of Noah, of which the Baris in Egypt was a reprefentation. Its very name fhews to what it alludes; for it fhould be expreffed Argus, which precifely fignified an Ark, and was fynonymous to Theba. Thofe who officiated at the fhrines termed Argus, were called Argeiphontai, from the Egyptian Phont, which fignified a Prieft. But the Greeks, interpreting this term by words in their own tongue, turned the Prieft into a Slayer; and Argo into a man; whom, from a confufed notion of the ftarry fyftem, they fuppofed to abound with eyes, and made Hermes cut off his head. 238. Schol. Vet. in Soph. Elect. v. 5. ταύτας γαρ (fc. Ειλειθυιας) ὁ Ζευς ςραςθεις, μεταβεβληκεν αυτην εις Βουν, λαθειν πειρωμενος την Ἡραν. ἡ δε γνουσα, τον Κυνα τον Αργον τον πανοπτην επεςτησε φυλαττειν αυτην, ὁν Ἑρμης ὑπο Διος πεμφθεις απεκτεινεν.

Argus, Κυν, or Canis, is precifely of the fame purport, as Argeiphontes; *a Prieft of the Ark.* 239.

ARGOS.

Its acropolis was fuppofed to have been founded by Danaus the Arkite. The Acropolis was certainly an Arkite temple, where the Laris, or Navis biprora, was reverenced. II. 453. The city was built by the Cyclopians;

Cyclopum facras
Turres, labore majus humano decus.
Seneca Thyeftes. Act. 2. v. 406.

I. 504. This city (befides many others) was faid to have been infefted by ferpents, till Apis came from Egypt and fettled there; and thefe ferpents
were

were Hivites from the same country. 485. There were accounts retained by the people of Argos concerning a deluge in the days of Inachus, but they did not imagine it to extend beyond their own country. II. 412.

ARGOS HIPPIUM.

There was one in Daunia, which had no relation to the animal, the horse; but to an emblem, under which, in many places the Ark was reverenced. II. 503.

ARGONAUTIC

Expedition. This has been always esteemed authentic, and admitted as a chronological æra. The Golden Fleece at Colchis was to be recovered. A ship was built at Pagafæ; the first that was ever attempted; it was built by Argus, instructed by Minerva. This ship (builded of sacred timber from Dodona) was said to have been oracular. A felect band of heroes, with Jafon at their head, engage in this enterprise. Chiron, or as some say Mufæus, made a sphere (the first ever made) for their use. They set sail at the rising of the Pleiades; but authors differ greatly as to their rout, both setting out, and returning. At the Bosphorus were two rocks, which used to clash together, and intercept whatever was passing. They let fly a Dove; which getting through, they followed, and, by the help of Minerva, escaped. After many difficulties and adventures they succeed, and Jafon brings off the prize, and Medea, the daughter of king Æetes; who, enraged, fits out some ships, purfues them, cuts off their retreat, and compells them to return another way, which by writers is differently reprefented. At length they arrive in Greece, facrifice to the gods, and confecrate the ship to Neptune.

The

The whole is a romantic detail; replete with inconfiftency and contradiction: yet it has been admitted as an hiftorical fact by Herodotus, Diodorus, Strabo, among the ancients; with every Græcian Mythologift; by Clemens, Eufebius, and' Syncellus, among the Fathers; and among the moderns, by Scaliger, and Petavius, Archbp. Ufher, Dr. Jackfon, and Sir Ifaac Newton, &c.

. A few remarks will be fubjoined; and

1ft. As to the fphere; it could not have been a Græcian work, defigned for the ufe of the Argonauts: for as Dr. Rutherforth obferves, Natural Philofophy, Vol. ii. p. 849.

" Befide Pagafæ, from whence the Argonauts failed, is about 39°; and Colchis, to which they were failing, is about 45° N. lat. The ftar Canobus of the firft magnitude, marked α by Bayer, in the conftellation Argo, is only 37° from the South pole, and great part of this conftellation is ftill nearer to the South pole. Therefore this principal ftar could not be feen, either in the place, that the Argonauts fet out from, or in the place to which they were failing. Now the fhip was the firft of its kind, and was the principal thing in the expedition: which makes it very unlikely, that Chiron fhould chufe to call a fet of ftars by the name of Argo, moft of which were invifible to the Argonauts. If he had delineated the fphere for their ufe, he would have chofen to call fome other conftellation by that name: he would moft likely have given the name Argo to fome conftellation in the Zodiac: however, certainly, to one that was vifible to the Argonauts, and not to one which was fo far to the South, that the principal ftar in it could not be feen by them, either when they fet out, or when they came to the end of their voyage." Hence it appears that the fphere could not be a Græcian work. It was the produce of Egypt,

from

from whence came the aſtronomy of Greece : and
the *Zodiac*, which Sir Iſaac Newton ſuppoſed to
relate to this expedition, was an aſſemblage of
Egyptian hieroglyphics.

2. As to the ſhip; there is a remarkable circumſtance relating to this expedition; that the
dragon ſlain by Jaſon was of the dimenſions of a
Trireme :

> Κειο γαρ οχμα, Δρακονος δ᾽
> Ειχειο λαϐροιαιαν γενυων,
> Ος ϖαχει μαχει τε ϖεν-
> τηκονορον ναυν κραιει.   Pind. Pyth. Ode 4.

by which muſt be meant, that it was of the ſhape
of a ſhip in general; for there were no Triremes at
the time alluded to. The writers of this ſtory do
not agree as to the perſon who built this ſhip, nor
as to the place where it was built. King *Æetes* is
ſaid to have purſued them, and intercepted their
retreat. Now what can be more ridiculous than
to ſee the firſt conſtructed ſhip purſued by a navy
which was prior to it? But to palliate the abſur-
dity it is ſaid, that the Argo was the firſt Long ſhip.
Here another difficulty ariſes; for Danaus, many
generations before, was ſaid to have come to Argos
in a long ſhip; Δαναον ϖρωιον (μακραν ναυν) καιαſκευ-
αſαι. Schol. in Apollon. L. 1. v. 4. And Minos
had a fleet of long ſhips, with which he held the
ſovereignty of the ſeas. Of what did the fleet of
Æetes conſiſt but of long ſhips? otherwiſe he could
not have gotten before them at the Boſphorus, or
overtaken them in the Iſter. To render the whole
more conſiſtent, Diodorus omits this and many
other circumſtances. But at this rate any thing
may be made out of any thing.

3. As to the Adventurers; the higheſt number
to which any writer makes them amount, is Fifty
and One. How is it poſſible for ſo ſmall a band of

men

men to have atchieved, what they are fuppofed to
have performed? How could they penetrate fo far
inland, raife fo many temples, and found fo many
cities? To have paffed over vaft continents, and
through feas unknown? And all this in an open
boat (Αργωον σκαφος) which they dragged over
mountains, and often carried for leagues upon their
fhoulders? Diodorus fuppofes Hercules to have
attended his comrades throughout (which other
accounts contradict); he further tells us, that the
Argonauts upon their return landed at Troas,
where Hercules made a demand upon Laomedon of
fome horfes, promifed to him; upon a refufal,
they attack the Trojans, and take the city;
Homer (Ιλ. Ε. v. 642.) fays Hercules had fix
fhips;

'Ος ποτε δευρ' ελθων, ἱνεχ' ἱππων Λαομεδοντος,
'Εξ οιης συν νηυσι, και ανδρασι παυροτεροισιν,
Ιλιου εξαλαπαξε πολιν, χηρωσε δ' αγυιας.

Here we find the crew of a little bilander in one
day perform what Agamemnon with a thoufand
fhips, and fifty thoufand men, could not effect in
ten years. Yet Hercules lived but one generation
before the Trojan war; and the event of the firft
capture was fo recent, that Anchifes was fuppofed
to have been witnefs to it;

———————— fatis una fuperque
Vidimus excidia, et captæ fuperavimus urbi.
Virg. Æn. L. 2. v. 642.

all which is very ftrange. For how can we believe,
that fuch a change could have been brought about
in fo inconfiderable a fpace, either in refpect to the
ftate of Troy, or the policy of Greece?

After many adventures, and long wandering in
different parts, the Argonauts are fuppofed to have

4   returned

returned to Iolcus; and the whole is faid to have been performed in *Four*, or as fome defcribe it, in *Two Months*.

If there were any truth in this hiftory, as applied by the Græcians, there fhould be found fome confiftency in their writers : but there is fcarce a circumftance, in which they are agreed. The Greeks borrowed their mythology and rites from Egypt ; which were founded on ancient hiftories, and which, by length of time, became obfcure, being tranfmitted in hieroglyphical reprefentations. Hence the fable of the bull of Europa, the ram of Helle, &c. in all thefe is the fame hiftory under a different allegory, and emblem. In thefe fables is figured the feparation of mankind by their families, and their journeying to their places of allotment. At the fame time the difperfion of one particular race of men, and their flight over the face of the earth, is principally defcribed. Of this family were the perfons, who preferved the chief memorials of the Ark in the Gentile world.

In the account of the Argo we have undeniably the hiftory of a facred fhip, the firft that was ever conftructed, and faid to have been originally framed by divine wifdom : this was no other than the Ark.

The Græcians took the hiftory to themfelves; and in confequence of this affumption, wherever they heard that any people under the title of Arcades, or Argæi, had fettled, they fuppofed that their Argo had been. Hence they made it pafs not only through the moft diftant feas, but over hills and mountains, and through the midft of both Europe and Afia : there being no difficulty that could ftop it.

The chief title, by which the Argonauts were diftinguifhed, was that of *Minyæ*. II. 475.

ARIMASPIANS

Were Hyperborean Cyclopians; and had temples named Charis, or Charifia, in the top of which was preferved a perpetual fire. They were of the fame family as thofe of Sicily, and had the fame rites, and particularly worfhiped the Ophite deity under the name of Opis.

Αριμασπιους ανδρας μουνοφθαλμους.

Herod. L. 4. c. 13.

ARION,

Who was fuppofed to have been faved by a Cetus, or dolphin, feems to have been the fifh itfelf, and was thence named Hippos. Ἱππος Αρειων. Paufan. L. 8. II. 411. v. Palæmon.

ARK.

Theophilus (Ad Autol. l. 3.) exprefsly fays, that the remains of it were to be feen upon the mountains of Aram, or Armenia. Chryfoftom (De perfecta Charit.) afferts the fame. II. 217. The name of the fhip of Ifis, and of all the navicular fhrines was Baris, and this was the very name of the mountain on which the Ark of Noah refted. 219. It was alfo called Theba. Gen. vi. 15. 222. In other countries befides Egypt, an Ark or Ship was introduced in their myfteries, and often carried about upon their feftivals: at Eruthra in Ionia—at Smyrna—Athens at the Panathenæa—at Phalerus near Athens—Olympia, &c.

Ενθεν ατιζωονῖα Θεωριδος ιερα Φοιϐῳ
Κεκροπιδαι πεμπουσι τοτηῖα νηος εκανης.

Callim. H. in Delum. v. 314.

223. Probably in early times moft fhrines among the Mizraim were formed under the refemblance of a fhip, in memory of the Deluge. It was alfo
called

called by the Greeks Λαρναξ, Κιϐωθος, &c. Moſt of the principal perſons in the Græcian hiſtory are ſaid to have been preſerved in an Ark. 227. . As the ancients deſcribed the Ark, the ναυς αμφιπρυμ- ναις, like a Lunette; it was in conſequence of it called Μην and Σιληνη, which ſignify a Moon; and a Creſcent became its common ſymbol. 242. The principal terms, by which the ancients diſtinguiſhed the Ark, were *Theba, Baris, Arguz, Argus, Aren, Arene, Arne, Laris, Boutus, Bœotus, Cibotus,* (and alſo ſeems to have been ſometimes called *Centaurus,* from whence many of the Arkites had the name of Centauri. II. 440.) Out of theſe they formed different perſonages: and as there was apparently a correſpondence in theſe terms, they in conſequence of it invented different degrees of relation (of this innumerable inſtances occur among the Greeks). Hence a large family has ariſen from a few antiquated words, which related to the ſame hiſtory, and of which many were nearly ſynonymous. 251. When the ark was conſtructed, Noah made alſo a door in its ſide; a circumſtance continually commemorated by the Gentile writers. The entrance through it they eſteemed a paſſage to death and darkneſs; but the egreſs from it was repreſented as a return to life: hence the opening and ſhutting of it were religiouſly recorded. II. 257. The hiſtory of the Ark was preſerved in all countries, as far as we can obtain evidence, with the greateſt care and veneration. 443. v. Προθυραια.

ARKITE DEITY,

(Noah) was called deus Lunus, Luna, and Selene; and by different nations Meen, Man, Menes, and Manes. The word is ſometimes exhibited Archæus; which may be referred to a different idea. Theſſaly was ſaid to have been originally named

Purrha,

Purrha, from the wife of Deucalion, called by the ancient poet Rhianus Αρχαια αλοχος.

Archæa may fignify ancient; but it often feems to be the fame as Archia, and Architis, from the Ark, from which both people and places were indifferently ftiled Αρχαιοι, and Αρχαιοι, Arkites, and Archites. II. 244.   There were innumerable colonies of Arkites, who went abroad, and made various fettlements: but the Græcians have afcribed the whole to the Arcades, Argæi, and Argonautæ of their own country.   When we read of people of Argos performing fuch and fuch things, we fhould underftand Argoï, and Arkitæ, or as it is fometimes rendered Architæ.   People of thefe denominations did fettle in Paleftine; and occupied a great part of Syria.   From thence they came to Greece and Italy: though the Græcians have reverfed the hiftory; and would perfuade us, that they proceeded from Hellas, and more particularly from Argos. Yet even among the Græcians the term Argivus was not of old confined to Argos.   Αργειοι, οι Ελληνες. Hefych.   It is ufed in this fenfe continually by Homer. 505.   Eufebius, in defcribing the people to the eaft of Babylonia, among others, mentions the Αρχαιοι, by whom, I am perfuaded, were meant an Arkite nation, who were worfhipers of the Lunar god. 310.

Αρχαιος, Archaius, is alfo another term for the Ark; and although, as the hiftory is of the higheft antiquity, it might be applicable to any part of it in the common acceptation; yet it will be found to be induftrioufly introduced, and to have a more immediate reference to the Ark.   For it is found continually annexed to the hiftory of Pyrrha, Pelias, Aimonia, and the concomitant circumftances of the Ark, and Deluge.   It was ufed alfo for a title.

Αρχη, πολις Φοινικης· το εθνικον Αρχαιος. Steph. Byzant. in Parutæ Sicilia. p. 104. is the reprefentation of
the

the Sicilian Tauro-Men ; with this inscription, Αλ Αρχαιος, which is literally *deus Arkitis*; and the term Αρχαιος is of the same purport, an *Archite*. II. 493.

ARLES,

The city in Provence, was famed for its medicinal waters ; the true name was Ar-Ales, the city of Ales. It was also called Ar-El-Ait, or Arelate. I. 33. n.

ARMENIA.

This region seems to have been particularly well calculated for the reception of the Patriarch's family, and for the re-peopling of the world. Strabo, who was a native of Asia Minor, (L. 11. p. 800.) speaks of the fertility of Armenia, and especially of the region of Gogarene, which he particularly mentions as productive of the olive. Arene was one name of the Ark. It is to be observed, that there is scarcely any eastern name, which begins with a vowel or common aspirate, but is at times found with a guttural. Thus Ham was expressed Cham ; Habor Chabor ; Arene Carene (hence the Carina of the Romans); the term Go-Carene (Γω-Γαρηνη) signifies literally the place or region of the Ark.

Armenia, for the most part, seems to have been of a very high situation. One province was styled, on this account, Armenia Alta ; of which Moses Choren. Geogr. p. 358. gives the following account : " inter omnes regiones revera altissima est ; quippe quæ ad quatuor cœli partes fluvios emittit. Habet præterea montes tres, feras plurimas, aves utiles, thermas, salinas, atque aliarum rerum ubertatem, et urbem *Carinam*." A country of this nature and situation must, after the flood, have been soonest dried, and consequently the soonest habi-

table.

table. The mountain ftill retains the name of
Ararat: and the province beneath is at this day
peculiarly ftyled Ar-Meni.

The mountain was alfo called Mafis, and likewife Thamanim and Tfhamanim; and there was a
town towards the foot of the mountain of the fame
name, which was fuppofed to have been built by
Noah. Now Thaman is faid in the ancient language of the country to have fignified Eight
(v. *Ogdoas.*) and was analogous to the Shaman of
the Hebrews, which denoted the fame number.
(Bochart. Geog. Sacra. L. 1. p. 18.) The Terra
Thamanim fignifies the region of the eight perfons.
(Ebn Patricius. v. 1. p. 40. 43.) III. 7.

ARPI,

There was a region in Apulia fo called; and in
its neighbourhood were the iflands of Diomedes,
and the birds, which were fabled to have been
Swans; and which were Amonian priefts. II. 44.
v. Harpies. Arpi-ai—'Αρπυιαι.

ARSINOE,

Arfene, Arfine, Arfiana. They are all the fame
name, only varied in different countries; and are
of the fame import. Arfinöe is a compound of
Arez-Ain, *fons Solis*; and moft places fo denominated will be found famous for fome fountain.
I. 208.

ARTEMIS

Was properly a city, Ar-Themis, the fame as
Thamus of Egypt. What was called Artemis, and
Artemifium, was in fome places reverfed, and ex-
preffed by Kir fubjoined; hence Themifcir, and
Themifcura in Pontus. I. 92.

ARX.

‘ ARX.

Every place stiled Arx and Ακροπολις, were in
reality facred eminences, where of old they worfhiped; and which in aftertimes were fortified.
The fame is to be obferved of thofe ftiled Purgoi.
I. 295. n.

AS,

(V. Ees.) One of the titles of the Sun; and related to Fire: it is fometimes compounded with
itfelf, and rendered Afas, and Azaz, expreffed by
the Greeks Αζαζος, and Αζιζος. In Adefa, the deity
was worfhiped under the name of Azizus. It was
a title not unknown to the Greeks;

Αζησια, η Δημηλης. Hefych. Proferpine was likewife fo called.

Azaz, and Afifus, are the fame as Afis, and Ifis
made feminine in Egypt, and fuppofed to be the
fifter of Ofiris the Sun.

Αζα fignified Ασβολος. Hefych. Hence Affo,
Affare of the Romans.

As is often compounded with Or; as in Aforus
and Eforus, titles of the deity in Syria, Sicily, and
Carthage, of which laft he was fuppofed the
founder.

Azor, Azur, common names for places, where
Puratheia were built. It is often compounded with
El and Il; as in Alefa, Azilis, Azila, Afyla.

Aziz *lightning*; any thing fuperlatively bright;
analogous to Adad and Rabrab.

As or Az, from this ancient term many Greek
words were derived; as Αζομαι veneror, Αζω, ξηραινω,
Αζαλιον, θερμον, Αζα, ασβολος, Αζωπες, αι ξηραι εκ της
θεωριας. Hefych.

Azania, a region fo called in Arcadia; famous
for the excellency of its waters. Hanes in Egypt
was the reverfe of Azan, formed of the fame terms,
and of the fame import precifely. I. 26.

E 4   ASCLEPIUS.

ASCLEPIUS,

The god of health, and reftorer of life. By
Sanchoniatho he is defcribed as the chief of the
Eight whom the Deluge fpared. Damafcius
(apud Photium. p. 1073.) fpeaks of him as a perfon, of whom the mother of the gods was ena-
moured: one, who had been configned to darknefs, but out of that gloom, difplayed a wonderful
light. He alfo makes him the Eighth, and principal of the Cabiri. II. 465.

ASIA

Proper comprehended little more than Phrygia,
and a part of Lydia; and was bounded by the
river Halys. It was of a moft inflammable foil.
The country about the Cäyfter was particularly
named Afia.

Ασιω εν λειμωνι Κανσ]ριου αμφι ρεεθρα.

Hom. Ιλ. B. 461.

See Strab. L. 13. I. 29.

The Afiatic Greeks, after a long æra of darknefs, began to beftir themfelves. They had a
greater correfpondence than the *Helladians*, and
they were led to exert their talents from examples
in Syria, Egypt, and other countries. The fpecimens, which they exhibited of their genius, were
amazing; and have juftly been efteemed a ftandard
for elegance, and nature. I. 151.

The reverfe of moft of the Afiatic coins relate to
the religion and mythology of the places where
they were ftruck. II. 231.

ASOPIANS

Were worfhipers of the Serpent; being fo denominated from places confecrated to Ops, and Opis,
the Serpent. II. 177. Afopus, Anopus, Europus,
Ellopis, Ellopia, Charopus, Oropus, all nearly of
the

the fame import, and named from the fame object of worſhip, the Serpent. II. 164.

AST, ASTA,

Eſta, fignified Fire, and alſo the deity of that element. The Greeks expreſſed it Ἑσ]ια, the Romans Veſta.

> Nec tu aliud Veſtam, quam vivam intellige flammam.
> Ovid. Faſti. L. 6. v. 291.

Aſta, and Eſta, fignified alſo a ſacred hearth. In early times every diſtrict was divided according to the number of ſacred hearths; each of which conſtituted a community, or pariſh. They were in different parts ſtiled Puratheia, Empureia, Prutaneia, Prætoria, Phratriai, and Apaturia: but Aſta the moſt common name. Theſe were all places of general rendezvous for people of the ſame community. Here were kept up perpetual fires: and places of this ſort were made uſe of for courts of judicature, where the laws of the country, Θεμιϛ]αι, were explained, and enforced. Hence Hom. Ιλ. A. 63. ſpeaking of a perſon not worthy of the rights of ſociety, calls him Ανεϛ]ιος, Αθεμιϛ]ος, Αφρη]ωρ. I. 62.

Aſta was in aftertimes by the Greeks expreſſed Αϛ]υ, and appropriated to a city; and this at firſt was the name for Athens.

Aſtus is the god of Fire. I. 503.

Aſtes and Eſtes, equally relate to fire. II. 463. Hence Apha-Aſtus, or Hephaſtus, the Hephaiſtus of the Greeks.

Aſtabeni are *Sons of Fire*.

ASTACHAN.

The deity was ſo ſtiled, which as a maſculine, fignified *Sol Dominus* ſive *Vulcanus Rex*. This we

may infer from a province in Parthia, remarkable
for eruptions of fire, which was called Afta-Cana,
rendered by the Romans Aftacene, the region of
the god of Fire.   I. 227.

ASTARTE

And Cronus are faid to have gone over the whole
earth, difpofing of the countries at their pleafure,
and doing good wherever they came. II. 82. She
was the fame as Europa.   II. 305.

ASTER.

Seven Cyclops are faid to have walled round the
harbour of Tiryns, which undoubtedly were feven
Cyclopian towers.   Some of them ftood towards
the harbour to afford light to fhips.   They were
facred to After and Aftarte, and ftiled Aftro-Caer,
and Caer-After, out of which the Greeks formed
Γαςροχιιρ and Εγχιιρογαςηρ; a ftrange medley made
up of hands and bellies. Strabo in particular
(L. 8.) having converted thefe buildings into fo
many mafons, calls them Γαςιροχιιρας, *belly-banded
men*.   Thefe towers were erected alfo for Purait, or
Puratheia, where the rites of Fire were performed.
Purait the Greeks turned into Πρoιlος, and made him
a king of that country.   I. 507.

After among many nations fignified *a Star*.
II. 121.

ASTERIE,

The daughter of Belus (faid to be married to
Perfeus) the fame as Afhtaroth, and Aftarte of
Canaan.   II. 64.

ASTERION.

Paufanias (L. 1.) reprefents him as the fon of
Anac, and of an enormous fize. I. 72.   What was
fuppofed to be his tomb in the ifland Lade, was
only a confecrated place.   465.

ATARBEC,

ATARBEC,

In Egypt, is the temple of Atar or Athar; called Atarbechis by Herodotus, L. 2. and by Strabo, L. 17. ftiled Athribites. I. 97.

ATESH,

To this day one of the names of Fire, among thofe in the eaft, who worfhip it. And Atefh-Pereft is a prieft of Fire. I. 26.

AΘAN

ὁ Θεος. Euftath. in Dionyf. Perieg. v. 915. The great fountain of Light; ftiled both Anath, and Athan, the fame as Athana, and Athena of Greece, and Anaith of Perfis. II. 305.

AΘANATOI,

Were no other than the three fons of Noah, the Baalim of the Scriptures. II. 278. v. Triad.

ATH-EL. ATH-AIN.

From hence the Greeks formed Aθηλα, and Aθηνα, titles, by which they diftinguifhed the goddefs of wifdom. Proferpine was called alfo Athele. Ath was an oriental term, which came from Babylonia and Chaldea to Egypt; and from thence to Syria and Canaan.

Ovid (Met. L. 5. v. 162.) fpeaking of an Ethiopian, introduces him by the name of Eth-Amon, foftened into Ethemon. So Virgil (Æn. L. 10. v. 126.)

— — — comites Sarpedonis ambo,
Et clarus Ethemon Lycia comitantur ab alta.

Or, Clarus et Ethemon——

Ath was fometimes joined to the ancient title *Herm*; which the Græcians with a termination made Ἑρμης. From Ath-Herm, came Θερμαι,
Θερμος,

Θερμος, Θερμαινω. These terms were sometimes re-versed, and rendered Herm-Athena. I. 20. v. Ait.

ATHEMANES.

There was a province of these in Thesprotia, who were so denominated from their deity Ath-Man or Ath-Manes. II. 170.

ATHENS.

Its first name was Asta; and then Athenæ of the same import; for it is a compound of Ath-En, *Ignis fons:* in which name there is a reference both to the guardian goddess of the city; and also to the perpetual fire preserved within its precincts. I. 63.

ATHENIANS,

Who came from Sais in Egypt, were denomi-nated from the deity Anath, whom they expressed Ath-An, or Αθηνη, after the Ionian manner. I. 57. n. The ancient Athenians worshiped Isis; and were in their looks, and in their manners, par-ticularly like the Egyptians. Diod. Sic. L. 1. The whole of their policy was plainly borrowed from that country. It is said by Sanchoniathon, Euseb. P. E. lib. 1. c. 10. that Cronus, in his tra-vels over the earth, in company with his daughter Athena, came to Attica; which he bestowed upon her. The Sch. on Lycophron. v. 111. has these remarkable words: Ελθων αρ (ὁ Κεκροψ) απο Σαεως πολεως Αιγυπ]ου τας Αθηνας συνῳκισε. Σαις δε κα]' Αιγυπ]ιους ἡ Αθηνα λεγ[ε]αι, ὡς φησι Χαραξ. Hence it is, that almost the whole of the mythology of Greece is borrowed from Egypt. All their rites and ceremonies from the same quarter. 185. They were esteemed Serpentigenæ; and they had a tra-dition, that the chief guardian of their Acropolis was a Serpent. Ægeus of Athens, according to Androtion, was of the Serpent breed; and the first king of the country is said to have been Δρακων, a

Dragon.

Dragon. Others make *Cecrops* the firſt who reigned. 483.

ATHYR,

One of the Egyptian months: the term is formed of Ath-Ur. It was alſo one of the names of that place, where the ſhepherds reſided in Egypt; and to which the Iſraelites ſucceeded. It ſtood at the upper point of Delta, and was particularly ſacred to Ur, or Orus: and thence called Athur-ai, or the place of Athur.

One of the moſt ancient names of Rhodes was Aithraia, or the land of Athyr; ſo called from the worſhip of the Sun. Lemnos was' denominated Aithalia, for the ſame reaſon, from Aith-El. Ethiopia was named both Aitheria, and Aeria, from Aur, and Athyr. I. 20.

ATLAS,

The great Aſtronomer, is repreſented as a ſhepherd. II. 183. Noah, among other titles and characters, is repreſented as Atlas. 253. Mythologiſts ſay that he ſupported heaven; one reaſon for this notion was, that upon mount Atlas ſtood a temple to Cœlus. The temple was undoubtedly a Cavern; but the name is to be underſtood in its original acceptation, as Coël, the houſe of God; to which the natives paid their adoration. This mode of worſhip among the Atlantians betrays a great antiquity; as the temple ſeems to have been merely a vaſt hollow in the ſide of the mountain; and to have had in it neither image, nor pillar, nor ſtone, nor any material object of adoration. To this cavern the people paid their adorations, and this was the heaven which Atlas was ſuppoſed to ſupport. I. 221. This notion took its riſe from ſome verſes in Homer, Od L. A. 52. ſtrangely miſconſtrued;

Ατλαντος

Ατλαντος Θυγατηρ ολοοφρονος, οστε Θαλασσης
Πασης βενθεα οιδεν, εχει δε τε ΚΙΟΝΑΣ αυτος
Μακρας, αι Γαιαν τε και Ουρανον αμφις εχουσιν.

Thefe Κιονες Κοσμου were certainly maps and hiftories of the univerfe; in the knowledge of which
the Atlantians feem to have inftructed their brethren the Herculeans. And obferve that when
the ancients fpeak of the feats of Hercules, we are
to underftand the Herculeans; of Cadmus, the
Cadmeans; fo under the name of Atlas, is meant
the Atlantians. Thefe alfo were ftiled Ουρανιωνες,
or fons of heaven. They fettled in Phrygia and
Mauritania; and like the Colchians, were of the
family of Ham: and had great experience in fea
affairs. The Græcians efteemed them barbarous;
but they were in reality of the fame family. Their
chief anceftor was the father of the Peleiadæ, or
Ionim. They were heads of moft families
upon earth; perfons of great confequence and
learning; founders of nations; &c. and from them
proceeded all thofe, who upon account of their
eminence were in aftertimes efteemed gods and
heroes. (Diod. Sic. L. 3.) I. 387.

Atlas, Battus, Cadmus, Pollux, &c. are faid to
have been turned into ftones. Thefe ftories relate
to perfonages, enfhrined in temples ftiled Petra,
who had a ϛυλος, or rude pillar erected to their
honour. This was the ufage in all parts, before the
introduction of images. II. 174.

ATTICA

At firft was divided into feparate and indepen-
dant hamlets; each of which had its own Prutaneion
and Archon. Thefe Archons were priefts of the
Prutaneia; and were denominated from their office.
Archon is the fame as Orchon, and like Chon-Or
fignifies the god of Light, and Fire; from which
title

title the priests had their name. In Babylonia, and Chaldea, they were called Urchani. II. 40.

AUR,

or Or, Our, Ur, *Light*, and *Fire*; hence Orus, an Egyptian title of the Sun.

From Aur, confidered as an element, were derived Uro, Ardeo; as a deity, Oro, Hora, Ὦρα, Ἱερον, Ἱερευς. I. 13.

AURELIA,

After its firſt ſtage as an Eruca, or worm, lies for a ſeaſon in a manner dead, and is incloſed in a ſort of coffin. In this ſtate of darkneſs it remains all the winter; but at the return of ſpring it burſts its bonds, and comes out with new life, and in the moſt beautiful attire. The Egyptians thought this a very proper picture of the ſoul of man, and of the immortality to which it aſpired. But they made it more particularly an emblem of Oſiris, who having been confined in an Ark, or coffin, and in a ſtate of death, at laſt quitted his priſon, and enjoyed a renewal of life. II. 388.

AURITÆ.

Under this title the ſons of Chus came into Egypt. They ſettled in a province named from them Cuſhan, which was at the upper part of Delta; and in aftertimes called Nomos Arabicus. It was in the vicinity of Memphis, and Aphroditopolis, which places they likewiſe occupied. I. 362. [See Mr. BRYANT's *Diſſertation concerning the Shepherd Kings in Egypt.*]

The title of Shepherds was peculiar to them. H. 181. This people ſpread themſelves over Egypt like a deluge, but were in time forced to retreat, and to betake themſelves to other parts; in conſequence of this they were diſſipated over regions far remote. They were probably joined

9 by

by others of their family, as well as by the Canáá-
nites, and the Capthorim of Palæftina. II. 189.

Oritæ, or Auritæ, were the fame as the Heliadæ,
denominated from the great object of their worfhip,
the Sun. II. 177.

AZONACES.

Zoroafter is faid to have been under his care. I
fhould imagine it was the name of the chief deity,
the reputed father of Zoroafter. II. 116. 124, 125.
He feems to have been the chief of the Azoni, or
Zoni, and to have been named Azon-Nakis, *Sol Rex*,
vel *Dominus*.

The Azoni and Zoni, feem to have been fecondary deities. The term fignifies Heliadæ : and
they were looked upon as æthereal effences, a kind
of emanation from the Sun. The fillet, with
which the Azoni were girded, is defcribed as of a
fiery nature; and they were fuppofed to have been
wafted through the air. This facred girdle was
efteemed an emblem of the orbit defcribed by Zon,
the Sun. The eaftern deities were reprefented
either as girded round with a Serpent, which was
an emblem of the fame meaning ; or elfe with this
bandage, denominated Zona. 124.

AZORA,

A temple in Affyria fo named. I. 419.

B.

THE fame as Dione, the Dove. II. 465.

BABEL.

This city was begun by Nimrod, and enlarged by his pofterity. It feems to have been a great feminary of idolatry : and the tower, a ftupendous building, was erected in honour of the Sun, and named the Tower of Bel. Upon the confufion of fpeech, both the city and tower were called Babel; the original appellation not being obliterated, but contained in the latter. And as the city was devoted to the worfhip of the Sun, it was alfo called the city of Bel-On, five civitas Dei Solis ; which was afterwards changed to Babylon. From thefe terms, I think, we may learn the nature of the judgment inflicted at the time of the difperfion. It did not confift in an utter change of language; but it was a Labial failure; an alteration in the mode of fpeech. It may be called the prevarication of the lip; which had loft its precifion, and perverted every found that was to be expreffed. Inftead of Bel, it pronounced Babel; inftead of Bel-on, Babylon : hence Babel, amongft other nations, was ufed as a term to fignify a faulty pronunciation. Ἑϐραιοι γαρ την συγχυσιν Βαϐελ καλουσι. Jofeph. Ant. L. 1. c. 4. Thefe terms feem ever afterwards to have been retained, even by the natives, in confirmation of this extraordinary hiftory : and the city, as long as it exifted, was called Babylon, or *The City of Confufion.*

F   The

The tower of Babel was probably a rude mound of earth, raifed to a vaft height, and cafed with bricks, which were formed from the foil of the country, and cemented with afphaltus or bitumen. There are feveral edifices of this fort to be feen in the region of Babylonia. They are very like the brick pyramids in Egypt. Many have been led to think, that one or other of thefe buildings was the original tower of Babel. But ancient writers are unanimous, that it was overthrown, and that Nimrod perifhed in it. (Syncellus. p. 42. Cedrenus. p. 11. Jofeph. Ant. L. 1. c. 4.) But this, I think, could not be true: for the term of Nimrod's life, extend it to the utmoft of Patriarchic age after the flood, could not have fufficed for this. And though writers do affert, that the tower was overthrown, and the principal perfon buried in its ruins: and it muft be confeffed, that ancient mythology had continual allufions to fome fuch event: yet I fhould imagine, that this related to the overthrow of the deity there worfhiped, and to the extirpation of his rites and religion, rather than to any real perfon. The fable of Vulcan, who was thrown down from heaven, and caft into the fea, is founded upon this ftory. III. 45. See *Vulcan.*

BACCHUS,

Who was no other than Chus, is faid to have firft inftituted triumphs. I. 257. The Egyptian and Afiatic Greeks had fome imperfect traditions about Ham, and Chus, the latter of whom they efteemed Bacchus. 273. There are few characters, which at firft fight appear more diftinct, than thofe of Apollo and Bacchus, yet the department, which is generally given to Apollo, as the Sun, I mean the conduct of the year, is by Virgil (Georg. I. 6.) given to Bacchus, or Liber. He joins him with

Ceres,

Ceres, and calls them both the bright lumina-
ries of the world.

———Vos, O, clariſſima mundi
Lumina, labantem cœlo qui ducitis annum,
Liber, et alma Ceres.

Quidam ipſum ſolem, ipſum Apollinem, ipſum
Dionyſium eundem eſſe volunt. Schol. in Horat.
L. 2. O. 19. Hence we find that Bacchus is the
Sun or Apollo, though generally ſuppoſed to have
been a very different perſonage. In reality they
are all three the ſame ; each of them the Sun. In
Thrace the Sun was eſteemed, and worſhiped as
Bacchus, or Liber. 308.

He was often miſtaken for Dionuſus, and in
many countries called Bochus, and in Mauritania
and Numidia was expreſſed Bocchus. II. 266.

Nonnus in his forty firſt book under the repreſentation of Bacchus coming into the country about
Libanus, and planting the vine and introducing
agriculture, gives the true hiſtory of the ſons of
Chus, who really came into theſe parts, and performed theſe things. 366. The vine was eſteemed
ſacred both to Dionuſus and Bacchus ; for they
were two different perſonages ; though confounded
by the Grecians. Indeed the titles of all thoſe, who
were originally ſtiled Baalim, are blended together.
I. 273.

BAI,

The name in Egypt for the branch of the Palm-
tree. (v. John c. xii. v. 13.) Homer ſays Iλ. Ϋ.
454. that one of Diomede's horſes was Phœnix,
of a Palm colour, which is a bright red : we call
ſuch horſes Bays, which probably is a term of the
ſame original. From Bai the Grecians formed the
word Baιη. The Romans called the ſame colour
Badius. As the Palm-tree was ſuppoſed to be

immortal, the Egyptians gave the name of Bai to the Soul. I. 327.

BAIÆ

Was properly Baian. I. 201.

BAL-AIN,

The fountains of the great lord of heaven. Hence Gr. and Lat. Βαλανηα and Balnea. And alfo hence *Whales* were called Bal-Ain, or Balænæ, as they fpout water in a large ftream through their noftrils. I. 53.

BAL, BAAL,

Names for Noah given to him by fome of his defcendants, who together with him, were ftiled the Baalim; Chus was one of thefe. I. 2.

The Baalim had a great regard paid to their memory, which at laft degenerated into the moft idolatrous veneration. II. 372.

BAAL-BERITH,

A deity in Canaan in very early times, of no fmall repute, and worfhiped by the men of She-chem. This, I fhould think, was no other than the Arkite god; with whofe idolatry the Ifraelites in general were infected, foon after they were fettled in the land. The place is ftiled Beth-Baal-Berith, *the temple of the god Berith.* See Judges viii. 33. ix. 4. 46—49. II. 358.

BAAL-SAMEN

Is *the lord of heaven.*

BALBEC

In Syria, is fuppofed to be the fame as Balbeth, the temple of Bal, or the Sun. I. 96.

BALSAM,

BALSAM,

Was ftiled by the Egyptians Baal-Samen. I. 332.

BARIS,

According to the Græcian manner of expreffion, the facred fhip of Egypt was fo ftiled, and was another name for the Ark or Thebah. Originally it was Barit, or Barith, or Berith. It was the name of the Ark, but fignified properly a *Covenant*. By this name mount Ararat was fometimes diftinguifhed; as well as the temple of the Ark, upon that eminence: and it related to the *Covenant* made by God with man.

Near Sidon was an ancient city, Berith, or Barith, of like import with Beth Baal-Berith, and facred to the fame deity. It was by the Greeks called Berytus, and fometimes by the poets Beröe. II. 357.

BARSANES.

According to Diod. Siculus, L. 2. the name of an ancient king of Armenia; it fignifies the offfpring of the Sun. I. 36.

BARSIPPA,

Ancient names are often eclipfed by later titles. Thus I am perfuaded, that Erech, or Arech, has been loft in Barfippa; which is a compound of Bars, or Baris-Ippa, two terms of precifely the fame purport as Arech, whofe inhabitants are ftiled Ἀρχυαιοι, or Arkites. Befides it was famous for weaving, and fo was Erech; it lay in the land of Shinar, and in the province now called Irac. Strabo fays (L. 16) that it was facred to Artemis and Apollo. The Arab tranflator Saad juftly renders Arach by El-Bars, or Baris. II. 525.

F 3

BATTUS, BOUTUS, BOEOTUS,

Though names conferred upon the Patriarch, yet originally related to the machine in which he was preserved. II. 328.

BEES.

When the Athenians sent their first colony to Ionia, the Muses led the way in the form of Bees. Herodotus says, that all the northern side of the Danube was occupied by Bees. When the shepherd Comatas was inclosed in an Ark, he was supposed to be fed by Bees. Jove upon mount Ida was said to have been nourished by Bees. When the temple at Delphi was a second time erected, it was built by Bees; who composed it of wax, and feathers, brought by Apollo from the Hyperboreans. Such are the strange accounts given by the Greeks; all owing to their misinterpreting the term Melissæ, who were certainly female attendants in the Arkite temples. II. 376.

BEL, BAL, BAAL,

Is a Babylonish title, appropriated to the Sun; and made use of by the Amonians in other countries, particularly in Syria and Canaan. It signified Κυριος, or lord. It is often compounded with other terms; as in Bel-Adon, Belorus, Bel-hamon, Belochus, Bel-On, hence the Bellona of the. Romans; and also Baal-Shamaim, the great lord of the heavens. The Syrians gave this title to the Sun. I. 45. The chief Syrian god had the title of Bel, Bal, and Belial: which last the Greeks rendered Βελιαρ. This Belial, or Beliar, was the same as Belorus, and Osiris, who were worshiped under the symbol of a Serpent. Βελιαρ—δρακων. Hesych. II. 166.

BELIDÆ,

BELIDÆ

Of the Greeks, an Arkite colony from Egypt. II. 443.

BELIN,

The deity of whom Aufonius fpeaks, Ode 4. was the fame as *Bel* and Balen of Babylonia and Canaan, the Orus and Apollo of other nations. I. 285. v. Herodian. L. 8. Æfchylus, Perfæ. p. 156.

BELUS

And Phœnix feem to be the fame. They were titles, not perfons. Under the character of thefe two fuppofed perfonages, colonies, named Belidæ and Phœnices, went abroad, and fettled in various parts. I. 325.

BENDIS

The deity, whofe rites were fo celebrated in Phrygia and Thrace, was a compound of Ben-Dis, *the offspring of God.* The natives of this country reprefented Bendis as a female; and fuppofed her to be the fame as Selene, or the Moon. I. 59.

BEROE,

Called Berytus by the Greeks, before the Romans were acquainted with that part of the world.

Under the character of Beröe, which by Nonnus (Dionys. L. 41.) is fuppofed to be the fame as Barit, he manifeftly alludes to the Ark and Deluge, and the Covenant afterwards made with man. He fpeaks of Beröe as coeval with the world: for all hiftory, and time itfelf according to the Græcians, commenced from the æra of the Ark. He fpeaks of her as a nymph, who had the whole ocean for her poffeffion; the feat of juftice, from whence all laws were derived. The Ark, fraught with the whole of animal life, and toffed about by an unruly flood, is defcribed under the character of Beröe in

F 4 labour;

labour; to whose delivery Hermes the chief deity
administered.   He next mentions the approach of
an ancient and respectable person called Æon.
Upon Beröe, whom Nonnus stiles both Paphie, and
Κυθερηα, being delivered, there was an immediate
joy throughout the whole creation.   The delivery
of Beröe was manifestly the opening of the Ark.

Nonnus mentions that there was a twofold Beröe:
one, πρωτοφανης Βερoη—κοσμω συγχρονος: this gave
name to the other, a nymph in aftertimes.   He
speaks of them sometimes as two places; the one
the work of Cronus, ην Κρονος αυτος εδειμε; *formed before the clouds were gathered, &c.*

> Ουδε συνερχομενων νεφεων μυκητορι ρομβω
> Βροντaιη βαρυδουπος εβομβεεν ομβριος ηχω.
> Αλλα πολις Βερoη πρoτερη πελεν, ην αμα γαιη
> Πρωτοφανης ενοησεν ομηλικα συμφυτος αιων.
> Ουποτε ταρσος εην τερψιμβροτος, ουποτε Θηβη,
> Ουποτε τις πολις ηεν Αχαιιας, ουδε και αυτη
> Αρκαδιη προσεληνος.

In this description we may, I think, plainly see
the history of the prototype, which was not a city,
but the original Beröe or Berith, from whence the
other Beröe, stiled also Berytus, was named.

The Ark was the ultimate, from whence all
things were to be deduced.   All religion, law, and
justice, were from thence derived: particularly the
seven Noachite precepts, which were supposed for
some ages to have obtained universally.   To this
memorable history he more than once alludes; but
attributes the whole to the city of Berytus.   Of
which this could not be true, as a city; for it never
had that extensive influence.   I cannot help
thinking that he has confounded two cities, and two
emblems.   He through the whole speaks of Beröe
and Berytus as the same: and thinks, that the
names are of the same purport.   But I think, that

3   Berytus

Berytus and Beröe were not the fame. The latter
I take to have been the city in Syria called Beroea,
at no great diftance from the former. Both places
were denominated from circumftances relating to
the Ark: and indeed from the fame object under
different types. Berytus was named from Berith,
the Covenant; from whence Baal Berith had this
title. But Beröe was fo called from the Ark being
efteemed a *bier*, or *tomb*, ϐαρις και σορος Οσιριδος.
II. 357.

BETARMUS,

A religious dance, denominated from fire, with
which it was accompanied. It was originally an
Egyptian dance in honour of Hermes; and practifed
by the Pataræ or Priefts. In fome places it was
efteemed a martial exercife; and exhibited by perfons in armour, who gave it this name.

Αμυδις δε νεοι Ορφνος ανωγη
Σκαιρονlες Βηlαρμον ενοπλιον ορχησανlο,
Και σακεα ξιφεεσσιν υπεκluπον.

Apoll. Rhod. L. 1.

The name was given to the dance from the temple
of the deity, where it was probably firft practifed.
It is a compound of Bet-Armes, or *Armon*, called
more properly Hermes, and Hermon. I. 286.

BETH,

Is a houfe, or temple; as in Beth-El, Beth-
Dagon, Beth-Shemefh, Beth-Oron, or Beth-Or-
On, &c. &c. It is fometimes fubjoined, as in
Phar-beth, Elifa-beth.

In different countries it was expreffed Bat, Bad,
Abad, as now in Perfia, and other parts of the
eaft; e. g. Pharfabad, Aftrabad, Amenadab, Mou-
ftafabad, &c.

The

The inner recefs of a temple is by Phavor. and Hefych. called Βαιλης, Βιλης, Βιλις, fimilar to בית אש among the Chaldeans. It was the Crypta or facred place where the everlafting fire of old was pre-ferved. Bet-Is fignifies the place of fire. I. 96.

BETH-ANATH

Occurs Jofhua xix. 38. A temple of the god-defs An-Ait. I. 52.

BETH-ARBEL.

The LXX (Hofea x. 14.) according to fome of their beft copies render it οικον Ιερο-Βααλ, which is no improper verfion of Beth-Aur-Bel. I. 100. n.

BETH-BAAL-BERITH,

The temple of the god Berith. II. 358. See Judges viii. 33. ix. 4. 46—49.

ΒΗΤΑΓΩΝ.

The author of the Etym. Magn. confounds Dagon with his temple; and fuppofes him to have been the god Cronus. But Βηαγων is for Bet-Dagon, the temple of the deity. II. 300. n.

ΒΟΕΣ ΛΑΡΙΝΟΙ.

The facred bulls of Egypt were the faireft to the fight that could be procured. They were emblems of the Patriarch, and the Ark, called, among many other names, Laren. Hence probably it was that the Græcians ufed to ftile fine looking oxen, Βοες λαρινοι: which in a fecondary acceptation fignified oxen, that were in flefh and well fed; Βοες ευγραφαις. Hefych. II. 452.

BOLATHES,

So Damafcius (ap. Photium. c. 243.) ftiles the Sun. It is a compound of Bal-Ath, or Bal-Athis, the fame as Atis, and Atifh of Lydia, Perfis, &c. I. 46.

BOT.

BOT.

Homer, Iλ. Z. v. 134, has thefe lines ; .

$$— \text{αἱ δ' ἅμα πᾶσαι}$$
$$\text{Θυσθλα χαμαι καⁱτεχευαν ὑπ' ανδροφονοιο Λυκουργου}$$
$$\text{Θειομεναι βουπληγι.}—$$

The Græcians were wont to change every foreign term, which came under their view, to fomething of fimilar found in their own language,
though it were ever fo remote in fenfe. A remarkable inftance may be found in the above paffage
from Homer: which manifeftly alludes to the
vengeance of the Deity, and the difperfion of the
fons of Chus. The term βου, Bou, in the Amonian language, fignified any thing large and noble.
The god Sehor was called Bou-Sehor. This was
the Bufiris, Βουσιρις, of the Greeks, who retained this
term in their own language; and ufed it in the
fame fenfe. Accordingly, Βουταις was a jolly fine
boy: Βουθυσια, a great facrifice: Βουπρηονες, vaft
rocks: Βουγαιος, a great boafter: Βουλιμος, great
hunger, or famine. Hence Hefychius tells us, Βου,
το μεγα και πολυ δηλοι. The term Pleg, or Peleg,
related to feparation and difperfon: and when
Homer mentions Θειομεναι δουπληγι, the original
word was Bou-pleg, or Bou-peleg, which means
literally a great difperfion. In the Hebrew tongue,
of which the Amonian was a collateral branch,
Pelach is to feparate; and Peleg to fever, and divide. The fon of Heber was named Peleg, *becaufe
in his days the earth was divided* (Gen. x. 25.) and
his name accordingly fignified divifion, and feparation. But the poet, not knowing, or not re-
garding, the true meaning of the word Pleg, or
Peleg, has changed it to an inftrument of hufbandry. And inftead of faying, that the Deity
purfued the rebels, and fcattered them with (Bou-
pleg) a great diffipation, he has made Lycurgus
follow

follow and beat them, Βουπληγι, with an ox-goad. III. 43.

BOUN.

One species of sacred bread, which used to be offered to the gods, was of great antiquity, and called Boun. The Greeks, who changed the Nu final into a Sigma, expressed it in the nominative Βους, but in the accusative more truly Βουν. Hesych. αιδος πεμμαιος κεραια εχοντος. So Phavor. See Jeremiah vii. 18. xliv. 18, 19. I. 298.

ΒΟΥΣ,

Βαρις, Αργος. Hesych. By an Ox or Bull is signified Baris, and Argus. II. 424.

BOZRAH,

The same term in different languages conveyed different and opposite ideas; and as the Greeks attended only to the meaning in their own tongue, they were constantly mistaken. e. g. Bozrah, *a citadel*, they changed into Βυρσα, *a skin*. I. 169. v. Orion.

BRENNER,

Great; a name of mount Pyrene.

ΒΡΕΦΟΚΤΟΝΟΣ

Infanticida, an epithet given to Palæmon by Lycophron, v. 229. on account of the children, which were offered at his shrine. II. 458.

BRITAIN

And Ireland, abound with sacred Amonian terms, which have been greatly overlooked. I. 213. The original religion of the former, was the worship of the Sun.

The British Antiquarian should observe that the names of places, especially of hills, promontories and rivers, are of long duration, and suffer little change,

change; the fame may be faid of every thing, which was efteemed at all facred, fuch as temples, towers, and high mounds of earth; which in early times were ufed as altars. More particularly all mineral and medicinal waters, will be found in a great degree to retain their ancient names; and among thefe there may be obferved a refemblance in moft parts of the world. For when names have been once determinately affixed, they are not eafily effaced. I. 213.

BULLS

Were facred to Ofiris (who was Noah) the great hufbandman. They were looked upon as living oracles, and real deities; and to be in a manner animated by the foul of the perfonage, whom they reprefented. II. 422.

As the Egyptians imagined that the Ark re-fembled the New Moon, and which was a favourite emblem, they ufed fome art to imprefs the figure of a crefcent on the fides of thefe facred animals, as it is certain, that white marks of this form were feen upon them; they were therefore chofen uni-formly of a black colour. The like is faid of the Apis. The Ark was called Theba, Baris, Argus; and we find that thefe terms, and the name of an Ox or Bull, were fynonimous among the Eaftern nations. The Syrians, like the people at Mo-Memphis, held a Cow in great reverence. Ib.

BUCENTAUR.

There feem to have been fhips of old denomi-nated from the Ark Centauri, and Βουχεηαυροι. The Amonians occupied all the upper part of the Adri-atic Gulf: and the Veneti at this day call their principal galley the Bucentaur. II. 441.

BUSIRIS.

BUSIRIS.

Diodorus, L. 1. and Strabo, agree that there was no fuch king. The word is only a variation of Ofiris; both were a compound of the Egyptian Sehor, and related to the god of day.

Bou-Sehor, and Uch-Sehor, are precifely of the fame purport, and fignify *the great lord of Day.* I. 462. On, Ofiris, and Bufiris, were the Sun. 468.

BUTO, BUDO.

The Indians have a perfon whom they greatly reverence, and efteem a deity: and whom they call by thefe names. They are the fame as Botus, Battus of Cyrene, and Bœotus of Greece. The account given of him is fimilar to that of Typhon. His hiftory, though now current among the Indians, is of great antiquity. The name Boutas, &c. though apparently conferred upon the Patriarch, yet originally related to the machine, in which he was preferved.

Boutus, the city in Egypt, where was the floating temple, fignified properly the city of the float, or Ark.

The Bœotians who in the Dionufiaca fo particularly commemorated the Ark, were fuppofed to be defcended from an imaginary perfonage Bœotus; and from him likewife their country was thought to have received its name: but Bœotus was only a variation of Boutus, and Butus, the Ark. II. 327.

Boutoi. As the confinement during the Deluge was efteemed an interval of death, the Ark from thence was reprefented as a bier, or coffin: and Boutus had the fame fignification. Hence places of fepulture among the Egyptians had the name of Boutoi: but this was only in a fecondary fenfe, being derived from fome refinements in hiftory. 330.

BUTZAN.

BUTZAN.

So is Boutas called at this day by fome nations, and efteemed contemporary with Vifhnou. But-Zan, is Zeus Bœotius ; Deus Arkitis. Ib.

C.

CAϒ, XAI, CAIA, CAIAS,

SIGNIFIED a Cavern, or Houfe; for the firft houfes in the infancy of the world are fuppofed to have been caves or grottoes :

Tum primum fubiere domos; domus antra fuere.

Ovid. Met. L. 1. 121.

terms fimilar to the Cava, Cavus, Cavea, of the Romans. They do not relate merely to a cavern; but to temples founded near fuch places : oftentimes the cave itfelf was a temple.

Caieta, Καιήτη, in Italy near Cuma, was fo denominated on this account. It was a cave in the rock, abounding with variety of fubterranes, cut out into various apartments. Thefe were of old inhabited by Amonian priefts : for they fettled in thefe parts very early.

Καιαδις, or Καιαδας, a compound of Cai-Adas, the houfe of Death. It was a cavern of great depth, or extent at Lacedæmon, with a building over it; of which in aftertimes they made ufe to confine malefactors.

Cacus,

Cacus, his den, was properly a facred cave, where Chus was worfhiped, and the rites of fire were practifed. It is the fame name as Cufcha in Ethiopia, only reverfed. I. 113.

CAANTHUS,

His hiftory contains an epitome of the voyage undertaken by Cadmus, though with fome fmall variation. He is faid to have been the fon of Oceanus; which in the language of Egypt is the fame as the fon of Ogus, and Oguges; which latter is the fame as Ogyges, in whofe time the Flood was fuppofed to have happened. Caanthus was fent by his father to find his fifter Melia who had been ftolen. He paffed into Bœotia, and here he found that his fifter was detained by Apollo in the grove of Ifmenus. There was a fountain of the fame name near the grove, guarded by a dragon. He is faid to have caft fire into the facred recefs; on which account he was flain by Apollo. His ταφος, or tomb, was in after times fhewn by the Thebans. Some make Melie to be the mother of Europa, which, with other circumftances, fhew that the hiftories of Caanthus and Cadmus are one and the fame. His throwing fire into the facred grove, relates to the firft eftablifhment of Fire-worfhip at Thebes in the grove of Apollo Ifmenius. The fame hiftory is told under the character of a perfon called Curnus.

Caanthus, Cunthus, Cunæthus, were all titles of the fame deity called Can-Thoth in Egypt. II. 154.

CABALLIS,

The city of the Solymi, was named from Ca-bal, the place of the god Bal, or Baal.

Caballion in Gallia Narbonenfis, is a compound of Ca-Abelion, a well known deity, whofe name is is made up of titles of the Sun. The region was called Χαουαρα, from Cha-Our, some temple of Ur, erected by the Amonians who settled here.

Canoubis in Egypt, was a compound of Ca-Noubis.

Cabasa in the same country; a compound of Ca-Basa, called by many Besa, the Beseth of the Scriptures, a goddess well known in Egypt. She had a temple in Canaan called Beth Besa. I. 106.

CABEIRA

In Armenia; here was one of the most superb temples that ever existed, of which Strabo (l. 12.) gives a particular description. He stiles it the temple of Meen, and adds, εστι δε και τουτο της Σεληνης το ιερον. He stiles several of these, in different places, the temples του Μηνος Αρχαιου, Dei Luni Arkæi; by which is certainly meant *the Lunar deity of the Ark*. II. 310.

CABIRI.

The supposed Genius of the Ark was represented as a goddess; and worshiped under the titles of Melitta, Rhea, Cybele, and Damater; also of Isis and Athena. Of her priests the principal were the Cabiri; whose office and rites were esteemed particularly sacred, and of great antiquity. They were the same as the Curetes, Corybantes, Telchines, and the Idæi Dactyli of Crete. In treating of these much confusion has ensued from not considering, that both the deity, and priests, were comprehended under the same title. The original Cabiritic divinity was Zeuth, the same as Dionusus. Pausanias (l. 9.) calls him Prometheus, the father of mankind. This was no other than the Patriarch who was of so great repute for his piety and justice. Hence the other Cabiri, his immediate offspring, are said to be the sons of Sadyc; by which is signified *the just man*. This is the very title given to

G Noah.

Noah. (Gen. vi. 9.) All fcience, and every ufeful
art was attributed to him; and through his fons
tranfmitted to pofterity. Hence the author of the
Orphic Argonautica mentions (v. 17.) αγλαα δωρα
Καβειρων. They were reprefented as dæmons, and
in number three. Many times they arc reprefented as Heliadæ, or the offspring of the Sun,
ftiled Cam-Il; alfo the defcendants of Proteus, the
great prophet, and deity of the fea. According to
Varro (l. 4.) they were particularly ftiled Divi
Potes; by Caffius Hermina (Macrob. Sat. L. 3.)
Θεοι δυναλοι, Θεοι χρηςοι, Θεοι μεγαλοι. According to
Sanchoniathon they were the fame as the Corybantes and Diofcuri, the offspring of the juft man
Sadyc (Noah). They lived in the time of Elion,
furnamed the Moft High; and of a perfonage
named Barith. Befides many other cities, they are
faid to have built Berytus, and to have there confecrated Πονlου λειψανα; no doubt all that the Deluge had fpared. Thefe rites confifted in memorials of the Ark Berith, and of the perfons therein
preferved; who were the original Cabiri, or Baalim. By Sanchoniathon they are defcribed as
eight in number; the chief of whom was Afcle-
pius, the god of health, and reftorer of life. There
were many cities, and thofe in parts very remote,
where the Cabiritic rites were for a long time preferved. They were the fame as the Cabarni of the
Parians, who were equally priefts of Damater, who
with Ifis had the title of Cabiria. It is obfervable,
that the chief province of the Cabiri related to the
fea, and fhipping. Their influence was particularly implored by mariners for fuccefs in their
voyages. II. 461.

The fhrines, where the facred fhip of Ofiris was
reverenced, were efteemed oracular: and the priefts
who officiated, had among other titles that of
Cabiri. And it is probable, that both they and
their

their oracle are alluded to by Mofes (Gen. x. 10.)
when he prohibits that particular kind of divination, which he ftiles Chabar, Chabar. 519.

CADMUS.

The account of this fuppofed perfonage as given
by the Greeks is full of inconfiftencies: and if we
confider the whole hiftory of this celebrated hero,
we fhall find, that it was impoffible for one perfon
to have effected what he is fuppofed to have performed. His expeditions were various and wonderful; and fuch as in thofe early times would not
have been attempted, nor could ever have been
compleated. In ancient times but little correfpondence was maintained between nation and
nation; depredations were very frequent; and
every little maritime power was in a ftate of piracy:
fo that navigation was attended with great peril.
It is not therefore to be believed, that a perfon
fhould fo often rove upon the feas amid fuch
variety of nations, and refide among them at his
pleafure: much lefs that he fhould build temples,
found cities (an hundred in Lybia) and introduce
his religion, wherever he lifted; and this too only
in tranfient vifits. The truth feems to be this.
The travels of Cadmus, like the expeditions of
Perfeus, Sefoftris, and Ofiris, relate to Colonies,
which at different times went abroad, and were
diftinguifhed by this title. But what was the
work of many, and performed at various feafons,
has been attributed to one perfon. All who em-
barked under the fame name or title, were in aftertimes fuppofed to have been under the fame leader;
and to him was attributed the honour of every
thing performed. And as Colonies of the fame
denomination went to parts of the world widely
diftant; their ideal Chieftain, whether Cadmus, or
Bacchus, or Hercules, was fuppofed to have traverfed

verfed the fame ground ; and the atchievements of different ages were conferred upon a fancied hero of a day.

Cadmus was one of the names of Ofiris, the chief deity of Egypt. Both Harmonia and Europa are of the like nature. They were titles of the deity; but affumed by Colonies, who went out, and fettled under thefe denominations. He was the fame as Hermes of Egypt, called alfo Thoth, Athoth, and Canathoth : and was fuppofed to have been the inventor of letters. He was fometimes ftiled Cadmilus, another name for Hermes. That he was the fame as Ham will appear from the etymology of his name. Achad, Achon, and Achor were names of the Sun ; and the name of which we are treating, is a compound of Achad-Ham, rendered by the Greeks Acadamus, and Aca-demus, and contracted Cadmus.

The ftory then of Cadmus, and Europa, relates to people from Egypt, and Syria, who went abroad at different times, and fettled in various parts. They are faid to have been determined in their place of refidence by an ox, or cow : by which is only meant, that they were directed by an oracle : for without fuch previous enquiry no Colonies went abroad.

The Cadmians extended themfelves very far, quite to the Euphrates ; and weftward to the coaft of Greece, and Aufonia; and ftill farther to the great Atlantic. They went under the name of Ellopians, Oropians, Cadmonites, Hermonians, and more particularly Ophitæ, or Hivites; and therefore many places whither they came, were faid to fwarm with Serpents, as they introduced the Serpent-worfhip. Another of their titles was Heliadæ, or children of the Sun. They were looked upon as adepts in every branch of fcience, and particularly famed for their fkill in Aftronomy.

They

They were the first navigators of the feas; and the division of time with the notification of feafons is afcribed to them.

Cadmus is reprefented as a giant; and Nonnus fays that he planted in Greece a Colony of Giants. Hence the Cadmians were ftiled Ανακες, and Ανακίες, and the temples of their gods Ανακλορια. Thefe terms were imported from the Anakim of Egypt and Canaan. As they were alfo Auritæ, they were of the Shepherd race. And Cadmus is thus defcribed by Nonnus,

Κλινας γειλονι νωλον υπο δρυι φορβαδος υλης,
Και φορεων αγραυλον ανθεος ειμα Νομνος

———— —— —— ——

Θελξω δενδρεα παντα, και ουρεα, και φρενα θηρων·
Ωκεανον σπευδοντα παλινδινητον ερυξω.   L. 1.

It is faid of Cadmus, that at the clofe of his life he was, together with his wife Harmonia, changed to a Serpent of ftone, at Encheliæ. The true hiftory is this. Thefe two perfonages were enfhrined in a temple, or Petra, and worfhiped under the fymbol of a Serpent. II. 138.

CALLIMACHUS

Abounds with ancient Amonian terms. He and Lycophron lived in Egypt, and have continual allufions to the antiquities of that country. I. 86. 143.

CALPE

Is now called Gibel-Tar, or Gibraltar: which name relates to the hill where of old the pillar ftood. I. 263. n.

CAMARINA,

Upon the fouthern coaft of Sicily; here fome of the Cyclopians fettled; fome have fuppofed this to be the Hupereia of Homer (Od. Z. 5.) where the

Pheacians

Pheacians once refided. But there is no reafon to think that Hupereia was in Sicily; or that the Pheacians came from that country. I. 407.

CAMESE.

The Amonians fettled upon the Tiber; and the ancient town Janiculum was originally named Camefe; and the region about it Camefene (Cam-ees-ain) undoubtedly from the fountain fo called, afterwards called Aqua Perenna, whofe waters ran into the facred pool Numicius: and whofe priefts were the Camœnæ, for Cam-Ain is the fountain of the Sun; and they wete fo named from their attendance upon that deity. The hymns in the temples of that god were fung by women: hence the Camœnæ were made prefidents of mufic. I. 53. 64.

CAMPE, CAMPI,

A name for fome Amonian temples. The term afterwards fignified the parade before the temple, where the facred games were celebrated, and was expreffed Campus, which among the Latins came to fignify any open and level place; but the Sicilians preferved the true meaning; Καμπος, Ιππoδρομος, Σικυλοι. Hefych. It was indeed a place for exercifes in general. Hence a combatant was ftiled Campio, and the chief perfons, who prefided, Campigeni. Arpe, and Campe were mifinterpreted by the ancient Mythologifts, and reprefented as fo many dragons and Monfters. Nonnus thus fpeaks of the latter,

$$\text{———————— } \text{ης απο δειρης}$$
$$\text{Ηνθει πεν]ηκον]α καρνα]α ποικιλα θηρων. } \text{L. 18.}$$

Thefe fifty heads, were fifty priefts, who were efteemed as fo many wild beafts for their cruelty. There were many of thefe Campi in Greece, and
elfe-

elfewhere; for the Amonian religion obtained further than we are aware.   In our Ifland the exhibi-
tion of thofe manly exercifes, wreftling, &c. in
vogue among country people is called *Camping*, and
the inclofures for that purpofe, Camping clofes.
In Germany the name of Kæmpenfelt fignifies, I
imagine, a field for fports, and exercifes, like the
Gymnafium of the Greeks, and a Camping place in
Britain.

Campanians in Italy were an Amonian colony,
and denominated from Campe, or Campus, which
was probably the firft temple they erected. II. 53.

CAMPHIRE.

This the Egyptians ftiled Cham-phour, the
Καμφουρα of Greece. I. 333.

CAMPSA.

One name for the Crocodile; it fignifies an ark,
or receptacle, like Aren, Argus, &c. II. 398.

CAMULUS, CAMILLUS.

Under this name the deity of the gentile world
was worfhiped.   He was worfhiped by the Hetrurians, and efteemed the fame as Hermes.   Cham-
El, the fame as Elion, ὁ ὑψιϛος.   He was fometimes
expreffed Cafmillus, but ftill referred to Hermes.
I. 14.

Cam-Il, a title of the deity brought from Chaldea to Egypt, and from thence to Greece.   His
priefts were called Camilli. 101.

CANAAN.

It is probable, that the Canaanites had been in
the fame original rebellion in Babylonia, as the
fons of Chus; and that they were a part of the
difperfion.   It is alfo probable, that they came into
Canaan about the fame time that the others betook
themfelves to Egypt.   This is certain, that when

G 4   Abraham

Abraham traverfed the country, it is repeatedly
faid, that *the Canaanite was then in the land*. (Gen.
xii. 6. xiii. 7.)   From whence we may infer, that
they were but lately come.   And the facred writer,
fpeaking of Hebron, a feat of the Anakim, or
Titans, fays, that it *was built feven years before
Zoan in Egypt* (i. e. Heliopolis, towards the apex
of the Delta) Numbers xiii. 22.   By this we may
infer, that the two nations in fome degree corre-
fponded in their operations, and began building
about the fame time.

The diftribution of the whole earth was by
divine appointment; and the land of Canaan was
particularly allotted to the fons of Ifrael.   They
accordingly have this ftrongly inculcated to them,
that in the divifion of countries, *the Lord's portion
is his people; Jacob is the lot of his inheritance.*
(Deut. xxxix. 9.   Sirach xvii. 17.   Pfalm cv. 11.
Gen. xiii. 15. xv. 18.)   And yet even to Abraham, and to his pofterity, it was rather a loan than
a gift: for God feems always to have peculiarly
referved the property of this country to himfelf.
The Ifraelite therefore had never a full command
of it: he only held it at will, and was fubject to
God as proprietor.   In fhort, it was *the Lord's
portion.* (See Numbers xxv. 23.)   It was however
invaded, as were other places, in oppofition to the
divine appointment.   The fons of Chus firft
ufurped the region allotted to Afhur; and afterwards tranfgreffed ftill farther upon the property
of their neighbours.   Of all others the tranfgref-
fion of Canaan was the moft heinous; for he knowingly invaded God's peculiar portion, and feized
it to himfelf.

Sanchoniathon (ap. Eufeb. P. E. L. 1. p. 35.)
fpeaking of the people, who were diffipated at
Babel, and of the great works which they performed, concludes with this fhort, but remarkable
                                    character

character of them; *thefe are the people, who are
defcribed as exiles and wanderers, and at the fame
time are called the Titans.* The event of the difperfion feems to have been very happy in its confequences to thofe of the family of the Patriarch
Abraham; as it muſt have facilitated their conver-
fion; and given them an opening to retreat. They
lived in the land of Ur of the Chaldees; which lay
upon the Tigris, to the fouth of Babel and Babylonia. There was no paſſage for them to get
away, but through the above country : nor would
they have thought of migrating, fo long as they
followed the religion of their fathers. But when
Terah and his family had feen the tower fhaken to
its foundation, and the land made a defart ; it was
natural for them to obey the firſt call from heaven;
and to depart through the opening, which Providence had made. They therefore acceded to the
advice of Abraham, and followed him to Haran in
Mefopotamia, in his way to Canaan. The rout,
which the Patriarch took, was the true way to that
country; a circumſtance, which has been little
confidered.

Note : Terah and Nahor, and all the fons of
Heber had feparated themfelves from the ſtock of
their fathers, and dwelt in a forbidden land. Here
they ferved other gods. But the faith of Abraham
was at laſt awakened : to which perhaps nothing
contributed more than the demolition of the tower
of Babel, and the difperfion of the fons of Chus :
and laſtly, the wonderful and tremendous interpofition of the Deity in producing thefe effects. This
event not only infpired them with an inclination to
get away, but alfo afforded them an opening for
their retreat. III. 265.

CANEBRO.

CANEBRO.

We read in Artapanus, as quoted by Eufebius
(Hiſt. Synag. p. 230. edit. Scal. 1658.) that the
Cæn of Heliopolis had a daughter who married
one Canebro: in which the hiſtory of Joſeph is
obſcurely alluded to; who married Aſenath the
daughter of Potifera or Petifra, called by Eutychius
(Annales. ed. Pocock. tom. 1. p. 87.—See Gen.
xli. 45.) the Caen of Heliopolis. Canebro is the
Hebrew prince or ruler; Caen, Cohen, Con, having in many languages that ſignification. (*Chaan
auguſtum nomen eſt regum Tartariæ appellativum.*
Kæmpfer. Amœn. Exotic. p. 136.) Sabacon the
Ethiopian means Sabœ rex, " the Arabian king of
Saba;" and is not properly the name of the perſon
mentioned. Canoubis, or, as it ſhould be expreſſed, Can-Ouph, is " the lord Ouph;" Chiniladanus, the name of a king of Babylon, is Caen al
Adon, or Adonai. Thonos Concoleros, whom
Africanus ſpecifies by his twofold titles, Θωνος Κογ-
κολιρος, ὁ και Ἑλλνιςι Σαρδαναπαλος is Thonos Con
Oue Al Orus: which laſt has been by inexperienced
writers contracted to Coleros. Thamas Couli, the
late conqueror of Perſia, was diſtinguiſhed by the
ſame title, and called Couli Chan: which is ſtill
in uſe in great part of India and Tartary. The
German *koning* is ſimilar to it; and we ſeem to retain it in our word king, but more apparently in
the feminine. Maundeville calls the emperor of
China the Chane of Cathay. Chingis Chan, the
celebrated Tartar emperor, called Changius Chan
by Hatho, is interpreted the *king of kings*; and ſuch
is its purport; anſwering very nearly to words of
the ſame ſignification in the plural of the very old
Engliſh, *king-es king*. Obſervations. 163.

CANOBUS.

As the hiftory of the Argo related to an ancient event, which the Egyptians commemorated with great reverence; the delineation in the fphere was intended as a lafting commemoration of a wonderful deliverance: on which account one of the brighteft ftars in the Southern hemifphere is reprefented upon the rudder of the Ship. The ftar the Egyptians called Canobus, which was one of the titles of their chief deity, and it was placed on the rudder to fhew that Providence was its guide.

Vitruvius calls it Canopus; it was utterly invifible in all the celebrated places of Greece; which alone would prove that the fphere could not be the work of a Græcian; and that this afterifm could have no relation to that country.

Cahobus was alfo the name of a city upon the moft weftern branch of the Nile, much frequented by failors. II. 498.

CAPH, CAP, CEPHAS,

Signify a Rock; and alfo · a Promontory, or · Headland. As temples ufed to be built upon eminences of this fort; we find this word often compounded with the titles of the deity there worfhiped, as Caph-El, Caph-El-On, Caph-Aur, Caph-Arez, Caph-Is, Caph-Is-Ain, Caph-Ait; whence come Cephale, Cephalonia, Cephareus, Capifa, Capiffene, Cephene, Caphyatæ, Capatiani. In Iberia was a wonderful edifice upon the river Bœtis, mentioned by Strabo, and called Turris Capionis. It was a Pharos, dedicated, as all fuch buildings were, to the Sun; hence it was named Cap-Eon, Petra Solis. It feems to have been a marvellous ftructure. Places of this fort, which had towers upon them, were called Caphtor. Such a one was in Egypt, or in its vicinity; whence the Capthorim had their name.

name. It was probably near Pelufium, which they quitted very early for the land of Canaan. I. 95.

CAPHISUS

Is a compound of Caph-Ifis, which fignifies Petra Ifidis, and relates to the fame deity as Metis, for we muft not regard fexes, nor difference of appellations, when we treat of ancient deities.

Cephifus, its ftream and lake in Bœotia were ftiled ὑδαλα και λιμνη Κηφισσιδος, by the ancient Dorians expreffed Καφ-ισιδος. I. 511.

CAPPADOCIA.

Here were many Puratheia; and the people followed the fame manner of worfhip as was prac-tifed in Perfis.

CASTABALA,

A city in Cappadocia; it is a compound of Ca-Afta-Bala, the place or temple of Afta Bala, the goddefs of Fire; the fame as by the Syrians was called Baaltis. The fame cuftoms prevailed here as at Feronia in Latium. The female at-tendants in the temple ufed to walk with their feet bare over burning coals. I. 230.

CASTOR,

The fuppofed difciple of Chiron, was in reality the fame; being a facred tower, a Chironian edi-fice, which ferved both for a temple and Pharos. As thefe for the moft part ftood on ftrands of the fea, and promontories; he was efteemed in confe-quence of it a tutelary deity of that element. The term was fo abbreviated from Ca-Aftor, the temple or place of Aftor, by the Greeks, who continually miftook the place and temple for the deity, to whom it was confecrated. The whole hiftory of Caftor and Pollux, is very ftrange and inconfiftent. They were both the fame perfonage; and the deity

deity alluded to, under the name of Caftor, was the Sun;

Ηελιος, ὁς παντ᾽ εφορα, και παντ᾽ επακουει·

On this account the fame province of fupreme judge was conferred on his fubftitute Caftor, in conjunction with his brother Pollux: and they were accordingly looked upon as the confervators of the rights of mankind. I. 441. v. Cic. in Verrem. Or. 7. fect. ult. v. Anac.

CAVERNS.

Men repaired in the firft ages, when fuperftition increafed, either to the lonely fummits of mountains, or elfe to caverns in the rocks, and hollows in the bofom of the earth; which they thought were the refidence of their gods. At the entrance of thefe they raifed their altars, and performed their vows. When they began to erect temples, they were ftill determined in their fituation by the vicinity of thefe objects, which they comprehended within the limits of the facred inclofure. Thefe melancholy recefles were efteemed the places of the higheft fanctity; and even in after times the innermoft part of the temple was denominated *The Cavern.* I imagine that the word Caverna, was denominated originally Ca-Ouran, Domus cœleftis, or Domus Dei, from the fuppofed fanctity of fuch places. I. 217. The reverence paid to caves and grottos, arofe from a notion that they were a reprefentation of the world. 232.

CAUONES, ΧΑΤΩΝΕΣ,

Sacred cakes at Cha-On, which fignifies the houfe of the Sun. I. 297.

CAUCASUS

Mount, was fo denominated, as is fuppofed, from the Shepherd Caucafus; the women who officiated

ficiated in the temple, were ftiled his daughters, and reprefented as Furies; by which was meant prieft-efles of Fire. II. 42. n.

CECROPS,

By fome made firft king of Athens. He is faid to have been διφυης· συμφυες εχων σωμα ανδρος και δρα-κονος. This Diodorus and Euftathius in vain endeavour to explain. Some had mentioned, that he underwent a metamorphofis, απο οφιως εις ανθρωπον ελθειν, by which Euftathius fays (on Dionys. p. 56.) was meant that by coming into Hellas he became more civilized and humane. But this does not agree with the then infant ftate of Greece. The learned Marfham therefore animadverts with great juftice, eft verifimilius illum ex Ægypto mores magis civiles in Græciam induxiffe. Chron. Canon. p. 109. His mixed character may be eafily accounted for. Cecrops was certainly a title of the deity, who was worfhiped under this emblem. It may not perhaps be eafy to decipher the name; but thus much is apparent, that it was a compound of Ops, and Opis, and related to his fymbolical character. I. 484.

CENTAURUS.

The Ark feems to have been fometimes fo called; from whence many of the Arkites had the name of Centauri: and were reputed of the Nephe-lim race. Chiron was faid to be the fon of the Centaur Cronus, but the reft were the offspring of Ixion and Nephele. They are defcribed by Nonnus as horned, and as infeparable companions of Dio-nufus. II. 440.

CERAMICUS

At Athens, was alfo called Academia. The common notion was, that it was denominated from the hero Ceramus, the fon of Dionufus (the ufual miftake miſtake of place for perſon) but Ceramus was Cer-Ham, the tower, or temple of Ham, which gave name to the incloſure. II. 159.

CERBERUS,

The dog of hell, was denominated from Kir-Abor; and from this term, and of the deity Chan-Ades, the Greeks formed τον Κερβερον χυνα αδου, and fabled, that he was forced into upper air by Her-cules. The notion both of Cerberus and Hades being ſubterraneous deities took its riſe from the temples of old being ſituated near vaſt caverns, which were eſteemed paſſages to the realms below. I. 350.

Euſebius from Plutarch ſays that Cerberus was the Sun. Cerberus was properly Kir-Abor, the place of the Sun, the parent of light. The ſame temple had different names from the diverſity of the god's titles, who was there worſhiped. It was called Tor-Caph-El, which the Greeks changed to Τριχεφαλος: it was alſo called Tor-Keren, Turris Regia, which they expreſſed Τριχαρηνος; hence Ca-hen-Ades or Cerberus was ſuppoſed to have been a triple-headed monſter. (See Palæphatus, p. 56, and p. 96.) 409.

CERCETUS,

A remarkable mountain in Samos; ſo named undoubtedly from ſome building ſacred to the Cetus. II. 505.

CERCUSORA,

The iſland at the point of Delta, where ſtood the city Cercuſora, is called Gierat Eddahib, or the *Golden* iſland at this day. Diodorus mentions, that this appellation of Chruſe was derived from *a very ancient tradition.* This tradition undoubtedly related to the Shepherds, thoſe ſons of Chus who

9   were

were fo long in poffeffion of the country; and whofe hiftory was of the higheft antiquity. I. 363.

KEREN

Originally fignifies *a Horn*; it was efteemed an emblem of power; and made ufe of as a title of fovereignty. Hence the Greeks, who often changed the final Nu into Sigma, formed Κερας, Κεραλος, and from thence deduced the words Κραλος, Κραλερος, and alfo Κοιρανος, Κρεων, Καρηνον, all relating to ftrength and eminence.

The Egyptian Crane, for its great fervices to mankind was held in high honour, being facred to the god of light, Abis, or Ibis. It was alfo called Keren and Kerenus, by the Greeks Γερανος, the noble bird, being moft honoured of any. It was a title of the Sun himfelf: for Apollo was named Craneus, and Carneus, which was no other than Ceraneus, the fupreme deity, the lord of light; his feftival was ftiled Καρνεια, an abbreviation of Κερενια. The prieft of Cybele in Phrygia was ftiled Carnas; which was a title of the deity, whom he ferved, of the fame purport as Carneus. I. 46.

CERES,

The benefactrefs, and lawgiver, was fometimes enrolled in the lift of the Furies. Antimachus as quoted by Paufanias, L. 8.

Δημητρος, τοθι φασιν Εριννυος ειναι εδεθλον.

Schol. on Lycophron, v. 1225. Εριννυς η Δημητηρ εν Ογχαις πολει της Αρχαδιας τιμαται. Her temple ftood upon the river Ladon, and fhe had this name given to her by the people of the place, Καλουσι δε Εριννυν οι Θελπουσιοι την θεον. Neptune is faid to have lain with Ceres, when in the form of a Fury; fhe is faid from thence to have conceived the horfe Αρειον. II. 42. She is faid to have placed a dragon for a

guardian

guardian to her temple at Eleufis; and appointed
another to attend upon Erectheus. I. 483.

The rites however of this benefactrefs, and lawgiver, this innocent and rural goddefs, were fo
cruel, that fome of her temples were as much
dreaded, as thofe of Scylla, and the Cyclops. The
towers of Ceres were P'urtain, or Πρύ]ανπα; fo
called from the fires, which were perpetually there
preferved. The Greeks, through ignorance, interpreted this πυρου ταμπιον; and rendered, what
was the temple of Orus, *a granary of corn*: thus
Ceres became the goddefs of corn. In early times
the corn there depofited feems to have been for
the priefts and diviners. But this was only a
fecondary ufe, to which thefe places were adapted.
They were properly facred towers, where a perpetual fire was preferved. (Paufan. L. 8.—L. 5.)
As in thefe temples there was always a light, and a
fire burning on the hearth, fome of the Græcians
have varied in their etymology, and have derived
the name from Πυρ, *fire*. (Suid. Schol. in Thucyd.
L. 2.) Thefe temples were alfo courts of juftice:
hence we find, that in the Prutaneion at Athens, the
laws of Solon were engraved. (Paufan. L. 1.
Plutar. in Solone.)

The perfons who refided in thefe temples were
of great ftrength and ftature; many were of the
race of Anac. There is reafon to think, that
ftrangers were obliged to fight with fome of the
priefts, who were trained up for that purpofe, with
the cæftus, or by wreftling: and this was looked
upon as a more fpecious kind of facrifice. Cercyon of Megara was famed for wreftling; and flew
many. Cercyon was the name of the place; and
they were the Cercyonians, the priefts, who were
noted for thefe atchievements. (Paufan. L. 1.)
Ancient hiftory affords numberlefs inftances of
this ungenerous and cruel treatment of ftrangers;

H   and

and the laws of hofpitality were evaded under the undue fanction of a facrifice to the gods. Thefe attributes of wreftling and boxing have been conferred upon fome of the chief divinities. Hercules and Pollux (thofe imaginary beings) were of that number; yet they are reprefented upon earth as fturdy fellows, a kind of honourable banditti, who righted fome, and wronged many; who would fuffer nobody to do any mifchief, but themfelves. From thefe cuftoms were derived the Ifthmian, Nemean, Pythic, Olympic, and Delian games (v. Hom. H. in Apoll.) Thefe contentions had always in them fomething cruel, and favage; but in later times they were conducted with an appearance of equity.

When the Spaniards got accefs to the weftern world, there were to be obferved many rites, and many terms, fimilar to thofe, which were fo common among the fons of Ham. Among others was this particular cuftom of making the perfon, who was defigned for a victim, engage in a fight with a prieft of the temple. In this manner he was flaughtered: and this procedure was efteemed a proper method of facrifice. (Purchafs. V. 5. Garcilaffo d. Vega. Ryc.) II. 37. v. *Temple Rites.* Cercyon, above mentioned, is compounded of Ker-Cuon, and fignifies the temple of the deity.

CETUS, ΚΗΤΟΣ, GATUS,

Names of the Fifh, under the femblance of which, the Ark was figured, in which mankind was preferved: and compounded Atargatis, and Atargatus: whence came Dercetus, and Dercetis of the Greeks. Macrobius makes Atargatis the mother of the gods. (Saturn. L. 1.) That this emblem related to the Ark, is manifeft from its being reprefented as a facred receptacle, wherein
the

the gods were inclofed. See Simplic. on Ariftot. de Occul. Phyfic. L. 4. The machine which was figured by the Atargatis did really contain the perfons alluded to; all thofe, who were ftiled Θεοι, και Δαιμονες; thofe reputed gods, the Baalim of the firft ages. II. 311.

The Ark was defcribed under the emblem of a large fifh, which Pliny terms fabulofa Ceto; and from this reprefentation fhips, which were unwieldy, and of great burthen, were often called Cetenæ. Καλ]νη, πλοιον μεγα ως Κηλος. Hefych. II. 408.

In ancient times great depredations were committed by rovers at fea, who continually landed, and laid people under contribution upon the coaft. Piracy and plunder were of old efteemed very honourable. Many migrations were made by perfons, who were obliged to fly, and leave their wives and effects behind them. Such loffes were to be repaired, as foon as they gained a fettlement. Hence, when they infefted any country, and made their levies upon the natives, one of their principal demands was women; and of thefe the moft noble and fair. (v. Diod. Sic. L. 5. p. 432.) Thefe depredations gave rife to the hiftories of princeffes being carried away by banditti; and of king's daughters being expofed to fea-monfters. The monfters alluded to were nothing more than mariners and pirates, ftyled Cetei, Ceteni, and Cetones, from Cetus; which fignified a fea-monfter, or whale; and alfo a large fhip. (Hefych.) They were Ceteans, and Cetonians; fome of whom fettled in Phrygia, and Myfia, where they continued the like practices, and made the fame demands. Κηλειοι, γενος Μυσων. Hefych. Their hiftory is undoubtedly alluded to by Homer in a paffage (Od. Λ. v. 518.) which Strabo (L. 13. p. 915.) looked upon as an enigma. The poet is

fpeaking

ſpeaking of Neoptolemus, whoſe great exploits are related by Ulyſſes to the ſhade of Achilles in the regions below. Among other things he ſeems to refer to ſome expedition made againſt the Myſians. He tells him, that he cannot enumerate all the actions of his ſon:

> Αλλ' οιον Τηλεφιδην κατενηρατο χαλκῳ
> Ἡρω Ευρυπυλον, πολλοι δ' αμφ' αυτον εταιροι
> Κητειοι κτεινοντο, Γυναικων εινεκα δωρων.

i. e. *on account of the unjuſt gifts, which they extorted, and which conſiſted in women.* Now when we know, that the Ceteans were people, who uſed to make theſe demands; and that the Myſians were Ceteans: I think we may be aſſured of the true meaning of the poet. In ſhort, theſe Myſians were Cuthites, and by race Nebridæ. Νεβρωδ ὁ κυνηγος και γιγας, ὁ Αιθιοψ, εξ ὁυ Μυσοι. (Heſych.) III. 549.

CEYLON.

The Cuthites ſent out many colonies, into various parts of the world. Some of them ſeized upon the province of Suſiana and Chuſiſtan, and poſſeſſed the navigation of the Tigris downward. They got footing in India, where they extended themſelves beyond Gedroſia and Carmania. The author of the Periplus takes notice of them under the name of Scythians. (Arriani Perip. 2. Geog. Vet. v. 1. p. 21.) They occupied alſo that inſular province, called in their language from its ſituation, Giezerette, or the iſland: and from their anceſtor, as well as from their worſhip, Cambaiar, or the Bay of Cham, which name it retains to this day. They ſettled alſo upon the promontory Comar, or Comarim: and were lords of the great iſland Palæſimunda, called afterwards Seran-dive.

They

They were all ftyled the Southern Scuthæ. (Dion.
Perieg. v. 1088. Prifcian. v. 996.)

In the ifland Palæfimunda or Ceylon, called alfo
Taprobane, the adoration of Fire and the worfhip
of the Sun were introduced very early. In this
ifland is an high mountain, held very facred; the
fummit of which is called the Pike of Adam. This
had no relation to the great Protoplaft: and I am
perfuaded, that there are very few allufions in
ancient hiftory to the antediluvian world. The
Pike of Adam is properly the fummit facred to
Ad Ham, the king, or deity Ham. This is plain
to a demonftration from another name given to it
by the native Cingalefe, who live near the mountain, and call it Hamalel. This without any
change, is Ham-al-El, *Ham the Sun*; and relates
to the ancient religion of the ifland. In fhort,
every thing in thefe countries favours of Chaldaic
and Egyptian inftitution. III. 192.

CHABARENI,

The name of a people, who lived in a province
near Colchis; and were fo called from Cha-Baren,
Domus Arcæ. They ufed to behave very inhu-
manly to all ftrangers, whom chance brought upon
their coaft: and feem to have been very refined in
their cruelty. (Steph. Byzant. Χαϐαρηνοι.) They
were probably the fame as the Thebeans, called
Tibareni: for they all have a reference to the fame
worfhip of Theba, and Arene. III. 546.

CHALDEANS,

Who were particularly poffeffed of the land of
Ur, and were worfhipers of Fire, had the name of
Urchani. There feems to have been particular
colleges appropriated to the aftronomers and priefts
in Chaldea, which were called Conah. I. 41.

H 3   Ham,

temple for the deity. Charon was the very place; the ancient temple of the Sun. It was therefore called Char-On, from the god who was there worshiped; and after the Egyptian custom an eye was engraved over the portal.

These temples were sometimes called Charis, a compound of Char-Is, which signifies a prutaneion, or place sacred to Hephastus. The Grecians rendered it by Χαρις, a term in their own language, which signified grace and elegance. They were attached to ancient terms, but were strangers to their true meaning. I. 498. As *Charis* was a tower sacred to Fire, some poets have supposed a nymph of that name, who was beloved of Vulcan. The Graces were said to be related to the Sun, who was the same as Vulcan. The Sun among the people of the East was called Hares, and with a guttural Chares, and his temple Tor-Chares, which was expressed by the Greeks Τριχαρες; and from thence they formed the notion of the three Graces. The Χαρις of the Greeks, was the same personage as Ceres of the Romans. I. 500.

CHARONIUM,

And Plutonium, names of a sacred cavern, which sent up pestilential effluvia. Εν Ἱεραπολει της Φρυγιας Ἱερον ην Απολλωνος, ὑπο δε τον ναον καταβασιον ὑπεκειτο, θανασιμους αναπνοας παρεχομενον. Damascius ap. Photium in vita Isodori. c. 242. Strabo, L. 14. mentions four caverns of this sort, and so named in this part of the world. Pliny, N. H.. L. 2. speaking of some Charonean hollows in Italy, says, Spiracula vocant, alii Charoneas scrobes, mortiferum spiritum exhalantes. I. 29.

CHAROPS.

Near the mount Laphystium in Bœotia the god Charops was worshiped, and stiled Hercules Charops.

Charops. But Char-Ops, or Char-Opis, fignified
the temple of the Serpent deity; and was undoubtedly built of old by the people named Charopians,
and Cyclopians, who were indeed the ancient
Cadmians. II. 159.

CHEMMIS,

The floating ifland, near the temple of Boutus
high in Upper Egypt. This was probably a large
Ark, or float, a beautiful place, and of uncommon
conftruction. There were feveral altars erected
to Ofiris, together with a ftately temple. It was
undoubtedly a memorial of the firft fhip, and defigned alfo for a repofitory, where the Arkite rites
and hiftory were preferved. II. 329.

CHERES.

There were feveral kings in Egypt of the name
of Cheres: fome are ftiled Acheres or Acherres;
which is " the mighty Cheres:" others are ftiled
Conchares and Achencheres, i. e. Ouc Cahen
Cheres, " the great lord and ruler Cheres."
Acheres and Achencheres is, according to the
Greek acceptation, " the great lord Mars:" but
it is properly Arez, *a lion*; from whence the Αρης
of the Greeks was derived. Αλκης μεν και ρωμης
συμβολον αυτοις ο Λεων. (Clem. Strom. L. 5. p. 671.)
It was a title firft conferred upon the third king of
Affyria. The Egyptians, who called Ham, Cham,
pronounced Arez, Charez and Cherez: hence
Acchencherez, or Ouc-cahen-charez. So Hala,
Habor, Haran, were at times pronounced Chala,
Chabor, Charan. Thefe titles were retained by
the Egyptians even in later times. *Obfervations,*
165. v. *Iconuphy.*

4   CHIMÆRA

CHIMÆRA

Is a compound of Cham-Ur, the name of the deity, whofe altar ftood towards the top of the mountain. I. 206.

CHINA.

The fame mythology, and the fame hierogly-phics relating to the Ark, which are to be met with in divers countries, were carried as far as China and Japan, where they are to be found at this day. II. 327.

Ar-Chota is the fame as Cothopolis, or the city of Cutha. The Arachotians are ftiled Λινοχλαινοι, from their particular habit, which was of linen. This circumftance is a ftrong characteriftic of the Amonians. In every place where they fettled, it feems, that they were famous for this manufacture. (1 Kings x. 28. Ifaiah xix. 9.) Colchis was fa-mous for its flax and linen; fo was Campania in Italy; the linen habit prevailed in Bœtica, efpe-cially among the priefts. (Sil. Ital. L. 3. v. 25.) It feems to have been univerfally the garb of the Cuthic Indians. (Philoft. Vita Apollon. L. 2. p. 79.) This was the exprefs habit of the Egyptians, whom this people refembled in many other refpects.

From circumftances of this nature, many learned men have contended that the Indians, and even the Chinefe, were a colony from Egypt. (Memoire dans lequel on prouve, que les Chinois font une colonie Egyptiene, &c. Par M. de Guignes, de l'Academie Royale, a Paris. 1760.) While others have proceeded as warmly upon the oppofite principle; and have infifted that the Egyptians, or at leaft their learning and cuftoms, are to be derived from the Indi and Seres. But neither opinion is quite true; nor need we be brought to
                                                        this

this alternative; for they both proceeded from one central place: and the fame people, who imported their religion, rites, and fcience into Egypt, carried the fame to the Indus and Ganges; and ftill farther into China and Japan. Not but that fome colonies undoubtedly came from Egypt; but the arts and fciences imported into India came from another family, even the Cuthites of Chaldea. Ex Χαλδαιων γαρ λεγεται φοιτησαι ταυτα προς Αιγυπτιους, χακειθεν προς Ελληνας. (Zonar. v. 1. p. 22.) III. 199.

One of the moft confiderable colonies, which went from Babylonia, was that of the Indi, or Sindi; who were further diftinguifhed by the name of the eaftern Ethiopians. They fettled between the Indus and Ganges, and one of their principal regions was Cuthaia, by the Græcians rendered Cathaia. They traded in linen and other commodities. A large body paffed inland towards the north, under the name of Sacæ and Sacaians (Σακαι. τους Σκυθας ουτω φασι. Steph. Byz. Plin. L. 6. c. 18.) and got poffeffion of Sogdiana, and the region upon the Iaxartes. The Tartarian nations are defcended from them. They got poffeffion of the upper part of China, which they denominated Cathaia: and there is reafon to think, that Japan was in fome degree peopled by them.

The Chinefe were the ancient Sinæ, and Seres; who were fo famous for their filk. Paufanias (L. 6. p. 519.) defcribes two nations of the Seres; who were of an Ethiopic, Indic, and Scuthic family. The firft was upon the Ganges; the other region of the Seres, is the fame as China; and lies oppofite to the iflands of Japan, called by Paufanias Abafa and Sacaia. The latter name ftill remains. The capital is fo named, and is famous for the worfhip of the god Dai-Maogen (which probably is Deus Magog, five Deus Magus.)

The

The names of the deities in Japan and China, and the form of them, as well as their mythology, point out the country, from whence they originally came. The people, who introduced these things in the upper region of this country, were the northern Seres, a branch of the Cathaian Sacæ. They were a different people from the Sinæ and Sinenses, though at last incorporated with them. They called the chief city Sera, and the region Cathaia.

In China the deity upon the Lotos in the midst of waters has been long a favorite emblem, and was imported from the west. The insigne of the dragon was from the same quarter. The Cuthites worshiped Cham, the Sun; whose name they variously compounded. In China most things, which have any reference to splendour, and magnificence, seem to be denominated from the same object. Cham is said in the language of that country to signify any thing *supreme*. Cum is a fine building, or palace; similar to Coma of the Amonians. Cum is a lord or master; Cham a sceptre; by Cham is also signified a priest, analogous to the Chamamim and Chamerim of Cutha, and Babylonia. The country itself is by the Tartars called Ham. The cities Cham-ju, Campion, Compition, Cumdan, Chamul, &c. are manifestly compounded of the sacred term Cham. Chambalu, the name of the ancient metropolis, is the city of Cam-Bal : and Milton stiles it very properly, *Cambalu, seat of Cathaian Chan*. By this is meant the chief city of the Cuthean monarch ; for Chan is a derivative of Cahen, a Prince. It seems sometimes in China and Japan to have been expressed Quan, and Quano. The Lama, and Lamas, those priests of Thibet and Tartary, are of the same original as the Lamii in the west.

Hamelton

Hamelton (Account of the Eaſt Indies. v. 2. p. 57.) takes notice of two temples near Syrian in Pegu : one was called Kiakiack, or *the god of god's temple*. The image was in a ſleeping poſture, and ſixty feet in length. The other is called the temple of Dagun; and the doors and windows. are continually ſhut; ſo that none can enter but the prieſts. They will not tell of what ſhape the idol is; but only ſay, that it is not of a human form. I make no doubt, but the true name of the temple was Iäch-Iäch, and dedicated to the ſame god, as the Iächuſi in Japan. It is very certain that the worſhip of Dionuſus prevailed very early in the eaſt. (v. Bayer. Hiſt. Bactrian. p. 2, 3.) As to Dagun, or Dagon in the other temple; we may conclude, that it was no other than that mixed figure of a man and a fiſh, under which he was of old worſhiped both in Palæſtine and Syria. He is expreſſed under this ſymbolical repreſentation in many parts of India; and by the Brahmins is called Wiſtnou, and Viſhnou. Dagon and Noah are the ſame. Viſh-nou is repreſented, like Dagon, under the mixed figure of a man and a fiſh; or rather of a man, a princely figure, proceeding from a fiſh. The name of the diſtrict, near which the temples above ſtand, we find to be called Syrian : juſt as the region was named, where ſtood the temples of Atargatus and Dagon. Syrus, Syria, and Syrian, are all of the ſame purport, and ſignify Cœleſtis, and Solaris, from Sehor, the Sun.

It is remarkable, that in Japan, the prieſts and nobles have the title of Cami (Kæmpfer. L. 2. p. 153.) The emperor Quebacondono, in a letter to the Portugueſe viceroy, 1585, tells him, *that Japan is the kingdom of Chamis; whom we hold to be the ſame as Scin, the origin of all things*. By Scin is probably ſignified San, the Sun; who was the ſame as Cham, rendered here Chamis. The founder of

the

the empire is said to have been Tensio Dai Sin, or *Tensio, the god of light.* Near his temple was a cavern, religiously visited, upon account of his having been once hid: when no sun, nor stars appeared. He was esteemed the fountain of day, and his temple was called the temple of Naiku. Near this cavern was another temple; in which the Canusi, or priests, shewed an image of the Deity, sitting upon a cow. It was called Dainits No Ray, *the great representation of the Sun.*

One of their principal gods is Iakusi; similar to the Iacchus of the west. Kæmpfer (L. 5. p. 493.) says, that he is the Apollo of the Japonese; and they describe him as the Egyptians did Orus. His temple stands in a town called Minnoki: Iachusi is here represented upon a gilt Tarate flower; which is said to be the nymphæa palustris maxima; or faba Ægyptiaca of Prosper Alpinus. One half of a large scallop shell is like a canopy placed over him; and his head is surrounded with a crown of rays. They have also an idol Menippe, much reverenced. It certainly relates to the same person; and is a compound of the two terms, Μην Ἱππα, Meen Hippa.

Kæmpfer, a writer of great credit, saw likewise the temple of Dabys, more truly rendered by him Daibod (and still more precisely by Lewis Almeida, Dai-But.) Dai, in the ancient language of the eastern countries, signified *Deus,* and *Divus,* any thing divine. By Dai-Bod was meant the god Budha; whose religion was styled the Budso. By Budha we are certainly to understand the idolatrous symbol, called by some nations Budda; the same as Argus and Theba. In the mythology transmitted concerning it, we may see a reference both to the machine itself, and to the person preserved in it. In consequence of which we find this person also styled Bod, Budha, and Buddo;

and

and in the weft Butus, Battus, and Bœotus. He was faid by the Indians not to have been born in the ordinary way; but to have come to light indirectly through the fide of his mother. By Clemens of Alexandria (Strom. L. 1. p. 359.) he is called Bouta : and in the hiftory of this perfon, however varied, we may perceive a relation to the Arkite deity of the fea, called Pofeidon : alfo to Arcalus, and Dionufus; ftyled Bœotus and Thebanus.

The Ark was reprefented under the fymbol of an Egg, called the Mundane Egg. It was alfo defcribed under the figure of a Lunette, and called Selene, the Moon. The perfon by whom it was framed, and who through its means was providentially preferved, occurs under the character of a fteer, and the machine itfelf under the femblance of a cow or heifer. Traces of thefe hieroglyphics may be obferved in Japan; which were carried thither by the Indic Ethiopians. They introduced the worfhip of their deified anceftors, and the events of thefe firft ages, which were couched under thefe well known fymbols. Confult Ambaffades memorables de la Compagnie des Indes Orientales des Provinces Unies, vers les Empereurs du Japon. Amfterd. 1680. tom. 1. p. 206.

The hiftory of Japan is divided into three æras, gods, demigods, and mortals. (Kæmpfer. L. 2. p. 143.) ' The perfon, whom the natives look upon as the real founder of their monarchy, is named Syn Mu ; in whofe reign the Sinto religion was introduced. To the Sinto was afterwards added the Budfo, together with the worfhip of Amida. This deity was commonly reprefented with the head of a dog : and they efteemed him the guardian of mankind. This religion was more complicated than the former ; and abounded with hieroglyphical reprefentations, and myfterious rites.

rites. It is the fame, which I term the Arkite idolatry; wherein the facred fteer and cow were venerated: the deity was reprefented upon the lotus, and upon a tortoife; and oftentimes as proceeding from a fifh. In this alfo, under the character of Buddha, we may trace innumerable memorials of the Ark; and of the perfon preferved in it. Kæmpfer (L. 2. p. 163.) having mentioned the eleventh emperor inclufive from Syn Mu, tells us, that in his time thefe rites began. *In his reign Budo, otherwife called* KOBOTUS, *came over from the Indies into Japan, and brought with him, upon a White Horfe, his religion, and doctrine.* We find here, that the object of worfhip is made the perfon, who introduced it; (a miftake, which has almoft univerfally prevailed:) otherwife in this fhort account what a curious hiftory is unfolded! III. 553. v. *Cibotus. Horfe of Neptune.*

CHIRON,

So celebrated for his knowledge, feems to have been a meer perfonage formed from a tower, or temple of that name. It ftood at Nephele in Theffaly; and was inhabited by a fet of priefts, called Centauri. They were fo denominated from the deity they worfhiped, who was reprefented under a particular form. They ftiled him Cahen-Taur; he was the fame as the Minotaur of Crete, and the Tauromen of Sicilia. Chiron is a compound of Chir-On, in purport the fame as Kir-On, the tower and temple of the Sun. In places of this fort people ufed to ftudy the heavenly motions; and they were made ufe of for feminaries, where young people were inftructed; on which account they were ftiled παιδότροφοι. Hence Achilles was fuppofed to have been taught by Chiron, and fo were numberlefs others. (v. Xen. de Venat.) But this could not be true of Chiron as a perfon; he

could

could not have had pupils of fuch different ages, and fo many different countries; befides many of them were manifeftly ideal perfonages: fuch as Apollo himfelf, and Æfculapius in the medicinal arts. Now Æfculapius was the Sun; by fome called the fon of Apollo; by others introduced rather as a title, and annexed to the names of different gods. Thofe who were inftructed partook only of Chironian education; and were taught in the fame academy: but not by one perfon, nor probably in the fame place; for there were many fuch towers for the purpofe of education in the fciences. Thefe places were likewife courts of judicature, where juftice was adminiftered: whence Chiron was faid to have been φιλοφρονιων, και δικαιοlαloς. Right was probably more fairly determined in the Chironian temples, than in others. Yet the whole was certainly attended with fome inftances of cruelty: for human facrifices are mentioned as once common, efpecially at .Pella in Theffaly. I. 435.

CHO, CHOA.

From hence probably was derived the word Χοϊκος, ufed by the Apoftle, 1 Cor. xv. 47, 48.— επλινος, γηινος. Hefych. I. 117. v. Κωοι.

CHUS

Was rendered by the Greeks Χυσος, but more commonly Χρυσος, and the places denominated from him were changed into Χρυση, and to Chrufopolis.

His name was often compounded Chus-Or, rendered by the Greeks Χρυσωρ, and Chrufaor, which among the Poets became a favourite epithet, continually beftowed upon Apollo. Hence there were temples dedicated to him, called Chrufaoria.

Chus, in the Babylonifh dialect, feems to have been called Cuth. And many places, where his

I   pofte-

posterity settled, were stiled Cutha, Cuthaia, Cutaia, Ceuta, Cotha, and compounded Cothon.

He was sometimes expressed Casus, Cessius,
Casius; and was still farther diversified. I. 5.

Chusistan, to the east of the Tigris, was the land
of Chus; it was likewise called by different writers,
Cutha and Cissia.

Chus was the father of all those nations stiled
Ethiopians (v. Joseph. Ant. Jud. l. 1. c. 6.) who
were more truly stiled Cuthites, and Cuseans. They
were more in number, and far more widely extended, than has been imagined. .ib. Chus was
the son of Ham; and though the names of the
Græcian deities are not uniformly appropriated, yet
Ham is generally looked upon as Ἥλιος, the Sun;
and had the title Dis, and Dios: hence the city of
Amon in Egypt was rendered Diospolis. If then
Chrusus and Chrusor be Chus; the person so denominated must have been, according to the more
ancient mythology, the son of Helius, and Dios.
And accordingly the Scholiast on Pindar expressly
says, Διος παις ὁ Χρυσος—εκ δε Ἡλιου ὁ Χρυσος. Magic
and incantations are attributed to Chus, as the
inventor; and they were certainly first practised
among his sons. (v. Sanchon. ap. Euseb. Pr. Ev.
l. 1. c. 10.) He was however esteemed a great
benefactor; and many salutary inventions were
attributed to him. He had particularly the credit
of being the first who ventured upon the seas.
Whether this can be said truly of Chus himself, is
uncertain: it agrees full well with the history of
his sons; who, as we have the greatest reason to be
assured, were the first great navigators in the world.
I. 365.

There were in India several cities, and temples,
dedicated to the memory of Chus. Some of these
are famous at this day, though denominated after
the

5

the Babylonifh dialect Cutha and Cuta.   Witnefs
Calcutta and Calecut. 364.

CIBOTUS, ΚΙΒΩΤΟΣ,

Is a term under which the Græcians reprefénted
the Ark, though the word feem not to be of
Græcian original; as both an haven in Egypt, and
a city in Phrygia of great antiquity, were fo denominated. It was called Apamea in latter times.
It was undoubtedly the fame as Celæne; though,
I fhould imagine, this was the name of the city,
and Cibotus was properly the temple.   There
feems to have been a notion that the Ark itfelf
refted upon the hills of Celænæ, where the city
Cibotus was founded. (See Orac. Sibyllin. p. 180.)
The people were called Magnetes.   The rites of
Damater related to the Ark and Deluge, like thofe
of Ifis : and the facred emblems, whatever they
may have been, were carried in an holy machine,
called Κιϐωτος. II. 229.

Strabo (l. 17.) fpeaks of a city Cibotus in Egypt,
which he reprefents as a dock, where were all con-
veniences for fhips to be built and repaired. 329.

CINNABAR,

Κινναϐαρις was denominated from Chan-Abor.

CINNAMON,

From Chan-Amon : for whatever the Egyptians
efteemed falutary, or of great value, they diftinguifhed by the title of facred, and confecrated to
fome god. I. 333.

CINNOR.

So was ftiled *the Harp*, and was fuppofed to have
been found out by Cinaras; which terms are compounded of Chan-Or, and Chan-Arez; and relate
to the Sun or Apollo, the fuppofed inventor of the
lyre. ib.

CIPPI.

The more difficult the navigation was, the more places of fanctity were erected upon the coaft. The Bofporus was efteemed a dangerous pafs; and upon that account abounded with Cippi, and altars. Thefe were originally mounds of earth, and facred to the Sun; upon which account they were called Col-On. It was not only upon rocks and mountains, that thefe Cippi and Obelifks were placed by. the ancients; they were to be ·found in their temples, where for many ages a rude ftock or ftone ferved for a reprefentation of the deity. They were fometimes quite fhapelefs; but generally of a conical figure. I. 267. v. Paufan. l. 9. Clem. Alexand. l. 1.

KIR, CAER, KIRIATH,

Are words of the like import, and fignify *a city*. We read in Scripture of Kiriath Sepher, Kiriath Arba, Kiriath Jearim. It was in fome parts pronounced Kirtha, and Cartha.

Carthage was Καρχηδων, from Car-Chadon, the fame as Adon. It was alfo called Carthada from Cartha-Ada, the city of the queen, or goddefs, who was by the Romans fuppofed to be Juno, but was properly the Amonian Elifa. [Carthage was alfo called Cadmeia. II. 147.]

Caer among many ancient nations fignified a *City*, or *Fortrefs*, as we may learn from the places called Carteia, Carnaim, Caronium, Caroura, Carambis. ·

Among the Britons were places of old exactly analagous, as Caerlifle, Caerdiffe, Caerphilly, Caernarvon, and Caeuriah in Cornwall. In Scripture we meet with Kir Harefh, Kir Harefeth, Kir Heres, of the fame purport as Kir Harefh.

In

In Cyprus was Kironia, rendered by Ptolemy
Κιρωνια; the true name was Kir-On, the city of
the Sun; where was a temple to Our-Ain, ſtiled
Urania. Kir-On was often rendered Cironis,
Coronis; and the deity Coronus and Cronus.   By
theſe means the place was ſubſtituted for the deity,
and made an object of worſhip; an abuſe which
frequently occurs. I, 91.

There is an inſcription in Gruter, p. 57. n. 13.
Marti Ciradino, &c. where there is a mixed title
of the deity formed from his place of worſhip.
Cir-Adon was the temple of Adon, or Adonis; the
Amonian title of the chief god. II. 159.

CNA.

Canaan ſeems, by the Egyptians and Syrians, to
have been pronounced Cnaan; rendered by the
Greeks Cnas, and Cna.   Steph. Byzant. ſays, that
the ancient name of Phenicia was Χνα. (See alſo
Euſeb. Pr. Ev. l. 1. c. 10.) Iſiris, the ſame as
Oſiris, is ſaid to have been brother to Cna; Ισιρις-
αδιλφος Χνα.   The purport of which is conformable
to the Scripture account, that the Egyptians were
of a collateral line with the people of Canaan; or
that the father of the Mizraïm, and of the Canaanites, were brothers. I. 6.

CNOPIA

Is a contraction for Can-Opia; and the temple
was certainly founded by people in Egypt. It took
its name from Can-Ope, or Can-Opus, the Ophite
god of that country; and of the people likewiſe by
whom the building was erected. II, 168.

CNUPHIS,

And Thermuthis, are generally crowned with the
flower of the Lotus. II. 400,

COCUTUS,

Which we render Cocytus, was undoubtedly a temple in Egypt; it gave name to a ſtream on which it ſtood, and which was alſo called the Charonian branch of the Nile, and the river Acheron. Cocutus was the temple of Cutus or Cuth: for ſo Chus was called by many of his poſterity. A temple of the ſame name was to be found in Epirus, upon a river Cocutus. I. 108.

COHEN,

Of the Hebrews; and which ſeems among the Egyptians, and other Amonians, to have been pronounced Cahen. Chan ſignified a Prieſt; alſo a Lord or Prince: theſe two offices being formerly united.

> Rex Anius, Rex idem hominum, Phœbique
> Sacerdos.

The term was ſometimes uſed with a greater latitude, and denoted any thing noble and divine. Hence we find it prefixed to the names both of deities and men; and of places denominated from them. It is often compounded with Athoth, as Canethoth; and we meet with Can-Oſiris, Can-Ophis, Can-Ebron, &c.

It was ſometimes expreſſed Cun; and among the Athenians was the title of the ancient prieſts of Apollo, whoſe poſterity were ſtiled Κυννιδαι; and Apollo himſelf was ſtiled Κυννιος, hence Κυνην, προσκυνην, προσκυνησις, well known terms of adoration. It ſeems to have been alſo a title of the true God, who is by Moſes (Gen. xiv. 19.) ſtiled Konah. This term is ſometimes ſubjoined. I. 40.

It was ſometimes expreſſed Con, which ſignifies the great Lord; which the Greeks made Caucon, a hero; it was properly a temple of the Sun; there was one in Bithynia; hence the country was called Cauconia. Strabo (l. 8.) mentions Caucones

in

in Elea. And they are mentioned by Homer. Od. γ. 366. They were Cuthite colonies. 108.

The term Cahen was not confined to men only; it is frequently annexed to the names of deities, to fignify their rule and fuperintendency over the earth. From them it was derived to their attendants, and to all perfons of a prophetical or facred character. However plain the meaning was, yet the Greeks and Romans conftantly mifapplied it. As the found approached near to their Κυων, and Canis, they imagined it had fome reference to a *dog*, which gave rife to many abfurd ftories. See Ælian de Animalibus, l. 7. Plutarch adv. Stoicos. Vol. II. p. 1064. Lycophron, who has continual allufions to obfolete terms, calls the two diviners Mopfus and Amphilochus, Κυνες, (v. 459.) upon which the Scholiaft obferves, Κυνες, οι Μανλεις.

The name of the deity Canouphis, expreffed alfo Canuphis, and Cnuphis was compounded with this term, Can-Uph, from his ferpentine reprefentation; and the whole fpecies of ferpents were made facred to him, and ftiled Canyphian. Canuphis was fometimes expreffed Anuphis, and Anubis: but however rendered, was always by the Greeks and Romans fpoken of as a dog; at leaft that he had a dog's head; and they often mention his barking; fo Propertius, L. 3. El. 11.

Aufa Jovi noftro latrantem opponere Anubim.

The Egyptians had many emblematical figures, fet off with the heads of various animals; among thefe was this canine figure; which I have no reafon to think was appropriated to Canuph, or Cneph. And though upon gems and marbles his name may be fometimes found annexed to that character, yet it muft be looked upon as a Græcian work, and fo denominated in confequence of their miftaken notion. Horus Apollo affures us (l, 1, c. 14.) that this canine figure was an emblem

I 4

blem

blem of the earth; Οικουμενην γραφονίες Κυνοκεφαλοι ζωγραφουσι. In fhort, whatever the Egyptians deemed falutary, or of great value, they diftinguifhed by the title of facred, and confecrated to fome god. e. g.

The fweet reed of Egypt was named Canah, and Conah, by way of eminence; alfo Can-Ofiris.

Cantharus, the facred beetle from Can-Athur; and the like.

Priefts and magiftrates were particularly honoured with the additional title of Cahen: and many things held facred were liable to have it in their compofition. Horus Apollo mentions the great veneration paid by the Egyptians to dogs; and adds, that in many temples they kept Κυνοκεφαλοι, a kind of baboons, or animals with heads like thofe of dogs, which were wonderfully endowed; that they did not die at once, but by piecemeal, &c.

The term Κυνοκεφαλος, is an Egyptian compound, and this ftrange hiftory relates to the priefts of the country, ftiled Cahen; alfo to the novices in their temples. As they much ftudied aftronomy, they ufed in upper Egypt to found their colleges and temples upon rocks and hills, called by them *Caph*. Thefe, as they were facred to the Sun, were ftiled Caph-El, Caph-Aur, Caph-Arez. The term Caph-El, which often occurs in hiftory, the Greeks uniformly changed to Κεφαλη; and from Cahen-Caph-El, the facred rock of Orus, they formed Κυνοκεφαλη, and Κυνοκεφαλος; which they fuppofed to relate to an animal with the head of a dog. But this Cahen-Caph-El was fome Royal feminary in Upper Egypt; from whence they drafted their novices to fupply their colleges and temples. They were denominated Caph-El, and Cahen-Caph-El, from the Academy, where they received their firft inftruction: and this place,
though

though facred, yet feems to have been of a clafs
fubordinate to others. It was ufed as a kind of
inferior cloifter and temple, fuch as Capella in the
Romifh church; which, as well as Capellanus,
was derived from Egypt: for the church in its
firft decline, borrowed largely from that country.

It is faid of the Cunocephali, that when one part
was dead and buried, the other ftill furvived. This
can relate to nothing elfe but a fociety, or body
politic, where there is a continual decrement, yet
part ftill remains, and the whole is kept up by
fucceffion. The facred offices in Egypt were hereditary, being vefted in certain families; and when
part was dead, a refidue ftill furvived, who admitted others in the room of the deceafed.

The Cunocephali are to be found in other parts
of the world. Many places were named Cunoce-
phale; all which will be found to have been
eminences, or buildings fituated on high.

Similar to the above hiftory, is that of the Cu-
nodontes. They are a people mentioned by Solinus and Ifidorus, and by them are fuppofed to
have had the teeth of dogs. Yet they were probably denominated from the object of their
worfhip, the deity Chan-Adon; which the Greeks
expreffed Κυνοδων, and ftiled his votaries Cuno-
dontes.

The Greeks pretended, that they had the ufe of
the fphere, and were acquainted with the Zodiac,
and its afterifms, very early. The contrary is plain
from their miftakes. They borrowed all from the
Egyptians; who had particularly conferred the
titles of their deities upon thofe ftars, which appeared the brighteft in their hemifphere. One
of the moft remarkable they called Cahen Sehor,
which was mifconftrued and changed by the Greeks
to Canis Sirius, *the Dog's Star*; fo P'urcahen to
Procyon, and Cahen Oura to Cunofoura, *the Dog's*
tail,

tail. But what relation had this laſt to a dog? or how came it to be the name of a ſtar in the tail of a bear? There were promontories in Attica and Bœotia of that name. It was a term brought from Sidon and Egypt; and the purport was to be ſought for from the language of the Amonians.

Apollo and Bacchus were ſtrangely repreſented, gaping with open mouths. They were both the ſame as the Egyptian Orus, who was ſtiled Cahen-On Rex, vel *Dominus Sol*; out of which the Græcians ſeem to have formed the word Χαινων: and in conſequence of it, theſe two deities were repreſented with their jaws widely extended. This term was ſometimes changed to Κοινος, *communis*; hence Κοιναι Θεοι, Κοινοι Βωμοι; alſo Κοινος Ἑρμης; and as he was eſteemed the god of gain, every thing that was found was eſteemed Κοινος, or *common*. And yet among the Græcians themſelves this term was an ancient title of eminence. Κοινος, ὁ Δεσποτης. Heſych. Undoubtedly from Cohinus, and that from Cohen.

We read of the brazen dog of Vulcan, of the dog of Erigone, Orion, &c. They were the titles of ſo many deities, or of their prieſts. Diod. Sic. L. 1. ſays, that at the grand celebrity of Iſis, the whole was preceded by dogs; more probably by the prieſts of the goddeſs. The Cuſean prieſts of Vulcan were ſtiled by the Greeks, Χρυσοι Κυνες. The god of Light, among other titles, was ſtiled Cahen, or Chan-Ades, but was changed into a dog, and ſaid to reſide in the infernal regions. Yet he was the god of Light, Κυν-ᾳδης, and ſuch was the purport of that name.

In ſhort the Cahen of Egypt were no more Dogs, than the Pateræ of Amon were Baſons. I. 329, &c.

Chan-Ait is nearly the ſame as *Sar-Qn*.

KOIΛΛ,

ΚΟΙΛΑ,

ΚΟΙΛΑ,

Cava, fo were many places and regions rendered by the Greeks, which were held facred, and called by the Amonians Coel. Hence we read of Κοιλη Λακεδαιμων, Κοιλη Ηλις, &c. Syria was by them ftiled Κοιλη, *the hollow*; but the true name was Coëla, *the heavenly* or *facred*. It was fo denominated from the Cuthites, who fettled there, on account of the religion eftablifhed.

COILUS,

In the original acceptation fignified *heavenly*. Whence in Hefych. and Suid. Κοιολης, ὁ Ἱερευς. So we learn, that by Coioles was meant a facred and heavenly perfon; or a prieft of Cœlus. In Coioles there is but a fmall variation from the original term, which was a compound from Coi-El, or Co-El.

COVELLA.

So is Juno ftiled, by Varro de Ling. Lat. L. 5. Here, as often, the place of worfhip is taken for the perfon worfhiped. The term is only a variation for Cou-El, or Co-El, the houfe or region of the deity, and fignifies *heavenly*. It is accordingly interpreted by Varro, Urania, Ουρανια: whence *Juno Covella* muft be rendered Cœleftis.

From the fubftantive Cou-El, the Romans formed Cœl, *heaven*; in aftertimes expreffed *Cælus*, and *Cælum*: I fay, in aftertimes; for they originally called it Co-El, and Co-Il, and then contracted it to Cœl.

Cœlus in aftertimes was made a deity: hence there are infcriptions dedicated Cœlo Æterno. The Perfians worfhiped Cœlus; which is alluded to by Herodotus, when he fays, that they facrificed upon eminences: τον κυκλον παντα του Ουρανου Δια καλεοντες, καλιονίες, L. 1. c. 131. The ancient deity Celeus, mentioned by Athenagoras (Legat. p. 290.) and said to have been worshiped at Athens, was the same as the above. I. 109, &c.

Coel, the name of a city in Lybia, which the Romans rendered Coëlu. They would have expressed it Coëlus or Cœlus; but the name was copied in the time of the Punic wars, before the S final was admitted into their writings. I. 221.

COINS.

Upon those of Syria and Tyre are allusions to Ophite temples, and Στυλοι. The deity is represented between two rough stones, with two serpents on each side of him. A temple of this sort, which betrayed great antiquity, stood in the vicinity of Thebes, and was called the Serpent's head. Pausan. L. 9. speaks of it as remaining in his time. II. 174.

As the Arkite rites prevailed greatly in Syria, and in the regions nearest Ararat, and Armenia, the coins of these countries are filled with emblems which relate to the history of the Ark. Hence the Ram of Colchis, and of Ammonia in Upper Egypt, will be found upon the money of Singara, Nisibis, and Edessa, and of other cities in the east. For the Ram seems like the sacred Bull, to have been an emblem of the Patriarch, the great husbandman, and shepherd, stiled γεωργος, and ανθρωπος γης. But above all other symbols the Lunette will most frequently occur upon coins of this country; especially upon those of Carrhæ, which was the Charan, or Haran of Moses. Under this semblance they did not worship the planet; but the Selenite deity; Σελανην μηίερα ὁλου κοσμου. 444.

COL, CAL, CALAH, CALACH,

Signify properly an Eminence, like Collis of the Romans; but are often ufed for a fortrefs fo fituated. We fometimes meet with a place ftiled abfolute Calah: but the term is generally ufed in compofition, as Calah-Nechus, Cala-Anac, Cala-Chan, Cala-On, Cala-Es, Cala-Ait, Cala-Ur, Cala-Ope, Cala-Ham, Cala-Amon, Cala-Adon; whence came the names of people and places. I. 93.

COLCHIS,

Was called Aia fimply, and by way of eminence; and Egypt had the fame name, for the Colchians were from Egypt. I. 91. n. It was alfo called Aﬕa. 116.

Colchis was properly Col-Chus; and therefore called alfo Cuta, and Cutaia. But what was Colchian being fometimes rendered Chalcion, Χαλκιον, gave rife to the fable of brazen bulls; which were only Colchic Tor, or towers. There was a region named Colchis near Comar in India: for where the Cuthites fettled, they continually kept up the memory of their forefathers, and called places by their names. Calecut feems to have been the capital of the region called of old Colchis. I. 363.

The Cuthites who fettled at Colchis, which they called Cutaia, built a temple which was called Ca-Cuta, and from which the region was alfo denominated; for it is certain, that it has that name at this day. I. 108.

COL-ON,

Or altars of the Sun. (v. Cippi.) Hence the terms Colona, and Κολωνη. It came at laft to fignify any nees or foreland; but was originally the name of a facred hill, and of a pillar which was placed upon it. Indeed there was hardly of old

any

any headland, but what had its temple, or altar. These Colonæ were sacred to the Apollo of Greece; and as they were sea-marks and beacons, which stood on eminences near the mouths of rivers, and at the entrances of harbours, it caused them to be called Ωρια, Ουρια, and Ὁρμοι. I. 268.

COLOPHON.

Jamblichus de Myster. Sect. 3. c. xi. "Some procure a prophetic spirit by drinking the sacred water, as is the practice of Apollo's priest at Colophon." He adds, "in respect to the oracle at Colophon, that the prophetic spirit was supposed to proceed from the water. The fountain, from whence it flowed, was in an apartment underground; and the priest went thither to partake of the emanation." From hence we may learn the purport of the name, by which this oracular place was called. It is Col-Oph-On, *tumulus dei Solis Pythonis*, and corresponds with the character given. The river into which this fountain ran, was sacred, and called Anelon, and Halesus: composed of well known titles of the same god. I. 205.

COLUMBKIL, or COLUMBA,

(One of the Scottish isles, the Hebrides of the ancients) is said to have been in old time a seminary; and was reputed of the highest sanctity. It is plainly a contraction of Columba-kil; which was not originally the name of the island, but of the temple there constructed. The island was simply Columba. And what is truly remarkable, it was also called Iöna (q. v.) a name exactly synonymous, which it retains to this day. II. 473. v. *Mona.*

COMAH,

Is ufed for a wall; but feems to be fometimes taken for thofe facred inclofures, wherein they·had their Puratheia; and particularly for the facred mount, which ftood within. h. gr. Χωμα, a round hill or mound of earth; called alfo Taph and ταφος, and thence often miftaken for a tomb; but it was originally a high altar. I. 93.

COMATAS,

The fhepherd, when inclofed in an Ark, was fuppofed to have been fed by Bées. II. 376. v. Theocr. Id. 7.

COMPARISON.

Moft of its irregular degrees are derived from Egypt and Chaldea; being derived from the Sun, the great deity of the pagan world, and from his titles and properties : e. g. Αρκων and Αρισος, from Αρης, the Arez of the eaft.

Βελιων, Βελισος, from Bel and Baaltis.

Αμανων, an inflection from Amon.

Αωιος, Αωίερος, Αωισος, from the god Aloeus.

Κρισσων, Κρισσων, Κραίερος, Κραίισος, from Κιριν changed to Κιρας, Κιραίος. I. 88.

CONAH.

So were called particular colleges appropriated to the aftronomers and priefts in Chaldea, as may be inferred from Ezra. (v. 6. iv. 9—17.) I. 42.

CONTEST SACRED.

As the Ark was reprefented under the fymbol of Hippos, and was preferved from the violence of the fea, by the wifdom, and influence of divine Providence, the ancients defcribed this hiftory under the notion of a conteft, wherein Minerva and Neptune were engaged. Each of thefe deities,

in

it feems, laid claim to a region : and upon com-
promifing the difpute, Minerva is faid to have
given birth to the olive tree; and Neptune produced a Horfe.

Sometimes, inftead of Minerva, Juno is introduced as a principal in the conteft. Thefe notions
arofe from emblematical defcriptions of the Deluge,
which the Græcians had received by tradition; but
what was general, they limited, and appropriated
to particular places. e. g. Argos, Mycene, Træ-
zen, Corinth, Attica.

In the difpute about Attica, Minerva is faid to
have had the advantage; and in confequence of it
an olive-tree fprang up in the Acropolis at Athens,
and at the fame time Neptune produced the Horfe
Scuphius. It feems manifeft, that thefe accounts,
however limited, relate to one general event: but
the hiftory has been adopted, and varied, according
to the mythology of different places.

There were many reprefentations of this hiftory
among the αναθημαῖα in the Acropolis. II. 412.

As the Ark was preferved by divine Providence
from the fea, which would have overwhelmed it ;
and as it was often reprefented under the fymbol
of an Horfe, it gave rife to the fable of the two
chief deities contending about Horfes. Orph.
Argon. v. 1275.

'Ως ποῖε δι δηρισσαν αιλλοποδων ὑπερ Ιππων
Ζευς ὑψιβρεμεῖης, και πονῖιος Εννοσιγαιος.

It was upon this account that the cities named
Argos, had the title of Ιππιοι και Ιπποβόϊοι. II. 503.

ΚΩΟΙ

Caves. v. Ορισχυος. Co and Coa fignified a
houfe in a mountain. Strabo fays, that this term
is alluded to by Homer, Οδ. Δ. v. 1.

Οιδ᾽ ιξον ΚΟΙΛΗΝ Λακεδαιμονα ΚΗΤΩΕΣΣΑΝ.

For

For it was by many thought to have been so called on account of the caverns. From hence we may fairly conclude, that Κηλωισσα was a mistake, or at least a variation for Καιτλωισσα, from Cai-Atis. I. 115.

CORA, ΚΟΡΑ,

So was Persephone stiled; which the Greeks absurdly interpreted Παρθενος. Κορα, which they understood was the same as Cura, was a feminine title of the Sun, by which Ceres was called at Cnidos. II. 41.

CORINTH

Seems to have abounded with Arkite emblems more than most places in Greece. II. 411.

CORONIS

Is said to have been the daughter of Phlegyas; Cronus the son of Apollo; Chiron the son of Saturn; Charon of Erebus and Night; Charisius the hero, of Lycaon, who was Apollo: these were all places, but described as personages; and made the children of the deity, to whom they were sacred. I. 501. n.

CORYBANTES.

They were called Αναχτοτελιςαι, as being of a royal, or supereminent priesthood. Their mysteries were stiled Cabiritic, in which the Rhoia was introduced: and they were often celebrated in woods, and upon mountains; and the whole was attended with shouts, and screams, and every frantic manœuvre. The persons concerned were crowned with serpents; and by their fury and madness exhibited a scene shocking to imagination: yet no one was thought compleatly happy, who did not partake in these mysteries.

K   The

The noife and diffonance at thefe celebrities are finely defcribed in the Edoni of Æfchylus.

Ψαλμος δ' αλαλαζει·
Ταυροφθογγοι δ' υπομαχωνlαι πανlοθεν
Εξ αφανους φοβεριοι μιμοι·
Τυμπανω δ' ηχω,
'Ωσθ' υπογκου βρονlης, φερεlαι βαρυlαρβης.
[vulg. leg. υπομηκωνlαι ποθεν.]

This wild joy, attended with fhouts and dancing, and the noife of pipes and cymbals, feems to have been exhibited in memorial of the exit from the Ark; when the whole of the animal fyftem iffued to light upon the fummit of Mount Baris.

Corybas the father and head of the band, was the fame as Helius, and in the Orphic hymns (h. 38.) is farther defcribed with the attributes of Dionufus. His offspring were twofold. Strabo. L. 10. p. 723. fpeaks of them both as priefts and divinities; and undoubtedly both were comprehended under this title. II. 468. The Tityri, Satyri, Mænades, Thyades, Lycaones, Sileni, Lenæ, were of the fame order. 470.

COSET.

This word the Græcians tranflated τοξος. The LXX uniformly ufe τοξος for the bow in the heavens. II. 347. n.

COTHON,

The name of the harbour at Carthage; alfo of an ifland in that harbour. I. 6.

ΚΟΘΟΣ,

Και Αρχλος, δι Ξουθου παιδες ως Ευβοιαν ηκον οικησανlες. Plut. Quæft. Græcæ. p. 296. By Cothus and Arclus are meant Cuthites and Herculeans, who fettled in that ifland. II. 177.

COTTIUS.

COTTIUS.

ellinus thinks, that a king Cottius gave
he Alpes Cottiæ in the time of Auguftus;
was the national title of the king, as
the nation; far prior to the time of
he paffage through the Alpes is faid
have been the work of Hercules, by
Cottus, and Cottius. From hence this
iar branch of the mountains had the name
Alpes Cottiæ. The country was called Regio
Cottiana, wherein were twelve capital cities. Some
of that ancient and facred nation, the Hyperboreans, are faid by Pofidonius to have taken up their
refidence in thefe parts. Here inhabited the
Taurini; and one of the chief cities was Comus.
Strabo (l. 4.) ftiles the country the land of Ideonus,
and Cottius. I. 212.

COTYS,

People of the Hyperborean family fettled in
Thrace under the name of Scythæ: alfo of Sithonians, Pæonians, Pierians, and Edonians. They
particularly worfhiped the firft planter of the vine
under the known title of Dionufus, and alfo of
Zeus Sabazius. They had alfo rites, which they
called Cotyttia, from the deity Cotys; and others
named Metroa, and Sabazia, which were celebrated
in a moft frantic manner by the Edoni upon mount
Hæmus. (Strabo. L. 10. 721, &c.) The deity
was alfo called Sabos, which term, as well as the
title Sabazius, was derived from סבא, Saba, *wine*.
Hence, amid all their acclamations, the words,
Ευοι Σαβοι, were to be particularly diftinguifhed.
He was worfhiped in the fame manner by the
Phrygians, who carried on the fame rites and with
the like fhouting and wild geftures upon mount
Ida. (Strabo. L. 10. p. 721.) The priefts alfo
were called Sabi; and this name feems to have

K 2   prevailed

prevailed both in Phrygia and in Thrace. (Sch. in Ariftoph. Vefp. v. 9.) III. 497.

CROCODILE

Was greatly reverenced by the Egyptians, for having faved from drowning, according to Diod. (l. 1. p. 80.) their king Menas; who in memorial thereof founded a city, called the city of the Crocodile. Now this fuppofed king was the Deus Lunus, called alfo Meen and Man, a deity equally known to the Perfians, Lydians, and Cappadocians, and worfhiped under the fame title. This legend about a Crocodile was taken from fome reprefentation in the city of the fame name; and hence it was fuppofed to have happened in Egypt. It was a facred hiftory, like that of Orus, and Helius, upon a Crocodile; for thefe were all titles, which at different times were conferred upon the fame perfonage, and related to the fame event.

The Crocodile had many names; Caimin, Souchus, Campfa; this laft fignified an Ark, or receptacle: Καμψα, Θηκη. Hefych. From hence the purport of the hieroglyphic may be proved. II. 397.

CRONUS.

So was the great Patriarch called by the Greeks, and his defcendants, the Baalim, *Cronidæ*, Κρονιδαι; who were alfo peculiarly ftiled, Αθαναλοι και Δαιμονες. II. 288. Orpheus (Hymn 13.) thus fpeaks of him:

Αιθαλιης, Μακαρων τε Θεων παλερ, ηδη και ανδρων,
ΑΙΩΝΟΣ ΚΡΟΝΕ, ΠΑΓΓΕΝΕΤΟΡ—
Γαιης τε Ϭλασημα, και Ουρανου αςεροεντος
Γεννα, Φυης μαιωσι, 'Ρεας ποσι, σεμνε ΠΡΟΜΗΘΕΤ.

In fhort, he is the fame perfon, in whom mankind was faid to be renewed. II. 256.

CUAMON,

CUAMON,

Near Efdraelon, is a compound of Cu-Amon, the houfe or place of Amon. There was a temple in Attica called *Cuamites*; and (according to a common, but fatal error) a perfonage denominated from it. The hiftory of the place, and of the rites, in time grew obfolete; and Paufanias (l. 1.) fuppofes that the name was given from Κυαμος, *a bean: to the memory of fome perfon who firft fowed beans.* I. 106.

CUBELA

Was another name of Damater, who is mentioned as mother of the gods. Cubeba was the fame deity (both the Cybele and Cybebe of the Ionians.) The former is Cu-Bela, the temple of Bela, the feminine of Belus, the title of the chief Chaldaic god: and Cu-Baba, is the temple of Baba, the mother of the infant world, the fame as Rhoia (the Ionian Rhea) and Damater. As the perfons in the Ark were fuppofed to return by a renewal of life to a fecond ftate of childhood, this machine was on that account ftiled Cubaba, or, the houfe of Infants; for that was the purport of Baba.

In the coins of Syria, we find this deity with a tower upon her head (to fhew that all nations were derived from her) fitting upon a rock in a ftate of fecurity. In her right hand fhe holds fome ears of corn, to denote the promife of plenty and return of the feafons; and there is often near her the myftic hive. At fome diftance ftands an altar; over her head a bird; below her feet are water, waves, and a perfon ready to fink. Thefe reprefentations are found upon the coins of many cities, at a diftance from each other; and undoubtedly are taken from the religion of the Syrians and Mefopotamians; and from the emblems in their feveral

temples;

temples; all which related to one great event. II. 384.

Cybele, Dyndamena, and Rhea, were no other than feminine titles of the Lunar deity, called Mon, or Maon, and there will be found a correspondence in their several histories. II. 447.

CUMA

(Properly Cuman) in Campania was certainly denominated from Chum, *beat*, on account of its soil, and situation. Its medicinal waters, Aquæ Cumanæ, are well known.

The term Cumana consists of the term Cumain, and signifies a hot fountain; or a fountain of Chum, or Cham, the Sun. Here was a cavern, which of old was a place of prophecy. It was the seat of the Sibylla Cumana; who was supposed to come from Babylonia. I. 200.

What in one part of the world was termed Cumana, was in another rendered Comana. Of this name there was a grand city in Cappadocia, where stood one of the noblest Puratheia in Asia. 202.

CUPRIS, CUPRA.

Under this title Juno was worshiped by the Hetrurians. II. 344. The Archite deity was worshiped under the symbol of a Dove, called Cupris, Jonah, Oinas, Venus. Of this Epicharmus (ap. Athæn. l. 12.) very truly takes notice in speaking of the worship in the first ages.

Ουδε τις ην κηνοισιν Αρης Θεος, ουδε κυδοιμος,
Ουδε Ζευς βασιλευς, ουδε Κρονος, ουδε Ποσειδων,
Αλλα Κυπρις βασιλεια.———371.

CUPSELIS.

A word of the same purport as Seira, and was an appellation of the Ark. At Corinth was a
family

family named Cupfelidæ, who were originally
priefts of the Ark; and who firft introduced the
rites of it into that city. Cupfelus, the father of
Periander, was of this order.

Hefych. makes Κυψιλις, or Κυψιλη, a bee-hive;
but it was more in the fhape of an Ark, or box.
It was made of cedar; and dedicated on account of
the great deliverance, which Cupfelus had experienced from the waters. II. 378.

CUR, KUR, ΚΥΡΟΣ.

So was the Sun named. Many places were
facred to this deity, and called Cura, Curia, Curo-
polis, Curene, Curefchata, Curefta, Cureftica regio.
Many rivers in Perfis, Media, Iberia, were denominated in the fame manner. The term is fometimes expreffed Coros, hence Corufia in Scythia.
I. 40.

ΚΥΡΟΣ.

The Greeks, who received their theology from
Egypt and Syria, often fuppreffed the leading
vowel, and thought to atone for it by giving a new
termination. Κυρος, the name of Cyrus, feems to
have fuffered fuch an abridgment. It was probably a compound of Uch-Ur, the fame as Achor,
and Achorus of Egypt, the great luminary, the
Sun. Achorus was abbreviated to Chorus, Curus.
We fometimes find it rendered, Κυρις; but ftill with
reference to the Sun, the Adonis of the Eaft. In
Phocis was Κυρρα, where Apollo Κυρραιος was honoured; which names were more commonly expreffed Κιρρα, and Κιρραιος.

CURETES

Were Heliadæ. Great confufion has arifen
from not confidering, that the deity and prieft
were named alike; and that the people often were
K 4   compre-

comprehended under the fame title. The god Helius was ftiled Cur-Ait, and his priefts had the fame name. (And the term Quirites, among the Romans, had the fame origin.) The ancient inhabitants of Ætolia, Eubœa, and Acarnania were ftiled Curetes, and their country Curetica. II. 472.

CUSCHA,

A place in Ethiopia (analogous to Cau-Come in Egypt) doubtlefs fo named from Chus, the great anceftor, from whom the Ethiopians were defcended, I. 104,

CUSHAN, *ftyled* ETHIOPIA,

The Ethiopians were Cuthites or Cufeans (Zonaras, p. 21, Syncellus, p. 47. Jofeph. Ant. L. 1. c. 6. Eufeb. Chron. p. 11.) The name is fuppofed to have been given to this people from their complexion; as if it came from αιθω and οψ: but it is not a name of Græcian original. It was a facred term; a title of the chief deity: whence it was affumed by the people, who were his votaries, and defcendants. Διος επιθέλον Αιθιοψ. (Euftath. in Hom. Od. A. v. 22.) Prometheus was ftyled Æthiops. Pliny (L. 9. p. 345.) fpeaking of the country, fays, that it was firft called Ætheria; then Atlantia; and laftly Ethiopia. Homer (Od. A. v. 22.) fpeaks of two nations only, which were named Æthiopes: but this is much too limited. The Scripture feems to mention three countries of this name. One was in Arabia, upon the verge of the defert, near Midian, and the Red fea. (Habakkuk, iii. 7.) A fecond lay above Egypt to the fouth. (Ezek. xxix. 10.) A third comprehended the regions of Perfis, Chufiftan, and Sufiana. (Zeph. iii. 10.) Even Chaldea was efteemed Ethiopia; and Tacitus (Hift. L. 5. c. 2.) fpeaking
of

of the Jews, whose ancestors came from Ur in
Chaldea, styles them *Æthiopum prolem.* Beyond
Carmania was another region of this name. (Euseb.
Chron. p. 12.) Even the Indi themselves were
Ethiopians. [The Cuthites, styled Æthiopes,
were the original Indi: they gave name to the
country which they occupied. Hence Iarchus of
India (Philostrati vita Apollon. L. 3. p. 125.)
tells Apollonius, ότι Αιθιοπες μεν ωχουν ενlαυθα, γενος
Ldικον. And almost in every place, where their
history occurs, the name of Indi will be found
likewise. Diod. Sic. L. 1. p. 17. The chief inhabitants upon the Indus were Cuseans. III. 212.]

The sons of Chus came into Egypt under the
name of Auritæ and Shepherds, as also of Ethiopians: hence Egypt also inherited that name.
(Eustath. Com. in Dionyf. v. 241.) The Cuthites
settled at Colchus, the Colchis of the Greeks; in
consequence of which it was called Cutaia and
Ethiopia. The sons of Chus came, under the
titles of Casus and Belus, into Syria and Phenicia,
where they founded many cities: and Strabo
(l. 1. p. 73.) informs us, that this country was
called Ethiopia.

The Cadmians came into Eubœa, and here was
an Ethiopium. (Strabo, L. 10. p. 683.) Samothrace was called Ethiopia. (Hesych.) Lesbos had
the name of Ethiope and Macaria. (Plin. N. H.
L. 5. c. 31.)

The extreme settlement of this people was in
Spain, upon the Bœtis, near Tartessus and Gades:
and Ephorus tells us, that colonies of Ethiopians
traversed a great part of Africa; some of which
came and settled near Tartessus; and others got
possession of different parts of the sea-coast.
(Strabo, L. 1. p. 57.) They lived near the island
Erythea, which they held. (Dionyf. Perieg. v. 558.)

It

It is on this account, that we find fome of the fame family on the oppofite coaft of Mauritania.

The original Ethiopia was the region of Babylonia and Chaldea, where the firft kingdom upon earth was formed, and the moft early police inftituted. Here alfo the firft idolatry began. As the Scythæ, or Cuthites, were the fame people, no wonder that they are reprefented as the moft ancient people in the world; even prior to the Egyptians. III. 179.

CUSHITAE.

All the Ethiopic race were great archers. Their name was fometimes expreffed Cufhitæ; and the ancient name of a bow was Cufhet: which it probably obtained from this people, by whom it was invented. There is reafon to think, that by their fkill in this weapon they eftablifhed themfelves in many parts, where they fettled. III. 497.

CYCLOPIANS

Were originally Ophitæ, who worfhiped the fymbolical ferpent. They are reprefented as of a gigantic ftature, rude and favage; and as having only one large eye, in the middle of their foreheads. In lieu of the deity of the place, the poets have introduced thefe ftrange perfonages, the ideas of whofe fize were borrowed from facred edifices, where the deity was worfhiped. They were Petra, or temples of Orion. Some of them had the name of Charon, and Tarchon; and they were efteemed Pelorian, from the god Orus, the fame as Cœlus, and Python. The Græcians confounded the people, who raifed thefe buildings, with the ftructures themfelves. They are faid to have efteemed above all things the flefh of ftrangers. This character arofe from the cruel cuftom of facrificing ftrangers, whom fortune brought upon their coafts.

This

This was practifed in many parts of the world. Polyphemus was fuppofed to be the chief of thefe people, and to have refided towards the foot of mount Ætna.

Οικης ὑπ' Αιlνη τη πυροςαχlῳ Πίlρα.

Eur. Cycl. v. 297.

The poets have confined them to Sicily; but memorials of them are to be found in many parts of Greece, where they were recorded as far fuperior to the natives in fcience and ingenuity. The Græcians by not diftinguifhing between the deity, and the people, who were called by his titles, have brought great confufion into hiftory. The Cyclopians were denominated from Κυκλωψ, the fame as Cœlus, the god Nilus of Egypt, the fame as Zeus, and Ofiris. (Athæn. L. 5.)

They were defcended from the fons of Anac; and were particularly famous for Architecture, which they introduced into Greece. (Herodot. L. 5.) And in all parts whither they came, they erected noble ftructures, which were remarkable for their height and beauty; and were often dedicated to the chief deity, the Sun, under the name of Elorus, and P'elorus. Hence every thing great and ftupendous became to be called Pelorian. And when people defcribed the Cyclopians as a lofty towering race, they borrowed their ideas of this people from the towers, to which they alluded. They fuppofed them in height to reach to the clouds; and in bulk to equal the promontories on which they were founded. Homer (Od. 10.) fays of Polyphemus,

Και γαρ θαυμ' ἐlἐlευκlο πελωριον, ουδε εῳκει
Ανδρι γε σιlοφαγῳ, αλλα ῥιῳ ὑλϙευlι.

and Virgil (Æn. L. 3.)

Ipfe arduus, altaque pulfat fidera,

As

As thefe buildings were oftentimes light-houfes, and had in their upper ftories one round cafement, Argolici clypei, aut Phœbææ lampadis inftar, by which they afforded light in the night feafon; the Greeks made this a characteriftic of the people. They fuppofed this aperture to have been an eye, which was fiery, glaring, and placed in the middle of their foreheads. Hence Callimachus (in Dian.) defcribes them as a monftrous race:

> αινα Πελωρα,
> Πρηοσιν Οσσηοισιν εοικο]α˙ πασι δ᾽ υπ᾽ οφρυν
> Φαια μουνογληνα σαχη ισα τε͡ιραϐοειω.

The Græcians have fo confounded the Cyclopian deity with his votaries, that it is difficult to fpeak precifely of either. They fometimes reprefent him as a fingle perfon; at other times they introduce a plurality, whom they reprefent as of the higheft antiquity, and make the brethren of Cronus.

There were certainly Cyclopians near Ætna; but thofe mentioned by Homer (Od. Z.) were of another country, and are reprefented as natives of the continent, though his account is obfcure. There were probably fome of this family about the city Camarina, ftiled Camarin. There was a city Camarina in Chaldea, the Ur of the Scriptures.

We learn from Bacchylides (Natalis Comes, l. 9.) that Galatus, Illyrius, and Celtus were the fons of Polyphemus. By this was fignified, that the Galatæ, Illyrii, and Celtæ, were of Cyclopian original, and of the Anakim race; all equally Amonians.

Though the Amonians were highly fkilful in building, yet of them, the Cyclopians were by far the moft eminent. They founded many cities in Greece; and conftructed many temples to the gods, which were of old in high repute. Quicquid mag-
nitudine

nitudine fua nobile eft, Cyclopum manu dicitur fabricatum. Schol. in Statii Theb. L.   p. 26.

The nature of the works, which they executed, and the lake near Hermione, which they named A-cherufia, fhew plainly the part of the world from whence they came.   When Euripides (Herc. Fur. v. 944.) fpeaks of the walls of ancient Mycene, as built by the Cyclopians after the Phœnician rule and method; the Phœnicians alluded to were the Φοινικες of Egypt, to which country they were primarily to be referred.

I imagine, that not only the common idea of the Cyclopians was taken from towers and edifices; but that the term Κυκλωψ, and Κυκλωπις, fignified a building or temple; and from thence the people had their name.   They were of the fame family as the Cadmians, and Phœnices; the Hivites, or Ophites who came from Egypt.   They worfhiped the Sun under the fymbol of a ferpent: hence they were ftiled in different parts, where they in time fettled, Europians, Oropians, Anopians, Inopians, Afopians, Elopians.   What may be the precife etymology of the term Κυκλωψ, I cannot prefume to determine.   Cuclops, as a perfonage, was faid to be the fon of Ouranus; who among the Amonians was often ftiled Cœl, or Cœlus; and was worfhiped under the emblem of a ferpent.   Hence the temple of the deity may·have been originally called Cu-Cœl-Ops, Domus Cœli Pythonis; and the priefts and people Cucelopians.   Their hiftory is however fufficiently determinate.

The Sicilian Cyclopes were three, becaufe there were three towers only, erected upon the iflands called Cyclopum fcopuli; and that they were light-houfes is apparent from the name which ftill re-mains, *Faraglioni*, according to Fazellus. (v. Tiryns.) From this circumftance we may prefume, that the ideas of the ancients concerning the Cyclopians

were

were taken from the buildings, which they erected. There was a place in Thrace called Cuclops.

As the Cyclopians were great artifts, they probably were famous for works in brafs and iron: and that circumftance in their hiftory may have been founded in truth. The Idæi Dactyli were Cyclopians; and they are faid to have firft forged metals, and to have reduced them to common ufe; the knowledge of which art they obtained from the fufion of minerals at the burning of mount Ida. From this event the Curetes, and Corybantes, who were the fame as the Idæi Dactyli, are fuppofed to have learnt the myftery of fufing and forging metals.

Their chief deity, among other titles, was ftiled Acmon, and Pyracmon :· but as αχμων fignified among the Greeks an anvil; thefe Cyclopians, fo eminent in fcience and fkilled in architecture, who were accounted Αριϛοι Τιχνιται (Schol. in Eurip. Oreft. 966.) were by the poets degraded to fo many Blackfmiths: they forged indeed thunderbolts for Jupiter;

ʹΟι Ζηνι ϐρονϊην τʹ ιδοσαν, τιυξαν τι κιραυνον.

and as fome of them refided near Ætna, the burning mountain was made their forge.

Ferrum exercebant vafto Cyclopes in antro,
Brontefque, Steropefque, et nudus membra
    Pyracmon.
I. 491.

ΚΥΚΝΟΣ.

Cycnus is faid to have been the brother of Phaeton, and to have been changed into a Swan. Lucian de Electro tells the ftory with great humour. Some make feveral Swans, and fuppofe them to have been the minifters, and attendants of Apollo,

who

who affifted at his concerts: others mention only
one perfon. The real hiftory feems to be this.
It alludes to Canaan, the fon of Ham, and to the
Canaanites his pofterity. They fent out many
colonies; which there is great reafon to think,
fettled in thofe places, where thefe legends about
Swans prevailed. The name of Canaan was by
different nations greatly varied, and ill expreffed:
and this mifconftruction among the Greeks gave
rife to the fable. The meafures and harmony of
the Canaanites in their religious hymns feem to
have been very affecting, and to have made a wonderful impreffion on the minds of their audience.

There is reafon to think that the word Canaan
was by the Egyptians and other neighbouring nations expreffed Cnaan. This by the Greeks was
rendered Χναας, and Χνας: and in later times Χνα,
Cna. There is a particular term, Υκ, Uc, which
is often found in the compofition of many words;
efpecially fuch as are of Amonian original. Uch,
fays Manethon, fignifies, in the facred language of
Egypt, a King. Cnas, or Canaan, was ftiled Uc-
Cnas, and the gentile name or poffeffive was Uc-
Cnaos, Υκ-χναος. The Greeks, whofe cuftom it
was to reduce every foreign name to fomething
fimilar in their own language, changed Υκ-χναος to
Κυκνος, Uc Cnaos to Cucnaos; and from Υκ Χνας
formed Κυκνος. (v. Ichnaia.) Befides, there was a
Canaanitifh temple called both Ca-Cnas, and Cu-
Cnas, and adjectively Cu-Cnaios; which, there is
reafon to think, were rendered Κυκνος, and Κυκνειος.
And further, the Swan was undoubtedly the infigne
of Canaan. It was certainly the hieroglyphic of
the country. Inftead of Υκχναον ασμα, the mufic of
Canaan, the Greeks have introduced Κυκνιον ασμα,
the finging of Swans. The Cycni were indeed the
priefts. One part of the world, where this notion
about Swans prevailed, was in Liguria upon the
banks

banks of the Eridanus. Here Phaeton met with his downfal; and here Cycnus was said to be changed into a Swan. In these parts some Amonians settled very early: among whom it appears that there were many from Canaan. I. 367.

CYPRUS,

Island of, was of old called Cerastis, and Cerastia; and had a city of the same name. This city was more known by the name of Amathus: and mention is made of cruel rites practised in its temple. As long as the former name prevailed, the inhabitants were stiled Cerastæ. The priests were particularly so denominated; and who were at last extirpated for their cruelty. The poets imagining, that the term Cerastæ related to a horn, fabled that they were turned into bulls:

Atque illos gemino quondam quibus aspera cornu
Frons erat, unde etiam nomen traxere Ceristæ.

Ovid. Met. L. 10.

Caryſtus, (name of a city in Bœotia) Cerastis, Cerasta, are all of the same purport: they betoken a place, or temple of Astus, or Asta, the god of fire. Cerasta in the feminine is expresly the same, only reversed, as Astrachar in Chusiſtan. I. 228.

The Βουκιυταυροι, and ships in general, are supposed to have been first formed in Cyprus: and here Nonnus supposes the Centaurs to have first existed. This notion arose from the original ship, the Ark, being built of Gupher wood. This has been interpreted the wood of the island Cupher, which was the ancient name of Cyprus. II. 440. It was also stiled Ophiusa, and Ophiodes, from the serpents with which it was supposed to have abounded. By these serpents is meant the Ophite race, who came from Egypt, and Syria. I. 482.

The people here were originally Ethiopians or Cuthites. They worſhiped the Sun under the title of Achur, and Achor. Acurana was abbreviated to Curana and Curene, but was always ſuppoſed to relate to the Sun, and Heaven; hence the Greeks, who out of every obſolete term formed perſonages, ſuppoſed Cyrene to have been the daughter of the ſupreme deity. Here was a fountain of great ſanctity, called Κυρη πηγη, which terms are equivalent to Kur-Ain, and Achar-Ain of the Amonians, and ſignify the fountain of the Sun. I. 80.

D.

DA.

Chaldaicè, *hæc, iſta, hoc, illud.* Buxtorf. II. 249.

Da, this Chaldaic particle is equivalent to *De, Die, The,* of the Saxon, Teutonic, and other languages. Of the ſame purport is *Da* in

DAMATER,

(Δημητηρ of the Ionians.) This name related to the Ark, and was a compound of Da Mater; the ſame as Mather, Methuer, Mithyr of Egypt, and other countries. This name, or *the mother,* was given to it, becauſe it was eſteemed the common parent, the mother of all mankind. From its connection with waters, Damater and Poſeidon, the deity of the ſea, were often found in the ſame temple. As a perſonage ſhe was the ſame as

L

Μητηρ

Μητηρ Θεων; to whom Orpheus gives the fovereignty of the main; and from whom he deduces the origin of all mankind.

Εκ σεο δ' αθανατων τε γενος, θνητων τ' ελοχευθη,
Σοι πολαμοι κραιτονται αει και πασα θαλασσα.

Hymn. 26.

II. 338.

As the prieftefles of Damater, who fang the facred hymns, were called Meliffæ, fo fhe and Perfephone had the title of Μελιτωδης from thefe fongs made to their honor. 377. She is reprefented with an handful of corn; and the divine Hope, which was gracioufly afforded to mankind immediately after the flood, being many ways recorded, fhe is reprefented with proper emblems, under the character of Spes Divina. v. Gruter. Vol. I. p. 102. She was the fame as Selene, Ifis, Ceres, Rhea, Vefta, Cybele, Archia, Niobe, and Meliffa. They are mere titles, by which a female perfonage was denoted, who was fuppofed to be the genius of the Ark, and the mother of mankind. 268. Near the olive-mount in Arcadia fhe was worfhiped by the Phigalians in a dark cavern. She was defcribed as a woman, but with the head of an horfe, and hieroglyphical reprefentations of ferpents and other animals. She fat upon a rock, clothed to her feet; with a dolphin in one hand, and a dove in the other. (Paufan. L. 8.) 411.

Near the temple of Eleufinian Damater in Arcadia, were two vaft ftones, called Petroma: one of which was erect; and the other was laid over, and inferted into the former. There was a hollow place in the upper ftone, with a lid to it. In this, among other things, was kept a kind of mafk, which was thought to reprefent the countenance of Damater, to whom thefe ftones were facred. This circumftance is mentioned, becaufe there was a

notion

notion among the Pheneatæ, who were the inhabitants of this diftrict, that the goddefs came into
thefe parts in an age very remote, even before the
days of Naos : Φινεαΐων ιςι λογος, και πριν η Ναον αφι-
κισθαι, &c. (Paufan. L. 8. p. 630.) But here
Ναος is certainly a tranfpofition for Νωας, Noah.
II. 203.

DAMASCUS

Is called by the natives Damafec, and Damakir.
The latter fignifies the town of Dama, or Adama :
by which is not meant Adam, the father of mankind ; but Ad Ham, the lord Ham, the father of
the Amonians. Sec, or Shec, is a prince. Damafec fignifies principis Ad-Amæ (Civitas). From
a notion however of Adama fignifying Adam, a
notion prevailed that he was buried at Damafcus.
This is fo far ufeful, as to fhew that Damafcus
was an abbreviation of Adamafec, and Damakir of
Adama-kir. I. 56. n.

DANAUS

Was a native of the city of Chemmis, from
whence he made his expedition into Greece.
Herod. L. 1. Navem primus ex Ægypto Danaus
advexit : Pliny, L. 7. He brought a colony with
him. Diodor. L. 1. I. 184. The place of defcent
from the Ark on mount Ararat, was called Αποβατηριον : (Jofephus, Antiq. L. 1.) The place where
Danaus made his firft defcent in Argolis, was called Αποβαθμος. (Pauf. L. 2.) He is fuppofed to
have brought with him the Amphiprumnon, or
facred model of the Ark, which he lodged in the
Acropolis of Argos, called Lariffa. II. 329. The
hiftories of Danäe, Danaus, and the Danaïdes, all
relate to the fame event, the Deluge, and the Ark.
Danae, is faid to be the mother of Perfeus, who
was conceived in fhowers, expofed in an Ark, and

at laft a king of Argos. She is alfo faid to be the mother of Argus, the founder of Ardea, and Argiletum in Italy; i. e. they were founded by people called Arkites. The ftory of Danaus does not feem to allude to the arrival of any particular perfon from Egypt; but to the firft introduction of rites from that country; and efpecially to the memorial of the Argo, from whence Argos took its name. If, as I fuppofe, the words ναυς and ναυς are derived from נו, Nau, or Noah; the name of Danaus relates not to a man, but is in reality Da Näus, *the Ship*.

Danäidæ, his fifty daughters were fifty priefteffes of the Argo, who bore the facred veffel on feftivals. They are faid to have been fent in queft of water; to have brought water to Argos; to have invented ὑδριας; and laftly, to have been condemned to draw water in buckets full of holes. Now the Egyptians were very affiduous in conveying water from one place to another. They had particular jars, facred to the god, called by the Greeks Canobus, and formed like him: they were fometimes made of earth with fmall holes at the bottom, to filter the water of the Nile, when it was turbid or faline. The Greeks, not underftanding this, have invented a ridiculous ftory. II. 249.

DANUBE.

A colony of Amonians fettled in Thrace, and in thefe parts are to be found many plain traces of their original hiftory. The Danube was properly the river of Noah, expreffed Da-Nau, Da-Nauos, Da-Nauvas, Da-Naubus. v. Herod. L. 4. Valerius Flaccus, L. 4. has

Quas Tanais, flavufque Lycus, Hypanifque, NOAfque;

which

(which is the true reading. v. L. 6. v. 100.)
By thofe who live upon its banks, it is now called
Danau. Not far off is the Borifthenes, called alfo
the Nieper. (Ναπαρος. Herod. L. 4.) This river
was alfo expreffed with the particle prefixed,
Danaper. In the fame part of the world is the
river Niefter; this likewife has been expreffed
Danafter, and Danefter: people not underftanding
the prefix have ufed it as part of the name.
II. 339.

DAUNIA,

(In Italy, where the Arkite worfhip was introduced by people ftiled Arcades, and Argæi) is a
compound of Da-Ionia, and fignifies. the land of
the Dove. In this region there was an Argos
Hippium. II. 503.

DECANI.

So were ftiled the priefts in Egypt. This term
feems to be a compound of De-Cani, *the Caben*, or
Priefts. II. 338.

DAGON.

The great Patriarch is fometimes defcribed as
an animal of the fea, but endowed with reafon;
who appeared twice, and preached to the fons' of
men about righteoufnefs and truth. He was alfo
depicted as a fifh; and fometimes as half a fifh and
half a man, of an amphibious nature. This being
is faid to be Ωδαχων, which is a blunder for ὁ Δαχων,
or Δαγων. It is a compound of Dag-On; and denotes the god On, in the femblance of Dag, *a fifh*.
And we find that the chief deity of Gath and
Afcalon in Paleftine, and of many cities in Syria,
was worfhiped under this form. Dag-On is Ofiris
in the fhape of a fifh. Deus Cetus. Dagon fru-
menti repertor, et aratri. Sanchon. ap. Eufeb.
P. E. L. 1. c. 10. II. 299. 335. 442.

ΔAIMONEΣ,

ΔΑΙΜΟΝΕΣ,

and Αθανατοι, the Baalim of the Scriptures, were
no other than the three sons of Noah. As all
mankind proceeded from the three families, of
which the Patriarch was the head; we find this
circumstance continually alluded to by the ancient
Mythologists. And the three persons, who first
constituted those families, were looked upon both
as deities and kings. They were the *Royal Triad*.
The whole religion of the ancients consisted in
Δαιμονολατρεια, the worship of Dæmons: and to those
personages their theology continually refers. They
were, like the Manes and Lares of the Romans,
suppoſed to be the souls of men deceaſed. Heſiod
(Op. et D. 111.) tells us who they were and when
they lived; οἱ μεν ὑπο Κρονου ησαν; in whose reign
was the golden age, when the life of man was at its
greatest extent. They were the Βασιλεις, or Royal
personages of Orpheus and Plato. II. 278.

Who these Dæmons, or Baalim were, could not
be a ſecret to Moſes; nor to many of the ſacred
writers. Yet though they ſpeak of this worſhip
with deteſtation, it is curious to obſerve, with
what delicacy they treat the ſubject, and what a
veil is drawn over this myſterious iniquity. Not
a word is ſaid about the origin of this idolatry:
nor the leaſt hint given to ſhew, who they were,
to whom this undue reverence was tendered. For
of all reverential regard, none is ſo liable to lapſe
into an idolatrous veneration as that, which is paid
to the memory of friends departed: more eſpecially
if ſuch perſons were the founders of families, and
benefactors; men, who had endeared themſelves
by their good works, and been a bleſſing to poſterity: this is evident from the adoration ſtill paid to
their anceſtors by many people in the eaſt. It is
a ſeeming duty the moſt plauſible of any: and at
the

the fame time the moft captivating. Hence the filence of the Sacred Writers upon a fubject of fuch feeming importance: whofe purpofe it appears to have been; that, if ever the great object of this idolatry fhould be loft, it might lie in oblivion, and never again be retrieved; at leaft to no ill purpofe. The Jews by thefe means loft fight of the original, and were weaned from the worſhip: and the Gentiles, who continued the rites, did not know to whom they were directed: fo blind was their procefs. In fhort, they were plunged in the depth of darknefs for ages: till they became at laft confcious of their fituation. This rendered them the more ready to return to the light, as foon as an opening was made. II. 531.

DEITY.

The cuftom of carrying the deity in a fhrine, placed in a boat, and fupported by priefts, was in ufe among the Egyptians, as well as the Ammonites. There are three curious examples of it in Biſhop Pocock's Egypt. Vol. I. Pl. XLII. The perfon in the fhrine, was their chief anceftor, and the whole procefs was a memorial of the Deluge; the hiftory of which muft have been pretty recent when thefe works were executed in Egypt. I. 251.

The ancients often reprefented the fame deity both as mafculine and feminine. They had both Cacus and Caca, Lunus and Luna, Janus and Jäna. II. 342.

DELOS.

This ifland was famous for its oracle; and for a fountain facred to the prophetic deity. I. 206. It was famous alfo for the worſhip of the Sun; and we learn from Callimachus (h. in Del.) that there were traditions of fubterraneous fires burſting forth in

many

many parts of it. Hence it was called Pirpile, and
by the fame poet Hiftia, and Heftia. 227.

This ifland was particularly frequented for its
oracle; and the failors feem to have undergone
fome fevere difcipline at the altar of the god, in
order to obtain his favour. Callim. in Del. v. 316.
A wonderful concourfe of people from all nations
continually reforted to its temple. The priefts in
confequence of it had hymns compofed in almoft
all languages. It is faid that the female attendants could imitate the fpeech of various people;
and were well verfed in the hiftories of foreign
parts, and of ancient times. (v. Hom. h. in Apoll.)
I. 264.

DELPHI.

The people were of old called Lycorians; and the
fummit of Parnaffus, Lycorea. Near it was a
town of the fame name; both facred to the god of
light. I. 79. The fituation of Delphi feems to
have been determined on account of a mighty
chafm in the hill; and Apollo is faid to have chofen
it for an oracular fhrine, on account of the effluvia
which from thence proceeded.

Ut vidit Pæan vaftos telluris hiatus
Divinam fpirare fidem, ventofque loquaces
Exhalare folum, facris fe condidit antris,
Incubuitque folo : vates ibi factus Apollo.

Lucan. L. 5. v. 82.

Here alfo was the temple of the Mufes, which
ftood clofe upon a reeking ftream. But what rendered Delphi more remarkable, and more reverenced, was the Corycian cave, which lay between
that hill and mount Parnaffus. Paufanias (l. 10.)
thus fpeaks of it; αντρον Κωρυκιον σπηλαιων, ων ειδον,
θεας αξιον μαλιςα. I. 219.

7

DERCETUS,

And Dercetis of the Greeks, came from Κῆτος, and Gatus; and compounded Atargatis, and Atargatus. Macrobius makes Atargatis, the mother of the gods, like Gaia, Rhea, and Cybele. That this emblem related to the Ark, is manifest from its being represented as a sacred receptacle, wherein the gods were inclosed. The Græcians, not knowing that their mythology arose from hieroglyphics, formed personages out of every circumstance. They supposed that Semiramis was the daughter of Dercetus; 'and that the latter was changed into a fish, as the former was into a pigeon. (Ovid. Met. L. 4.) These notions arose from the feminine emblems of the Ark, which were exhibited at Ascalon, Azotus, Joppa, and in the cities of Syria. Diodor. (L. 2.) thus represents her; Θια, ἣν ονομαζουσιν οἱ Συροι Δερκεῖουν,—το μεν προσωπον ἐχη γυναικος, το δε αλλο σωμα παν ιχθυος. He adds that she was esteemed the same as Venus, or Cupris. (v. Lucian. de Suria dea.) II. 312.

DEUCALION,

Phoroneus, Apis, Inachus, Zeuth, Prometheus, were all one person: and with that person commenced the Gentile history, 'not of Greece only, but of the world. II. 268.

We are assured by Philo (de præm. et pœna.) that Deucalion was Noah. Ἑλληνες μεν Δευκαλιωνα, Χαλδαιοι δε ΝΩΕ επονομαζουσιν, εφ' ου τον μεγαν καῖακλυσμον ςυνεβη γενεσθαι. That Deucalion was unduly adjudged by the people of Thessaly to their country solely, may be proved from his name occurring in different parts of the world. II. 212.

DEUS LUNUS.

The Mneuis, or as the Dorians exprefs it Mneuas, is a contraction of Men-Neuas, the Lunar god Neuas, the fame as Noas, or Noah. The Mneuis, and Apis, were both dedicated to Ofiris (Noah) who among other titles had that of Helius: but they related more to him under the character of the Deus Lunus, and from hence the Mneuis was denominated. Under this character the Egyptians did not refer to the planet, but to a perfon; and to the machine, in which he had been preferved: the fame, which was ftiled Rhea and Damater. II. 422.

The fame deity was often mafculine and feminine; what was Dea Luna in one country, was Deus Lunus in another. I. 39.

DI, DIO, DIS, DUS,

Common names for the deity; analogous to Deus, and Θεος of other nations. The Sun was called Arez in the eaft, and compounded Dis-Arez, and Dus-Arez; which fignifies Deus Sol. Hefych. fays, Δουσαρην τον Διονυσον Ναβαταιοι (καλουσιν) ως Ισιδωρος. There was a high mountain or promontory in Arabia, denominated from this deity; analogous to which there was one in Thrace, which had its name from Duforus, or the god of light, Orus, Δους, Dous, is the fame as Deus. I. 38.

DIVI POTES,

So were the Cabiri particularly ftiled. Hi, quos Augurum libri fcriptos habent fic, Divi Potes, funt pro illis, qui in Samothrace Θεοι δυνατοι. (Varro de ling. Lat. l. 4.) II. 463.

DIANA.

DIANA.

She was called Saronia; and by the Perfians was named Sar-Ait. I. 75. She was ftiled πολυπ7ολις, becaufe the office was particularly afcribed to her of conducting colonies. 281. Many thought that Janus was the fame as both Apollo and Diana; the fame alfo as Helius, and with good reafon. II. 264. Diana is a compound of De Iäna, and fignifies the goddefs Jäna; hence with the prefix was formed Diana, the fame, I imagine, as Dione. 342.

DIESPATER,

The god of day. Macrob. Saturn. L. 1. Cretenfes Δια την ημεραν vocant. The word Dies of the Latins was of the fame original. I. 309. n.

DIOMEDES.

The rites of Dionufus Hippius were carried into Thrace, where the horfes of Diomedes were faid to have been fed with human flefh. Abderus, the founder of Abdera, is fuppofed to have been a victim to thefe animals. (v. Scymnus Chius. Geogr. Vet. V. 2.) Thefe horfes, ξενοκ]ονοι, which fed upon the flefh of ftrangers, were the priefts of Hippa, and of Dionufus, ftiled Hippus, or more properly Hippius. They feem to have refided in an ifland, and probably in the Thracian Cherfonefe: which they denominated Diu-Medes, or the ifland of the Egyptian deity Medes. II. 34.

DIONE,

Was fometimes looked upon as the mother of Venus; at other times as the goddefs herfelf, ftiled Dione, and Venus Dionæa. She was faid to have been the mother of Niobe, and under the name of Pleione, was efteemed the mother of the Peleiades, who form the conftellation, fo aufpicious to mariners.

ners. She had joint rites with Zeuth or Jupiter at
Dodona; where the Dove was said to have given
out oracles. Adione, Idione, Dione, Hermione,
Pleione are all compounded of Ione, and relate to
doves. II. 316. Dione is a compound of Ad, or
Ada, Ione. 340.

DIONUSUS.

In Arcadia, near the eruption of the river Era-
finus, was a mountain, clothed with beautiful trees,
and facred to Dionufus. It was called Chaon, *the
place of the Sun*; for Dionufus was of old efteemed
the fame as Ofiris, the Sun, I. 106. Apollo, Bacchus, Dionufus, are all three the fame; each of
them the Sun. 308.

He was a great traveller, a founder of cities and
a lawgiver; he taught men to plant the vine, and
other falutary arts. He had many attendants;
among whom were the Tityri, Satyri, Thyades, and
Amazons. The whole of his hiftory is very inconfiftent in refpect both to time and place.
Writers therefore have tried to remedy this by introducing different people of the fame name.
Hence he is multiplied into as many perfonages as
Hercules. According to the Græcian mythology,
he is reprefented as twice born; and to have had
two fathers, and two mothers. He was alfo expofed in an Ark, and wonderfully preferved. As
his rites came originally from Chaldea, and the land
of Ur, he is in confequence of it often ftiled Πυρι-
γενης, and Πυρισπορος. The Indians gave the fame
account of Dionufus, as the Egyptians did of
Ofiris,

We muft confider the account given of Dionufus,
as the hiftory of the Dionufians. This is twofold.
Part relates to their rites and religion; in which the
great events of the infant world, and the prefervation of mankind in general, were recorded. In the
other

other part, which contains the expeditions and conquefts of this perfonage, are enumerated the various colonies of the people, who were denominated from him. They were the fame as the Ofirians and Herculeans; all of one family, though under different appellations.

Many places claimed his birth; and many fhewed the fpot of his interment. For the Græcians, whereyer they met with a grot or a cavern facred to him, took it for granted that he was born there; and wherever he had a Taphos, or high altar, fuppofed that he was buried there. The fame alfo is obfervable in the hiftory of all the gods. II. 77.

The name of Dionufus relates not to Νοος, *mens,* but to Nufos, Noah; being a compound of Dios-Nufos, for fo his name was properly expreffed. 274.

Semele, the mother of Dionufus, was called Thyone; by which was certainly meant *the Ïone,* or Dove. The poet, from hence ftiled Dionufus Thyoneus. This is analogous to the former, and fignifies *the Ioneus, the god of the Jonah,* or Dove. He was alfo called Ὑας, as Ζευς was ftiled Ομβριος; both which terms fignify the deity of rain. The prieftefs of the god had hence the name of Hyas, and alfo Thyas. Thyas fignifies *The Hyas:* Thyades, *The Hyades.* Why Dionufus had this title, and why at his myfteries and orgies they echoed the terms Hyas Atis; or as the Greeks expreffed it Ὑας Ατλης, *the lord of fhowers,* need not be explained. The conftellation of the Hyades was a watry fign, and fuppofed to have been a memorial of fome perfonages, who are reprefented as the nurfes of Dionufus. They were the daughters of Oceanus and Melitta, and refided once at Nufa. It is faid of them, that they had a renewal of life. 340. Dionufus alfo himfelf was fuppofed to have been twice born; and thence was ftiled διφυης. Sometimes

times the intermediate ſtate is taken into the account; and he is repreſented as having experienced
three different lives:

Οργιον, αρρηῖον, τριφυες, κρυφιον Διος ερνος.

Κικλησκω Διονυσον, εριβρομον, ευαςηρα,

Πρωῖογονον, διφυη, τριγονον.   Orphic. H. 51—29.

His laſt birth was from Hippa, certainly the Ark,
at which time nature herſelf was renewed. 410.
Athenæus (l. 15.) tells us, that the perſon, whom
the Greeks invoked after ſupper by the title of
Ζευς Σωῖηρ, was no other than Dionuſus. And he
adds, what points out the perſon more particularly,
that he was ſtiled not only the ſaviour, but τον και
των Ομβρων αρχηγον. 406.

The moſt ancient prieſts of Dionuſus were called
Saturi and Tituri, from Sat-Ur, and Tit-Ur: the
former were ſo named from the object, the latter
from the place of their worſhip. Tit-Ur, μαςος
ηλιου; the name of thoſe high altars, where the rites
of Orus were celebrated. The Tituri were properly Titurians; the Saturi, Σαῖυροι, Saturians.
II. 265.

DIONUSIA,

An Ark, or Ship, was made uſe of as a ſacred
emblem in the rites of Iſis and Oſiris. The like
cuſtom prevailed in the Dionuſia, and at the feſtivals of other deities. II. 284.

DIU,

Sometimes, but ſparingly, occurs for an Iſland;
and is generally by the Greeks changed into Δια,
Dia. The iſland Ναξος, was called Dia. (Schol. in
Theocr. Idyl. 2. v. 45.) It is ſtill common in the
Arabian Gulf, and in India; and is often expreſſed
Dive, and Diva; as in Laodive, Serandive, Mal-
dive. Before Goa is an iſland called Diu καῖ εξοχην.
I. 95.

I. 95. and n. The Greeks not knowing that Diu in the east fignified an ifland, out of Diu-Socotra in the Red-Sea, formed the ifland of Diofcorides: from Diu-Ador, or Adorus, they made an ifland Diodorus. The ifland Socotra they fometimes called the ifland of Socrates. I. 169. n.

DODONA.

As the Dove was efteemed the interpreter of the will of the deity; the priefts and foothfayers were ftiled Iönah, or Doves. And as Theba in Egypt was originally the temple of the Ark, we muft look for priefts of this denomination in a fanctuary of that name; accordingly we find that there were perfons in this place called Iönah; which the Greeks rendered Πιλειαι and Τρηρωνις.

It is faid, that fome of this order carried the rites of Theba, or the Ark, to Libya: and that others brought them to Dodona in Epirus; where Deucalion is fuppofed to have fettled; and where was the moft ancient oracular temple of Greece. It was founded by Cuthites, who were ftiled Ellopians, Pierians, Cadmians. They brought with them the memorials of the Dove, and the Ark; and the whole hiftory of the Deluge, from the Thebäis of Egypt. The women, who officiated in thefe temples, were, from the nature of their department, called Πιλειαι, and Πιλειαδις; which the Latins rendered Columbæ. See Silius Ital. L. 3. v. 678, who fays, that they originally came from Theba.

Paufanias mentions, that the Peleiades were the moft ancient prophetefles at Dodona in Chaonia, even antecedent to the celebrated Phæmonoe. He fays that they were women: and the firft oracle, which they exhibited, feems to relate to the re-eftablifhment of Zeuth, and the reftoration of the earth to its priftine ftate.

Ζευς

Ζευς ην, Ζευς ετι, Ζευς εσσέται· ω μεγαλε Ζευ·
Γα καρπους ανιη, διο κληζέτε μήτερα γαιαν.

Servius in Virg. Æn. L. 3. v. 466. takes notice
of the Doves at Theba: but, as it was usual with
the ancients to form personages out of every obsolete term, he makes Theba a woman; and supposes
her to have been the daughter of the deity, who
gave her two prophetic Doves for a present. One
of these, it is said, flew away to Dodona. But
Herodotus, l. 2. c. 54. gives the best account of
this oracle. He relates the Græcian history of it;
and that which he received from the people of
Egypt, who explain very satisfactorily the story of
these black Doves. εφασαν δι ιρεες του Θηβαιος Διος,
δυο γυναικας ιρηιας εκ Θηβεων εξαχθηναι υπο Φοινικων· και
την μεν αυτεων πυθεσθαι ες Λιβυην πρηθεισαν, την δε ες
τους Ελληνας. ταυτας δε τας γυναικας ειναι τας ιδρυσαμενας
τα μαντηια πρωτας εν τοισι ειρημενοισι εθνεσι. II. 286.

DORIANS.

The more simple the terms, the more ancient
and genuine we may for the most part esteem them:
and in the language of the Dorians we may perceive more terms relative to the true etymology of
the country, and those rendered more similar to the
ancient mode of expression, than are elsewhere to be
found. We must therefore, in all etymological
inquiries, have recourse to the Doric manner of
pronunciation, to obtain the truth. They came
into Greece, or Hellotia, under the name of
Adorians; and from their simplicity of manners,
and their little intercourse with foreigners, they
preserved much of their ancient tongue. For this
there may be another additional reason obtained
from Herodotus, L. 6. c. 53. who says, φαινοιατο αν
εοντες δι των Δωριεων ηγεμονες Αιγυπτιοι ιθαγενεες. The
ancient hymns, sung in the Prutaneia all over
Greece,

Greece, were Doric : fo facred was their dialect esteemed. I. 112.

As every colony, which went abroad, took to themfelves fome facred title, from their particular mode of worfhip; one family of the Hellenes ftyled themfelves accordingly Dorians. They were fo named from the deity Adorus, who by a common aphærefis was expreffed 'Dorus. The country, when they arrived, was inhabited by a people of a different race; whom they termed, as they did all nations in contradiftinction to themfelves, Βαρβαροι. With thefe original inhabitants they had many conflicts; of which we may fee fome traces in the hiftory of the Heraclidæ. For the Dorians, were the fame as the Herculeans ; and did not fettle in Greece only ; but in many parts of the world, whither the Amonians in general betook themfelves.

Paufanias imagines that the Dorians were comparatively of late date: yet he fhews, from many evidences in different parts of his antiquities, that they were high in the mythic age : and informs us of one curious particular, that all the ancient hymns of Greece in every province were in the dialect of this people. (L. 2. p. 199.) From hence I fhould infer, in oppofition to this learned antiquary, that they were as ancient as any branch of their family; that their language was the true Hellenic ; and that it was once univerfally fpoken. Their hiftory is not to be confined to Greece; for they were to be found in Phenicia, Caria, Crete, and Hetruria. They forced themfelves into Laconia, and Meffenia; in the latter of which provinces the Dorian language was retained in the greateft purity : and from their hiftory are to be obtained more ancient terms than can be elfewhere collected.

We learn from almoft every writer upon the fubject, that the Dorians, like their brethren the

M   Iönim,

Iönim, were not the firſt occupiers of Greece.
They were colonies from Egypt: and Herodotus
(L. 6. c. 53, 54.) ſpeaks of all the heads and
leaders of this people as coming directly from
thence. He takes his epocha from the ſuppoſed
arrival of Perſeus and Danae: and ſays, that all the
principal perſons of the Dorian family upwards
were in a direct line from Egypt. But it was not
Perſeus, nor Iön, nor Dorus, who came into Greece:
but a race of people, ſtyled Iönians, Dorians, and
Pereſians. Theſe were the Αιγυπίιοι ιθαγινεες; but
who came originally from Babylonia and Chaldea,
which countries in aftertimes were included under
the general name of Aſſyria.

When theſe colonies ſettled in Greece, they dif_
tinguiſhed themſelves by various titles. Some
were called Caucones; and were ſo denominated
from their temple Cau-Con, Ædes Herculis, ſive
Domus Dei. They reſided about Meſſenia, near
the river Minyas, and the city Aren.

Others were called Leleges, and were a people of
great antiquity. They were ſuppoſed to have been
conducted by one Lelex, who by Pauſanias is mentioned as the firſt king in Laconia; and ſaid to
have come from Egypt. (L. 3. p. 203. L. 1. p. 95.)
There was a remarkable paſſage in Heſiod, which
is taken notice of by Strabo (L. 7. p. 496.) concerning theſe Leleges. They were ſome of that
choſen family, whom Jupiter is ſaid in his great
wiſdom to have preſerved, out of a particular regard to that man of the ſea, Deucalion.

Τους ρα πoίε Κρονιδης Ζευς, αφθιία μηδεα ειδως,
Λεκίους εκ γαιης άλιω ποpε Δευκαλιωνι.

The Iönim are ſometimes ſpoken of under the
name of Atlantians; who were the deſcendants of
Atlas, the great aſtronomer, and general benefactor. (v. Diod. Sic. L. 3. p. 194.)

3   Some

Some of them were ftyled Myrmidones; particularly thofe who fettled in Æmonia, or Theffaly. They were the fame as the Hellenes, and Achivi. (v. Plin. L. 4. c. 7. Hom. Iλ. 6. v. 684.) They firft fettled about the cities Iäolcus, and Arene; and they had a tradition of their being defcended from one Myrmidon, a king of the country. This term was not only a proper name, but alfo fignified an ant or pifmire; (Hefych.) which gave occafion to much fable. It was by the ancient Dorians expreffed Murmedon. Now Mur, Mar, Mor, however varied, fignified of old the Sea: and Mur-Medon denotes Maris Dominum. It is. a title, which relates to the perfon, who was faid to have firft conftructed a fhip, and to have efcaped the waters. He was the fame as Deucalion.

The Myrmidons are fometimes reprefented as the children of Æacus: and are faid to have firft inhabited the ifland of Ægina. It is mentioned of this perfonage, that having loft all his people by a public calamity, he requefted of Jupiter, that the ants of the ifland might become men, which was granted. Who Æacus was may be learnt from his character. He is reprefented as a perfon of great juftice; and for that reafon to have been made judge of the infernal world: he is faid to have collected people together; to have humanized them; to have enacted laws; and to have firft eftablifhed civil polity. (Sch. in Pind. Nem. Od. 3. v. 21.) This is precifely the fame character, as was given to Uranus, Atlas, Ofiris, Dionufus, Saturnus, Phoroneus, Janus: all which are titles of the fame perfon, by whom the world was renewed, and from whom law and equity were derived. III. 385. v. *Pelafgi.*

DORSANES.

DORSANES.

This name is an abridgment of Ador-San, or Ador-Sanes, that is Ador-Sol, *the lord of light*. It was a title conferred on Ham; and alfo upon others of his family, who, collectively, were called the Baalim. I. 35.

DRACO.

His laws in the thirty ninth Olympiad were certainly the moſt ancient writing, to which we can ſecurely appeal. I. 152.

DRAGON.

We often read of virgins, who were expoſed to Dragons, and ſea-monſters; and of Dragons, which laid waſte whole provinces, till they were encountered and ſlain by ſome perſon of prowefs. This relates to women, who were immured in towers by the ſea-ſide; and to Banditti, who got poſſeſſion of theſe places, from whence they infeſted the adjacent country. Theſe Dragons are repreſented as ſleepleſs; becauſe in ſuch places there were commonly lamps burning, and a watch maintained. In thoſe ſet apart for religious ſervice, there was a fire, which never went out. What were ſtiled the eyes of the Dragon, were windows in the upper part of the building, through which the fire appeared. I. 433.

The Dragon ſaid to be ſlain by Jaſon, was of the dimenſions of a Trireme; by which muſt be meant that it was of the ſhape of a ſhip in general : for there were then no Triremes; indeed all theſe Dragons were really Dracontia; where, among other rites, the worſhip of the Serpent was inſtituted. II. 221.

DURA,

DURA,

And Amphipolis, cities upon the Euphrates in Mesopotamia, were both called of old Oropus. The people were addicted to Serpent-worship. II. 165.

DYNDAMENA.

As she, Cybele, and Rhea, were no other than feminine titles of the Lunar deity, called Mon, and Moon, we shall find a correspondence in the histories of those personages. Diodorus, (l. 3.) according to the custom of the Greeks, supposes Dindyma to have been the mother of Dindymene and Cybele, and the wife of Maon: which, though an idle distribution of persons, yet shews, that some relation subsisted between the terms. II. 447.

E.

EAGLE.

IT was one of the insignia of Egypt; and was particularly sacred to the Sun. It was called Ait, or Aἶτος. And Homer alludes to the original meaning of the word, when he terms the Eagle Aἶτος αιθων. I. 19.

EANUS.

This, according to Cornificius (Macrob. Sat. L. 1. c. 9.) was properly the name of Janus; and, as he would insinuate, from eo, I go: but Eanus was undoubtedly the same as Οιναс of the Greeks, and the Jönas of the eastern nations; by which was signified the Dove. II. 260.

M 3

EARTH,

Partition of. After Mofes has defcribed the prefervation of Noah and his family, and their de-fcent from the Ark, he gives a fhort hiftory of the Patriarch. (Gen. ix.) He afterwards proceeds to fhew how the reparation of mankind was effected in that family, and how they multiplied upon the earth. When they were greatly increafed, he gives a lift of their generations, and defcribes them with great accuracy upon their feparating, according to their places of deftination. (Gen. x.) And this diftribution was by the immediate appointment of God. (Deut. xxxii. Acts xvii.)

The Greeks had fome traditions of this partition of the earth, which they fuppofed to have been by lot, and between Jupiter, Neptune, and Pluto. Callim. H. in Jov. v. 61.

Φαυλο παλον Κρονιδησι δια τριχα δωμαια νειμαι,

Homer Iλ. O. v. 187.

Τρεις γαρ τ' εκ Κρονου ειμεν αδελφεοι, ους τεκε Ρειη
Τριχθα δε παυια δε δαςαι, εκαςος δ' εμμορε τιμης.

See alfo Plato in Critia. V. 3. p. 109.

At the diftribution of families, and the allotment of the different regions upon earth, the houfe of Shem ftood firft, and was particularly regarded. The children of Shem were Elam and Afhur, Ar-phaxad, Lud, and Aram. Their places of defti-nation feem to have been not far removed from the region of defcent, which was the place of fepara-tion. They in general had Afia for their lot, as Japhet had Europe, and Ham the large continent of Africa. And in Afia, the portion of Elam was to the eaft of the river Tigris, towards the mouth of it, which country, by the Gentile writers, was
ftyled

ftyled Elymaïs: and oppofite to him, on the
weftern fide, was Afhur. In like manner, above
Afhur, upon the fame river was Aram, who poffeffed the countries called Aram and Aramea: and
oppofite to him was Arphaxad, who in aftertimes
was called Arbaches and Arbaces, and his country
Arphacitis. Lud probably retired to Lydia, and
bordered upon the fons of Japhet, who were poffeffed of fome regions in Afia Minor. This was
the original difpofition of thefe families.

During the refidence of mankind in the parts
adjoining to the place where the Ark refted, we
may imagine, that there was a feafon of great happinefs. They for a long time lived under the mild
rule of the great Patriarch, before laws were enacted or penalties known. When they multiplied,
and were become very numerous, it pleafed God to
allot to the various families different regions, to
which they were to retire: and they accordingly,
in the days of Peleg, did remove, and betake themfelves to their different departments. But the fons
of Chus would not obey. They went off under the
conduct of the arch-rebel Nimrod; and feem to
have been for a long time in a roving ftate; but at
laft they arrived at the plains of Shinar. Thefe
they found occupied by Affur and his fons; for he
had been placed there by divine appointment: but
they ejected him, and feized upon his dominions;
which they immediately fortified with cities, and
laid the foundation of a great monarchy. Their
leader is often mentioned by the Gentile writers,
who call him Belus. He was a perfon of great
impiety; who finding, that the earth had been
divided among the fons of men by a divine decree,
thought proper to counteract the ordinance of God,
and to make a different diftribution. This is often
alluded to in the Ethnic writers: and Abydenus
(Eufeb. P. E. L. 9. p. 457.) particularly mentions,

M 4

tions, that Belus appointed to the people their place of habitation. Dionyſius (v. 1173.) refers to this Belus and his aſſociates, when he is ſpeaking of the deities, who were the anceſtors of the Indo-Cuthites.

$$———— εκληρωσαν\]ο δ' ἱκαςῳ$$
$$Μοιραν ιχҽν πον\]οιο, και ηπҽιροιο Ϭαθҽιης.$$

This is the beginning of that period, which, upon account of the rebellion then firſt known, was by the Greek writers alluded to under the title of Σκυθισμος. This ejectment of Aſſur ſeems to ſhew, that theſe tranſactions were after the general migration; for he was in poſſeſſion of the province allotted to him, till he was ejected by this lawleſs people. III. 13.

. See more upon this important ſubject, p. 261, of Obſervations and Inquiries relating to various parts of Ancient Hiſtory.

ECHETUS

Was a title of Apollo, rendered by the Greeks more commonly Ἐκαῖος, as if it came from the word ἱκας. King Echetus was a prieſt of Orus, and Oſiris. Homer (Οδ. Σ. v. 83.) calls him Ϭρο\]ων δηλη-μονα παν\]ων, from his cruelty to ſtrangers. II. 49.

EDESSA.

So was Adeſa called by the Greeks. It was the name of one of the chief, and moſt ancient cities in Syria, ſaid to have been built by Nimrod. It was undoubtedly the work of ſome of his brotherhood, the ſons of Chus; who introduced there the rites of fire, and the worſhip of the Sun. I. 26. Adeſa is the proper name, from Hades, the god of light. This city was alſo from its worſhip ſtiled Ur, Urhoe and Urchoë, which laſt was probably the name of the temple: Ori domus, vel templum; Solis Ædes. I. 208.

5

The true Phenicians were the fons of Efau, who was called Edom : and they fettled firft at mount Seir; and upon the Rèd Sea, which received its name from them.   Both Phoinic and Edom fignify *red*; which the Greeks changed to Erythrus, a word of the fame meaning.   There are continual allufions in Scripture to their power, wifdom and experience. (Obed. 8, 9. Jer. xlix. 7. Ifaiah lxiii. 1. Zech. ix. 2.)   They were very rich and powerful, carried on an extenfive commerce, and engroffed all the trade of the eaft. This people in procefs of time got poffeffion of Tyre and Sidon, and the adjacent country; which from them was called Phenicia : but how early they fettled here is uncertain.   They fent out many colonies : and traces of them are to be found, as far as Gades and Tarteffus. (v. Herodot. L. 7. c. 89. Dionys. Περιηγ. v. 905.)   Thofe, who fettled at Gades and the remoter parts of Spain, carried thither many memorials of their original country; particularly the name of Edom, by tranflation Erythra, which they conferred upon that part where they inhabited, and efpecially upon an ifland, Erythia, mentioned by Pliny. (Nat. H. L. 4. c. 22.) Solinus, c. 26. calls it Erythra.   The original Phenicians therefore were the people of Edom; who lived near the Arabians and Amalekites, and intermarried with their families, and are often confounded with them.   They feem to have carried their knowledge with them, wherever they fettled.   Thus the Carthaginians are reprefented as a knowing and politic people.   It is remarkable, that their chief city Carthage was originally called Bofra, the name of the capital of Edom.   Their language alfo was a dialect of the Hebrew : and the above city is faid by Philiftus (Eufeb. Chron. Can. p. 31.) to have
been

been built by Efor, to whom he fubjoins one Car-
chedon of Tyre.

Poffibly Spain might receive the name of Iberia
from them; who, when they fettled in the parts
particularly fo called, were diftinguifhed by their
moft ancient family name Ebræi.　The original
name of the river Iberus feems to have been Ebor,
called at prefent Ebro.　They fettled in many parts
of this country, but chiefly near Gades; and it is
obfervable, that here was the principal feat of the
Iberi. (v. Steph. Byz. Dion. Περιηγ. v. 282.)　The
Iberians therefore appear to have been the fame
nation as the Erythreans or Edomites; who came
from Tyre, and were generally mentioned by the
name of Phenicians, yet they loft not their original
gentile name from Heber; but were at times termed
Eberi, or Iberi, according to the Greek manner of
expreffing it. · The chief city of this country is at
this day called Ebora; and is near the ancient
Gades.　So wide did this active people extend
themfelves; and they were for ages very powerful;
till by degrees they were weakened in every part,
and infenfibly funk into oblivion.　In the time of
the Greeks, the Arabians were in poffeffion of
Edom, the original country of the Phenicians, and
they retain it to this day.　Hence it is that they
have been mentioned as coming from Phenicia; and
fometimes called Phenicians.　Such mifnomers are
very common in the writings of both Greeks and
Romans. Obferv. 222.

EES,

Rendered As, and Is, like אש of the Hebrews,
related to light, and fire. I. 26.　It is often compounded with El, and Il.　Hence many places
denominated Alefia, Elyfa, Eleufa, Halefus, Elyfus,
Eleufis; by apocope Las, Lafa, Læfa, Lafaia; alfo
Liffe, Liffus, Liffia.　And fometimes reverfed;
instead

inſtead of El Ees, Ees El; hence places named Azilis, Azila, Aſyla, contracted Zelis, Zela, Zeleia, Zelitis; alſo Sele, Sela, Sala, Salis, Sillas, Silis, Soli. All theſe places were founded, or denominated by people of the Amonian worſhip. I. 28. Hence alſo Ασυλον, Aſylum. From El-Ees came Elis, Eliſſa, Eleuſis, Eleuſinia ſacra, Elyſium, Elyſii campi in Egypt and elſewhere. 32. n. Ees was one of the titles of the Sun.

EES—AIN

Is the reverſe of Ain-Ees, or Hanes. I. 53.

EGBATANA

In Media. Here was an eruption of fire. I. 202.

EGNATIA,

The name of a town in Italy, which ſeems to have been of the ſame purport as Hanes: for Hanes was ſometimes expreſſed with a guttural, Hagnes; from whence came *Ignis* of the Romans. In Arcadia near mount Lyceus was a ſacred fountain; into which one of the nymphs, who nurſed Jupiter, was ſuppoſéd to have been changed. It was called Hagnon, the ſame as Ain-On, *the fount of the Sun.* From Ain of the Amonians, expreſſed Agn, came the Αγνος of the Greeks, which ſignified any thing pure and clean. Hence was derived Αγνειον, ωη-γαιον· Αγναιον, καθαρον· Αγνη, καθαρα. Heſych. Pauſanias (L. 8. p. 678.) ſtiles the fountain Hagno: but it was originally Hagnon, *the fountain of the Sun.* The town Egnatia ſtood in campis Salentinii, and at this day is called Anazo, and Anazzo. It was ſo named from the rites of Fire which were here practiſed. Reperitur apud auctores in Salentino oppido Egnatiâ, impoſito ligno in ſaxum quoddam ibi ſacram protinus flammam exiſtere.

exiftere. Pliny, l. 2. c. 110. From hence undoubtedly came alſo the name of Salentum, which
is a compound of Sal-En, *Solis fons*; and aroſe from
this ſacred Fire to which the Salentini pretended.
They were Amonians, who ſettled here, and who
came laſt from Crete. (Strabo. l. 6. p. 430.) The
ancient Salentini worſhiped the Sun under the
title of Man-zan, or Man-zana : by which is meant
Menes, Sol. (Feftus in v. Octobris.) I. 202.

EGG.

In many hieroglyphical deſcriptions, the Dove,
Oinas, was repreſented as hovering over the *Mundane Egg*, which was expoſed to the fury of Typhon.
This doubtleſs was an emblem of the Ark; whence
proceeded that benign perſon, the preacher of
righteouſneſs, who brought mankind to a more
mild kind of life. Dicitur et Euphratis fluvio
Ovum piſcis Columbam aſſediſſe dies plurimos, et
excluſiſſe Deam benignam et miſericordem hominibus ad vitam bonam. Lucius Ampel. in lib. ad
Macrinum. The Ark reſted upon mount Baris in
Armenia, the Ararat of Moſes; and in this country
are the fountains of the Euphrates.

An Egg, as it contains the elements of life, was
thought no improper emblem of the Ark, in which
were preſerved the rudiments of the future world.
Hence in the Dionuſiaca, and in other myſteries,
one part of the nocturnal ceremony conſiſted in the
conſecration of an Egg. By this, as we are informed by Porphyry, was ſignified the world.
This world was Noah, and his family; even all
mankind, incloſed and preſerved in the Ark. The
το Ορφικον Ωον, και το Πλατωνος Ωον, were undoubtedly
of the ſame purport. It ſeems to have been a
favourite ſymbol, very ancient, and adopted among
many nations. It was ſaid by the Perſians of
Oromaſdes, that he formed mankind, and incloſed
them

them in an Egg. The Syrians (v. Arnobius, l. 1.) uſed to ſpeak of their anceſtors, the gods, as the progeny of Eggs. Helladius Beſantinous (ap. Photium. p. 1594.) takes notice of one Oan, who was repreſented as a juſt man; who lived at the renewal of time, and was ſuppoſed to have proceeded εκ του Πρωτογονου Ωου. This very perſon is thus addreſſed; Orphic. Hymn. 5.

Πρωτογονον καλεω διφυη, μεγαν, αιθεροπλαγκτον,
ΩΟΓΕΝΗ, χρυσεαισιν αγαλλομενον πτερυγεσσιν.
II. 31'9.

In the temple of the Dioſcouri in Laconia there was ſuſpended a large hieroglyphical Egg. This Egg was ſometimes attributed to Leda, and ſometimes to Nemeſis the deity of juſtice. This Egg the poets ſuppoſed to have been hatched by Leda: and the Διοσκουροι were produced. At other times a Serpent was deſcribed around it; either as an emblem of that Providence, by which mankind was preſerved; or elſe to ſignify a renewal of life from a ſtate of death: as the ſerpent, by caſting his ſkin, ſeems to renew life. By the burſting of the Egg was denoted the opening of the Ark; and the diſcloſing to light whatever was within contained. II. 360.

EGYPT

Was one of the moſt ancient and extenſive kingdoms: it ſeems to have been reſpectable from the beginning; and the moſt early accounts bear witneſs to its eminence and power. The firſt inhabitants ſeem to have ſettled in the upper parts, near the Thebais: but they ſoon got poſſeſſion of the whole. They were eſteemed a very wiſe and learned people: (Acts vii. 22.) they were very powerful and populous: and there are ſaid to have been in the days of Amaſis thirty thouſand cities in Egypt.

Egypt. But it was doomed to a fatal change. It was to become *a bafe . kingdom*, (Ezekiel xxix. 14, 15.—xxx. 13.) and for above two thoufand years it has been *the bafeft of kingdoms* : neither in all that vaft interval of time has there been once *a prince* of that nation.

The antiquity of this kingdom may be feen by it's founders Ham and Mizraim; by whofe names the country was of old called, nor are they obliterated at this day. Plutarch (de Is. et Os.) tells us that the priefts of Egypt in the myfteries of Ifis called their country Chemia. Hefychius terms it Hermochemia, as its ancient name. Stephanus gives it the name of Mifore or Myfora. In refpect to its extent ; the Greeks defcribe it under three large and principal divifions, which comprehend Lower Egypt, Upper Egypt, and a third which was uppermoft of all ; which extended to Philæ and Syene. Thefe were termed ἡ κατω, ἡ ανω, and ἡ ανωτατη χωρα. Delta, fituated among the branches of the Nile, was efteemed the loweft of all. How Egypt was fituated and bounded, we are very clearly informed by Leo Africanus : *Ægyptus, clariffima regio, ab occidente defertis Barcæ, Lybiæ, ac Numidiæ clauditur* ; *ab oriente defertis, quæ Ægypto et Mari Rabro interjacent.* The whole extent of this country from N. to S. was computed to be about fix hundred miles : and confifted of three principal divifions, fubdivided into fmaller provinces, called by the Greeks Νομοι, by the natives *Tabir*. Of thefe there were reckoned thirty-fix.

The river that waters the whole country is the Nile ; which is fingle for fome hundred of miles downwards, running in one direction. When it arrives at the extremity of Lower Egypt, called Delta, where ftood the city Cercafora ; it is divided into very confiderable branches, which inclofe all the country below, and never unite again. They

are

are called the Canobic and Pelufiac branches. The river ftill however keeps on its courfe downward; having a fupply of water fufficient to fill the Sebennitic channel, which forms one of the moft confiderable mouths of the Nile. (Herodot. L. 2. c. 17.)   As long as the Nile ran in a fingle channel, which was about four hundred miles, it was inhabited both on the Arabian and Libyan fide; having all the way a ridge of mountains to the eaft and to the weft, which were a fecurity to the natives.   A few miles below Memphis, juft where Lower Egypt commenced, the mountains (or as Herodotus fpeaks *the mountain*) of Arabia ceafed: reaching no farther downward to the north, though eaftward they extended to the Red Sea.   -

The provinces of Delta generally referred to *Arabia*, were within the precincts of the Nile, and in the beft of Egypt.   Thefe were the provinces of Arabia (the fame as Phacufa, q. v.) Bubaftus and Heliopolis.   Thefe were all contiguous to each other, and towards the fummit of Lower Egypt.

Of thefe three provinces, the moft remarkable was that of Heliopolis, whofe capital was likewife fo called. (There was another city of the fame name to the eaft of the Nile in *Arabia*.)   Here was the city On (of the Scriptures, the fame with Heliopolis) fo famous for its temple and religious rites; whofe inhabitants are reported to have been the wifeft of the Egyptians.   The temple is faid to have been very magnificent : and its original name was Ain Shems, or Shemefh, *the fountain of the Sun:* from whence the whole province received its name, being called at different periods Ain, Aven, and On.

Bubaftus was to the eaft of this, and likewife a noted province, feparated from the former by the great Sebennitic branch, and from *Arabia* by the Pelufiac.

Pelufiac. This alfo was renowned for its magnificent temple, which was dedicated to the goddefs
Befheh or Befhet, the Αρτεμις αγρια, or Diana agreftis
of the Greeks and Romans. This nome and the
chief city of it are the Phibefeth (q. v.) of the
Scriptures : and they are often mentioned in conjunction with On or Heliopolis, which was next in
fituation. Obferv. 100.

The third great province was the nome of
Arabia; fo called, not becaufe it was in *Arabia*,
which it was not, but from the Arabian fhepherds,
who had formerly fettled in thefe parts, and held
them for many years. The true Arabian nome was
nothing more than the land of Gofhen, called by
the *Seventy* Γισσιμ της Αραβιας. Egypt had been in
fubjection to a threefold race of kings : the Meftræi, who were undoubtedly the genuine defcendants of Mizraim, who firft gave name to the
country, the traces of which are not yet effaced;
Al Cahira, and, indeed, the whole of Egypt being
called Mezré to this day. The Auritæ, who were
the Arabian fhepherds, and their kings; thefe
reigned here a confiderable time, maintaining
themfelves by force; till, after many ftruggles, they
were finally expelled by the natives. Laftly, the
Egyptian kings.

The Auritæ were called by the Greeks and
Romans Arabians : but their true name was Cufhan
or Cufeans; the fame which they gave to the
province where they fettled, which was *the beft of
the land*; and was fituated, within the Delta, at the
extreme and higheft part of Lower Egypt.

To this place the children of Ifrael fucceeded,
after it had been abandoned by its former inhabitants; but at what interval of time is uncertain.
Jofephus, out of a defire to aggrandize his own nation, fuppofes that the Shepherds who bore rule in
Egypt were his anceftors; and that hence arofe
the

the hatred that the Egyptians bore to them. For this reason he makes no difference between the twofold race of shepherds, which Manetho, even as he quotes him, sufficiently distinguishes. The first were the Cuseans and their *Pastor* kings, who held the country in bondage : the others were the Israelitish shepherds, who succeeded to the first, and were theirselves held in bondage. *Ibid.* 140.

EGYPTIANS.

They were of a collateral line with the people of Canaan; for the father of the Mizraim and the Canaanites were brothers. Josephus calls the country of Egypt Mestra. Ant. Jud. L. 1. c. 6. I. 7. As it was the land of Ham, who, as the Sun, was stiled Ait, it also was called Ait, rendered by the Greeks Aἴλια. As the heart in the body may be esteemed what the Sun is in his system, the source of heat and life, it was therefore called Ait, which word having these two senses was the reason why they made a heart over a vase of burning incense, an emblem of their country. 19. The principal rites in Egypt were confessedly for a person lost, and for a time consigned to darkness, who was at last found. This was Osiris. Hence those exclamations at the feasts of Isis; Ευρηκαμεν· Συγχαιρομεν. See a curious account of this in Plutarch. Is. et Osiris. V. 1. the ultimate to which which we can apply is Egypt. To this country we must look up for the original of those much mistaken people, the Ionim, Arkitæ, and Argonauts. II. 333. 508.

The native Egyptians seldom left their country, but by force. This necessity however did occur; for Egypt at times underwent great revolutions. It was likewise in some parts inhabited by people of a different cast; particularly by the sons of Chus. 150.

N   Every

Every sacred animal in Egypt was distinguished by some title of the deity. I. 78. The Egyptians had many subordinate deities, which they esteemed so many emanations, *απορροιαι*, from their chief god. These derivatives they called fountains, and supposed them to be derived from the Sun; whom they looked upon as the source of all things. I. 52. They were of all nations the most extravagant in their grief. 303. They were refined in their superstition, above all nations in the world; and conferred the names and titles of their deities upon vegetables, and animals of every species; and not only upon these, but also on the parts of the human body; and the very passions of the mind. Whatever they deemed salutary, or of great value, they distinguished by the title of sacred, and consecrated to some god. 333.

They had many emblematical personages, set off with heads of various animals, to represent particular virtues, and affections; as well as to denote the various attributes of their gods. 331. They esteemed a renewal of life, a second state of childhood. II. 327. The Egyptian priests seem to have been denominated from their complexion Crows, or Ravens. Hence Strabo. L. 17. says, that upon Alexander's expedition to the temple of Ammon, he was conducted by two Crows; Curtius, L. 4. c. 7. says, that a good number went out to meet him. These Crows, like the black Doves, were certainly the priests of the place. 291.

EIRAS.

The Rainbow and the Dove were certainly depicted together in hieroglyphics. What the Græcians called Iris seems to have been expressed Eiras by the Egyptians; and was a favourite name among that people. The two female attendants upon Cleopatra, who supported her in her last moments, were

were named Eiras and Charmion, which may be interpreted the Rainbow, and Dove. II. 346. Columba, Οινας, a Syris dicta est Charmion, vel Charmiona. Bochart. Hieroz. pars 2da. L. I. c. I.

EL, AL, HA, ELI,

Was the name of the true God; but by the Zabians was transferred to the Sun: whence the Greeks borrowed their Ἥλιος, and Ἠέλιος.

ELEES, or EESEL,

Was an ancient title of Mithras and Osiris in the east, the same as Sol, the Sun. I. 31.

EL, ELION,

Were titles, by which the people of Canaan distinguished their chief deity. El was a title given to Cronus. Elion is a compound of Eli-On, both titles of the Sun: hence the former is often joined with Aur, and Orus. Elorus, and Alorus, were names both of persons and places. It is sometimes combined with Cham; hence Camillus, &c. The deity El was particularly invoked by the eastern nations, when they made an attack. They used to cry El-El, and Al-Al; now changed to Allah. I. 13. Ελελευ, επιφωνημα πολεμικον.

EL-APHAS,

Was one of the titles of the Sun, Sol Deus Ignis. This El-aphas the Greeks rendered Ελαφος, and supposed it to relate to a *deer*; and the title El-Apha-Baal, given by the Amonians to the chief deity, was changed to Ελαφηβολος, a term of quite different import. El-aphas, and El-apha-baal, related to the god Osiris; the deity of light; and there were sacred liba made at his temple, called Ελαφοι. I. 298.

    ΗΛΙΒΑΤΟΣ,

ΉΛΙΒΑΤΟΣ,

A favourite term with Homer and other poets, though they knew not the purport of it, and uniformly joined with Petra. It is an Amonian compound of Eli-Bat, Solis domus, vel templum.

Ήλιβάτοι πέτραι. The Greeks derived Ήλιβάτος from βαίνω, *descendo*; hence the idle story of the Petra falling from the Sun. I. 288.

ELIS COELA,

Was the moft facred part of Greece; efpecially the regions of Olympia, Cauconia, and Azania. It was denominated Elis from Ηλ, the Sun; and what the Greeks rendered Κοιλη, of old meant *Heavenly*. Hence Homer (Ιλ. B. v. 615.) peculiarly ftiles it Ήλιδα δίαν, *Elis the facred*. I. 111.

ELIZABETH,

Or temple of Eliza. It was a Canaanitifh name, the fame as Elifa, Eleufa, Elafa of Greece and other countries. It was a compound of El-Ees, and related to the god of light. It was made a feminine in aftertimes, and was a name affumed by women of the country ftiled Phenicia, as well as by thofe of Carthage. Hence Dido has this as a fecondary appellation; and mention is made by the Poet of Dii morientis Elizæ, though it was properly the name of a deity. Elifa, quamdiu Carthago invicta fuit, pro dea culta eft. Juftin. L. 18. c. 6. The worfhip of Elifa was carried to Carthage from Canaan and Syria; in thefe parts fhe was firft worfhiped; and her temple from that worfhip was called Eliza-Beth. I. 55.

ELLOPIA.

Solinus, c. 17. fays, Caryftos aquas calentes habet, quas Ellopias vocant. (See Pliny, L. 4. c. 12.)

c. 12.) Caryftos is Car-yftus, the deity of fire, to whom all hot fountains were facred. Ellopia is a compound of El-Ope, Sol Python, another name of the fame deity. I. 229.

EL-UC, EL-UC-OR, EL-UC-AON,

Were all titles of the Sun; which terms were all foftened by the Greeks into Λυκος, Λυκωριυς, Λυκαων. As this laft perfonage was the fame as El-Uc, Λυκος; it was fabled of him, that he was turned into a Wolf. The caufe of this abfurd notion arofe from hence: every facred animal in Egypt was diftinguifhed by fome title of the deity. But the Greeks never confidered whether the term was to be taken in its primary, or in its fecondary acceptation: whence they referred the hiftory to an animal, when it related to the god, from whom the animal was denominated. I. 78.

ELYSIAN PLAIN,

Near the Catacombs in Egypt, ftood upon the foul Charonian canal. I. 29.

EMESA,

Is a compound of Ham-Ees: the natives are faid by Feftus Avienus (Defcr. Orbis, v. 1083.) to have been devoted to the Sun.

Denique flammicomo devoti pectora Soli
Vitam agitant ——————. I. 208.

ENCHELIÆ,

A town in Illyria. Here Cadmus with his wife Hermione are faid to have been changed to a Serpent of ftone. Lucan (l. 3. 187.) fpeaks of the name as of great antiquity. It undoubtedly was of long ftanding; and a term from the Amonian

language.

language. It is the place of En-Chel, by which
is fignified the fountain of heaven, fimilar to Hanes,
Anorus, Anopus in other parts. The temple was
an Ophite Petra; which terms induced people to
believe, that there were in thefe temples Serpents
petrified. II. 172.

ENDOR.

The woman at Endor, who had a familiar fpirit,
is called אוב, Oub, or Ob; and it is interpreted
Pythoniffa. The place, where fhe refided, feems
to have been named from the worfhip there inftituted : for Endor is compounded of En-Ador, and
fignifies Fons Pythonis, the fountain of light, the
oracle of the god Ador. This oracle was probably
founded by the Canaanites; and had never been
totally fuppreffed, I. 49.

ERECH.

The Arkite rites were of high antiquity; and
though they began very foon in Egypt, yet they
feem to have been of ftill earlier date among the
people of Babylon and Chaldea. Perhaps they
commenced in the ancient city Erech which was
built by Nimrod. It was called by the Greeks
Erecca, and Aracca. The name Arca feems to be
a contraction of Arecca; and Arcas, Argos, Arguz
were perhaps the fame term with different terminations.

The deity of Erech was the original Erectheus.
The Chaldeans expreffed it Erech-Thoth, analogous to Pirom-Thoth, or Prometheus; and by it
they denoted the Arkite god. The Græcians took
this perfonage to themfelves, and fuppofed him to
have reigned in Attica. But Solon, when he came
to Egypt, found that he had been known there
long before. [και τον Ερεχθεα λεγουσι το γενος Αιγυπτιον
αναι. Diod. Sic. L. 1. I. 183.] Zeus by Lycophron

phron is ſtiled Erectheus; v. 158. It was alſo a title of Poſeidon; and the Athenians worſhiped him as the deity of the ſea.

Erichthonius was the ſame perſonage, whom Minerva was ſuppoſed to have incloſed in an Ark. (Pauſan. L. 1. See Ovid. Met. L. 2.) The word ſeems to be compounded of Erech, the Arkite title, and Thon, or Thonius, an oriental term, and probably had the ſame meaning as γηγενης. Erectheus likewiſe had the title of γηγενης. There were two cities called Erech, at no great diſtance from each other. The natives took care to diſtinguiſh them. The one they ſtiled And-Erech, the other Ard-Erech, the Anderica and Arderica of Herodotus. (l. 6.) Fiery pools were near both.

Erech (the ſame as Barſippa) was particularly famous for weaving. Hence the ſpider for its curious webb was ſtiled Arachana, contracted Arachna. And the poets fabled that this inſect was once a virgin, who, for ſkill in weaving, vied with the goddeſs of wiſdom. Ovid makes her to have been of Lydia, but other writers ſtile her Babylonica. The poet Nonnus ſpeaks of Erech by the name of Arachne, and mentions the manufactures, for which it was ſo famed: but repreſents it as a Perſic city, and near the Tigris;

Και ωορς ωοικιλα ωιπλα, τα ωιρ ωαρα Τιγριδος ὑδωρ
Νημαλι λιπlαλιω τιχνηςαlο Πιρςις Αραχνη.

There were in Babylonia canals of communication, which led from the Euphrates to the Tigris: ſo that the cities ſituated upon them might be referred to either river. What the poet means by ſtiling Arachne, which was of Babylonia, Perſic, may be known from his giving the ſame title to the Euphrates, upon which river the city was properly ſituated; and from whence he mentions theſe valuable commodities to have been ſent abroad.

Νηρευς μεν ταδε δωρα πολυθροκα· δωκε δε κωρη
Περσιχος Ευφρηλης πολυδαιδαλου ειμαῖ Αραχνης.

II. 519.

ERIDANUS.

This river betrays its original in its name; for it has no relation to the Celtic language; but is apparently of Egyptian or Canaanitish etymology. This is manifest from the terms, of which it is made up: for it is compounded of Ur-Adon, five Orus Adonis; and was facred to the god of that name, The river fimply, and out of compofition was Adon, or Adonis. And it is to be obferved, that this is the name of one of the principal rivers in Canaan. It is faid that the Eridanus was fo called firft by Pherecydes Syrus: and that this etymology is true, may in great meafure be proved from the Scholiaft upon Aratus. (p. 48.) He fhews that the name was of Egyptian original, at leaft confonant to the language of Egypt; for it was the fame as the Nile. It is certain, that it occurred in the ancient fphere of Egypt, from whence the Greeks received it. The great effufion of water in the celeftial fphere, which Aratus fays was the Nile, is ftill called Eridanus: and as the name was of oriental original, the purport of it muft be looked for among the people of thofe parts. I. 376.

EROS.

The Greeks out of Eiras formed Eros, a god of Love; whom they annexed to Venus, and made her fon. And finding that the bow was his fymbol, inftead of the Iris, they gave him a material bow, with the addition of a quiver and arrows. Being furnifhed with thefe implements of mifchief he was fuppofed to be the bane of the world. This was different from his original character. He is ftiled by Plato (Sympos.) Μεγας θεος, a mighty god; and it is faid Ερωτα μεγιστην αγαθων ημιν αιτιον ειναι. The bows of Apollo, and Diana, were probably formed from the fame originals.

Mofes informs us (Gen. ix.) that the bow in the clouds was inftituted as the token of a covenant, which God was pleafed to make with man. To this covenant Hefiod (Theog. v. 780.) alludes, and calls it the great oath. In all probability Iris and Eros were originally the fame term; and related to the Divine Love exhibited in the difplay of the bow, which it pleafed God to make a teft of his covenant with man. But a difference arofe in time; and the former was appropriated to the rainbow; and of the latter was formed a boyifh deity: by which means it was made to vary from its original purport. There was a particular kind of chaplet, familiar among the Greeks; and compofed, εκ παντων ανθεων. It was called Eros: undoubtedly from having all the variety of colours, which are confpicuous in the Iris. This beautiful phænomenon in the heavens was by the Egyptians ftiled Thamuz, and feems to have fignified, *The Wonder*. The Greeks expreffed it Thaumas; and from hence were derived θαυμαζω, θαυμασιος, θαυμαςος. This Thaumas they did not immediately appropriate to the bow, but fuppofed them to be two perfonages, and Thaumas the parent. Homer Ιλ. Λ. 27. thus fpeaks;

——Ιρισσιν εοικοτες, ας τε Κρονιων
Εν νεφει στηριξε, Τερας Μεροπων ανθρωπων,

and Ιλ. Ρ. 547.

Ηυτε πορφυρεην Ιριν θνητοισι τανυσση
Ζευς εξ ουρανοθεν Τερας εμμεναι.——

After the defcent from the Ark, the first wonderful occurrence was the bow in the clouds, and the covenant,

covenant, of which it was made an emblem. To this purpose there seems to be a verse of Parmenides, quoted by Plutarch (Amator.)

Πρωίτον μεν Ερωία Θεων μηίιζΘο παυίων.

At this season another æra began: the earth was supposed to be renewed; and time to return to a second infancy. They therefore formed an emblem of a child with the rainbow, to denote this renovation in the world; and called him Eros, or Divine Love. But however like a child he might be expressed, the more early mythologists esteemed him the most ancient of the gods.

Πρεσβυίαίον τι, και αυίοίελη, πολυμηίιν Ερωία

Orphic. Argon. v. 422.

Phædrus in Plato (Sympos.) says, μεγας θεος ο Ερως, και ΘΑΥΜΑΣΤΟΣ — εν πρεσβυίαίοις των θεων. Plato here in the term θαυμασος has an eye to the ancient Amonian name Thaumaz, and Thamuz.

Eros is made by some the son of Cronus; by others, of Zephyrus; and again by others, of Venus, or the Dove. Which variety of notions arose from the different manner of expressing, and also of interpreting, the ancient hieroglyphics. Eros, who was first the wonderful phænomenon, seems sometimes to be spoken of as Phanes, who was also called Dionusus. (Orphic. Fragm. ap. Macrob. Sat. L. 1. c. 18.) Among other titles he was stiled Maneros, which signified Lunus Cupido. Under this character the Egyptians reverenced a person who seems to have been the same as Thamas, or Thamuz: and his rites were attended with lamentations and dirges. They esteemed him a disciple of the muses, a great husbandman, and the inventor of the plough. (See Plut. If. et Ofir.) II. 343.

ERYX,

ERYX,

In Sicily, was proply Erech. Upon the mount was a celebrated temle of Venus. Doves were here held as facred, ashey were either in Paleftine, or Syria. There we two days of the year fet apart in this place for ftivals, called Αναγωγια, and Καλαγωγια; at which thes Venus was fuppofed to depart over fea, and afr a feafon to return. There were alfo facred Pigeis, which then took their flight from the ifland but one of them was ob-ferved upon the ninth ιy to come back from the fea, and to fly to the fhrιe of the goddefs. This was upon the feftival of the αναγωγια. Upon this day it is faid that there we great rejoicings. On what account can we iagine this veneration for the bird was kept up, id this celebrity to have been inftituted, but foα memorial of the Dove fent out of the Ark, andf its return from the deep to Noah? The hiftor is recorded upon the ancient coins of Eryx; hich have on one fide the head of Janus Bifrons,ɔn the other the facred Dove. Il. 319. 527.

ERYTREANS

Was another title, by hich the Cuthites were diftinguifhed: and the pces, where they refided, received it from them. 'c are apt to confine the name of the Erythrean feto the Red fea, or Sinus Arabicus; but that was oιy an inlet, and a part of the whde. The Cuthite Erythreans, who fettled near Midian, upon the Sιnus Elanitis, conferred this name upon that gulf but the Perfic fea was alfo denominated in the fine manner, and was in-deed the original Erythrea fea.

Thofe of this family wh fettled in India, con-ferred this name upon he great Indic ocean.

People

People of this family found many places weft-
ward, which were called Erhra, in Ionia, Libya,
Cyprus, Ætolia, and Bœot.. There were Ery-
threans about Tarteffus : Gdes itſelf was called
Erythia ; a ſmall variationfor Erythria. (Pliny,
N. H. L. 4. p. 230.) Ĺre lived the Σκυθεις
Αιθιοπης of Dionyſius (v. 59.) under which cha-
racter the Cuthites are partularly denoted.

In ſhort the Cuthites, Ethiopians, and Erythreans were the ſame peop.: and they had a ſtill
more general name of Σκυθι III. 185.

ESORUS.　EORUS,

Under theſe titles theicity was worſhiped in
Syria, Sicily, and Carthag I. 28.

ESTA anASTA,

Hence come the term Æſtas, Æſtus, Æſtuo,
Αςυ, Εςια, Εςιαζειν. I. 62.

ESTACHAR, o ISTACHAR,

Is the place or templeof Efta, or Ifta. That
the term originally relaid to fire, we have the
authority of Petavius. in Epiphanium, p. 42.)
Herbert, therefore, withgreat propriety ſuppoſes
the building to have bee the temple of Anaia, or
Anais, (Travels, p. 139) who was the ſame as
Hanes, as well as Hcia, Procopius (Perfica,
L. 1. c. 24.) ſpeaking ſ the Perfians, ſays ex-
preſsly, that it was the ery ſame which is aftertimes the Romans worſlped, and called the fire of
Heftia, or Vefta. Hye renders the term after
Kæmpfer, Ifta : but itwas more commonly expreſſed Efta, or Afta. I 126. Iftachar then was a
name given to the grancPureion in Chufiftm from
the deity there worſhipd. A miftake in Maximus
Tyrius (Differt. 8.) may hhence corrected. He ſays,

￼χ4᥊

και θυουσι Περσαι πυρι, περφουσιες αυλω την πυρος τροφην, επιλεγοντες, Πυρ, δεσπολαμεθα; *O Fire, come, and feed:* it fhould be, Ω Πυρ, δεσπολα, Εσιε; *O mighty Lord of Fire, Heſtius.* I. 228.

ESTES, STES, ASTUS,

All are variations o the fame term, and equally relate to fire. II. 463.

HΩIOΣ.

Ait and Aith were tems not only of high honour but of endearment. Vnus in Apollonius Rhodius (L. 3. v. 52.) calls Jup, and Minerva, by way of refpect, Hθεαι. Menſaus fays to his brother Agamemnon (Il. K. v. 7.) Τιφθ' ουλως, Hθεε, κορυσσεαι; and (Ψ. v. 94.) 'ιπλε μοι, Hθεεη κεφαλη, δευρ' αελελουθας, are the words of Achilles to the fhade of his loſt Patroclus. Hθεα, in the original acceptation, as a title, fignified olaris, Divinus, Splendidus; but in a fecondary fenfe it denoted any thing holy, good, and praife-wrthy. From this ancient term were derived the εθ; and ηθικα of the Greeks. I. 21.

ETHEION.

Ovid, though his whle poem be a fable, yet copies the modes of thofe countries, of which he treats. Speaking therefce of an Ethiopian, he introduces him by the nme of Eth-Amon, but foftened by him into Ethemon. (Metam. L. 5. 162.)

——— inſtabant pæte finiſtra
Chaonius Molpeus, dexta Nabathæus Ethemon.

So Virg. Æn. L. 10. 126.

——— comites

———— comites Sarpedonis ambo,
Et clarus Ethemon Lyc comitantur ab alta,
Or, *Clarus et Ethemon,*————. 22.

ETHIOPIANS,

Were defcended from Chs, who was their great
anceftor. I. 104.

The worfhip of the Serpnt began among them;
and they were from thence enominated Ethopians,
and Aithopians, which the Greeks rendered Aιθιοπις.
It was a name which they id not receive from their
complexion, as has been ommonly furmifed; for
the branch of Phut, and the Lubim, were probably
of a deeper die; but they vere fo called from Ath-
Ope, and Ath-Opis, the gd, which they worfhiped.
(See Pliny, L. 6.) 481.

ETYMOLOGY;

Euftathius upon Dionfius has laid down a rule,
which fhould be carefull remembered: Ει CαρCαρον
το ονομα, ου χρη ζηλειν Ελληνικην ετυμολογιαν αυτου.
This is a plain and goldn rule, pofterior indeed to
Ariftotle, Plato, and oher Greek writers; which
however common fenfe might have led them to
have anticipated, and to have followed: but it was
not in their nature. Euftathius who gave the
advice was a Greek, and could not for his life abide
by it. It is true that Scrates is made to fay fomething very like it. (Plato in Cratylo.) Εννοω γαρ,
οτι πολλα οι Ελληνες ονομla, αλλως τε και οι υπο τοις
BαρCαροις οικουντες παρα τν BαρCαρων ειληφασι—ει τις ζητοι
ταυτα κατα την Ελληνικην φωνην, ως εοικοτως κειται, αλλα
μη κατ ικεινην, εξ ης το ονμα τυγχανει ον, οισθα οτι απορει
αν. Who would think, when Plato attributed to
Socrates this knowlee, that he would make him
continually act in contradiction to it? Or that
other writers, when his plain truth was acknowledged, fhould deviat fo fhamefully?

Some

Some neceffary Rules and Obfervations in refpect to Etymological inquiries; and for the better underftanding the Mythology of Greece.

1. We muft never deduce the etymology of an Egyptian, or Oriental term from the Greek language. Euftath. fupra.

2. We fhould recur to the Doric mode of expreffion, as being neareft to the original.

3. All terms of relation between the deities are to be difregarded.

4. We muft have recourfe to the oblique cafes, efpecially in nouns imparafyllabic, when we have an ancient term tranfmitted to us either from the Greeks or Romans. The nominative in both languages, is often abridged: fo that from the genitive, or from the poffeffive, the original term is to be deduced. This will be found to obtain even in common names. e. g. Mentis, and not Mens, was the true nominative of mentis, menti, mentem.

Iftic eft de fole fumptus ignis, ifque mentis eft.

Ap. Ennii fragm.

5. All the common departments of the deities are to be fet afide, as inconfiftent, and idle.

6. Obferve that people of old were ftiled the Children of the god, whom they worfhiped; hence they were at laft thought to have been his real offspring: and that the Priefts were reprefented as fofter-fathers to the deity, before whom they miniftered; and Priefteffes were ftiled τιθηναι, or nurfes.

7. Obf. that Colonies always went out under the patronage and title of fome deity; that this conducting god was in aftertimes fuppofed to have been the real leader. That therefore the whole merit of a tranfaction was imputed to this deity folely; who was reprefented under the character, e. g. of Perfeus, Dionufus, or Hercules; but that, if,

if, inftead of one perfon, we put a people, the hiftory will be found confonant to truth.

8. As the Græcians made themfelves principals in many great occurrences, which were of another country, we muft look abroad for the original, both of their rites and mythology; and apply to the nations, from whence they were derived. Their original was foreign; and ingrafted upon the hiftory of the country where they fettled. This is of great confequence, and repeatedly to be confidered.

9. One great miftake alfo too frequently prevails among people, who deal in thefe refearches, which muft be carefully avoided. We fhould never make ufe of a language, which is modern, or comparatively modern, to deduce the etymology of ancient, and primitive terms.

10. It has been the cuftom of thofe writers, who have been verfed in the Oriental languages, to deduce their etymologies from roots; which are often fome portion of a verb. But the names of places and of perfons are generally an affemblage of qualities, and titles. The terms were obvious, and in common ufe; taken from fome well known characteriftics. Thofe, who impofed fuch names, never thought of a root: and probably did not know the purport of the term. I. 129—175. v. Græcians. Hebrew.

EVA.

Clemens Alexandrinus fays (and Epiphanius fays the fame) that this term fignified a Serpent, if pronounced with a proper afpirate. There were places of this name in Arcadia, Argolis, and Macedonia. And a mountain called Eva, or Evan, near the city Meffene, noticed by Paufanius. (l. 3.) I. 487.

Some think that the invocation, Eva, Eva, related to the great Mother of Mankind, who was

deceived

deceived by a Serpent: but I fhould think, that
Eva was the fame as Eph, Epha, Opha, which the
Greeks rendered Οφις, Ophis, and by it denoted a
Serpent. I. 474.

EUBOEA.

The worfhip of the Serpent begañ among the
fons of Chus. They brought thefe rites into
Greece; and called the ifland where they firft
eftablifhed them Ellopia, Solis Serpentis infula.
It was the fame as Eubœa, a name of the like purport, in which ifland was a region named Æthio-
pium. Eubœa is properly Oub-Aia; and fignifies
the Serpent ifland. I. 479.

EUDOXUS.

Until he had been in Egypt, the Græcians did
not know the fpace of which the true year confifted.
I. 167.

EUMOLPIDÆ.

Diodorus Siculus (l. 1.) fays, that the priefts at
Athens fo ftiled, came from Egypt. I. 186.

EUROPA.

Under the charaċter of Europa may be underftood people ftiled Europeans from their worfhip of
the Serpent. Europa (the fame as Rhea, and
Aftarte) was a deity: and the name is a compound
of Eur-Ope, analogous to Canope, Canophis, and
Cnuphis of Egypt; and fignifies Orus Pytho. It
is rendered by the Greeks as a feminine, upon fup-
pofition that it was the name of a woman; but it
related properly to a country; and we find many
places of the like etymology in Media, Syria, and
Babylonia: which were expreffed in the mafculine

O   Europus,

Europus, and Oropus. The fame alfo is obfervable in Greece. II. 163.

EUROPUS,

Is the fame as Oropus, and fignifies Orus Pytho. Ops, Opis, Opus, Opas, all fignify a Serpent. Zeus was the fame as Orus, and Ofiris: hence ftiled Europus, and Europas; which Homer has converted to Ευρυοπας, and accordingly ftiles Jupiter Ευρυοπα Ζευς. II. 179. n.

EURUNOME.

Under this name Dercetus was worfhiped by the Phigalians in Arcadia. Her ftatue was of great-antiquity; and reprefented a woman as far as the middle, but from thence had the figure of a fifh. She had a chain of gold, and was denominated by the natives Eurunome Diana: which Euronome is reprefented as the moft ancient of the female divinities, and the wife of Ophion. II. 314.

F.

FABA ÆGYPTIACA.

MOST of the Aquatics of the Nile were efteemed
facred: among thefe was this Faba. It was a
fpecies of bean, ftiled Colocafia; and was reverenced on account of its fhape. The common bean
is particularly like the Navis biprora, or facred
fhip of Ifis. The Faba Ægyptiaca had the fame
appearance; and this perhaps was the reafon why
Pythagoras abftained from beans; for his whole
fyftem feems to have been borrowed from Egypt.
It was undoubtedly on account of this refemblance,
that it was alfo ealled Cuamon, and Cibotium,
from Cibotus, Κιϐωδος, *a boat*. Some fuppofe it to
have been a fpecies of Ciborium; of whofe fruit
they made cups to drink. Athenæus, L. 11.
p. 477. Και ταχα αν ειη τα λεγομενα σκυφια δια το εις
ςενον συνηχθαι, ως τα Αιγυπλια Κιϐωρια. II. 399.

FANUM.

From Ph' Hanes, the fountain of light was derived Phanes of Egypt; alfo φαινω, φανεις, φανερος;
and from Ph'ain on, Fanum. I. 124.

FATHERS.

Almoft all the Fathers, and many other learned
men, fuppofe the gods of the heathen to have been
deified mortals, who were worfhiped in the countries where they died. It was alfo the opinion of
the heathen themfelves; the very people, by whom
O 2   thefe

thefe gods were honoured: yet ftill it is a miftake. For thefe ταφοι were not tombs, but λοφοι μαϛοειδεϛ, conical mounds of earth; on which in the firft ages offerings were made by fire. Hence τυφω fignified *to make a fmoke,* fuch as arofe from incenfe upon thefe Tupha, or mounds. (*See more under* Taph.)

In refpect to the Fathers, the whole of their argument turns upon this point, the conceffions of the Gentiles. The more early writers of the church were not making a ftrict chronological inquiry: but were labouring to convert the heathen. They therefore argue with them upon their own principles; and confute them upon their own teftimony. It matters not whether the notion that thefe fuppofed deities had been mortals were true: the Fathers very fairly make ufe of it. They avail themfelves of thefe conceffions; and prove from them the abfurdity of the gentile worfhip, and the inconfiftency of their opinions. I. 454.

FERENTUM

Was Fer-En, Ignis, vel Solis fons. And here was a facred fountain, whofe waters were ftiled Aquæ Ferentinæ,—cui numen, etiam, et divinus cultus tributus fuit. Cluver. Ital. L. 2. Here was a grove equally facred; where the ancient Latines ufed to hold their chief affemblies. As this grand meeting ufed to be in a place denominated from fire, it was the caufe of thofe councils being called Feriæ Latinæ. I. 191.

FERONIA,

The name of a goddefs, and of the city denominated from her. It may be deduced from Fer-On, Ignis dei Solis: for the worfhip of the Sun, and the rites of fire were here practifed. One cuftom remained even to the time of Auguftus, that of the priefts walking barefoot over burning coals. (Strab. L. 5.)

L. 5.) The town stood at the bottom of mount Soracte, sacred to Apollo: and the priests were stiled Hirpi. The temple is said to have been founded on account of a pestilential vapour, which arose from a cavern: and to which some Shepherds were conducted by (Λυκος) *a wolf.* I. 190.

FOUNTAINS.

The ancient Cuthites, and the Persians after them, had a great veneration for Fountains, and streams. Which also prevailed among other nations, so as to have been at one time almost universal. If rivers were attended with any nitrous, or saline quality, or with any fiery eruption, they were adjudged to be still more sacred; and ever distinguished with some title of the deity. I. 192. It was an universal notion, that a divine energy proceeded from the effluvia; and that the persons, who resided in their vicinity, were gifted with a prophetic quality. Fountains of this nature, from the divine influence with which they were supposed to abound, were by the Amonians stiled Ain Omphe. I. 276.

FURIES.

Nonnus (l. 44.) says, Περσεφονη Θωρηξεν Εριννυας. The notion of which Furies arose from the cruelties practised in the Prutaneia alluded to. They were called by the Latines Furiæ; and were originally only the priests of fire; but were at last ranked among the hellish tormentors. II. 41.

G.

EXPRESSED *Cau*, *Ca*, and *Co*, fignifies a houfe, or temple; alfo a cave or hollow, near which the temple of the deity was founded. Some nations ufed it in a more extended fenfe; and by it denoted a town, or village, and any habitation at large. It is found in this acceptation among the ancient Celtæ, and Germans, as we learn from Cluverius. Germ. Antiq. L. 1. c. 13.—Hinc Brifgaw, Wormefgaw, Zurichgow, Turgow, Nordgaw, Andegaw, Rhingaw, Hennegaw, Weftergow, Oostergow. I. 97—117.

GAUGAMELA

Was not the houfe of a camel, οικος Καμηλου, as Plutarch (Vit. Alex.) and Strabo (l. 16.) would perfuade us: but it was the houfe and temple of Cam-El, the deity of the country. This title was brought from Chaldea to Egypt; and from thence to Greece, Hetruria, and other regions. It was the fame place with Arbelá. I. 99.

GAUZANITIS,

A region fo named from a city Gauzan, the Gofan of the fcriptures. Strabo (l. 16.) calls it Χαζηνη, Cha-Zene, and places it near Adiabene. Gauzan, or Go-zan, is literally the houfe of the Sun. Gofhen, or Gofhan, like Gauzan in Mefopotamia,

potamia, fignifies the temple of the Sun: hence it
was rendered by the Greeks Heliopolis. Artapanus, as we learn from Eufebius, expreſſes it
·Καισάν. Go-Shan, Gau-Zan, Caifan, Cazena, all
denote a place facred to the Sun. I. 104.

GAZA,

A city in Paleſtine; it was named both Iöna,
and Minoa: the latter of which names it was faid
to have received from Ion of Argos. (Steph.
Byzant.) II. 506.

GENTILE.

All the myſteries of the Gentile world feem to
have been memorials of the Deluge; and of the
events, which immediately fucceeded. They
confiſted for the moſt part of a melancholy procefs;
and were celebrated by night with torches in commemoration of the ſtate of darkneſs, in which the
Patriarch and his family had been involved. The
firſt thing at thefe awful meetings was to offer an
oath of fecrefy to all, who were to be initiated;
after which they proceeded to the ceremonies.
Thefe began with a defcription of Chaos; by
which was fignified fome memorial of the Deluge.
Chaos was certainly the fame as Βυθος, the great
abyfs. Of the rites above-mentioned we have an
account in the Orphic Argonautica. V. 11, &c.

> ————Μέλα δ' ορκια Μυςαις,
> Αρχαιου μεν πρωία Χαους αμεγαρίον αναγκην,
> Και Κρονον, ὁς ιλοχευσεν απειρισιοισιν ὑφ' ὁλκοις
> Αιθερα, και διφυη περιωπεα κυδρον Ερωία.

The poet adds afterwards, that Eros had the name
of Phanes, becaufe he was the firſt remarkable
object which appeared to the eye of man, in confequence of this great event. Noah is fpoken of
as a man of juſtice; and this part of his character

is continually alluded to by the mythologifts, whenever they treat of his hiftory. The author of the poem above, among many facred rites, to which he had been witnefs, mentions the orgies of Juftice, or the Juft perfon; and thofe of Arkite Athene, which were celebrated by night:

Οργια Πραξιδικης και Αρεινης νυκτος Αθηνης. v. 31.

by Αρεινη Αθηνη was meant Arkite Providence; in other words Divine Wifdom, by which the world was preferved. In thefe myfteries, after the people had for a long time bewailed the lofs of a particular perfon, he was at laft fuppofed to be reftored to life. Upon this the prieft ufed to addrefs the people in thefe memorable terms, "Comfort yourfelves, all ye, who have been partakers of the myfteries of the deity thus preferved: for we fhall now enjoy fome refpite from our labours." To thefe were added the following remarkable words: "I have efcaped a fad calamity; and my lot is greatly mended." At fuch times there feems to have been an invocation made by the people to the Dove, Iönah; which was probably introduced to their view; Ιω Μακαιρα, Λαμπαδηφορος; *Hail to the Dove, the Reftorer of Light.* II. 331.

ΓΕΡΗΝΙΟΣ,

An Amonian term; applied by Homer to Neftor. It fignifies a princely, and venerable perfon. I. 47.

ΓΕΡΑΙΣΤΟΣ,

The Cyclopians were undoubtedly a part of the people called Academians, who refided in Attica; where they founded the Academia, and Ceramicus, and introduced human facrifices. Hence we are informed, that the Athenians in the time of a plague facrificed three Virgins, daughters of Hyacinthus,

at

at the tomb of Geræftus, the Cyclops. But Geræftus is not a perfon, but a place. Γεραιϛος is a
fmall variation for Ker-Aftus; and fignifies the
temple of Aftus, the god of fire. It was certainly
the ancient name of the place, where thefe facrifices were exhibited. And the Taphos was a
Cyclopian altar, upon which they were performed.
I. 503.

GIB

Signifies an *Hill*. Gibeon was the hill of the
Sun; faid to be famous for its fprings. Gibethon
is a compound of Gib-Ethon, or Athon, titles of
the fame deity. I. 94.

GIWON.

In the ifland of Japan they have many fymbolical
reprefentations, which plainly allude to the Ark.
Among other inftances is that of a particular deity
called Giwon; who is alfo ftiled Gofo Tennoo, or
the Ox-headed prince of heaven. (Kæmpfer's
Japan.) II. 442.

GODS.

All the deities of Greece were αποϛασμαΊα, or
derivatives, formed from the titles of Amon, and
Orus, the Sun. Many of them betray this in their
fecondary appellations; for Vulcan, Diana, &c.
were called Apha, &c. I. 61. The blindnefs of
the Greeks, in regard to their own theology and to
that of the countries, from whence they borrowed,
led them to mifapply the terms which they had
received, and to make a god out of every title.
But however they may have feparated, and diftinguifhed them under different perfonages, they are
all plainly refolvable into one deity, the Sun. The
fame is to be obferved as to the gods of the Romans.
307. There was by no means originally that
diverfity

diverfity of gods, which is imagined, as Sir John
Marfham has very juftly obferved. Chron. Canon.
p. 32. Neque enim tanta πολυθεσΐης ·Gentium,
quanta fuit Deorum πολυωνυμια. 309.

Porphyry (ap. Eufeb. P. E. L. 3.) acknowledged,
that Vefta, Rhea, Ceres, Themis, Priapus, Profer-
pina, Bacchus, Attis, Adonis, Silenus, and the
Satyrs, were all one, and the fame. Nobody had
examined the theology of the ancients more deeply
than Porphyry. He was a determined Pagan; and
his evidence in this point is unexceptionable. 316.

GRÆCIANS.

The firft inhabitants of the country, called afterwards Hellas, were the fons of Iavan; who feem
to have degenerated very early, and to have become
truly barbarous. Hence the beft hiftorians of
Greece confefs, that their anceftors were not the
firft inhabitants : but that it was before their arrival
in the poffeffion of a people, whom they ftiled
Βαρβαροι. The Helladians were colonies of another
family; and introduced themfelves fomewhat later.
They were of the race, which I term Amonian;
and came from Egypt, and Syria : but originally
from Babylonia. They came under various titles,
all taken from the religion which they profeffed.
As foon as the Amonians were fettled, and incorporated with the natives, a long interval of darknefs
enfued. The very union produced a new language:
at leaft the ancient Amonian became by degrees fo
modified, and changed, that the terms of fcience,
and worfhip were no longer underftood. Hence
the titles of their gods were mifapplied : and the
whole of their theology grew more and more corrupted; fo that very few traces of the original were
to be difcovered. In fhort, almoft every term
was mifconftrued, and abufed. This æra of darknefs was of long duration : at laft the Afiatic Greeks
began

began to beſtir themſelves. They had a greater
correſpondence than the Helladians: and they
were led to exert their talents from examples in
Syria, Egypt, and other countries. The ſpecimens
which they exhibited of their genius were amazing:
and have been juſtly eſteemed a ſtandard for elegance and nature. The Athenians were greatly
affected with theſe examples. They awoke as it
were out of a long and deep ſleep: and as if they
had been in the training of ſcience for ages, their
firſt efforts bordered upon perfection. In the ſpace
of a century, out of one little confined diſtrict,
were produced a group of worthies, who at all
times have been the wonder of the world. They
did not however retrieve any loſt annals: nor were
any efforts made to diſpel the cloud in which they
were involved.

Among the various traditions handed down they
did not conſider, which really related to their
country, and which had been introduced from
other parts. Indeed they did not chuſe to diſtinguiſh, but adopted all for their own; taking the
merit of every ancient tranſaction to themſelves.
No people had a greater love for ſcience; nor diſ-
played a more refined taſte in compoſition. Their
ſtudy was ever to pleaſe, and to raiſe admiration.
Hence they always aimed at the marvellous; which
they dreſſed up in the moſt winning manner: at
the ſame time that they betrayed a ſeeming veneration for antiquity. But their judgment was perverted: and this veneration was attended with little
regard to truth. They had a high opinion of
themſelves and their country in general: and being
perſuaded that they ſprang from the ground on
which they ſtood; and that the Arcadians were older
than the moon, they reſted ſatisfied with this, and
looked no farther. In ſhort, they had no love for
any thing genuine, no deſire to be inſtructed.
Their

Their hiftory could not be reformed but by an acknowledgement which their pride would not fuffer them to make. They therefore devoted themfelves to an idle theology: and there was nothing fo contradictory and abfurd, but was greedily admitted, if fanctioned by tradition. Even when the truth glared in their very faces, they turned from the light; and would not be undeceived. They went fo far as to deem inquiry a crime; and thus precluded the only means, by which the truth could be obtained.

An idle zeal made them attribute to their forefathers the merit of many great performances to which they were utterly ftrangers. Wherever they got footing, or even a tranfient acquaintance, they in their defcriptions accommodated every thing to their own preconceptions; and expreffed all terms according to their own mode of writing, and pronunciation, that appearances might be in their favour. To this were added a thoufand filly ftories to fupport their pretended claim. In refpect to foreign hiftory, and geographical knowledge, the Greeks in general were very ignorant. (v. Strabo. L. 11. p. 774. L. 15. p. 1006.)

The ancient hiftory and mythology of Greece was partly tranfmitted by the common traditions of the natives: and partly preferved in thofe original Doric hymns, which were univerfally fung in their Prutaneia and temples. Thefe were in the ancient Amonian language; and were chanted by the Purcones, or priefts of the Sun, and by the female Hierophants; of whom the chief upon record were Phaënnis, Phæmonoe, and Bæo. The laft of thefe mentions Olen, as the inventor of verfe, and the moft ancient prieft of Phœbus. Thefe hymns grew, by length of time, obfolete; and fcarce intelligible. They were however tranflated, or rather imitated by Homer, and others. Many of
the

the facred terms could not be underftood, nor interpreted; they were however retained with great reverence; and many which they did attempt to decipher, were mifconftrued and mifapplied. Upon this bafis was the theology of Greece founded: from hence were the names of the gods taken: and various departments attributed to the feveral deities. Every poet had fomething different in his theogony; and every variety, however inconfiftent, was admitted by the Greeks without the leaft hefitation. Such were the principles which gave birth to the mythology of the Græcians; from whence their ancient hiftory was in great meafure derived. As their traditions were obfolete, and filled with extraneous matter, it rendered it impoffible for them to arrange properly the principal events of their country.

Another reafon may be given for the obfcurity in the Græcian hiftory, even when letters had been introduced among them. They had a childifh antipathy to every foreign language; and were equally prejudiced in favour of their own. This has paffed unnoticed; yet was attended with the moft fatal confequences. They were mifled by the too great delicacy of their ear; and could not bear any term which appeared to them barbarous, and uncouth. On this account they either rejected foreign appellations; or fo modelled and changed them, that they became in found and meaning effentially different. They explained every thing by the language in ufe; without the leaft retrofpect or allowance: and all names and titles from other countries were liable to the fame rule. If the name was diffonant, and difagreeable to their ear, it was rejected as barbarous: but if it was at all fimilar in found to any word in their language, they changed it to that word; though the name were of Syriac original, or introduced from Egypt,

or

or Babylonia. The purport of the term was by these means changed: and the hiftory which depended upon it, either perverted, or effaced. l. 143.

The Græcians, who received their religion from Egypt, and the Eaft, mifconftrued every thing which was imported; and added largely to thefe abfurdities. They adopted deities, to whofe pretended attributes they were totally ftrangers; whofe names they could neither articulate nor fpell. They did not know how to arrange the elements, of which the words were compofed. Hence it was, that Solon the Wife could not efcape the bitter, but juft, cenfure of the prieft in Egypt, who accufed both him, and the Græcians in general of the groffeft puerility, and ignorance. Ω Σολων, Σωλων, Ελληνις ιστ παιδες αει, γερων δε Ελλην ουκ ιστι, νεοι τε ψυχας απαντες· ουδεμιαν γαρ εν εαυτοις εχετε παλαιαν δοξαν, ουδε μαθημα χρονω πολιον ουδεν. (Cyril. contra Julian. p. 15. It is related fomewhat differently in the Timæus of Plato.) The truth of this allegation may be proved both from the uncertainty, and inconfiftency of the ancients in the accounts of their deities. Of this uncertainty Herodotus takes notice. (l. 2. c. 53.) Ενθεν δε εγενετο ικαστος των θεων, ειτε δ' αει ησαν παντες, οκοιοι τε τινες τα ειδεα, ουκ ηπιστεατο μεχρι ου πρωην τε και χθες, ως απειν λογω. The evidence of Herodotus muft be efteemed early; and his judgment valid. What can afford us a more fad account of the doubt and darknefs, in which mankind was enveloped, than thefe words of the hiftorian? How plainly does he fhew the neceffity of Divine interpofition; and of Revelation in confequence of it? I. 306.

GROTTOS,

Formed by nature, or artificially produced, were in reality temples, and not tombs; and what

have

have been fuppofed to be coffins, were cifterns for
water which the Perfians ufed in their nocturnal
luftrations. I. 222.

ΓΡΥΠΕΣ.

Towers for augury were the repofitory of much
treafure; and were often confecrated to the Ophite
deity. The temple was called Kir-Upis, which
the Greeks abridged to Γρυπες; and finding many
of the Amonian temples in the north, with the device of a winged ferpent upon the frontal, they gave
this name to the hieroglyphic. Hence, perhaps,
arofe the notion of Γρυπες, or Gryphons; which,
like certain Dragons, were fuppofed to be the guar-
dians of treafure, and to never fleep. The real
confervators of the treafure, were the priefts. They
kept up a perpetual fire, and an unextinguifhed
light in the night. From Kir-Upis, the place of
his refidence, a prieft was named Grupis; and from
Kir-Uph-On, Gryphon. The Poets have reprefented the Grupes as of the ferpentine kind; and
fuppofed them to have been found in countries of
the Arimafpians, Alazonians, Hyperboreans, and
other the moft northern regions, which the Amonians poffeffed. All the ftories about Prometheus,
Chimæra, Medufa, Pegafus, Hydra, as well as of
the Grupes, or Gryphons, arofe in great meafure
from the facred devices upon the entablatures of
temples. I. 446.

HAGNON,

H.

HAGNON.

IN Arcadia, near mount Lyceus, was a sacred fountain so called; into which one of the nymphs, who nursed Jupiter, was supposed to have been changed. It is the same as Ain-On, the fountain of the Sun. I. 202.

HAM.

He was esteemed the Zeus of Greece, and Jupiter of Latium. From Egypt his name and worship was brought into Greece; as indeed were the names of almost all the deities there worshiped. I. 3. He being the Apollo of the east, was worshiped as the Sun; and was also called Sham and Shem. This has been the cause of much perplexity, and mistake: for by these means many of his posterity have been referred to a wrong line, and reputed the sons of Shem; the title of one brother not being distinguished from the real name of the other. 66. His posterity esteemed themselves of the Solar race. The chief oracle in the first ages was that of Ham, who was worshiped as the Sun, and stiled El, and Or; hence these oracles are in consequence called Amphi, Omphi, Alphi, Elphi, Orphi, Urphi. 88.

In the very ancient accounts of Greece Ham is called Iämus, and his priests Iämidæ. His oracle in consequence of this was stiled Iämphi, and Iämbi, which was the same term as Amphi. From Iämbi came the measure Ιαμϐος, in which oracles of old were delivered. Ham among the Egyptians

I   was

was called Tithrambo, which is the fame name as the Dithyrambus of Diodorus. Μανΐειον ην εν Ολυμπια, ου αρχηγος γεγονεν Ιαμος, τη δια εμπυρων μανΐεια, ή και μεχρι του νυν οι Ιαμιδαι χρωνΐαι. Schol. in Pind. Olymp. Ode vi. Ἰαμος αρχηγος was in reality the deity: his attendants the Iämidæ were perfons of great power and repute. From the term Dithyrambus were derived the Θριαμβος of the Greeks and the *triumphus* of the Romans. 257.

He was the Hermes of the Egyptians, and his oracle was called Omphi, and when particularly fpoken of as *the* oracle, it was expreffed P'omphi, and P'ompi. The worfhip of Ham, or the Sun, as it was the moft ancient, fo it was the moft univerfal of any in the world. It was at firft the prevailing religion of Greece; and was propagated over all the fea coaft of Europe: from whence it extended itfelf into the inland provinces. It was eftablifhed in Gaul and Britain; and was the original religion of this ifland, which the Druids in aftertimes adopted. That it went high in the north is evident from Aufonius, who takes notice of its exifting in his time. (Ode 4—10.) 284. Ham was alfo the fame as Petor and Ofiris. q. v.

HAMATH.

The people of Canaan and Syria paid a great reverence to the memory of Ham: hence we read of many places in thofe parts named Hamath, Amathus, Amathufia. There was an Hamath in Cyprus, by the Greeks expreffed Αμαθους, of the fame original. I. 22.

HANES,

Is derived from An-Ees; and was a title of the Sun. I. 57. 90. Ζευς was worfhiped under this title in Greece, and ftiled Ζευς Αινησιος. (v. Schol. in Apollon. Rhod. l. 2. v. 297. Strabo, L. 10. p. 700.

P   where

where read Αυτη for Αυτος.) This title fometimes occurs with the prefix Ph'anes. 199.

HAR, and HOR,

Signify a mountain; ορος of the Greeks. I. 94. Har and Hara (rendered Ἡρα by the Ionians) were common titles, and particularly beftowed upon Juno, as Queen of heaven. And analogous to this Har-Mon, and Har-Monia, fignify Domina vel Regina Luna. II. 447.

HARMONIA,

The daughter of Mars and Venus, whom Cadmus is faid to have married. Bochart imagines that fhe had her name from mount Hermon: but fhe feems to have been an emblem of nature, and the foftering nurfe of all things. She is from hence ftiled by Nonnus, παντροφος Ἁρμονια. And when Venus is reprefented in the allegory as making her a vifit, fhe is faid to go εις δομον Ἁρμονιης παμμητορος. In fome of the Orphic verfes fhe is not only reprefented as a deity, but as the light of the world.

Ἁρμονιη, κοσμοιο φαισφορε, και σοφι Δαιμον.

Harmonia was fuppofed to have been a perfonage, from whom all knowledge was derived. On this account the books of fcience were called κυρβιας Ἁρμωνιας, the books of Harmonia, as well as the books of Hermes. Thefe were four in number, of which Nonnus (l. 12.) gives a curious account, and fays, that they contained matter of wonderful antiquity. The firft of them is faid to have been coeval with the world.

Πρωτην κυρβιν οπωπεν αιερμονος ηλικα κοσμου,
Ειν ενι παντα φερουσαν, οσα σκηπτουχος Οφιων
Ηνυσεν.

From

From hence we find, that Harmon, or Harmonia,
was a deity, to whom the firſt writing is aſcribed.
The ſame is ſaid of Hermes. The invention is alſo
aſcribed to Taut, or Thoth. Cadmus is ſaid not
only to have brought letters into Greece, but to
have invented them. From hence we may fairly
conclude, that under the characters of Hermon,
Hermes, Taut, Thoth, and Cadmus, one perſon is
alluded to.

The deity, called by the Greeks Harmonia, was
introduced among the Canaanites very early by the
people of Egypt: and was worſhiped in Sidon, and
the adjacent country, by the name of Baal Hermon.
II. 151.

Nonnus (l. 41.) gives an account of a Robe of
Pharos, which Harmonia is ſuppoſed to have worn,
when ſhe was viſited by the goddeſs of beauty.
Upon it were delineated the earth, the heavens, and
the ſtars. The ſea alſo, and the rivers were repreſented: and the whole was at the bottom ſurrounded by the ocean.

Πρωίην Γαιαν επασσε μεσομφαλον, αμφι δι γαιη
Ουρανον εσφαιρωσε τυπω κεχαραγμενον αςρων.
Συμφερίην δι θαλασσαν εφηρμοσε συζυγι Γαιη,
Και ποιαμους ποικιλλεν· επ' ανδρομεω δε μιίωπω
Τ αυρεφυης μορφουίο κερασφορος εγχλοος εικων.
Και τυμαίην παρα πεζαν ευκλωσοιο χιίωνος
Ωκιανος κυκλωσε περιδρομον ανίυγα Κοσμου.

All this relates to a painting either at Sidon or
Berytus; which was delineated in a tower or temple
ſacred to Hermon. I. 395.

HARPIES.

I imagine that the ſtory of the Harpies relates
to the prieſts of the Sun. They were denominated from their ſeat of reſidence, which was an
oracular temple called Harpi, and Hirpi, analo-
P 2   gous

gous to Orphi, and Urphi in other places. The ancient name of a prieft was Cahen, rendered miftakenly Κυν, and Canis. Hence the Harpies, who were priefts of Ur, are ftiled by Apollonius (l. 2.) *the Dogs of Jove :*

Ου Θεμις, ω υιης Βορεου ξιφιεσσιν ιλασσαι
'Αρπυιας, μεγαλοιο Διος ΚΥΝΑΣ.

This term in the common acceptation is not applicable to the Harpies, either as birds, for fo they are reprefented; or as winged animals. But this reprefentation was only the infigne of the people. The Harpies were certainly a college of priefts in Bithynia; and on that account called Cahen. They feem to have been a fet of rapacious perfons, who for their repeated acts of violence, and cruelty, were driven out of the country. Their temple was ftiled Arpi; and the environs Arpi-ai: hence the Græcians formed 'Αρπυιαι. II. 43.

HEBREW.

If a prophet were to rife from the dead, and preach to any nation, he would make ufe of terms adapted to their idiom and ufage; without any retrofpect to the original of the terms, whether they were domeftic, or foreign. The Sacred Writers undoubtedly obferved this rule towards the people, for whom they wrote; and varied in their expreffing of foreign terms, as the ufage of the people varied. For the Jewifh nation at times differed from its neighbours, and from itfelf. We may be fure, that the Jews, and their anceftors, as well as all nations upon earth, were liable to exprefs foreign terms with a variation; being led by a natural peculiarity in their mode of fpeech. They therefore are furely to be blamed, who would deduce the orthography of all ancient words from the Hebrew; and bring every extraneous term to that teft. It

requires

requires no great infight into that language to fee
the impropriety of fuch procedure. Yet no pre-
judice has been more common. The learned
Michaelis has taken notice of this fatal attachment,
and fpeaks of it as a ftrange illufion. He fays,
that *it is the reigning influenza, to which all are liable,
who make the Hebrew their principal ftudy.* The
only way to obtain the latent purport of ancient
terms is by a fair analyfis. This muft be difcovered by an apparent analogy; and fupported by
the hiftory of the place, or perfon, to whom the
terms relate. If fuch helps can be obtained, we
may determine very truly the etymology of an
Egyptian or Syriac name; however repugnant it
may appear to the orthography of the Hebrews.
I. 198. v. Etymology.

HELLENISMUS.

The firft innovation in religion was called by
this name; which had no relation to Greece, being
far prior to Hellas, and to the people denominated
from it. Though it began among the Cuthites in
Chaldea; yet it is thought to have arifen from fome
of the family of Shem, who refided among that
people. Epiphanius (Hæres. L. 1. c. 6.) accordingly tells us, that *Ragem, or Ragau, had for his fon
Seruch, when idolatry and Hellenifmus firft began
among men.* But Eufebius, Chron. p. 13. and
other writers mention, that he was the author of
this apoftacy. *Seruch was the firft, who introduced
the falfe worfhip, called Hellenifmus.* Some attribute alfo to him the introduction of images; but
moft give this innovation to his grandfon Terah.
(Epiphan. L. 1. p. 7.)
The people of Midian lived upon the upper and
eaftern recefs of the Red fea; where was a city called El Ain, the Elana of Ptolemy, and Allane of
Jofephus. It happens, that there are in the oppo-

fite recefs fountains, which retain the name of El
Ain at this day; and they are likewife called by
the Arabs Ain Mofh, or the fountains of Mofes,
Hence each bay has been at times called Sinus
Elanites; which has caufed fome confufion in the
accounts given of thefe parts. The nether recefs
had certainly its name from the celebrated fountains of Mofes, which ran into it : but the bay on
the other fide was denominated from the people,
who there fettled. They were Cuthites, of the
fame race as the Iönim and Hellenes of Babylonia,
from which country they came. They built the
city Elana; and were called Hellenes (the people
ftill retain their primitive name Ellanes. Dr,
Pocock calls them Allauni,) from the great luminary, which they worfhiped; and to which their
city was facred. In the days of Mofes the whole
world feems to have been infected with the rites of
the Zabians: and Jethro the Cuthite was probably
high-prieft of this order, whofe daughter Mofes
married. The very firft idolatry confifted in wor-
fhiping the luminary El Ain; which worfhip was
ftiled Hellenifmus. El Ain fignifies Sol Fons,
the fountain of light. [The Græcians, juft as they
ftyled the Bay of Fountains on the Red Sea Elanites
from El Ain, might have called this characteriftic
of the times Ελανισμος. But fuch a change would
not fatisfy them : they made fome farther alteration; and rendered it Ionicè Ἑλληνισμος with an
afpirate ; and made it by thefe means relate to
their own country.] III. 153.

When the Egyptians, fays Porphyry (Eufeb,
Pr. Ev. L. 3. p. 115.) would defcribe Helius,
they reprefent a man in a float, or fhip, which is
fupported by a crocodile. Orus is often defcribed
as ftanding upon a crocodile, and at the fame time
                              furrounded

furrounded with other fymbolical reprefentations.
For as the Egyptians in their rites referred to a
perfon preferved in the midft of waters; they accordingly, to defcribe that hiftory, made ufe of
types, which had fome analogy, and refemblance to
fuch prefervation. Some of thefe could fcarcely
be called fymbolical, the purport was fo manifeft.
We are told by Jamblichus, that the figure of a
man upon the Lotus in the midft of mud, was an
emblem of Helius. (Sect. 7. p. 151.) This philofopher, as well as Plutarch, and Porphyry, falfely
imagined that thefe hiftories related to the real
Helius, the Sun: and that the fymbols of Selene
had the like reference to the Moon. In confequence of which they have a great deal of idle refinement. But Helius and Selene, were names
given to objects which were immediately connected
with water; even with the ocean itfelf. They had
been expofed to water, and preferved in it: and to
this their real hiftory related.

The Lotus was made an emblem of their prefervation; becaufe in the inundation of the Nile its
broad leaf rifes with the flood, and is never overwhelmed. Hence it was, that the Egyptians
placed Helius upon the Lotus: and he was faid to
have arifen from the waters upon this plant in the
form of a new-born child. This could have no
relation to the Sun; but was a proper picture of
Ofiris, who had been looked upon as loft, but returned to life in the character of the boy Orus. By
Helius, the Egyptians meant a perfon fo denominated: and the Moon, to which they alluded, was
Μήτηρ Σελήνη του Κοσμου, the reputed mother of the
world, as Plutarch confeffes; which character cannot be made in any degree to correfpond with the
planet. Selene was the fame as Ifis, τοπος θεων: the
fame alfo as Rhea, Vefta, Cubele, and Da-Mater.
II. 394.

The Græcians were, among other titles, ftyled
Hellenes, being the reputed defcendants of Hellen.
The name of this perfonage is of great antiquity ;
and the etymology foreign. To whom the Greeks
alluded, may be found from the hiftories, which
they have tranfmitted concerning him. γινον]αι δε
εκ Πυῤῥας Δευκαλιωνι παιδες. Ἑλλην μεν πρωῖος, ὁν εκ
Διος γεγεννσθαι λεγουσι,—θυγαῖηρ δε Πρωῖογενεια ; fays
Apollodorus, L. 1. p. 20. (By Protogeneia is
fignified *the firft-born of women,*) by others he is
fuppofed to have been the fon of Prometheus, but
by the fame mother. Now Deucalion, Prometheus,
Xuth, and Zeuth were the fame perfon; fo the
hiftories are of the fame amount ; and relate to the
head of the Amonian family, who was one of the
fons of the perfon called Deucalion. He is
made coeval with the Deluge; and reprefented as
the brother to the firft-born of mankind: by which
is meant the firft-born from that great event: for
the Deluge was always the ultimate, to which they
referred. The Hellenes were the fame as the
Iönim or Ιωνες. (Hefych.) The fame is to be faid
of the Æolians, and Dorians : they were all from
one fource, being defcended from the fame Arkite
anceftors, the Iönim of Babylonia and Syria; as the
Phœnician women in Euripides acknowledge
(Phœniff. v. 256.)

> Κοινον αἱμα, κοινα τεκεα
> Τας κερασφορου πεφυκεν Ιους.

The term Hellen was originally a facred title:
and feems to have been confined to thofe priefts,
who firft came from Egypt; and introduced the
rites of the Ark and Dove at Dodona. They were
called alfo Elli and Selli. (Hefych.) This country
was the firft Hellas; and here were the original
Hellenes;

Hellenes; and from them the title was derived to all of the Græcian name. III. 382.

From Babylonia the Hellenes came into Egypt; they were the fame as the Auritæ, or Cuthite Shepherds; they introduced into that country their arts and learning, by which it was greatly benefited. Hence the learning of Egypt was ftyled Hellenic from the Hellenic Shepherds: and the ancient theology of the country was faid to have been defcribed in the Hellenic character and language. (Manethon. ap. Eufeb. Chron. p. 6.)   This had no relation to the Hellenes of Greece; being far prior to that nation.   The Græcians, it is true, were both Iönim and Hellenes; but by a long defcent, being the pofterity of the people here fpoken of.   This theology was faid to be derived from Agathodæmon (he was the fame as Cneph) that benign deity, the benefactor of all mankind.   He was fuppofed to have had a renewal of life; and on that account was reprefented under the figure of a ferpent crowned with the Lotus, and ftyled Noe Agathodæmon (the Greeks tranfpofed, and exprefled it Νοε Αγαθοδαιμων.)   The Græcians fuppofed, that by the Hellenic tongue was meant the language of Greece; and that the Hellenic characters were the letters of their own country.   But thefe writings were in reality fculptures of great antiquity: and the language was the Cuthite, ftyled by Manethon (v. Jofeph. c. Apion. L. 1. p. 445.) the facred language of Egypt.

Hellen was the fame as Ion; the fame alfo as Helius, Ofiris, and Apollo: by which titles were fignified the deity of light and of fcience. III. 156.

HERA,

The Græcian name for Juno: this was not originally a proper name, but a title, the fame as Ada

5   of

of the Babylonians, and fignified *a Lady*, or *Queen*. Heer, Herus, Heren, Haren, in many languages betokened fomething noble.   Hence Ἥρα, &λκη. Ἡρανος, βασιλευς. Hefych. II. 343.

HERCULES.

The fuppofed exploits of this ideal perfonage are well known.   He was efteemed the chief god, the fame as Cronus, and was faid to have produced the Mundane egg.   He was reprefented in the Orphic Theology under the mixed fymbol of a lion, and ferpent; and fometimes of a ferpent only (Athenag. Legat. p. 294.) I. 480.   Hefychius fays, that the Indian Hercules, by which is always meant the chief deity, was ftiled Dorfanes. 35.   He had alfo the name of Sandis, and Sandes, which fignifies Sol deus. 39.   Hercules, the chief deity of Tyre, and who was alfo highly reverenced in Egypt, was ftyled Con.   From hence we find, that it was a facred Egyptian title. 104.   He was faid, though falfely, to have been the firft who paffed the Alpes. 212.   To his dog is given the honour of difcovering the fine purple die. (v. Murex.)

There is room to think that pillars and obeliſks were made ufe of for beacons, and that every temple was a Pharos.   They feem to have been erected at the entrance of harbours; and upon eminences along the coaſts in moſt countries.   The pillars of Hercules were of this fort, and undoubtedly were erected for the purpofe of directing navigation. They were not built by him; but erected to his honour, by people called Herculeans, who worfhipped him.   Such pillars were by the Iberians called Herculean, becaufe they were facred to Hercules; under which title they worfhiped the chief deity. Two of the moſt celebrated ſtood upon each fide of the Mediterranean at the noted paffage called fretum Gaditanum.   That on the Mauritanian fide was called Abyla; the other in Ibera, Calpe, for it was built near a cave; and all such recesses were esteemed to be oracular. I. 262.

Sometimes he appears little better than a sturdy vagrant; at other times he is mentioned as a great benefactor; also as the patron of science, the god of eloquence with the Mufes in his train. On this account he had the title of Mufagetes. There are gems upon which he is reprefented as prefiding among the deities of fcience. He is faid to have been fwallowed by a Cetus, or large fifh, from which he was after fome time delivered. He was the chief deity of the Gentile world; the fame as Hermes, Ofiris, and Dionufus; and his rites were introduced into various parts by the Cuthites. In the detail of his peregrinations is contained, in great meafure, an hiftory of that people, and of their fettlements. Each of thefe the Greeks have defcribed as a warlike expedition; and have taken the glory of it to themfelves. Hercules is faid to have had many fons. Their names are manifeftly the names of nations: all defcended from that Hercules, who was the father of Archemagoras the chief of the Magi. II. 76.

It is faid of Hercules, that he traverfed a vaft fea in a cup, or fkiff, which Nereus, or Oceanus, lent him for his prefervation. The fame hiftory is given to Helius, who was faid to have traverfed the ocean in the fame vehicle. II. 404. In the neighbourhood of Tyre and Sidon the chief deity went by the name of Ourchol, the fame as Archel and Arcles of Egypt (he was of old ftiled Arcles in Greece) whence came the Ἡρακλης, and Hercules of Greece and Rome. Nonnus, who was deeply read in the mythology of thefe countries, makes all the various departments of the other gods, as well as their titles, center in him. He defcribes him (l. 40.) in fome good poetry as the head of all.

Αςροχι-

Αςροχιτων Ἡρακλις, Αναξ πυρος, Ορχαμι κοσμου,
Ὅτια Χρονου Λυκαβαντα δυωδικαμηνον ἑλισσων,
Ἱππευων ἑλικηδον ὁλον πολον αιθοπι δισκῳ,
Κυκλον αγεις μετα κυκλον————
Ομβρον αγεις φερεκαρπον, επ᾽ ευωδιτι δε γαιη
Ηερινς ηωον ερευγειται αρδμον ιερσης.————
Βηλος επ᾽ Ευφρητα, Λιβυς κικλημενος Αμμων,
Απις εφυς Νειλῳος, Αραψ Κρονος, Ασσυριος Ζευς.——
Εἴτε Σαραπις εφυς Αιγυπτιος, ανεφαλος Ζευς,
Ει Χρονος, ει Φαεθων πολυωνυμος, ειτε συ Μιθρης,
ΗΕΛΙΟΣ ΒΑΒΥΛΩΝΟΣ, εν Ἑλλαδι ΔΕΛΦΟΣ
ΑΠΟΛΛΩΝ.

All the various titles, we find, are at laſt compriſed
in Apollo, or the Sun. I. 312.

Selden de Diis Syris, p. 77. has theſe words
(though not ſpeaking of Hercules) Sit Oſiris, ſit
Omphis, Nilus, Siris, ſive quodcunque ab hiero-
phantis uſurpatum nomen, ad unum tandem *Solem*,
antiquiſſimum Gentium numen, redeunt omnia.
317.

HERMES.

Zeus and Hermes were originally the ſame.
Plutarch (in Numa) mentions Ἑρμην—Καμιλλον απο
της διακονιας, and ſuppoſes that Camillus had the
name of Hermes from the ſimilarity of his office,
which was waiting upon the gods. But the Chaldeans and Egyptians from whom theſe titles were
borrowed, eſteemed Hermes as the chief deity, the
ſame as Zeus, Bel, and Adon. They knew nothing
of Mercurius pediſſequus, nor Hermes the lackey.
I. 102. The Rupes Ægyptiaca ſeems to have been
a ſeminary, where the youth of Upper Egypt
were educated. And as the Cunocephali are ſaid
to have been ſacred to Hermes, this ſeminary was
probably in the nome of Hermopolis. Hermes
was the patron of ſcience; and particularly ſtiled
Cahen,

Cahen, or Canis : and the Cunocephali are faid to have been worfhiped by the people of that place. 33⁸.

HERMIONE.

Some of the Cyclopians built Hermione, one of the moft ancient cities in Greece. The tradition was, that it was built by Hermion the fon of Europs, or Europis, a defcendant of Phoroneus, and Niobe; and was inhabited by Dorians, who came from Argos. The city ftood near a ftagnant lake, and a deep cavern, where was fuppofed to be the moft commodious paffage to the fhades below. (Strabo. L. 8.) The lake was called the pool of Acherufia; near to which, and the yawning cavern, the Cyclopians chofe to take up their habitation. I. 504. The true name was Herm-Ione, a com- pound of two Egyptian titles; and was faid to be built by Argives; and it was by them denoted a city facred to the Arkite Dove. II. 505. The poets reprefented Ino as the daughter of Hermione and Cadmus. But Ino and Hermione are different names for the fame emblem. Herm-Ione is fimilar to Hermon, Hermonax, Hermonaffa, Hermodorus, Hermotubius, Hermeracles, Hermochemia. It was fometimes expreffed with the guttural, Cher- mion, Chermione, and Charmione. 311.

HETRURIA.

When the Hetrurians fettled in Italy, they founded many places of ftrength; and are reputed to have been the firft who introduced the art of fortification. (v. Schol. in Lycoph. v. 717.) They worfhiped the Sun, ftiled Zan, and Zeen; whofe temples were called Tur-Zeen: and in confequence of it one of the principal names by which their country was diftinguifhed, was Turzenia. (Ibid. v. 1242.) The Hetrurians occupied a large tract

of

of fea-coaft; on which account they worfhiped
Pofeidon. They erected upon their fhores towers
and beacons for the fake of their navigation, which
they called Tor-Ain; whence they had a ftill farther denomination of Tur-Aini, and their country
was named Tur-Ainia; the Τυρρηνια of the later
Greeks. All thefe appellations are from the fame
object, the edifices which · they erected. They
were thought to have been the inventors of trum-
pets : and in their towers upon the fea-coaft there
were people appointed to be continually upon the
watch both by day and night; and to give a proper
fignal, if any thing happened extraordinary. This
was done by a blaft from a trumpet : and Triton
was hence feigned to have been Neptune's trum-
peter. He is accordingly defcribed by Nonnus
(l. 17.)

Τυρσηνης ὑαρυδουπον εχων σαλπιγγα Θαλασσης;

However in early times thefe brazen inftruments
were but little known : and people were obliged to
make ufe of, what was near at hand, the conchs of
the fea, which every ftrand afforded. By founding
thefe they gave fignals from the top of the towers,
when any fhip appeared : and this is the inftrument, with which Triton is more commonly furnifhed. I. 403.

HIERAPOLIS

Of Syria, was called Magog, or rather the city of
Magog. It was alfo called Bambyce. I. 8. n. One
of the moft ancient cities of Afia Proper, and the
moft reverenced, was Hierapolis, famous for its hot
fountains. Here was alfo a facred cavern, ftiled
by Strabo (l. 13.) Plutonium, and Charonium ;
which fent up peftilential effluvia. Photius in the
life of Ifidorus (c. 242.) fays, εν Ἱεραπολει της Φρυγιας
Ἱερον

Ἱερὸν ἦν Ἀπόλλωνος, ὑπὸ δὲ τὸν ναὸν καταβάσιον ὑπέκειτο, ᾀσασίμους ἀναπνοὰς παρεχομένον. I. 29.

HIEROGLYPHICS.

We muſt make a material diſtinction between the hieroglyphics of old, when Egypt was under her own kings; and thoſe of later date, when that country was under the government of the Greeks ; at which time their learning was greatly impaired, and their ancient theology ruined. I. 332.

If any means can be found out to obtain the latent purport of the Egyptian hieroglyphics, they muſt ariſe from conſidering theſe emblems ſingly, and obſerving their particular ſcope, and deſtination. When we have aſcertained the meaning of ſome individuals, we may poſſibly diſcover their drift, when conſidered collectively. Theſe, I think, are the principles upon which we muſt proceed ; but after all it will be a dark reſearch, in which many have been bewildered.

There are authors who mention an ancient piece of hieroglyphical ſculpture, which was to be ſeen in the city Saïs of Lower Egypt. It conſiſted of a Child, an old Man; and near them ſtood an Hawk. After theſe a Cetus, or ſea-fiſh ; and laſt of all an Hippopotamus. Clemens of Alexandria (l. 5.) mentions the ſame hiſtory ; but ſays, that it was at Dioſpolis. Inſtead of the river horſe he introduces a Crocodile, which he ſays was an emblem of impudence. It is to be obſerved, that the Hippopotamus and Crocodile were ſymbols of the ſame purport ; both related to the Deluge: and however the Greeks might ſometimes repreſent them, they were both in different places reverenced by the ancient Egyptians. The interpretation given by Clemens is this : *All ye, who are juſt come into the world, and all ye, who are going out, remember, that God hates impudence.* As there are ſo many crimes of high

moment,

moment, which demand animadverfion, it is ftrange, that fo folemn a caution fhould be given merely againft impudence. The infcription feems to have been put up in two places: one of which was the temple of Ifis at Saïs; the other the temple at Diofpolis, called Theba. Thefe are two remarkable places; in confequence of which, one would imagine, that the infcription fhould contain fome memorial of more confequence: fomething which had a reference to the temples wherein it was found. Were I to attempt the decyphering of thefe hieroglyphics, which however diverfified feem to amount to the fame purport, I fhould begin from right to left, in a feries different from thofe, who have gone before me. I find according to this order, that the Hippopotamus or Crocodile ftands firft; and then the Cetus. Next comes the figure of the facred Hawk, under which femblance Divine Providence was always depicted: and after this an old Man, and a Child. It may feem prefumptuous to pretend to interpret what was a fecret two thoufand years ago: I fhall therefore only mention, what I have to fay, as matter of opinion. I apprehend it may be read in the following manner. *As the Hippopotamus, or Crocodile, furvives the inundation of the Nile, juft fo that facred receptacle, the Cetus, or Ark, through the interpofition of Providence, weathered the Deluge; by which means the aged Patriarch efcaped, and obtained a renewal of life.* How true this interpretation may be, I will not prefume to fay: it certainly correfponds with the hiftory of each emblem, as they have been feparately confidered; and is confonant to the general fcope of the rites and mythology of Egypt. What is ftill more to the purpofe, it perfectly agrees with the deftination of the two temples, where it is faid to have been found: for by Ifis was meant a facred receptacle; and Theba is literally the Ark. The

temples

temples were both of them built in memory of that event, which the hieroglyphic feems to defcribe. II. 400.

HIGH PLACES.

Many of old worfhiped upon hills, and on the tops of high mountains; imagining that they thereby obtained a nearer communication with heaven. Strabo fays (l. 15.) that the Perfians always performed their worfhip upon hills. (Some nations inftead of an image worfhiped the hill as the deity. Max. Tyr. Differt. 8.) v. Appian. de bello Mithridatico. In Japan moft of their temples at this day are upon eminences; and often upon the afcent of high mountains: commanding fine views, with groves and rivulets of clear water, for they fay, that the gods are extremely delighted with fuch high and pleafant fpots. Kæmpfer's Japan. V. 2. b. 5. This practice in early times was almoft univerfal; and every mountain was efteemed holy. The people, who profecuted this method of wor-fhip, enjoyed a foothing infatuation, which flattered the gloom of fuperftition. The eminences to which they retired were lonely, and filent; and feemed to be happily circumftanced for contem-plation and prayer. They, who frequented them, were raifed above the lower world; and fancied that they were brought into the vicinity of the powers of the air, and of the deity who refided in the higher regions. But the chief excellence for which they were frequented, was the Omphi, expreffed αμφη by the Greeks, and interpreted (Hefych.) Θεια κληδων, vox divina, being a particular revela-tion from heaven. In fhort, they were looked upon as the peculiar places where God delivered his oracles.

Many times when a reformation among the Jews was introduced by fome of the wifer and better

Q   princes,

princes, it is ftill lamented by the facred writer (1 Kings xxii. 2 Kings xii. xv. &c.) that *the high places were not taken away; the people ftill offered, and burnt incenfe on the high places.* I. 235.

HIPPA,

A goddefs of great antiquity. In the Orphic verfes fhe is faid to have been the foul of the world; and the perfon, who received and foftered Dionufus, when he came from the thigh of his father. This hiftory relates to his fecond birth, when he returned to a fecond ftate of childhood. Dionufus was the chief god of the Gentile world, and was worfhiped under various titles; which at length came to be looked upon as different deities. Moft of thefe fecondary divinities had the title of Hippius and Hippia: and as they had female attendants in their temples, thefe too had the name of Hippai. As to the term itfelf, which was become obfolete, the Greeks, who were but little acquainted with the purport of their ancient theology, uniformly referred it to *Horfes.* Hence we have Mars — Pofeidon Hippius; and Ceres — Minerva—Juno Hippia. Hippa was a facred Egyptian term, and as fuch was conferred upon Arfinoë, the wife of Ptolemy Philadelphus: for the princes of Egypt always affumed to themfelves facred appellations. As Ceres was ftiled Hippa, the Greeks imagined her to have been turned into a mare, and Hippius Pofeidon, in the fhape of an horfe, to have had intimate acquaintance with her. (Ovid. Met. L. 6.) The like is faid of Ocuroë. (lib. 2.) Phylera likewife was fo changed by Saturn, who is faid to have purfued her in the fame fhape over the mountains of Theffaly. (Virg. G. l. 3.)

Talia

Talis et ipfe jubam cervice effudit equina
Conjugis adventu pernix Saturnus, et altum
Pelion hinnitu fugiens implevit acuto.

All thefe legendary ftories arofe from this ancient term being obfolete and mifapplied. Homer makes mention of the mares of Apollo. (Il. B. v. 766.) Thefe Hippai, mifconftrued mares, were prieftefles of the goddefs Hippa, who was of old worfhiped in Theflaly, and Thrace, and in many different regions. They chanted hymns in her temples, and performed the rites of fire; but the worfhip growing obfolete, the very terms were at laft miftaken. Many places were denominated from Hippa. It was a title of Apollo, or the Sun; and often compounded Hippa On, contracted Hippon. Argos was of old called Hippeion (Hefych.) απο Ιππης του Δαναου; i. e. from a prieftefs who founded there a temple; and introduced the rites of the goddefs, whom fhe ferved. As a title of the Sun, it was fometimes expreffed Hippos. Paufanias (l. 3. p. 262.) takes notice of a very curious piece of antiquity, near mount Taygetus in Laconia, called the monument of Hippos, the purport of which he almoft ruins by referring to an horfe. The central part muft be defigned for the Sun; and however rude the whole may poffibly have appeared, it is the moft ancient reprefentation upon record, and confequently the moft curious one of the planetary fyftem.

Hence it appears that the titles Hippa, and Hippos, related to the luminary Ofiris; who was the fame as Dionufus. His worfhip was extenfive; we read of Montes Hippici in Colchis; Ιππου κωμη in Lycia; Ιππου ακρα in Libya; Ιππου ορος in Egypt; a town Hippos in Arabia Felix; alfo in compofition, Hippon, Hipporium, Hippouris, Hippana, Hipponefus, Hippocrene. This laft was a facred fountain, fo called from the god of Light, who was the patron of verfe, and fcience: but by the Greeks it was referred to an animal, and fuppofed to have been produced by the hoof of an horfe. II. 27.

HIPPOS.

I cannot help furmifing, that the Horfe of Neptune was a miftaken emblem; and that the an-cients in the original hiftory did not refer to that animal. What the Ἱππος alluded to in the early mythology was certainly a float or fhip, the fame as the Ceto; for in the firft place the Ceto was de-nominated Hippos: Ἱππον, τον μεγαν Θαλασσιον ιχθυν, i. e. the Ceto or Whale; 2dly, It is remarkable that the Hippos was certainly called Σκαφος και Σκυφιος. (Sch. in Lycoph. v. 766.) I therefore cannot help thinking that the fuppofed Horfe of Neptune, as it has fo manifeft a relation to the Ceto, and the Scyphus, muft have been an emblem of the like purport: and that it had originally a re-ference to the fame hiftory, to which the Scyphus, and Ceto related. The fable of the Horfe cer-tainly arofe from a mifprifion of terms; though the miftake be as old as Homer. The goddefs Hippa, is the fame as Hippos, and relates to the fame hiftory. There were many fymbols of an Horfe. The hiftory of Pegafus, the winged horfe, is pro-bably of the fame purport. So does Palæphatus, a judicious writer, interpret it: ονομα δ' ην τω πλοιω Πηγασος. This Hippos was in confequence faid to have been the offspring of Pofeidon and Da-mater. II. 408.

HIPPARENE,

Was one of the three Chaldaic feminaries of learning. It is a compound of Hippa-Arene, and relates,

relates, as I should imagine, to the Ark, Hippa-Aren. II. 409. n.

HIRPI,

Near Soracte in Latium, were Amonian priests; priests of fire. II. 44.

HISTORY.

All History, and Time itself according to the Græcians, commenced from the æra of the Ark. They stiled it the æra of Inachus. II. 359.

HIVITE.

Bochart has very justly observed, that an Hivite is the same as an Ophite. The Hivites settled at Rhodes, which place was said to swarm with serpents. It was called Ophiusa, on account of the Hivites, and the Serpent-Worship, which they introduced. II. 166.

HOMER.

Seven places in Greece contended for his birth: while many doubt whether he was of Græcian original. I. 166. He had been in Egypt; and was an admirer of the mythology of that nation. He adhered to ancient terms with a degree of enthusiasm; he introduced them at all hazards, though he many times did not know their meaning. 86. He abounds with mysterious lore, borrowed from the ancient Amonian theology; with which his commentators have often been embarrassed. 143. In the short hymns ascribed to Homer, the term Αμφι is industriously retained: and the persons who composed them, have endeavoured to make sense of it, by adopting it according to the common acceptation. These hymns were of late date, long after Homer; and introduced in Ionia, and also in

Cyprus, and Phenicia, when the Græcians were in
poffeffion of thofe parts. They were ufed in the
room of the ancient hymns, which were not underftood by the new inhabitants. 255.

HOMOURA,

Amora, Omoritæ, cakes made in honour of
Ham-Orus. I. 297.

HORN.

· There is no term, which occurs fo often figuratively in the facred writers, as that of a Horn. By
this they denoted any thing fuper-eminent and
powerful. The Ifraelites were forbidden to make
any reprefentation in ftone, or metal : fo that we
have no inftance from them of its being ever reprefented to the eye. The fame was a fymbol
among the Egyptians : they copied it in ftone and
brafs : and affixed the reprefentation of a horn to
the ftatues of their kings and deities. But though
this was a common emblem in thefe two nations, it
does not follow, that one borrowed it from the
other. It was a general type of early date, and in
almoft univerfal acceptation in every nation of
old, to whofe hiftory we can gain accefs : it was
an emblem of affluence and power. II. 530.

HYMEN,

At the celebration of marriage, to Iönah was added a Genius, called Hymen ; the purport of whofe
name is a veil or covering. In the hiftory of
Hymen, the fame object was probably referred to,
which was ftiled χίλων Φανήλος, *the covering of Phanes*:
from whence that deity after a ftate of confinement
was at laft difengaged. Saturn was often depicted
with his head under a covering, which had an allegorical meaning. Hymen as a perfonage was the
god of the veil : and faid to have been an Argive,
and the fon of Liber, the fame as Dionufus ; though

many

relates, as I should imagine, to the Ark, Hippa-
Aren. II. 409. n.

HIRPI,

Near Soracte in Latium, were Amonian priests;
priests of fire. II. 44.

HISTORY.

All History, and Time itself according to the
Græcians, commenced from the æra of the Ark.
They stiled it the æra of Inachus. II. 359.

HIVITE.

Bochart has very justly observed, that an Hivite
is the same as an Ophite. The Hivites settled at
Rhodes, which place was said to swarm with serpents. It was called Ophiufa, on account of the
Hivites, and the Serpent-Worship, which they introduced. II. 166.

HOMER.

Seven places in Greece contended for his birth :
while many doubt whether he was of Græcian original. I. 166. He had been in Egypt; and was an
admirer of the mythology of that nation. He adhered to ancient terms with a degree of enthusiasm;
he introduced them at all hazards, though he many
times did not know their meaning. 86. He
abounds with mysterious lore, borrowed from the
ancient Amonian theology; with which his commentators have often been embarrassed. 143. In the
short hymns ascribed to Homer, the term Αμφι is
industriously retained : and the persons who composed them, have endeavoured to make sense of it,
by adopting it according to the common acceptation. These hymns were of late date, long after
Homer; and introduced in Ionia, and also in

Q 3   Cyprus,

Cyprus, and Phenicia, when the Græcians were in possession of those parts. They were used in the room of the ancient hymns, which were not understood by the new inhabitants. 255.

HOMOURA,

Amora, Omoritæ, cakes made in honour of Ham-Orus. I. 297.

HORN.

· There is no term, which occurs so often figuratively in the sacred writers, as that of a Horn. By this they denoted any thing super-eminent and powerful. The Israelites were forbidden to make any representation in stone, or metal: so that we have no instance from them of its being ever represented to the eye. The same was a symbol among the Egyptians: they copied it in stone and brass: and affixed the representation of a horn to the statues of their kings and deities. But though this was a common emblem in these two nations, it does not follow, that one borrowed it from the other. It was a general type of early date, and in almost universal acceptation in every nation of old, to whose history we can gain access: it was an emblem of affluence and power. II. 530.

HYMEN.

At the celebration of marriage, to Iönah was added a Genius, called Hymen; the purport of whose name is a veil or covering. In the history of Hymen, the same object was probably referred to, which was stiled χιΤων ΦανιΤος, *the covering of Phanes:* from whence that deity after a state of confinement was at last disengaged. Saturn was often depicted with his head under a covering, which had an allegorical meaning. Hymen as a personage was the god of the veil: and said to have been an Argive, and the son of Liber, the same as Dionusus; though

many

many fuppofed him to have been the fon of Magnes, i. e. Manes, the Lunar god. At the celebration of nuptials the name of Hymen was continually echoed; at the fame time there were offerings made of fruit, and of meal; alfo of fefamum and of poppies; which ceremony was called Σημ*ιον, *the fign.* II. 390.

HYPERBOREANS.

This was another name by which the ancients diftinguifhed the Cuthites. They are placed, as many of the Cimmerians and Amazonians were, upon the Palus Mæotis, and Tanaïs; and in thofe regions, which lay near the Borifthenes and Ifter. But from a notion, that their name had a relation to the north, they have been extended upwards almoft to the Cronian fea. They were of the Titanic race, and called Sindi; a name common among the Cuthites. Strabo (l. 11.) fpeaks of them as called among other names Sauromatæ, and Arimafpians. By Herodotus they are reckoned among the Amazonians. (l. 4. c. 10.) They worfhiped the Sun, whom they held in high honour; and they had prutaneia, which were ftyled αιθρια. (Hefych.) They were great traders, and navigators.

The people of Cyprus were of the fame race, equally Cutheans. The Hyperboreans upon the Euxine at one time feem to have kept up a correfpondence with thofe of the Titanian race in moft countries. But of all others, they feem to have refpected moft the people of Delos. To this ifland they ufed to fend continually myftic prefents, which were greatly reverenced. (Callim. H. in D. v. 281.) Apollo, (Apollon. Arg. l. 4.) Perfeus, (Pind. Pyth. O. 10.) and Hercules (Olymp. O. 3.) are faid to have vifited the Hyperboreans.

They

They are fometimes reprefented as Arimafpians; and their chief priefteffes were named Oupis, Loxo, and Hecaërge; by whom the Hyperborean rites are faid to have been brought to Delos. They never returned, but took up their refidence, and offici-. ated in the ifland. Olen the Hyperborean is faid to have been the firft prophet of Delphi. (Paufan. 1. 10.) By other writers he is faid to have come from Lycia. (Herod. L. 4. c. 35.) Olen, was properly an Egyptian facred term; and expreffed Olen, Olenus, Ailinus, and Linus; but is of un-known meaning. If then this Olen, ftyled an Hyperborean, came from Lycia and Egypt, it makes me perfuaded, that the term *Hyperborean* is not of that purport, which the Greeks have affigned to it. There were people of this family in the north; and the name has been diftorted and adapted *folely* to the people of thofe parts. But as there were Hyperboreans from the eaft; as they firft in-ftituted the rites in Delos; as they firft founded the temple at Delphi; as people of this name and family not only came into Greece, but alfo into Italy, and extended themfelves even to the Alps; as the ancient Latines were defcended from them: (Dion. Hal. L. 1. p. 34.) as thofe who occu-pied Mons Palatinus are fuppofed to have been Atlantians, and alfo Arcadians, i. e. Arkites; it would be unnatural to fuppofe, that thefe rites, and thefe colonies, came all from the north: it is contrary to the progrefs of nations, and repugnant to the hiftory of the firft ages.

There muft have been fomething myfterious in the term Hyperborean: it muft have had a latent meaning, which related to the fcience and religion of the people fo called. Pythagoras, who had been in Egypt, and Chaldea, and who afterwards fettled at Croton, was by the natives ftyled the Hyperbo-rean Apollo. (Ælian. V. H. L. 2. c. 26.) And
though

though fome of this name were of the north, yet there were others in different parts of the world, who had no relation to that clime. Pindar (Pyth. Od. 10.) manifeftly makes them the fame as the Atlantians, and Amazonians of Afric : for he places them near the iflands of the Bleft, which were fuppofed to have been oppofite to Mauritania. He fpeaks of them, as a divine race.

The northern Hyperboreans, who were the fame as the Cimmerians, were once held in great repute for their knowlege. A large body came into Italy; fome of whom occupied the fine region of Campania, and went under the name of Cimmerians. It has been the opinion of learned men, that they were fo called from כמר, Cimmer, *Darknefs*. This may be fo; though moft nations feem to have been denominated from their worfhip and gods. Thus much however is certain, that this people had in many places fubterranean apartments, where their priefts and reclufes dwelt; and were fuppofed to be configned to darknefs; all which favours the opinion abovementioned. (v. Hom. Od. λ. v. 13.) Several apartments of this kind were about Cuma, and Parthenope, and near the lake Acherufia in Campania. Strabo (l. 5.) fpeaks of this part of Italy, and fays, that it was inclofed with vaft woods, held of old in great veneration; becaufe in thofe they facrificed to the Manes. According to Ephorus, the Cimmerians dwelt, and refided in fubterranean apartments, called Argilla, (referring to the great object of veneration, the Argo) which had a communication with one another. Thofe who applied to the oracle of the cavern, were led by thefe dark paffages to the place of confultation. Within the precincts were to be found all the requifites for an oracle : dark groves, foul ftreams, and fœtid exhalations : and above all a vaft and dreary cave. It was properly a temple, and formed by by the Cimmerians, and Herculeans, who fettled in thefe parts. (v. Lycophron. v. 1273.) Places of this nature were generally fituated near the fea, that they might more eafily be confulted by mariners, whom chance brought upon the coaft.

The many fubterranes which are met with, are probably in part natural; but they were enlarged by art; and undoubtedly defigned for a religious purpofe. They all related to the hiftory of that perfon, who was principally commemorated under the title of Cronus. He is faid to have had three fons; and in a time of danger he formed a large cavern in the ocean; and in this he fhut himfelf up together with thefe fons, and thus efcaped the danger. (Sanchon. ap. Eufeb. P. E. L. 1. c. 10. Porph. de Nymph. Antro. p. 109.)

One tribe of the Hyperboreans is taken notice of by Pliny (N. H. L. 6.) under the name of Arimpheans. They feem to have been reclufes, who retired to woods and wilds, that they might more ftrictly devote themfelves to religion. They wore their hair very fhort, both men and women; and are reprefented as very harmlefs; fo that they lived unmolefted in the midft of many barbarous nations. They were addicted to great abftinence, feeding upon the fruits of the foreft. In many of thefe circumftances they refembled the people, from whence they came. The fame monaftic life prevailed in India among the Sarmanes and Allobii. (Clem. Alex. Strom. L. 1.)

Thofe who fettled in Sicily feem to have been a very powerful and knowing people: but thofe of Hetruria were ftill far fuperior. At the time when they flourifhed, Europe was in great meafure barbarous: and their government was in a ftate of ruin, before learning had dawned in Greece; and long before the Romans had divefted themfelves of their natural ferocity. Hence we can never have an

hiftory

hiftory of this people, which will be found adequate to their merits.

The two moft diftant colonies of this family weftward were upon the Atlantic ocean; the one in Europe to the north; the other oppofite at the extreme part of Africa. The country of the latter was Mauritania; whofe inhabitants were the Atlantic Ethiopians. (Diod. Sic. L. 3. Mela. L. 3. c. 10.) They looked upon themfelves, as of the fame family as the gods; (Diod. Sic. L. 1.) and they were certainly defcended from fome of the firft deified mortals. Thofe who occupied the provinces of Iberia and Bœtica, on the other fide, went under the fame titles, and preferved the fame hiftories. (v. *Cufban*.) They were of Erythræan and Ethiopic race. III. 487.

HYRCANI.

There were many people fo called; and cities and regions, named Hyrcania: in the hiftory of which there will be uniformly found fome reference to fire. The name is a compound of Ur-chane, the god of fire. He was particularly worfhiped at Ur in Chaldea; and one tribe of that nation were called Urchani. Here was the fource of fireworfhip: and all the country was replete with bitumen and fire. There was a region Hyrcania inhabited by the Medes, which feems to have been of the fame inflammable nature. The people were called Hyrcani and Aftabeni; which latter fignifies the fons of fire. In Lydia there were Hyrcani, a city Hyrcania, and a Campus Hyrcinius; perhaps part of that region called καταχεχαυμενη. It was near Hierapolis, Caroura, and Foffa Charonea, all famed for fire. Perhaps the Hyrcinian Foreft was no other than the Hurcanian, fo called from the god Urcan, who was worfhiped here as well as in the Eaft. Eratofthenes, and Ptolemy, call it Δρυμος Ορχυνιος.

Οϼνντιος, the foreſt of Orcun. Among the Alpes Tridentini was a Regio Hercynia; and here the Hercynian Foreſt commenced, and from which it received its name. I. 209.

I.

IABOC.

THE ſame term in different languages conveyed different and oppoſite ideas: and as the Greeks attended only to the meaning in their own tongue, they were conſtantly miſtaken. Thus the river Iaboc, they expreſſed Io Bacchus. I. 169.

IANUS.

Among all the various perſonages, under which the Patriarch may have been repreſented, there are none, wherein his hiſtory is delineated more plainly, than in thoſe of Saturn and Janus. The latter of theſe is by ſome ſuppoſed to have been the ſame as Javan. But there is nothing to be obtained from the hiſtory of Javan to countenance this notion: whereas all the chief circumſtances in the life of Noah correſpond with the hiſtory of Janus. By Plutarch (in Numa. Quæſt. Rom.) he is called Ianos, and repreſented as an ancient prince, who reigned in the infancy of the world; and who brought men from a rude and ſavage way of life to a mild and rational ſyſtem: who was alſo the firſt former of civil communities, and introducer of national polity. He was repreſented with two faces;

faces; with which he looked both forwards and backwards: and from hence he had the name of Janus Bifrons. One of thefe faces was an aged man: the other was often reprefented as young and beautiful. About him were many emblems, to 'denote his different departments. There was particularly a ftaff in one hand, with which he pointed to a rock; from whence iffued a profufion of water. In the other hand he held a key. (See Albricus. c. 14.) He had generally near him fome refemblance of a fhip; particularly upon money, which in aftertimes was coined to his honor. Ovid (Faft. L. 1. v. 239.) feems to have been puzzled to find out the hiftory, and purport of this deity.

Quem tamen effe deum dicam te, Jane biformis?
Nam tibi par nullum Græcia numen habet.

The Romans indeed had in a manner appropri-ated him to themfelves. There were however many divinities fimilar to him both in Greece and Egypt. To him was attributed the invention of a fhip; and he is faid to have firft compofed a chaplet. Upon the Sicilian coins of Eryx his figure often occurs with a twofold countenance: and on the reverfe is a dove encircled with a crown, which feems to be of olive. (Parut. Sicil.) He was reprefented as a juft man, and a prophet: and the remarkable characteriftic of being in a manner the author of time, and god of the year. He was ftiled Matutinus; as if to him was owing the renewal of light and day. There was a tradition that he raifed the firft temple to Heaven; though they looked upon him as a deity, and one of the eight original divinities. In the hymns of the Salii (Macrob. Sat. L. 1.) he was ftiled the god of gods. In this and many other refpects he was fimilar to the Cronos of the Greeks. He was ftiled Patuleius
and

and Clufius: and he had the title of Junonius, from the Arkite dove Iönah, which the Latins expreffed Juno.   He is ftiled

Templorum pofitor, templorum fanĉte refeĉtor:

by which is meant, that he was a renewer of religious rites, and the worfhip of the Deity.   He was reputed the fame as Apollo; and had the title of Θυραιος, or the deity of *the door*, or *paffage :* and his altars were placed immediately before the door of the houfe, or temple, where his rites were celebrated.   In memorial of his hiftory every door among the Latines had the name of Janua: and the firft month of the year was named Januarius, as being an opening to a new æra, and in fome degree a renewal of time.

Ovid has continual allufions to this hiftory. Janus is by him fuppofed to be the Chaotic deity; and the fame time to prefide over every thing, that could be fhut, or opened; and to be the guardian of the doors of heaven. (Faft. L. v. 103.   See alfo Macrob. Sat. L. 1.) II. 253.

JASON

Has been efteemed as the chief in the Argonautic expedition.   But this is a feigned perfonage, made out of a facred title.   Many temples in the Eaft were called Jafonea. (Strabo. L. 1. and 11.)   In all thefe countries we may obferve names of cities, which had a reference to the Arkite hiftory; hence we may infer that thefe temples related to the fame event.   They were not built by him, but ereĉted to his honour.   It is faid, that, when a child, he underwent the fame fate as Ofiris, Perfeus, and Dionufus: in arca opertus, et claufus eft, tanquam mortuus. (Natalis Comes. L. 6.)   Juftin (l. 42. c. 3.) places him in the fame light as Hercules, and Dionufus: and fays that by moft of the people in the Eaft he was looked up to as the founder of their nations, and had divine honours paid to him. I fufpect that Æfon, Jafon, Jafion, and Jafius, were originally the fame title. Argos was ftiled Jafon; which confirms me, that it was an Arkite title. Αχαϊκον Αργος—η Ιασον, η Ἱππιον, η Ἱπποϐαιον, η Πελασγικον. Strabo. L. 8. The temple of Juno Argiva among the Lucanians in Italy, was faid to have been built by Jafon. Id. (l. 6.) II. 515.

ICONUPHY.

Eudoxus, who refided at Heliopolis, is faid by Laertius (l. 8.) to have ftudied under Iconuphy, a prieft of the country. Ικονουφι was, I apprehend, the name of the deity to whom he was prieft. It was Ouc Cahen Ouph, *the mighty prince Ouph,* or as the Greeks would have expreffed it, Canouphis. (Plut. de Genio Socrat.) He tells us that he was of Memphis (de If. et Ofir.) and mentions that Pythagoras ftudied under Oenuphis of Heliopolis. Neither Chonuphis nor Oenuphis are the names of men, but of the god Anubis, to whom the prieft was facred, as well as the college at Heliopolis. Obferv. 165. Chonuphis and Oenuphis are the fame names differently written, anfwering to the Anubis of the Romans, and the Canoubis of the Greeks. Ib. n.

IDMON.

What his attainments were, we find in the Orphic. Argonaut. v. 720.

Δη τοῖ' Αϐανλος παις νοθος ηλυθε καρτερος Ιδμων,
Τον ρ' ὑποκυσσαμενη τεκεν Απολλωνι ανακτι
Αμϐροσιον παρα κυμα φερελριος Αντιανειρα,
Τῳ και Μανλοσυνην επορε, και Θεσφαλον Ομφην.

Like Amphion, &c. was a deity, or rather a title of the Sun. I. 253.

JEZEBEL,

JEZEBEL,

Whofe father was Ethbaal, king of Sidon, and whofe daughter was Athaliah, feems to have been named from Aza-bel, for all the Sidonian names are compounds of facred terms. I. 28. n.

IGNETES.

The Telchines and Ignetes were the firft who fettled at Rhodes; and were efteemed Heliadæ. The latter were denominated from their god Hanes, who was at different times called Agnis and Ignis. But notwithftanding their relation to Hanes and Helius, they were at the fame time fuppofed to be defcended from the fea. Hence it was faid of them by Simmias Rhodius, (Clem. Alex. Strom. 5.)

———————— Αμμα
Ιγνηίων και Τελχινων εφυ η αλυκη Ζαψ.

(Αμμα fignifies *a mother*, and Ζαψ *the fea*.) The purport of the verfe is, that they carried their origin up to the Deluge. Though they had the character of Γηγενης and Ουρανιωνες, yet they univerfally took to themfelves the title of fons of the fea. ευίοι ησαν υιοι μεν Θαλασσης, ως ο μυθος παρεδωκε. (Diod. Sic. L. 5. Strabo. L. 10.) II. 470.

ILITHYA,

At Tegea in Arcadia there was a ftatue of this goddefs, the fame as Ifis; the fame alfo as Juno Lucina of the Latines: fhe was ftiled Ειλαθυια επι γονασι, Lucina Ingenicula, being reprefented in a fupplicating pofture upon her knees. She was the goddefs of the birth; and feemed an emblem of nature, pleading for her offspring, who were to be deftroyed. Hard by was an altar of earth. II. 335. Among the αναθηματα in the Acropolis at Athens, is a ftatue of the Earth in a fupplicating pofture; re-
queſting,

quefting, as Paufanias imagines (l. 1.) that Jupiter would fend her rain. The hiftory, doubtlefs, related to rain; but from the circumftances of the other furrounding ftatues, the purport of this entreaty was rather to avert it as an evil, than to implore it as a blefling. As the object of the fupplication was unknown, we may form conjectures as well as Paufanias. I fhould therefore think this ftatue had the fame reference, as that of Ilithya, επι γονασιν; and that they both related to the Deluge, and to the deftruction of mankind in the waters. 414. Ilithya, as goddefs of the birth, was the fame as Diana, Venus Lubentia, and Genetillis, who rofe from the fea. 455.

IMAGES.

In ancient times they had no images in their temples, but in lieu of them they ufed conical ftones, called Βαιτυλια; under which reprefentation their deity was often worfhiped. I. 49.

INACHUS,

Annachus, and Nannachus relate to Noachus, or Noah: by fome he was ftiled Inachus, a king of Greece; and Phoroneus, and Apis, brought in fucceffion after him. But the name is not of Græcian original. It is mentioned by Eufebius (Chron.) in his account of the firft ages, that there reigned *in Egypt Telegonus, a prince of foreign extraction; who was the fon of Orus the Shepherd, and the feventh in defcent from Inachus.* In the fame author we read, that a colony went forth from that country into Syria, where they founded the ancient city Antioch: and that they were *conducted by Cafus and Belus, who were fons of Inachus.* Thefe events were far more early than any hiftory of Greece, let it be removed as far back as tradition can be carried. But otherwife, what relation can a prince of

R   Egypt,

Egypt, or Cafus and Belus, who came originally from Babylonia, have with a fuppofed king of Argos? By Inachus is certainly meant Noah: and the hiftory relates to fome of the more early defcendants of the Patriarch. His name has been rendered very unlike itfelf, by having been lengthened with terminations; and otherwife fafhioned according to the idiom of different nations. II.206. Inachus, Oceanus, Ogugus, and Agenor, are all the fame perfonages, under different names; and the hiftories are all the fame. 156. Indeed Phoroneus, Apis, Zeuth, Deucalion, Prometheus, Inachus, were all one perfon, and with that perfon commenced the gentile hiftory; not of Greece only, but of the world. 268. Epiphanius (Hæres. L. 1.) tells us that Pappaius, the father of Apis, was the fame as Inachus, in whofe days the Deluge happened. 421.

INESSUS.

The city of Hanes in Egypt was of the fame etymology with Innefa (v. Ætna.) being denominated from the Sun, who was ftiled Hanes, Ain-Es, fons ignis five lucis. Stephanus Byz. calls it Inys; Ινσσος, πολις Αιγυπτον; but Herodotus (l. 3. c. 5.) renders it Iënis, better Doricè Ιᾱνις, for that was nearer to its real name. He however points it out plainly, by faying, that it was three days journey from mount Cafius; and that the whole way was through the Arabian defert. This is a fituation, which agrees not with any other city in all Egypt, except that, which was the Onium of the later Jews.. With this it accords precifely. There feem to have been two cities named On from the worfhip of the Sun. One was called Zan, Zon, and Zoan, in the land of Go-zan, the Gofhen of the Scriptures. The other was the city On in Arabia; called alfo Hanes. They were within eight or nine miles of each other: and are both mentioned together by Ifaiah xxx. 4. *For his princes were at*

Zoan,

Zoan; and his ambaffadors came to Hanes. The name of each of thefe cities, on account of the fimilarity of worfhip, has by the Greeks been tranflated Heliopolis: which has caufed great confufion in the hiftory of Egypt. The latter of the two was the Iänis, or Ιανσος, of the Greeks; fo called from Hanes, the Sun: who was worfhiped under that title by the Egyptians and Arabians. It now lies in ruins, clofe to the village Materea, which has rifen from it. It is very remarkable, that it is at this day called by the Arabians Ain El Sham, the fountain of the Sun. I. 195.

INO.

She was no other than Iöna, the fame as Venus, and reputed a goddefs of the fea, and the nurfe of Dionufus. II. 311.

INOPUS,

A fountain in Delos, facred to the prophetic deity. The name is a plain compound of Ain-Opus, fons Pythonis.

IO,

The fame as Jonah; her temple was at Argos, where was this infcription; Ιω Μαχαιρα, Δαμπαδη- φορος.—Ιω, η Σελην. Euftath. in Donyf. v. 95. II. 333. n.

IOLCUS,

The name of a fea port in Theffaly, in which the Argo was fuppofed to be laid up: and the name fhews the true hiftory of the place. It was denominated from the Ark, ftiled Ολκας; which was one of the Græcian names for a large ark or float. Iolchus was originally Jaolcus, which is a variation of Aia-Olcas, the place of the Ark.

Medea

Medea in Apollonius makes ufe of the true name, when fhe fpeaks of being wafted to Greece.

Γ.　Η αυίην με ταχειαι υπερ πονίοιο φεροιεν
- (　Ενθεν δ' εις Ιαολκον αναρπαξασαι αελλαι.
Σ.

Apoll. Rhod. L. 3. v. 1110. Homer alfo ftiles it Βαθυχαρος Ιαολχος. Οδ. Λ. v. 255. II. 502. As Iolchos was the city of the Ark, it was hence alfo called Lariffa; and the ancient inhabitants were ftiled Minyæ, and the country Magnefia. 513.

JONAH.

The fatal confequences of the Deluge muſt have left the deepeſt impreffions upon the few furvivors: the like muſt have been tranfmitted to their pofterity. Upon their defection from the worfhip of the true God, an undue reverence paid to the Patriarch might conftitute one fpecies of idolatry: rites and myfteries might be inftituted in allufion to his wonderful prefervation. This feems natural; and was indeed actually the cafe. Temples and cities were built in memory of the Ark and Deluge. The Dove and the Iris (v. Eiras, Eros) were not forgotten. The former, which returned to Noah with a leaf of olive, and brought the firſt tidings that the waters were abated, was held in many nations as particularly facred. It was looked upon as a peculiar meffenger of the deity; an emblem of peace, and good fortune. It was called by the ancient Amonians Iön, and Jönah; fometimes expreffed Iönas, from whence came the Οιας, Oinas, of the Greeks. It was efteemed an interpreter of the will of the gods; and on that account was early looked upon as a bird of prefage. Among mariners it was thought to be particularly aufpicious. From the prophetic bird Jönah, or Ionas, the Greeks formed many terms of augury; e. g. Οιας, Οιναξ, Οιωνος, Οιωνοι. Priefts and foothfayers were

ftiled

ſtiled Jönah, or Doves; which was rendered by the
Greeks Πελειαι και Τρηρωνες. Servius (in Virg. Æn.
L. 3. v. 466.) takes notice of the doves at Thebà.

The Dove was a ſacred emblem; and was once
univerſally received; and even admitted as an Hieroglyphic among the Hebrews. The Prophet, who
was ſent upon an embaſſy to the Ninevites, is ſtiled
Iönas: a title probably beſtowed upon him, as a
meſſenger of the Deity. The great Patriarch, who
preached righteouſneſs to the Antedeluvians, is by
Beroſus and Abydenus ſtiled Oan, and Oannes,
which is the ſame name as Jönah. The author of
the Apocalypſe is denominated in the like manner:
whom the Greeks ſtiled Ιωαννης. And when the
great forerunner of our Saviour was to be named;
his father induſtriouſly called him Ιωαννης, for the
ſame reaſon (ſee Lu. i. 1.) The Patriarch Noah ſeems
to have been the firſt who was in the Gentile world
typified under this emblem. He was a great
Prophet; and it was foretold at his birth, that he
ſhould bring peace and comfort to mankind. The
purport of his name was Reſt from labour. Hence
the Dove became an emblem of peace, as well as of
the perſon, through whom it was derived to the
earth. He was in conſequence of it called Oan and
Oannes, analogous to the Ιωαννης of the Greeks. We
find then, that the Dove was a truly ſacred ſymbol;
and ſo acknowledged in the times of the pureſt
worſhip. But the ſons of Ham perverted that,
which was intended to be only typical; and carried
their regard for it to a degree of idolatrous veneration.

The term Jönah is ſometimes found compounded;
and expreſſed Ad, or Ada Jönah, Regina, vel Regia
Columba: from which title a deity Adiona was
conſtituted; and particular rites were inſtituted.
This mode of Idolatry muſt have been very ancient;
as it is mentioned in Leviticus and Deuteronomy:

and is one species of false worship, which Moses forbade by name.

As Venus (of the Latines, the Οινας of the Greeks) was no other than the ancient Jönah, we shall find in her history numberless circumstances relating to the Noachite Dove, and to the Deluge. II. 283.

IONIC WORSHIP, and JONAH-HELLENIC COLONIES.

The worship of the Dove, and the circumstances of the Deluge, were very early interwoven among the various rites and ceremonies of the eastern world. The people, by whom these rites were kept up, were stiled Semarim, Iönim, and Dercetidæ; according to the particular symbol, which they venerated.

The Capthorim brought these rites with them into Palestine; where they were kept up in Gaza, Ascalon, and Azotus. They worshiped Dagon; and held the Dove in high veneration. Gaza was called Jönah. Their coast was called the coast of the Iönim: for the sea with which it was bounded, was called the Iönian sea quite to the Nile. (Steph. Byz. Ιονιον.) The like terms, and worship, and allusions to the same history, prevailed at Sidon, and in Syria. Antioch upon the Orontes was called Jönah. Who the Argeans were that founded it needs not any explanation.

Iö, among her various peregrinations, arrived at last at Gaza, from her called Jönah. Under the notion of her flight, as well as of Osiris, Damater, Astarte, Isis, Dionusus, the poets alluded to the journeying of mankind from mount Ararat; but more particularly to the retreat of the Iönim, upon their dispersion from the land of Shinar. The Greeks represented this person as a feminine, and made her the daughter of Inachus. They supposed her travels to commence from Argos (by which is signified the journeying of mankind from the Ark) and

and they defcribed her as proceeding in a retro‑
grade direction toward the eaft. The line of her
procedure may be feen in the Prometheus of Æf‑
chylus: which account, if we change the order of
the rout, and collate it with other hiftories, will be
found in great meafure confonant to the truth.
The like ftory was told by the Syrians of Aftarte;
by the Egyptians of Ifis: but they were all three
the fame perfonage, and their hiftories of the fame
purport. (v. Marfham. Can. Chron. Sæc. 1.
p. 42.)

    The Greeks, efpecially the Athenians, pretended
to be Aὐloχθονες; but their beft hiftorians ingenu‑
oufly own, that the whole region, called Hellas,
was originally inhabited by a people of another
race, whom they ftiled Βαρϐαροὶ: that their own an‑
ceftors came under different denominations, which
they took from their mode of worfhip. Among
others were the Iönim, called in after times
Ionians. They were fuppofed to have been led by
one Iön, the fon of Zeuth, ftyled by the Greeks
Xuthus (thefe were the fame perfons). This arri‑
val of Iön was a memorable æra among the Græ‑
cians; and always efteemed fubféquent to the firft
peopling of the country. Iön (in the play of
Euripides he is mentioned as the fon of Xuthus, but
claimed by Apollo, as his offspring: Xuthus and
Apollo were titles of the fame perfon) was expofed
in an Ark; and in the Ark faid to have been
crowned, not with *laurel*, as we might expect a fon
of Apollo would have been, but with *olive*;

     Στεφανον Ελαιας αμφιθηκα σοι τῆι. (v. 1434.)

From thefe two, Xuthus and his fon Iön, the Do‑
rians, Achæans, and Ionians were faid to be de‑
fcended. Some of the Hellenes, and efpecially the
Athenians were ftyled Säitæ; not, as is commonly

imagined from the city Saïs, but from the province of Saït, in upper Egypt, *the land of olives.*

It has been a prevailing notion, that the Ionïans were of the family of Javan. His fons certainly settled in Greece; but they were the original inhabitants: whereas the Dorians and Ionians confeffedly fucceeded to a country, which had been in the poffeffion of others. The author of the Chronicon Pafchale (p. 49.) fays, that, according to the moft genuine accounts, they were a colony brought by Jönan from Babylonia. This Iönan was one of thofe, who had been engaged in the building of Babel, at the time, when the language of mankind was confounded. The building of Babel is in Scripture attributed to Nimrod, the firft tyrant upon earth; and it was carried on by his affociates, the Cuthite Iönim. They were the firft innovaters in religion; and introduced idolatry wherever they came. We accordingly find (Eufeb. Chron. p. 13.) that they were the perfons, who firft infected Greece.

The invention of Aftronomy is attributed to Ham, ftyled Ionichus: and as titles were not uniformly confined to one perfon, it is probable that Chus was alfo included under this charaƈteriftic. Tonichus feems to be a compound of Ion-Nechus; and is undoubtedly a term, by which the head of the Iönim was diftinguifhed. The ancients give continually to one perfon, what belonged to many. Under the character of Ionichus are meant the Amonians; thofe fons of Ham, who came into Egypt; but particularly the Cuthites, the Iönim from Chaldea.

They feem to have been diftinguifhed from the fons of Javan, by being ftyled Ιωνες; whereas the others were ftyled Ιαονες: though this diftinction is not perhaps uniformly preferved. The people of Bœotia in the time of Homer were Iönim; and the

the Iäones feem by him to be mentioned as a different race. (Il. N. v. 685.)

Ενθα δε Βοιωloι και Iaovες ελκεχιlωνες.

And Attica is faid by Strabo to have been called
both Ionia and Ias. (L. 9. p. 600.) We find,
that it had two names; the latter I fhould imagine,
was that by which the primitive inhabitants were
called. The Græcians continually changed the
Nu final into the Sigma: whence Jan, or Javan,
has been rendered Ias. It was originally expreffed
Ιαν, and Ιαων: and this was the ancient name of
Hellas, and the Helladians; as we may infer from
its being fo called by people of other countries:
for foreigners abide long by ancient terms. (v.
Ariftoph. Schol. in Acharn. v. 106. Hefych. Steph.
Byz.) The Iaones then, or the fons of Javan,
were the firft who peopled the country, and for a
while a diftinct race. But when the Ionians afterwards joined them, and their families were mixed;
we muft not wonder, if their names were confounded. They were however never fo totally incorporated, but what fome feparate remains of the
original ftock were here and there to be perceived:
and Strabo fays (L. 7. p. 495.) that this was to be
obferved even in the age when he lived. III. 369.

ISIRIS,

The fame as Ofiris, was, according to Philo
Biblius from Sanchoniathon, the brother to Cna.
I. 7.

ISIS.

The worfhip of Ifis, and of her facred fhip, prevailed among the Suevi. (Tacitus de Mor. Ger.)
Her fhip was alfo reverenced at Rome; and is
marked in the calendar for the month of March.
(Grut. vol. 1. p. 655.) I. 212.

Orus

Orus was fuppofed to be the fon of Ifis; but Ifis, Rhea, Atargatis, were all emblems of the Ark, that *receptacle* (την Ισιν υποδοχον. Ifis et Ofir. Plut.) which was ftiled the Mother of mankind. II. 327. The genius of the Ark was worfhiped by the Ca-naanites under the title of Baal Maon. This deity was the fame as Ifis, and Rhea. Both Ifis and Juno were defcribed with the Labana, or Crefcent. 445. Ifis was the fame as Latona. II. 330.

ISMENIUS.

This term is compounded of Is-Men, *ignis Menis*. Meen, Menes, Manes, was one of the moft ancient titles of the Egyptian god Ofiris, the fame as Apollo and Caanthus. II. 155.

ISTA-CHAR,

Or Efta-Char (in Perfia) is the place or temple of Ifta, Efta, the 'Εςια of the Greeks, and Vefta of the Romans. Every fymbol, and reprefentation in it, relates to the worfhip of the country: and all hiftory fhews that fuch places were facred, and fet apart for the adoration of Fire, and the deity of that element, called Ifta, or Efta. Hyde therefore (de Rel. Vet. p. 306.) feems to be wrong, when he tells us, that it fignifies *e rupe fumptum, feu rupe ronftans faxeum palatium*; and that it is derived from the Arabic word *Sachr, rupes,* in the eighth con-jugation. The words *e rupe fumptum,* &c. are not at any rate materials, out of which a proper name could be conftructed; and what temple, or palace, is not built of ftone taken out of a quarry? Herbert (Travels, p. 158.) with great propriety fuppofes the building to have been the temple of Anaia, or Anais; who was the fame as Hanes, as well as Heftia. I. 225.

JUNO,

The fuppofed mother of all the deities, thus
fpeaks of her titles and departments in Apuleius.
(Metam. L. xi.) Me primigenii Phryges Peffi-
nuntiam nominant deûm matrem : hinc autoch-
thones Attici Cecropiam Minervam : illinc fluc-
tuantes Cyprii Paphiam Venerem : Cretes fagitti-
feri Dictynnam Dianam. Siculi trilingues Stygiam
Proferpinam : Eleufinii vetuftam deam Cererem.
Junonem alii: alii Bellonam: alii Hecaten : Rham-
nufiam alii : et qui nafcentis dei Solis inchoantibus
radiis illuftrantur Æthiopes, Ariique, prifcaque
doctrina pollentes Ægyptii, ceremoniis me prorfus
propriis percolentes, appellant vero nomine Regi-
nam Ifidem. I. 315.

Juno was the fame as Iönah ; and fhe was particularly called Juno Argiva. She was efteemed the
fame as Luna, and Selene, from her connexion with
the Ark : and at Samos fhe was defcribed as
ftanding in a Lunette, with the lunar emblem upon
her head. She was called Inachis and Inachia
(Ov. Met. L. 9.) and reprefented as the Queen of
heaven, the fame as Afhtaroth, and Aftarte of
Sidon and Syria. It is faid of Juno, that fhe was
fometimes worfhiped under the fymbol of an Egg,
fo that her hiftory had the fame reference, as that
of Oinas, or Venus. She prefided equally over
the fea. (Virg. Æn. l. 4. v. 120. Orph. H. in
Jun. 15.) Ifis, Io and Ino were the fame as Juno;
and Venus alfo was the fame deity under a different
title. In Laconia there was an ancient ftatue of
the goddefs ftiled Venus Junonia.

As Juno was the fame as Iönah, fhe had Iris for
her concomitant. As the peacock in the full ex-
panfion of his plumes difplays all the beautiful
colours of the Iris, or Rainbow ; it was probably
for

for that reason made the bird of Juno instead of the Dove, which was appropriated to Venus. II. 343.

JUPITER, or ZEUS,

Was originally the same with the Hermes of the Chaldeans and Egyptians, whom they esteemed the chief God. I. 102. The ancient name of Latian Jupiter was P'ur. 124. The ancients represented the Patriarch under a numberless variety of titles and characters, whereof Zeuth was one. II. 253. 268. 273. To the god Dagon was ascribed the invention of many arts; particularly, the construction of the plough, and the introduction of bread corn. These were benefits, attributed also to Zeuth, stiled Ζευς αγριος, Ζευς νομιος, Ζευς αροlριος, and likewise to Osiris. They were all the same deity, who was worshiped in Egypt under many titles, but particularly that of On. 299.

The ancients, which may seem very extraordinary, represented their chief god of all ages and sexes. A bearded Apollo, and a bearded Venus (Servius in Virg. Æn. l. 2. v. 632.) The poet Calvus speaks of Venus as masculine; (Macrob. Sat. L. 3.) and Valerius Soranus (ap. August. de Civ. Dei. L. 4. and L. 7.) among other titles calls Jupiter *the Mother of the gods.*

Jupiter omnipotens, Regum Rex ipse, Deûmque Progenitor, *Genetrixque Deûm*; Deus unus et idem.

Synesius speaks of him in nearly the same manner. (Hymn 3.)

> Συ πατηρ, συ δ' εσσι μητηρ,
> Συ δ' αρσην, συ δι θηλυς.

And the like character is given to the ancient deity Μητις. (Orph. Hymn 31.)

> Αρσην μεν και θηλυς εφυς, πολυωνυμε Μητι.

In

In one of the fragments of the Orphic poetry every
thing under this head is comprehended in a very
ſhort compaſs. (Orph. Fragm. vi. p. 366. Geſner's
ed.)

Ζευς αρσην γενεῖο, Ζευς αμϐροῖος επλεῖο Νυμφη,
Ζευς πυθμην γαιης τε και ουρανου ασεροεντος.—
Ζευς πονῖου ριζα, Ζευς Ἡλιος *, ηδε Σελμνη,
Ζευς Βασιλευς, Ζευς αυῖος ἁπανῖων αρχιγενεθλος.—
Και Μηῖις, πρωῖος γενεῖωρ, και Ερως πολυῖερπης.
Πανῖα γαρ εν Ζηνος μεγαλω ταδε σωμαῖι κηῖαι.
Ἐν κραῖος, εις Δαιμων, γενεῖαι μεγας αρχος ἁπανῖων.

Whom he meant under the title of Zeus, he explains
afterwards (Fragm. vii. p. 371.) in a ſolemn invocation of the god Dionuſus.

Κεκλυθι τηλεπορου δινης ἑλικαυγεα κυκλον
Ουρανιαις ςροφαλιγξι περιδρομον αιεν ἑλισσων,
Αγλαε ΖΕΥ, ΔΙΟΝΥΣΕ, παῖερ πονῖου, παῖερ αιης,
Ἡλιε, παγγενεῖορ, παναιολε, χρυσεοφεγγες,

I. 313. The common hiſtory of Jupiter (of which
name there are reckoned about three hundred) is
full of inconſiſtencies and impoſſibilities. 452, &c.

* Jupiter Lucetius, or god of light. Macrob. Sat. L. 1. c. 15.

L.

LABAN, LUBAN.

BY thefe terms the Arkite moon was denominated; by fome they feem to have been changed
into Labar, and Lubar. Epiphanius fays that the
Ark refted upon mount Lubar, (the fame as Baris,
and the Ararat of Mofes.) by which was meant the
mountain of Lunus Architis. From Labar the
Roman enfigns were ftiled Labara, quafi Infignia
Lunaria. This is evident from the Lunette, which
is continually to be found upon them. The name
Labarum however was not properly Roman; but
was adopted by the later Emperors, efpecially thofe
of Conftantinople. They borrowed it from fome
of the conquered nations, who had the fame kind
of military ftandard. II. 449.

LABANA.

As the worfhip of Labana, or Selene, prevailed
fo much at Carrhæ, or Haran; we may form a
judgment from the name of the perfon, by Mofes
called Laban, of the nature of his idolatry. We
may prefume, that he was fo named from this worfhip; and that it confifted in an undue reverence
to the Arkite emblem Labana. It is moreover
highly probable, that thefe images, which are fuppofed to have been invented by Terah, and from
him ramed Teraphim, the fame which Laban worfhiped, were lunar amulets, or types of the Ark in
the form of a crefcent. Both Terah, and Serugh,
are

are faid to have-been devoted to falfe worfhip : and
though people had been previoufly addicted to
Zabaifm, and other fpecies of idolatry, yet the introduction of images is attributed to them.   And
as the worfhip of the Arkite emblem prevailed fo
much at Charræ, the very city of Haran, and Laban, the defcendants of Terah; we may infer, that
it was the primitive idolatry of the place, and confifted in the worfhip of the Labana, or Arkite moon.
Both Ifis and Juno were defcribed with the Labana,
or Crefcent : and Venus was ftiled Lubentia, and
Lubentina, which certainly related to the fame
emblem; and fignified Venus Lunaris et Architis.
II. 445.   Lubentia by the Romans was derived
from Lubens, but erroneoufly.

LACEDÆMONIANS

Efteemed themfelves of the fame family as the
Capthorim of Egypt; hence they furmifed that
they were related to the Jews. I. 184.

LAMIÆ.

They are fuppofed to have delighted in human
blood, like the Cyclopians; but their chief repaft
was the flefh of young people and children, of
which they are reprefented as very greedy.   They
were priefts of Ham, called El Ham; hence
'Lamus and 'Lamia.   Their chief city, perhaps
Tauromenium, is mentioned by Homer (Od. K.)
as the city of Lamus, and the inhabitants as of the
Giant race.   They were Amonians, and came originally from Babylonia.   The Lamiæ were to be
found not only in Italy, and Sicily, but Greece,
Pontus, and Libya.   However widely they may
have been feparated, they are ftill reprefented in
the fame unfavourable light.

Τις τ'ουνομα τοδ' ιπονηδισον Ερολοις
Ουκ οιδι Λαμιας της Λιβυσικης γινος,

fays

fays Euripides (Cyclops. v. Philoftrat. Vit. Apollon. L. 4. Ariftot. Eth. L. 7. c. 6.) Formiæ was one of their principal places in Italy. (v. Horat. L. 3. Ode 17.) The chief temple of the Formians was upon the fea-coaft at Caiete; it ftood near a cavern, facred to the god Ait, called Ate, and Atis, and Attis: and it was hence called Caieta, and Caiatta. There were in the rock fome wonderful fubterranes, which branched out into various apartments. Here the ancient Lamii, the priefts of Ham, refided. They undoubtedly facrificed chil-·dren here: and probably the fame cuftom was common among the Lamii, as among the Lace-dæmonians, who ufed to whip their children round the altar of Diana Orthia. Fulgentius, and others affure us, that the ancient Latines called the whiping of children Caiatio. Caiat fignified a kind of whip, or thong; probably fuch was ufed at Caiate. II. 15.

LANGUAGE.

There was once but one language among the fons of men. Upon the difperfion of mankind, this was branched out into dialects; and thofe again were fubdivided: all which varied every age; not only in refpect to one another; but each language differed from itfelf more and more continually. It is therefore impoffible to reduce the whole of thefe to the mode, and ftanding of any one.—It is my opinion that there are two events recorded by Mofes, Gen. v. and Gen. xi. 8, 9. One was a regular migration of mankind in general to the countries allotted to them: the other was a difperfion which related to fome particulars [the fons of Chus. See Mr. Bryant's *Obfervations on the ancient Hiftory of Egypt.*] I. 54.

LAODICEA,

LAODICEA,

According to Euftathius (in Dionyf. Perieg. v. 915.) was called of old Ramæthan; of which he gives the true interpretation: Ῥαμαιθας, αφ᾽ υψους ὁ Θεος· Ῥαμαν γαρ εγχωριον το υψος· Αθαν δε ὁ Θεος. II. 304.

LAR, LAREN, LARIS.

Laren, and Laris, feem to have been ancient terms for the Ark. Indeed they are the fame, the n final being changed into an s; hence Lares and Laris. From Laren came Λαρναξ, Larnax, an Ark; alfo Larnaffus, Larina, Laranda; and Larunda, a goddefs well known to the Romans. She was ftiled Δαιμονων μηηρ: by fome fhe was called Lara; children were offered at her altar to procure her favour. Parnaffus was of old Larnaffus; εκαλειτο δε προτερον Λαρνασσος, δια το την Δευκαλιωνος λαρνακα αυτοθι προσεχθηναι. From Laris there were many places named Lariffa, and in all thefe places the Arkite rites prevailed. Lar, and Laren had a reference to the fea: *they who fifh in the fea, call the machine, which they ufe,* Λαριναιον, *Larinæum.* Hefych.

There was a fea bird called Lar, which outlived the moft tempeftuous ftorms; and hence, perhaps, was made an emblem of the Ark. Homer (Oδ. E.) compares Hermes to this bird;

Σευατ επειτ επι κυμας Λαρῳ ορνιθι εοικως.

The Lares, and Manes, thofe domeftic deities of the ancient Hetrurians, and Latines, were the fame perfonages under different names. By thefe terms are fignified Dii Arkitæ, who were no other than their Arkite anceftors (the Δαιμονες, the Baalim of the fcriptures) the perfons preferved in the Laren or Ark; the genius of which was Ifis, the reputed parent of the world. The feafts inftituted to thefe deities were ftiled Larentalia. The Lares were the fame as the Dii Penates, and the Dii Præftites; the latter, according to Macrobius (Saturn. L. 1.) were imported from Egypt. Arnobius (l. 3.) ftiles them quofdam Genios, et functorum animas; he fpeaks of Neptune as one of the Lares; and the reft of them are confeffedly deities of the fea. (v. Livy, l. 40. c. 52. Macrob. l. 1. c. 10.) II. 451.

LAURUS,

The Laurel, was denominated from Al-Orus: the berry was termed Bacca, from Bacchus. I. 333.

LEITUS.

Herodotus fpeaks of a Prutaneïon in Achaia Pthiotic, called Leïtus; of which he gives a fearful account: l. 7. § 197. Ανιλον δε καλιουσι το Πρυλανιον οι Αχαιοι· ην δε ισελθη, ουκ ιςι, οκως εξασι, πριν η θυσεσθαι μελλη· ωςε τι προς τουλοισι πολλοι ηδε των μιλλονλων τουλεων θυσισθαι, δισαντες οιχονλο αποδρανλες ες αλλην χωρην. χρονου δε απιονλος, οπισω καλελθονλες, ην αλισκωνλαι, ιςιλλονλο ες το Πρυλανιον, ως θυλαι τε εξηγεονλο, ςεμμασι πας πυκασθεις, και ως συν πομπη εξαχθεις. Xerxes, he adds, and his army, paffing through Theffaly, paid all due regard to this temple; fo awful, it feems, was myfterious cruelty. II. 42.

LETTERS. WRITING.

It is faid, that Oannes (*the man of the fea.* Helladius calls him Ωην, which Doricè would be Ωαν. By Ωον πρωλογονον is fignified the Ark.) and Sifuthrus inftructed men in the knowlege of letters, and committed many things to writing. Now if the people of the firft ages had been poffeffed of fo valuable a fecret, as that of writing; they would never have afterwards defcended to means lefs perfect for the explanation of their ideas. And it is to be obferved, that the invention of hieroglyphics was

certainly

certainly a difcovery of the Chaldeans; and made ufe of in the firft ages by the Egyptians; the very nations, who are fuppofed to have been poffeffed of the fuperior and more perfect art. They might retain the former, when they became poffeffed of the latter; becaufe their ancient records were en-trufted to hieroglyphics: but, had they been pof-feffed of letters originally, they would never have deviated into the ufe of fymbols; at leaft, for things, which were to be publifhed to the world, and com-memorated for ages. Of their hieroglyphics we have famples without end in Egypt; both on obe-lifks, and in their fyringes; as alfo upon their portals, and other buildings. Every mummy almoft abounds with them. How comes it, if they had writing fo early, that fcarcely one fpecimen is come down to us: but that every example fhould be in the leaft perfect character?

For my part, I believe that there was no writing antecedent to the Law at mount Sinai. Here the divine art was promulgated; of which other nations partook; the Tyrians and Sidonians firft, as they were the neareft to the fountain-head. And when this difcovery became more known; even then, I imagine, that its progrefs was very flow: that in many countries, whither it was carried, it was but partially received, and made ufe of to no purpofe of confequence. The Romans carried their pre-tenfions to letters pretty high; and the Helladian Greeks ftill higher; yet the former marked their years by a nail driven into a poft: and the latter for fome ages fimply wrote down the names of the Olympic victors from Coræbus; and regiftered the priefteffes of Argos.

Why letters, when introduced, were fo partially received, and employed to fo little purpofe, a twofold reafon may be given. Firft, the want of antecedent writings, to encourage people to proceed

in

in the fame track. The practice of writing, or, in other words, compofing, depends upon previous reading, and example. A fecond reafon feems to have been the want of fuch materials as are necef-fary for expedition and free writing. The rind and leaves of trees, and fhells from the fea, can lend but fmall affiftance towards literature: and ftones and flabs are not calculated to promote it much further. It is impoffible for people to receive any great benefit from letters, where they are obliged to go to a fhard or an oyfter-fhell, for information; and where knowlege is configned to a pantile. As to the high antiquity affigned to letters by Pliny, (N. H. l. 7.) no credence can be given to that au-thor, who from 720 years infers eternity, and fpeaks of thofe terms as fynonimous.

Note. From writing upon leaves and fhells, came *Petalifmus* and *Oftracifmus* of the Greeks: from the bark of trees, *Libri* of the Latines. III. 122.

LIBANUS,

Laban, Liban, and Libanah were names of the Lunette, the moft noted emblem of the Ark. They are only variations of the fame term. Mount Li-banus, doubtlefs, received its name from this type; for the city Arca ftood here towards the bottom; and upon the fummit was the temple of Venus Architis, where the moft ancient rites were pre-ferved of Libanah, or Selene. They were intro-duced by people ftiled Archites; who were colo-nies from Egypt, the Belidæ, Danaidæ, and Cad-mians of the Greeks; and the Hivites and Arkites of Mofes. II. 443.

LIBER.

This title given to Dionufus, was, I imagine, the fame as Labar; and conferred upon him, as the
deus

9

deus Lunus. For the horns of Dionufus, like the
horns of Ifis, were originally a crefcent. II. 450.

LION.

The Egyptians conferred the names and titles of
their deities upon animals of every fpecies. A Lion
was El-Eon; hence græce λεων. I. 333. The Sun
was called Arez; and the Lion, which was an
emblem of the Sun, had the fame denomination:
and there is reafon to think, that the device upon
Charopian temples was fometimes a Lion. Homer
had undoubtedly feen the fierce figure of this animal upon fome facred portal of Egypt; to which
he often alludes, when he fpeaks of a Charopian
Lion. (Οδ. Λ. 610.)

Αρχλοιτ', αγροτεροι τε συες, Χαροποι τε Λεονλες.

This term feems to have puzzled the commentators.
Χαροποι, επιπληκλικοι, φοβεροι. Sch. ib. It was certainly an Amonian term: and the Poet alluded to
a Charopian temple. Hefiod. Theog. v. 321.

Της δ'ην Τρεις κεφαλαι, μια μεν Χαροποιο Λεονλος.

Homer (Hymn εις Μηλερα Θεων, v. 4.) mentions

Λυκων κλαγγην, Χαροπων τε Λεονλων.

As a Lion was from hence ftiled Charops, fo from
another temple it was called Charon. Χαρων ὁ λεων.
Hefych. Achilles (Lycoph. v. 260.) is ftiled
Αιχμηλης Χαρων, a martial Charonian Lion. 512,
and n.

ΛΟΦΟΙ

Μαςοειδεις. Thefe mounts were not only in Greece,
but in Egypt, Syria, and moft parts of the world.
They were generally formed by art; being compofed of earth, raifed very high; which was floped
gradually, with great exactnefs; and the top of all

S 3   was

was crowned with a tower. They were held in great reverence, and therefore confidered as places of fafety, and were the repofitories of much treafure. (See Jofephus, Bell. Jud. l. 7. p. 417.) There were often two of thefe mounds of equal height in the fame inclofure. To fuch as thefe Solomon alludes, when he makes his beloved fay, (Song, c. viii. v. 10.) *I am a wall, and my breafts like towers.* Though the word Chumah, or Comah, be generally rendered a wall; yet I think that in this place it fignified the ground, which the wall furrounded: an inclofure facred to Cham, the Sun, who was particularly worfhiped in fuch places. The Mizraim called thefe hills Typhon, and the cities where they were erected, Typhonian. But as they ftood within enclofures facred to Chom, they were alfo called Choma. This, I imagine, was the meaning of the term in Solomon's Song, and in fome other places.

In thefe temples the Sun was principally adored, and the rites of Fire celebrated; and this feems to have been the reafon, why the judgment denounced againft them is uniformly, that they fhall be deftroyed by Fire. If we fuppofe Comah to fignify a mere wall, I do not fee why fire fhould be fo particularly deftined againft a part, which is the leaft combuftible. (See Jeremiah xlix. Amos 1.) As the crime, which brought down this curfe, was idolatry, and the term ufed is Chomah; I fhould think that it related to a temple of Chom, and his high places, called by the Greeks Λοφοι μαςοειδεις. The ground fet apart for fuch ufe was generally oval; and towards one extremity of the long diameter, as it were in the focus, were thefe mounds, and towers erected. As they were generally royal edifices, and held facred, they were termed Tarchon. I. 418.

LUNA.

The fame deity was often mafculine and femi-
nine: what was Dea Luna in one country, was
Deus Lunus in another. I. 39. From Labana and
Lavana, came Luna. It is remarkable that the
Portus Argous in Hetruria was hard by the Portus
Lunus. Strabo, L. 5. And the people of thefe
parts are by Silius Italicus, L. 8. called Mæonians.
II. 446. n.

M.

MA, MAS, MACON,

IN many countries, where the Rhoia was not
known, the Poppy was made ufe of as an emblem
for the Ark: and it is accordingly found with ears
of wheat, and other fymbols, upon coins and
marbles, where Juno, Venus, Mithras, and other
deities are commemorated. The Poppy was by
the ancient Dorians ftiled Μαχων. Now Ma, and
Mas, among the Amonians fignified water, and
with fome latitude the fea. Ma-Con denoted the
deity worfhiped under the name of Pofeidon; and
fignifies Marinus deus, five Rex aquarum. II. 383.

MACAR.

This was a facred title given by the Amonians to
their gods:

Κλυθι, Μακαρ Παιαν, τιʃυοχʃονε, Φοιϲε Λυκωρευ.
Κλυθι, Μακαρ, πανδερκες εχων αιωνιον ομμα,

Orph. H. 33. 7. So Ελθε Μακαρ, to Hercules, and
to Pan. Κλυθι Μακαρ, to Dionufus. Alfo Μακαρ

Νηρευς. Κλυθι, Μακαρ, φωνων, to Corybas the Sun.
Many people affumed this title, and were ftiled
Μακαρις. Colonies are fuppofed to have been led
by an imaginary perfonage Macar, or Macareus.
Hence many cities and iflands were very anciently
named Macra, Macris, and Macaria. The Macares, who were the reputed fons of Deucalion, after
a deluge fettled in Chios, Rhodes, &c. Diod. Sic.
l. 5. The Græcians fuppofed the term to fignify
happy: hence Μακαρις Θεοι was interpreted ευδαιμονες;
how far true, cannot now be determined. Some
made Macar the offspring of Lycaon, others of
Æolus.

Diod. Sic. l. 5. fpeaks of Macareus as the fon of
Jupiter. This term is often found compounded,
Macar-On. Hence people called Μακαρωνες, and
Μακρωνες, and places Μακρων: and hence probably
the original of Μακαρων νησοι. They were to be
found in the Pontus Euxinus, as well as in the
Atlantic. The Acropolis of Thebes in Bœotia
was called Μακαρων νησος. The inland city
Oäfis, in an Egyptian province, had the fame name:
fo that the meaning of it muft not be looked for
in Greece. It was fometimes expreffed feminine,
Macris, and Macra, and interpreted *longa.* It
was certainly an ancient facred Amonian word, and
had no relation to length; but was grown fo obfolete, that the original purport could not be retrieved. There was a cavern in the Acropolis of
Athens, called Macrai,

Προσβορρον αντρον, ας Μακρας κικλησκομεν.

Eurip. in Ione. Macrai was a contraction for
Macar-Ai, or the place of Macar, a title of the
deity. I. 67.

MAGUS.

By Magus is probably meant Chus, the father of
thofe worfhipers of Fire, the Magi: the father alfo
of

of the genuine Scythæ, who were ftiled Magog,
l. 8,

MANES.

This term is derived from Man, Manus, and
Mania. Apuleius (Metam. l. xi.) introduces Ifis,
(the genius of the Ark) as calling herfelf *Regina
Manium.* Huetius (Demonft. Prop. 4.) fays,
Lares Varro Manes effe vult, Maniæ filios, quæ
dicitur vulgo Larunda. Mela (L. 1. c. 9.) fays,
that the Augelenfes, who lived near the Syrtes in
Africa, held the Manes, as the fupreme and only
deities. That to them they directed their prayers,
and made their offerings: and alfo fwore by them.
The Greeks and Romans did the fame thing: and
it is wonderful, that they fhould be fo blinded, as
not to perceive the true meaning. Moft of their
deities were formed out of titles: and the whole of
their worfhip was confined to a few deified men,
the Lares, Manes, and Dæmones. They were no
other than their Arkite anceftors, the Baalim of the
Scriptures: to thefe they offered; and to thefe
they made their vows. II. 455.

MAPS.

The Egyptians were very famous for geometrical
knowlege: and as all the flat part of their country
was annually overflowed, it is reafonable to fuppofe
that they made ufe of this fcience to determine
their lands, and to make out their feveral claims,
at the retreat of the waters: and in confequence,
that charts and maps were firft delineated in this
country. Thefe did not relate only to private de-
mefnes, but included the courfe of the Nile, and all
the fea coaft, and its inlets, with which lower
Egypt was bounded. It is very certain, that
the people of Colchis, who were a colony from
Egypt, had charts of this fort, with written defcriptions

fcriptions of the feas and fhores, whitherfoever they traded : and they at one time carried on a moft extenfive commerce. The Scholiaft upon Apollon. Rhod. L. 4. v. 279. fays, that the Colchians ftill retain the laws and cuftoms of their forefathers ; that they have pillars of ftone, upon which are engraved maps of the continent, and of the ocean. Apollonius himfelf calls them ΚυρΕις : they were of a fquare figure, like obelifks. If then the Colchians had this fcience, we may prefume that their mother country poffeffed it in as eminent a degree: and we are affured, that they were very knowing in this article. Clemens Alexandrinus (Strom. 6.) mentions, that there were maps of Egypt, and charts of the Nile very early. And we are moreover told, that Sefoftris (by which is meant the Sethofians) drew upon boards fchemes of all the countries, which he had traverfed : and copies of thefe were given both to the Egyptians, and to the Scythians, who held them in high eftimation. Euftath. Præf. Ep. to Dionyf. Rerieg. p. 18. This is a curious account of the firft delineation of countries, and origin of Maps; which were firft defcribed upon pillars. I. 385. (v. Atlas.)

Though the origin of Maps may be deduced from Egypt ; yet they were not the native Egyptians, by whom they were firft conftructed. Delineations of this nature were the contrivance of the Cuthites, or Shepherds. They were firft engraved on pillars, and in aftertimes fketched out upon the Nilotic papyrus. There is likewife reafon to think, that they were fometimes delineated upon walls. Pherecydes Syrus (Laert. L. 1, Jofeph. c, App. L. 1. c. 2.) is faid to have ftudied in Egypt. He fays that Zas, or Jupiter, compofed a large and curious robe, upon which he defcribed the earth, and the ocean, and the habitations upon the ocean. Zas, or more properly Zan, was the Dorian title of

Amon.

Amon, And Ogenus, the Ocean, was the most ancient name of the Nile, from whence the Græcians
borrowed their Ωκιανος. The word was a compound of Oc-Gehon, and was originally rendered
Ogehonus. It signifies the noble Gehon, and is a
name taken from one of the rivers of Paradise. The
robe abovementioned, was indeed a Pharos: a
building, a temple, which was not constructed by
the deity, but dedicated to him: upon the walls of
which were described, and otherwise delineated,
Ωγηνος και Ωγηνου δωματα, the course of the Gehon,
or Nile; and the towns and houses upon that river.
I. 390.

MEDUSA.

The head of Medusa in Argolis is said to have
been the work of the Cyclopians. This seems to
have been an ancient hieroglyphical representation
upon the temple of Caphisus (from Caph-Isis,
petra deæ Isidis.) It was usual with the Egyptians and other Amonians to describe upon the
architrave of their temples some emblem of the
deity, who there presided. Among others the
Serpent was esteemed a most salutary emblem; and
they made use of it to signify superior skill, and
knowledge. A beautiful female countenance surrounded with an assemblage of Serpents was
made to denote Divine wisdom, which was stiled
Meed, or Meet, the Μητις of the Greeks. Μεδουσα
is from Meed-Ous, the temple of Metis, or Divine
wisdom. The devices upon temples were often
esteemed as talismans, and supposed to have an
hidden, and salutary influence, by which the building was preserved. In the temple of Minerva at
Tegea was some sculpture of Medusa, which the
goddess was said to have given herself, *to preserve
the city from ever being taken.* (Pausan. L. 8.) It
was probably from this opinion, that the Athenians
6   had

had the head of Medufa reprefented upon the walls
of their Acropolis : and it was the infigne of many
cities, as we may find from ancient coins. I. 510.

MELECH, MALECH, MOLOCH.

These terms mean the fame, though differently
expreffed : they betoken a King; as Malecha does
a Queen.   It was an old title given to many deities
in Greece : it became obfolete, and was mifunder-
ftood ; fo it was often changed to Μειλιχος, and
Μειλιχιος, fignifying the *fweet, gentle, benign* deity.
Paufanias (L. 1. c. 2.) mentions a Jupiter Μειλιχιος
in Attica, and at Argos, and another (l. 1.) with
Artemis at Sicyon.   Thefe two, he fays, were of
great antiquity, placed in the temple before the
introduction of images ; the one was reprefented by
a pyramid, and the other by a bare pillar.   He
(l. 10.) alfo fpeaks of fome unknown gods at
Myonia in Locris, called Θεοι Μειλιχιοι : and of an
altar with this infcription, Βωμος Θεων Μειλιχιων.

Rivers often had the name of Melech, changed by
the Greeks into Μαλιχοι.   Malaga in Spain was
properly Malacha, the royal city.   Perhaps
Amelek was Ham Melech contracted. (1 Chron.
iv. 40.)   Malchom, the god of the Sidonians, was,
I fuppofe, a contraction of Malech-Chom, Βασιλευς
Ἡλιος, a title given to the Sun ; but conferred alfo
upon the chief of the Amonian family. (Zeph,
i. 4.) I. 70.

MELES, MELAS.

The terms El, Ees, are fometimes combined
with the name of Ham; as Hameles, Hamelas;
contracted to Meles, Melas.   There were rivers of
thefe names.   A Meles in Pamphylia, another
near Smyrna, both noted for their moft cold and
pure water; a Melas in Cappadocia, which ran
through a hot, inflammable country, and formed
many

many fiery pools. In Pontus was Amafus, Amafia, Amafeæ, where the region abounded with hot waters. I. 33.

MELIBOCHI,

The name of a mountain in Germany (near which Crodo, the Saturn of the Latines, together with Ifis, was worfhipped,) feems to be a variation of the ancient terms Melech Bochus, the Lord Bochus. Bacchus was often miftaken for Dionufus, and in many countries called Bochus, and Bocchus; as in Mauritania and Numidia. II. 265.

MELICARTUS,

The Hercules of the Phenicians and Cretans, was properly Melech-Carta, the deity of the place. I. 92.

MELISSÆ, MELITTÆ.

The priefts of the Seira (who was alfo ftiled Me-litta and Meliffa) were called Meliffæ, and Melittæ, and the votaries in general had that appellation. Many colonies went abroad under this appellation; and may be plainly traced in different parts of the world: but the Græcians have fadly confounded the hiftories, where they are mentioned, by inter-preting Meliffæ, *Bees.* II. 375.

MEMPHIS,

In Egypt; even this city, if we may believe the Græcians, was built by Argives. But by this was certainly meant Arkites; for Argos itfelf in the Peloponnefus could not have fupplied perfons to have effected, what was fuppofed to have been done by them. II. 506.

MEN,

MHN, MENES, MANES, MENON,

Were all terms, by which the Lunar god (deus Lunus, i. e. Noah) was in different countries diſtinguiſhed. This deity was repreſented by a luſhette; which did not relate to the planet in the heavens, but to the Patriarch, and to the Ark: for the lunette greatly reſembled the ſacred ſhip, ναυς αμφιπρυμναῖς, under which ſemblance the Ark was deſcribed. It was accordingly reverenced under this type in many places. II. 310.

In the mythology of the Ark, and the Jonah, there is continually ſome reference to the moon; the former from its figure being ſtiled Μην. Hence it is, that the Moon by the Egyptians was eſteemed the mother of all beings: for the Moon and the Ark were ſynonimous terms. 333. Meno-Taurus, ſignifies Taurus Lunaris, and was a ſacred emblem. I. 403. n.

As the name of the deity Meen and Manes, was changed to Magnes, ſo the people thence denominated had alſo the title of Magnetes; which was the uſual appellation given to them by the natives of Aſia. II. 514. The Meneiadæ, who were prieſts and prieſteſſes of Menes, were ſaid to be changed into birds, becauſe, like the Peleiades and Trerones, they were Ionim. II. 291.

MENELAUS

Was of old, according to Heſychius, ſtiled Pitanates; and the reaſon of it may be known from his being a Spartan, by which was intimated one of the Serpentigenæ, or Ophites. Hence he was repreſented with a Serpent for a device upon his ſhield. I. 488.

MENTOR.

MENTOR.

As many facred towers were feminaries of learning, (v. Chiron.) Homer from one of them has formed the character of fage Mentor; under whofe femblance the goddefs of wifdom was fuppofed to be concealed. By Mentor, I imagine, that the Poet covertly alludes to a temple of Menes. It is faid, that Homer in an illnefs was cured by one Mentor, the fon of Alcimus. The perfon probably was a Mentorian prieft, who did him this kind office, if there be any truth in the ftory. I. 440.

MEROPES.

This was another name given to thofe of the difperfion. Epiphanius adv. Hær. l. 1. p. 6. And he further fuppofes that the language of mankind at Babel was changed. Many other writers have imagined, that there was at Babel an univerfal change of language. But the author of the Chronicon Pafchale (p. 49.) more truly confines the change to found and utterance; διὰ τὴν αἰτίαν καὶ Μέροπες πάντες κεκλῆναι, διὰ τὴν Μεμερισμένην τὴν φωνήν.

Many of the family of Chus came into Hellas, Myfia, and Ionia. They poffeffed fome of the beft iflands of the Ægean fea: Cos, or Cöus, by which is meant Χοͅς, the Græcian name of Chus, was particularly occupied by the Cuthites, who preferved many memorials of their original.

The two principal occurrences preferved by the Cuthites were the Deluge, and Difperfion: and they ftyled themfelves both Ogugians, and Meropians from thefe circumftances. Hence Cöus is fo characterized. Callim. H. in Del. v. 160. fpeaking of Latona;

Ὠγυγίην δ' ἥπειλα Κόων Μεροπηίδα ῆσον
Ἰκέτο——

The

The Meropidæ were the fuppofed defcendants
of Merope; and likewife of Merops. The latter
was by fome looked upon as the author of Dæmon
worſhip; confequently one of the firſt, who introduced innovations in religion. They were the
fame as the Heraclidæ, or Herculeans; though
Pindar (Iſth. Od. 6. v. 46.) fuppofes them to
have been conquered by Hercules, who fubdued
all the Meropians. But Hercules was the chief
deity of the firſt ages: and in the fubduing of the
Meropes we have an ancient tradition tranſmitted;
which the Coans had preferved. It related to their
difperfion, and to the Giant monarch (Nimrod)
who was by way of eminence ſtyled Al-Cuon, or
the great king. If therefore, inſtead of Hercules,
we fubſtitute *Divine Vengeance,* the purport of the
tradition will be plain. (v. Pind. Nem. Od. 4.
v. 42.)

Some feem to apply the term Merops to all
mankind: Μεροπες, ανθρωποι. Hefych. But they
were a particular ràce; Pindar (*fupra*) mentions
Μεροπων εθνεα, intimating, that there were feveral
nations of them. The Athenians were Meropians
by being Nebridæ. They were alfo ſtyled Erect-
heidæ, or the defcendants of Erectheus, who was
faid to be the father of Merope. A large body of
this family occupied a region far in the weft, called
Μεροπιδα γην: they were the Atlantians, who fettled
in Mauritania; and were of the Titanian race.
They were the fame as the Cuthite Erythreans:
and the ocean, upon which they lived, was called
the Erythrean fea. There was an Erythrean fea
alfo in the eaſt, where lived the Indo-Cuthites, a
people of the fame family as the Meropes, and
called Æthiopes, Mauri, and Erythræi. In ſhort,
in almoſt all places, where the Cuthites fettled, the
titles of Æthiopes, Titanes, Mauri, Erythræi, and
alfo of Meropes will be found.

The

The Trojans alſo were of this family: and Homer, ſpeaking of the foundation of Troy, mentions
it as πολις Μεροπων ανθρωπων (Ιλ. Υ. v. 215.) *a city of*
the Diſperſed. The Trojans, and Myſians, were of
a different family from the native Phrygians; being
of the ſame lineage, with the people of Hellas and
Ionia. The Phrygians were the deſcendants of
Japhet, and Javan: and poſſeſſed the whole country,
except ſome diſtricts upon the ſea-coaſt. As they
were of a different race, ſo they had a language of
their own diſtinct from that of Troas. They were
likewiſe in ſubjection to a king, who is repreſented
as monarch of the whole country. All this is to
be obtained from the evidence of Homer himſelf.
(Iliad. Τ. v. 295. H. to Venus, v. 109. See alſo
Strabo, l. 13. p. 910.) But the Græcians and
Trojans were of the ſame family, however they
may be repreſented, as in a ſtate of warfare: and
they are introduced as ſpeaking the ſame language.
Priam's people could converſe with their enemies:
but their allies differed from them in ſpeech, and
indeed from one another. As the Trojans were
Meropes and Titanians, they were conſequently
Αθαναλοι, or of the race of the Immortals. Their
language accordingly is characterized by Homer as
the language of the gods. It was the Amonian, or
Titanian tongue: and we often find it oppoſed
to that of men, which was the language of Japhet
and Javan. (See Hom. Il. Α. v. 402. Β. 811.
Ε. 289. Τ. 73. Od. Κ. 304. Μ. 61. Schol. in
Theocr. Idyl. 13. v. 22.) Hence we find, that
there were two languages alluded to by the Græcian writers; one of which was the Meropian, or
that of the Diſperſed; the other was the language
of Javan. III. 427.

METHANE.

Almoft all the places in Greece were of oriental etymology; or at leaft from Egypt. I fhould fuppofe that the name of Methane in the Peloponnefus had fome relation to a fountain, being compounded of Meth-An, the fountain of the Egyptian deity Meth, the Μητις of the Greeks. We learn from Paufanias (l. 2.) that there was in this place a temple, and a ftatue of Ifis, and of Hermes in the forum; and that it was fituated near fome hot fprings. We find this term fometimes compounded Meth-On, of which name there was a town in Meffenia. (Paufan. l. 4.) I. 204.

MINERVA.

The Athenians were Saïtæ; and Minerva was ftiled Saïtis; and was worfhiped under that title at Pontinus near Epidaurus. She was undoubtedly fo named from the Olive, Saït, which was peculiarly facred to her.———Minèrva dicitur navem feciffe biproram, in qua Danaus profugit. (Hygin. F. 168.) II. 453.

MINES

Were held facred; and like fountains were denominated from Ænon, and Hanes, thofe titles of the Sun. In Arabia near Petra was a mine, named Phinon, and Phænon. Epiphanius (Adverf. Hær. l. 2. tom. 2.) mentions Φανησια μέταλλα, or the mines of Hanes. I. 90.

MINUA, MANIA, MONIA,

Are all of the fame purport; and relate equally to Selene the Moon. Μινυα, πολις Θετίαλιας, η προτερον Αλμωνια. (Steph. Byzant.) II. 448.

MINYÆ.

MINYÆ.

The votaries of the Patriarch, who was called Meen, and Menes, were ftiled Minyæ; which name was given to them from the object of their worſhip. II. 242. We muſt not look for the original of this term in Greece; but from among thoſe people, through whom it was derived to the Helladians. There were Minyæ, or Minnæi on the Red ſea, who were Arabians, and worſhipers of the Lunar deity. They did not refer this to the Moon; but to the Genius of the Ark, whom they ftiled Menith, Maneth, and Mana. One of their chief cities was named Manna-Carta, from this goddeſs there worſhiped. They called her alſo Mather, and Mither, ſimilar to the Mithra of the Perſians; by which was ſignified the Mother of gods and men. The Menæi in Sicily were ſituated upon the river Menaïs. They had traditions of a deluge; and a notion, that Deucalion was ſaved upon mount Ætna; near which was the city Noa. There were of old Minyæ in Elis, upon the river Minyas. There were Minyæ, or Menians in other parts: they were all Arkites. The chief title of the Argonauts was that of Minyæ. The genealogies relating to the perſons from whom the Argonauts are ſaid to be deſcended are all fictitious, and inconſiſtent; they were Minyæ, that is, Arkites. II. 510.

MITHRAS.

All waters, which had any uncommon property, were ſacred to Elees, or Eeſel. It was an ancient title of Mithras and Oſiris in the Eaſt, the ſame as Sol, or the Sun. I. 31. Nothing was more common among the Perſians, than to have their temples formed out of rocks. *Mithras e Petra* was in a manner a proverb. Porphyry aſſures us, that the

deity

deity had always a rock, or cavern for his temple, that people, in all places, where the name of Mithras was known, paid their worſhip at a cavern. (de Antro Nympharum. 263.) 223. The temple named Iſtacher, and the caverns in the mountains of Chuſiſtan, were ſacred to Mithras, and were made uſe of for his rites. Some make a diſtinction between Mithras, Mithres, and Mithra, but they were all the ſame deity, the Sun, eſteemed the chief god of the Perſians. 230.

MIZRAIM.

This perſon is looked upon as the father of the Egyptians; but his hiſtory is ſo veiled under allegory and titles, that no great light can be obtained. Some conſider Mizraïm as a people, not as a perſon. This people were the Egyptians; and the head of their family is imagined to have been Miſor, or Metzor. It is certain that Steph. Byzant. among other names ſtiled Egypt Μυαρα, which doubtleſs is a miſtake for Μυσαρα, the land of Muſar, or Myſar. Joſephus called Egypt Meſtra; Euſebius and Suidas Meſtraia, by which is meant the land of Metzor, a different rendering of Myſor. Sanchoniathon alludes to this perſon under the name of Μισωρ; and joins him with Sydic: both which he makes the ſons of the Shepherds Amunus, and Magus. Amunus, I doubt not, is Amun, or Ham, the real father of Miſor, from whom the Mizraïm are ſuppoſed to be deſcended. I. 7.

Mizraim, who ſettled in Egypt, were branched out into ſeven families. Of theſe the Caphtorim were one; who ſeem to have reſided between Peluſium and mount Caſius, upon the ſea-coaſt. Caphtor, from whence the people were denominated, ſignifies a tower upon a promontory; and was probably the ſame as Migdol, and the original reſidence of the Caphtorim. This people made an

early

early migration into Canaan, where they were called Paleſtines, the Philiſtim of the Hebrews; and the country where they ſettled, was named Palæſtina. Whether the whole of their family, or only a part, are included in this migration, is uncertain. Be it as it may, they ſeem to have come up by Divine commiſſion, and to have been entitled to immunities, which to the Canaanites were denied. (Amos ix. 7.) In conſequence of this, upon the coming of the Iſraelites into Canaan, they ſeem to have been unmoleſted for years. They certainly knew from the beginning, that the land was deſtined for the Iſraelites, and that they only dwelt there by permiſſion. (Conſult Gen. xx. 15. xxi. 23. xxvi. 27. Joſhua xiii. 2.)

The other tribes of the Mizraim ſent out colonies to the weſt; and occupied many regions in Africa; to which part of the world they ſeem to have confined themſelves. The children alſo of Phut, the third of the ſons of Ham, paſſed very deep to the ſouthward: and many of the black nations are deſcended from them; more, I believe, than from any other family. Lybia proper, was peopled by the Lubim, or Lehabim, one of the branches from Mizraim. (Chron. Paſch. p. 29.) The ſons of Phut ſettled in Mauritania; where was a region and river called Phutia. Some of this family ſettled above Egypt near Ethiopia, and were ſtyled Troglodytæ. (Syncellus. p. 47.) Many of them paſſed inland, and peopled the Mediterranean country. In proceſs of time, the ſons of Chus, after their expulſion from Babylonia, and Egypt, made ſettlements upon the ſea-coaſts of Africa, and came into Mauritania. We accordingly find traces of them in the names, which they bequeathed to places; ſuch as Chuzis, Chuſarez, upon the coaſt; a city Cotta, a promontory Cotis, in Mauritania. By their coming into theſe parts the

T 3 memorials

memorials of the Phuteans were in some measure obscured. They are however to be found lower down; and the country upon one side of the river Gambia is at this day called Phuta.

It is not possible at this æra to discriminate the several casts among the black nations. Many have thought, that all those, who had *woolly* hair, were of the Ethiopian, or Cuthite, breed. But nothing can be inferred from this difference of hair: for many of the Ethiopic race had *strait* hair. (Herod. l. 5. c. 1.) And we are told by Marcellinus, that some of the Egyptians had a tendency to wool. From whence we may infer, that it was a circumstance more or less to be observed in all the branches of the line of Ham; but universally among the Nigritæ, of whatever branch they may have been. III. 293.

MNEUIS.

It is said of the Patriarch after the Deluge, that he became an husbandman. This circumstance was religiously recorded in all the ancient histories of Egypt. An Ox, so useful in husbandry, was, I imagine, upon this account, made an emblem of the Patriarch. Hence upon many pieces of ancient sculpture are seen the Ox's head with the Egyptian modius between his horns; and not only so, but the living animal was in many places held sacred, and reverenced as a deity. At Memphis they worshiped the sacred Bull Apis; at Heliopolis they held the Bull Mnevis, or Mneuis, in equal veneration. The like custom was observed at Momemphis, Aphroditopolis, and Chusa, except that in these places, the object of adoration was an Heifer or Cow.

That the Apis, and Mneuis, were both representations of an ancient personage is certain; and who that personage was, may be known from Diodorus. (l. 1.)

(l. 1.) He speaks of him by the name of Mneues: but confines his history to Egypt, as the history of Saturn was limited to Italy; that of Phoroneus and Inachus to Argos; of Deucalion to Theffaly.

Mneues, or as the ancient Dorians expreffed it, Mneuas, is a compound of Men-Neuas, and relates to the fame perfon, who in Crete was ftiled Minos, Min-Noas, and whofe city was Min-Noa: the fame alfo who was reprefented under the emblem of the Men-Taur, or Mino-Taurus. Diodorus fpeaks of Mneues, as the firft lawgiver; and fays, that he lived after the æra of the gods and heroes, when a change was made in the manner of life, among men. He defcribes him as a man of moft exalted foul; a great promoter of civil fociety, which he benefited by his laws, which were unwritten; thefe he received from the chief god Hermes, as of the greateft importance to the world. He was the fame as Menes, whom the Egyptians reprefented as their firft king; and a great benefactor. This was the perfon who firft facrificed to the gods, and brought about a great change in diet; a circumftance which occurs continually in the hiftory of the firft ages.

We find it made a characteriftic of almoft every ancient perfonage, *that he withdrew mankind from their favage and bloody repafts.* To this foul and unnatural manner of feeding, which prevailed in the Antideluvian world, the poets and mythologifts continually allude; and memorials of it were kept up in all their rites and myfteries, where one part of the ceremony confifted in eating raw flefh, which was often torn from the animal, when alive. [*See* Bruce's *Account of the Abyffinians.*] Menes, who put a ftop to this cruel practice, and introduced a more mild diet, is ftiled Meen by Herodotus, and was the fame as Men-Neuas above-mentioned: the fame alfo as the Men-Taur, and Taur-Men, of other countries. Diodorus

T 4   in

(in the prefent copies it is Ϛιουν Μνευην, without fenfe) calls this famous lawgiver Βουν Μνευην, Taurus Men-Neues; from whence we may judge, that he was the fame perfon, whom the Egyptians reverenced under the fymbol of the facred Bull; efpecially as it was called by the fame name Mneuas, and Mneues. II. 417.

MON.

The planet fo called was only made ufe of as a refemblance, and type of the Ark; and thence was called Mon, and Moon, as we may infer from the Hebrew: for מין, and מרנה, Mon and Monah, fignify in that language an image, or type. The name was at times differently expreffed, but related to the Genius of the Ark, who was worfhiped by the Canaanites under the title Baal Maon, (Ezekiel xxv. 9.) and whofe temple was the Beth-Meon of Jeremiah. (xlviii. 23.) This deity was the fame as Ifis, and Rhea. II. 444.

MONA.

Tacitus (De Mor. Germ.) takes notice, that the Suevi worfhiped Ifis: and he mentions that the chief object at their rites, was an Ark, or fhip; *fignum in modum Liburnæ figuratum*; which was held in great reverence. The like myfteries according to Artemidorus prevailed in one of the Britifh iflands: in which, he fays, that the worfhip of Damater was carried on with the fame rites as in Samothracia. (Strabo, l. 4.) I make no doubt, but that this hiftory was true; and that the Arkite rites prevailed in many parts of Britain; efpecially in the ifle of Mona, where in aftertimes was the chief feat of the Saronides, or Druids. Monai fignifies infula Selenitis, vel Arkitis. It was fometimes expreffed Menai; as is evident from the frith between the ifland and the main land
being

being ſtiled Aber Menai at this day. Aber Men-
Ai ſignifies fretum inſulæ dei Luni; which iſland
undoubtedly had this name from its rites. The
ſame worſhip was probably extended to ſome of the
Scottiſh Iſles, the Hebrides of the ancients, and
particularly into that called Columbkil. II. 473.

MONIMUS.

The emperor Julian acquaints us in his hymn to
the Sun, that the people of Edeſſa poſſeſſed a region, which from time immemorial had been ſacred
to that luminary: that there were two ſubordinate
deities, Monimus and Azizus, who were eſteemed
coadjutors, and aſſeſſors to the chief god. He
ſuppoſes them to have been the ſame as Mars and
Mercury: but herein this zealous emperor failed;
and did not underſtand the theology, which he was
recommending. Monimus and Azizus were both
names of the ſame god, the deity of Edeſſa, and
Syria. The former is undoubtedly a tranſlation of
Adad, which ſignifies μονας, or unitas; or more
properly primus. Azizus is a reduplication of a
like term, being compounded with itſelf; and was
of the ſame import as Ades, or Ad-Ees, from
whence the place was named. I. 27.

MONKS.

Plato ſays (de Repub. l. 10. p. 620.) that Orpheus out of diſguſt to womankind led the life of
a ſwan. The meaning certainly is, that he retired
to ſome cloiſter, and lived a life of celibacy, like a
prieſt. For the prieſts of many countries, but
particularly of Egypt, were recluſes; and devoted
themſelves to celibacy: hence Monkery came
originally from Egypt. I. 381.

MOSES.

MOSES.

Emblems in the firft ages feem to have been
fimilar in moft countries: and to have almoft univerfally prevailed.   The facred writers often allude
to them: and many of them were retained even in
the church of God.   For the fymbol thus admitted
was a very proper memorial: and all the emblems
were originally the beft which could be devifed, to
put people in mind of what had paffed in the infancy of the world.   The whole was defigned as a
difplay of God's wifdom and goodnefs: and to
tranfmit to lateft pofterity memorials of the prefervation of mankind.   The fymbols in ancient
times were inftead of writing; harmlefs, if not
abufed: nay of great confequence when directed to
a proper purpofe.   Such were the Serpent, the
Ark, the Iris, the Dove; together with many
others, to which there are apparent allufions in
Scripture.   Thefe were known to the Ifraelites before their defcent into Egypt: being originally
from that country beyond the flood, where their
fathers of old refided.   And when properly applied,
they were as innocent as the elementary characters,
by which the fame hiftories were in aftertimes recorded.   The lifting up of the Serpent in the wil-
dernefs was proper as a prophetic defignation, and as
pertinent to the people, to whom it was exhibited,
as the purport would have been, if expreffed by
letters, and written at length upon a tablet.   It is
true that thefe fymbols were at laft perverted; and
the memorials abovementioned degenerated into
idolatrous rites and worfhip.   It was accordingly
the purpofe of Providence, in its difpenfation to
the Ifraelites, to withdraw them from this idolatry
of the Gentiles: and this was effected, not by de-
nying them the ufe of thofe characters, which were
the current types of the world, and to which they
had

had been conſtantly uſed; but by adapting the ſame
to a better purpoſe, and defeating the evil by a
contrary deſtination.

Upon the reſting of the Ark upon Mount Baris,
and the appearance of the Bow in the clouds, it
pleaſed God to make a covenant with man, and to
afford him ſome gracious promiſes. A memorial
of this was preſerved in the Gentile world. They
repreſented this under the type of an Ark; which
they ſtiled Barith, in alluſion to the covenant.
Some ages after, another covenant of a more peculiar nature was made by the Deity with the
poſterity of Abraham: and a law was promulgated
from mount Sinai. In conſequence of this, another Ark by divine appointment was framed,
ſeemingly in oppoſition to the former; and this
too was called the Ark of the covenant. This I
mention, becauſe many perſons have been alarmed
at finding ſometimes the ſame ſymbols among the
Egyptians as were to be found in the ordinances of
the Iſraelites. Both Spencer and Marſham have
animadverted upon this: and ſeem to have carried
their notions too far; for from them one might be
induced to imagine, that the Law of Moſes was in
a manner founded upon the rites of Egypt. But
there is not the leaſt reaſon for ſuch a ſurmiſe. The
religion of the two nations was eſſentially different:
and though ſome ſymbols were ſimilar, yet it does
not follow, that they were borrowed from that
quarter. They were many of them general types,
of great antiquity, and known to the whole world.
II. 528.

MUREX.

Every deity was by the ancients gratefully looked
up to as the cauſe of ſome bleſſing. The Tyrians
and Sidonians were famous for the manufacture of
purple: the die of which was very exquiſite, and
the

the difcovery of it was attributed to Hercules of Tyre; the fame whom Palæphatus ftiles Hercules Philofophus. Some will not allow him this honour; but fay, that his dog was the difcoverer. For accidentally feeding upon the Murex, he ftained his mouth with the ichor of the fifh; and from hence the firft hint of dying was taken. Such is the ftory; too childifh to admit of credit. It is not likely that a dog would feed upon fhell-fifh: befides the Murex is of the turbinated kind, and particularly aculeated; having ftrong and fharp protuberances, with which a dog would hardly engage. This ftory is founded upon the ufual mifconception of the Greeks. Hercules of Tyre, like all other oriental divinities, was ftiled Cahen, and Cohen, as was allowed by the Greeks themfelves. By this intelligence however they could not abide; but changed this facred title to Κυων, *a dog*, which they defcribed as an attendant upon the deity. Johannes Antiochenus, who tells this ftory at large, fays, that purple was the difcovery Κυνος Ποιμενικου, which in the original hiftory was undoubtedly *a Shepherd King*. I. 343.

MYRINA.

From a notion that the Amazonians were a community of women, hiftorians have reprefented the chief perfonage of their nation as a female. She is mentioned by fome as having flourifhed long before the æra of Troy: and it is faid more precifely by others, that fhe lived in the time of Orus, the fon of Ifis and Ofiris. This removes her hiftory far back; fo as to make it coeval with the firft annals of time. Her dominions lay in the moft weftern parts of Africa, at the extremity of Atlas; where the mountain terminated in the ocean. This country, Mauritania, was fuppofed to have been poffeffed by the Atlantes and Gorgons. The
Græcian

Græcian writers, who did not know that the fame family went under different titles, have often made the fame nation at variance with itfelf. And as they imagined every migration to have been a war-like expedition, they have reprefented Myrina as making great conquefts: and what is extraordinary, going over the fame ground, only in a retrograde direction, which Ofiris had juft paffed before.

According to Homer (Ιλ. B. v. 811.) fhe died in Phrygia; for he takes notice of her tomb in the plains of Troas; and reprefents it as a notable per-formançe.

Εςι δε τις προπαροιθε πολεως αιπυια κολωνη,
Εν πεδιῳ απανευθε, περιδρομος ενθα και ενθα·
Την ῃοι ανδρες Βαℸιειαν κικλησκουσιν,
Αθαναℸοι δε τε σημα πολυσκαρθμοιο Μυρινης.

The tomb of this heroine was in reality a facred mound, or high altar (v. Taph.); and Myrina a gentile divinity. In her fuppofed conquefts we may in great meafure fee the hiftory of Ofiris, and Perfeus, reverfed, and in fome degree abridged; yet not fo far varied, but that the purport may be plainly difcerned. II. 68.

·MYRRH,

Μυρρα, was denominated from Ham-Ourah. The Egyptians ftiled it Baal. I. 333.

N.

There is a hiftory mentioned by Arnobius (1. 5.) of a king's daughter in Phrygia, named Nana; who lived near the mountain, where Deucalion was fuppofed after the deluge to have landed. She is faid to have found a pomegranate, which fhe put into her bofom, and by its influence became with child. Her father fhut her up with an intent to deftroy her: during her confinement fhe produced Atis, or Attis; the perfon who firft inftituted the facred rites of Rhea, and Cubele, and who was looked upon as the fame with Apollo.—Paufanias (1. 7.) tells the fame ftory with additional circum-ftances: from all which we may perceive that it was an ancient tradition, and related to an hiftory of confequence; but taken from fome allegorical defcription, when the terms were imperfectly un-derftood. Nana feems to be a miftake for Naua: though the Patriarch does appear to be fometimes alluded to under the name of Nun, which is not much unlike Nana. Epiphanius mentions fome heretics, who worfhiped Idal-Baoth. This was either a place or machine, where the holy man Nun was fuppofed to have been born under the fem-blance of a Serpent. (v. Lilius Gyrald. Syntag. 1.) II. 382.

NAUPLIANS.

- The Cyclopians muſt have reſided at Nauplia in Argolis; a place in ſituation not unlike Hermione. Near it were caverns in the earth, and ſubterraneous paſſages, conſiſting of labyrinths cut in the rock, like the ſyringes in Upper Egypt, and the maze at the lake Mœris: and theſe alſo were reputed the work of the Cyclopians. Pauſanias (l. 4.) thinks very truly, that the Nauplians were from Egypt. He ſuppoſes that they were ſome of thoſe emigrants, who came over with Danaus. The nature of the works, which the Cyclopians executed, and the lake, which they named Acheruſia, ſhew plainly the part of the world from whence they came. I. 505.

ΝΑΥΣ.

There is reaſon to think, that in early times moſt ſhrines among the Mizraïm were formed under the reſemblance of a ſhip, in memory of the Deluge, and the conſervation of one family in the Ark. Nay, farther, both ſhips and temples received their names from hence; being ſtiled by the Greeks, who borrowed largely from Egypt, Ναυς and Ναος, and Mariners Ναυlαι, in reference to the Patriarch, who was variouſly ſtiled Noas, Naus, and Noah. II. 227.

NEBRIDÆ.

There was a family of this name at Athens, and another at Cos; they were, as we may infer from their hiſtory, the poſterity of people, who had been prieſts to Nimrod. I. 11.

NEITH, NEIT,

One of the Egyptian deities was ſo called: her prieſts were ſtiled Pataneit. I. 45.

NEPHELIM.

Perfons of great ftrength and ftature were ftiled among the people of the eaft Nephelim : which in after times the Greeks fuppofed to relate to νεφελη, *a cloud.* In confequence of this, they defcribed the Centaurs as born of a cloud ; and not only the Centaurs, but Ixion, and others, were reputed of the fame original. The chief city of the Nephelim ftood in Theffaly, and is mentioned by Palæphatus (c. 2.) ; but through the mifconception of his countrymen it was expreffed Νεφελη. The Græcians in general were of this race. The Scholiaft upon Lycophron (v. 22.) mentions that the defcendants of Hellen were by a woman named Nephele, whom Athamas was fuppofed to have married. Αθαμας ὁ Αιολου του Ἑλληνος παις εκ Νεφελης γεννα Ἑλλην, και Φριξον. The author has made a diftinction between Helle, and Hellen ; the former of which he defcribes in the feminine. By Phrixus is meant Φρυξ, who paffed the Hellefpont, and fettled in Afia minor. However obfcured the hiftory may be, I think the purport of it is plainly this, that the Hellenes, and Phrygians were of the Nephelim, or Anakim race. I. 435.

NEREUS.

Noah was figured under the hiftory of Nereus, a deity of the fea ; and his character of an unerring prophet, as well as of a juft, righteous, and benevolent man is very plainly defcribed. Hefiod. Theog. v. 233.

Νηρεα δ' αψευδη και αληθεα γεινα]ο Πον]ος,
Πρεσβυ]α]ον παιδων· αυ]αρ καλεουσι Γερον]α,
Ὁυνεκα νημερ]ης τε, και ηπιος· ουδε θεμιστεων
Ληθε] αι, αλλα δικαια και ηπια δηνεα οιδεν.

He

He is termed by Æfchylus παλαιγενής; and is
mentioned by Orpheus as a fon of the ocean, but
of all others the moft ancient. Orp. Argon. v. 334.

Νηρεα μεν πρωτιςα καλω, πρεσβυσον απανίων.

II. 270.

NIMROD,

The fon of Chus, (Gen. x.) his hiftory is plainly
alluded to under the character of Alorus, the firft
king of Chaldea : but more frequently under the
title of Orion.   The Cuthite colonies, which went
weftward, carried memorials with them of this their
anceftor; and named many places from him;
where will be found fome peculiar circumftances,
which will point out the great Hunter, alluded to
in their name.   The Græcians generally ftile him
Νεβρωδ : hence Nebrodes, a mountain in Sicily, a place
famous for hunting ; Nebriffa a town in Spain near
the mouth of Bœtis, called by Pliny (N. H. l. 3.
c. 1.) Veneria, a miftake probably for Venaria, as
the rites and memorials alluded not to Venus, but
Nimrod, and Bacchus.

The term Νεβρος, which the Greeks fubftituted
for Nimrod, fignifying *a Fawn*, gave occafion to
many allufions about a fawn, and fawn-fkin, in the
Dionufiaca and other myfteries.   The hiftory of
Nimrod was in great meafure loft in the fuperior
reverence fhewn to Chus, or Bacchus : yet there is
great reafon to think, that divine honors were of
old paid to him.   He feems to have been worfhiped
in Sicily under the names Elorus, Pelorus, and
Orion.   He was likewife ftiled Belus; but as this
was merely a title, and conferred upon other perfons, it renders his hiftory difficult to be diftinguifhed.   Nimrod built Babylon according to the
Etym. Magnum. I. 9.

U   NIOBE

NIOBE

Is the fame as Noubi, though by the Greeks
mentioned as a woman. She is reprefented as one,
who was given up to grief, for the lofs of all her
children. Her tears flowed day and night; till fhe
at laft ftiffened with woe; and was turned into a
ftone, which was to be feen on mount Sipylus in
Magnefia. (Paufan. L. 1. l. 8.)

Ιω, ϖανλαμω
Νιοϐα, σε δ᾽ εγωγε κεμω θεον,
Ἀτ᾽ εν ταφω ϖιλραιω
Αι, αι, δακρυεις. .

Sophocles in this paffage (Elect. 150.) fpeaks of
her as a goddefs. By fome fhe was reprefented as
the mother of Argus, II. 241.

NOAH.

The hiftory of the Patriarch was recorded by the
ancients through their whole theology: but it has
been obfcured by their defcribing him under fo
many different titles, and fuch a variety of characters. They reprefented him as Thoth, Hermes,
Janus, Menes, Ofiris, Zeuth, Atlas, Deucalion,
Xuthus, Inachus, Nereus, Pofeidon, Proteus, Prometheus, Phoroneus, Saturn, Dionufus, to which
lift a farther number of great extent might be added.
All the principal deities of the fea, however diverfified, have a manifeft relation to him. But
among all the various perfonages, under which he
may have been reprefented, there are none, wherein
his hiftory is delineated more plainly, than in thofe
of Saturn and Janus. II. 253.

This hiftory would have been abundantly more
clear, if the Greeks had not abufed the terms tra-
ditionally delivered, and transpofed them to words
in their own language. Indeed nothing has produced

duced greater confusion in these ancient histories, than that fatal turn in the Greeks of reducing every unknown term to some word, with which they were better acquainted. They could not rest, till they had formed every thing by their own idiom, and made every nation speak the language of Greece. Among the people of the East the true name of the Patriarch was preserved: they called him Noas, Naus, and sometimes contracted Nous: and many places of sanctity, and many rivers were denomi-nated from him,

Anaxagoras had been in Egypt; and had there obtained some knowledge of this personage. He spoke of him by the name of Noas or Nous; and both he and his disciples were sensible that it was a foreign appellation: yet he has well nigh ruined the whole of a very curious history, which he had been taught, by taking the terms in a wrong acceptation, and then making inferences in consequence of this abuse. Ὁι δε Αναξαγοραιοι ερμηνευουσι Νουν μεν τον Δια, την δε Αθηναν Τεχνην—Προμηθεα δε Νουν ελεγον· Προμηθεια γαρ ισιν ανθρωποις ο νους διο και μυθευονlαι τους ανθρωπους μἱαπιπλασθαι, δηλονόlι απο ιδιωlιας εις γνωσιν. He then proceeds to inform us, why they looked upon Nous to have been Prometheus: *because he was the renewer of mankind, and was said*, μἱαπιπλασθαι, *to have fashioned them again*, after they had been in a manner extinct. All this is to be inferred from the words above. But the author, while he is giving this curious account, starts aside; and forgetting that he is confessedly treating of a foreign term, recurs to his own language; and from thence frames a solution of the story. He tells us that Nous, which he had been speaking of as a proper name, was after all a Græcian term, νους, the mind: that *the mind was Prometheia; and Prometheus was said to renew mankind, from new forming their minds; and leading them by cultivation from ignorance to*

know-

knowledge. Thus have the Greeks by their affectation continually ruined hiſtory: and the reader may judge, how difficult it is to ſee the truth through the miſt, with which it is environed. [*See this point more fully treated.* II. 272.]
Suidas has preſerved from ſome ancient author a curious memorial of this wonderful perſonage; whom he affects to diſtinguiſh from Deucalion, and ſtiles Ναννακος, παλαιος ανηρ προ Δευκαλιωνος, τουΐον φασι βασιλεα γενεσθαι,——ός προειδως τον μελλονΐα καΐακλυσμον, συναγαγων παΐΐας εις το ιερον μεΐα δακρυων ικεΐευσε. και παροιμια επι Ναννακου, επι των σφοδρα παλαιων και αρχαιων. Suidas has done great injury to this curious tradition by a miſapplication of the proverb in the cloſe. What he alludes to was τα Ναννακου κλαιω, vel οδυρομαι; a proverb, which had no relation to time, nor to ancient perſons; but was made uſe of in a general calamity; whenever it could with propriety be ſaid, *I ſuffer, as Noah ſuffered*; or, *the calamities of Noah are renewed in me.* Stephanus Byzant. (Ικονιον.) gives great light to this hiſtory, and ſupplies many deficiencies. He calls the perſon Annacus, and like Suidas, makes him of great antiquity, even prior to the reputed æra of Deucalion. He ſuppoſes him to have lived above three hundred' years; at which period, according to an oracle, all mankind were to be deſtroyed, (Noah lived above three hundred years after the flood; which this writer has ſuppoſed to have been his, term of life when the flood came) this event happened by a deluge, which this author calls the deluge of Deucalion, inſtead of Annacus. In conſequence of which unfortunate diſtinction between two characters, which were one and the ſame, he makes the aged perſon to be deſtroyed in the general calamity, and Deucalion to be ſaved. He takes notice of the proverb; αφ' ού παροιμια, το επι Αννακου κλαυσεν, επι των λιαν οικΐιζομενων; and mentions the renewal

renewal of the world. However the story may have been varied, the principal outlines plainly point out the person who is alluded to in these histories. Many personages having been formed out of one has been the cause of great confusion both in these instances, and in numberless others. It seems manifest that Annacus and Nannacus, and even Inacus, relate to Noachus, or Noah. And not only these, but the histories of Deucalion, and Prometheus have a like reference to the Patriarch; in the sixth hundredth year of whose life (and not in the three hundreth) the waters prevailed upon the earth. He was the father of mankind, who were renewed in him.

Noah was the original Cronus, and Zeus; though the latter is a title conferred sometimes upon his son, Ham.

There is a very particular expression recorded by Clemens of Alexandria (Strom. l. 5.) and attributed to Pythagoras; who is said to have called the Sea Κρονου δακρυον; and there was a farther tradition concerning this person, καταπινειν τα τεκνα. The tears of Isis are represented as very mysterious. They are said to have flowed, whenever the Nile began to rise, and to flood the country. The overflowing of that river was the great source of affluence to the people: and they looked upon it as their chief blessing; yet it was ever attended with mystical tears, and lamentations; all this was certainly said, and done, in memorial of a former flood, of which they made the overflowing of the Nile a type.

As to the Deluge, as transmitted to us by Moses, (Gen. vi. vii. viii.) though it may appear short and concise; yet abounds with matter: and affords us a thorough insight into the most material circumstances with which that calamity was attended. The machine, in which Noah, &c. were secured,

was

was of fuch a make and conftruction, that it was never defigned to be managed, or directed by the hands of men. And it feems to have been the purpofe of Providence throughout to fignify to thofe, who were faved, as well as to their lateft pofterity, that their prefervation was not in any degree effected by human means. We may reafonably fuppofe that the particulars of this extraordinary event would be gratefully commemorated by the Patriarch himfelf; and tranfmitted to every branch of his family. In procefs of time, when there was a falling off from the truth, we might farther expect that a perfon of fo high a character as Noah, fo particularly diftinguifhed by the Deity, could not fail of being reverenced by his pofterity: and when Idolatry prevailed, that he would be one of the firft among the fons of men, to whom divine honours would be paid. We might conclude that thefe memorials would be interwoven in the mythology of the Gentile world: and that there would be continual allufions to thefe ancient occurrences in the rites and myfteries; as they were practifed by the nations of the earth. And in conformity to thefe fuppofitions, the diligent inquirer will find, that thefe things did happen: that the hiftory of the Deluge was religioufly preferved in the firft ages; that every circumftance of it is to be met with among the hiftorians and mythologifts of different countries; and that traces of it are to be particularly found in the facred rites of Egypt, and of Greece.

The moft particular hiftory of the Deluge, and the neareft of any to the account given by Mofes, is to be found in Lucian (De dea Syria.) He was a native of Samofata, a city of Commagene upon the Euphrates: a part of the world where memorials of the Deluge were particularly preferved; and where a reference to that hiftory is continually

to be obferved in the rites and worfhip of the
country. His knowledge therefore was obtained
from the Afiatic nations, among whom he was
born; and not from his kinfmen the Helladians,
who were far inferior in the knowledge of ancient
times. He defcribes Noah under the name of
Deucafion: and fays, " that the prefent race of
" mankind are different from thofe, who firft
" exifted; for thofe of the antedeluvian world were
" all deftroyed. The prefent world is peopled
" from the fons of Deucalion; having encreafed to
" fo great a number from one perfon. In refpect
" to the former brood, they were men of violence,
" and lawlefs in their dealings. They regarded
" not oaths, nor obferved the rites of hofpitality,
" nor fhewed mercy to thofe, who fued for it. On
" this account they were doomed to deftruction:
" and for this purpofe there was a mighty eruption
" of waters from the earth; attended with heavy
" fhowers from above; fo that the rivers fwelled,
" and the fea overflowed, till the whole earth was
" covered with a flood, and all flefh drowned.
" Deucalion alone was preferved to repeople the
" world. This mercy was fhewn to him on ac-
" count of his juftice and piety. His prefervation
" was effected in this manner: he put all his fa-
" mily, both his fons and their wives, into a vaft
" ark, which he had provided; and he went into
" it himfelf. At the fame time animals of every
" fpecies, boars, horfes, lions, ferpents, whatever
" lived upon the face of the earth, followed him by
" pairs: all which he received into the ark, and
" experienced no evil from them: for there pre-
" vailed a wonderful harmony throughout, by the
" immediate influence of the Deity. Thus were
" they wafted with him, as long as the flood en-
" dured." After this he proceeds to mention
that, upon the difappearing of the waters, Deuca-

lion went forth from the ark, and raifed an altar to
God : but he tranfpofes the fcene to Hieropolis in
Syria ; where the natives pretended to have very
particular memorials of the Deluge. II. 195.

As the Patriarch was efteemed the author of the
firft fhip, which was navigated, he was in confequence of it made the god of feamen ; and his temple
was termed ἱερον Ποσειδωνος Κανωβου. He was efteemed
the fame as Serapis : and infcriptions in the city,
or rather temple, called Canopus, Canobus, Canoubis, upon the moft weftern outlet of the Nile,
have been found dedicated to him under the title of
Θεος Σωτηρ.　In this temple, or rather college, was a
feminary for aftronomy, and other marine fciences.
Ptolemy, the great Geographer, ftudied here. The
name of the temple was properly Ca-Noubi : the
latter part, Noubi, is the oracle of Noah. II. 240.

NYMPHA.

Hot fprings were imagined to be more immediately under the infpection of the Nymphs : whence
Pindar (Olym. Od. 12.) ftiles fuch fountains Θερμα
Νυμφαν λουτρα.　The temple of the Nymphæ Ionides
in Arcadia ftood clofe to a fountain of great efficacy.
The term Numpha will be always found to have a
reference to water.　As the Greeks changed Ain
Omphe to Nympha, a goddefs, they accordingly
denominated the place itfelf Nymphæum, and
wherever a place occurs of that name, there will be
found fomething particular in its circumftances,
e. g. there was a method of divination at Rome,
mentioned by Dion Caffius, in which people
formed their judgment of future events from the
fteam of lighted frankincenfe. The terms of enquiry were remarkable : for their curiofity was
indulged in refpect to every future contingency,
excepting death and marriage. The place of divination was called Nymphæum. I. 277.

NYMPHÆA.

NYMPHÆA.

Above all other aquatics of the Nile the Nymphæa feems to have been regarded: which is reprefented as the flower of the Lotus. It was efteemed a facred ornament by the priefts ; and we find it continually ufed for a kind of coronet upon the figures of Orus, when he is defcribed on the Lotus. It is alfo to be feen upon the heads of Ifis and Ofiris; and the ferpents Cnuphis and Thermuthis are generally crowned with this flower, II. 400.

O.

OB.

A SERPENT in the Egyptian language was ftiled Ob, or Aub; though poffibly it may be only a variation of Oph. It was an emblem of the Sun; alfo of time and eternity: it was worfhiped as a deity, and efteemed the fame as Ofiris; by others the fame as Vulcan. Orus Apollo (c. 1.) fays, that the bafilifk or royal Serpent was named Ουβαιος: it fhould have been rendered Ουβος; for Ουβαιος is a poffeffive, not a proper name. The deity fo denominated was efteemed prophetic ; and his temples were applied to as oracular.

This idolatry is alluded to by Mofes (Levit. xx.) who in the name of God forbids the Ifraelites ever to enquire of thofe dæmons Ob and Ideone: which
shews

fhews that it was of high antiquity. The fymbolical worfhip of the ferpent was in the firft ages
very extenfive; and was introduced into all the
ceremonies wherever celebrated. This term was
alfo compounded with On: and Kircher fays that
Obion is ftill among the people of Egypt the name
of a ferpent. I. 48. From Ob-El, Pytho deus,
came Obelia; Οϐιλιαι, placentæ. Athenæus (l. 14.)
I. 298. On-Ob, is Sol Pytho. Onoba, regio Solis
Pythonis. I. 263. n.

OCEANUS.

As time with the ancients commenced at the
Deluge; and all their traditions, and all their genealogies terminated here: even the birth of mankind went with them no higher than this epocha:
they made the Ocean in confequence of this the
Father of all things. Under this character, which
was no other than that of Nereus, Proteus, and Pofeidon, they reprefented the Patriarch, the real
Father of the poftdiluvian world. He was the Θιος
Γινισιος, Γινιθλιος, Φυἶαλμιος; and was worfhiped alfo
as Oceanus. The poets often allude to him under
this title: (Orphic. Hymn. 82.)

Ωκιανον καλιω, ϖαἰιρ' αφθἰἶον, αιιν ιοἶα,
Αθαναἶων τι Θιων γινισιν, Θνηἶων τ' ανθρωπων.

Juno tells Jupiter, that fhe is going to pay a vifit
to Tethys and Oceanus, from whom the gods were
derived. (Homer. Ιλ. Ξ. v. 200.)

Ειμι γαρ οψομινη ϖολυφορϐου ϖιιραἶα Γαιης,
Ωκιανον τι Θιων γινισιν, και μηἶιρα Τηθυν,
'Οι μ' ιν σφοισι δομοισιν ιυτριφον, ηδ' αἶιἶαλλον.

Hence, when it was faid in the early hiftories,
which Thales, and other Græcians copied, that all
things were derived from water; I do not believe,
that the ancient Mythologifts referred to that
element,

element, as the material principle; but to the
Deluge, as an epocha, when time, and nature, and
mankind were renewed. Plutarch (If. et Ofir.)
mentions it, as an Egyptian notion, that all things
proceeded from water: but at the fame time tells
us, that Ofiris was Oceanus. Hence the doctrine
amounts to no more than this; that all were derived from Ofiris, the fame as Pofeidon, the fame
alfo as Dionufus, the Father of mankind. II. 271.

OENONE.

This nymph was in reality a fountain, Ain-On,
in Phrygia. The ifland Ægina was named
Oenone, and Oenopia, probably from its worfhip,
I. 52.

OKTΩ.   OGDOAS.

The Ark according to the traditions of the
Gentile world was prophetic; and was looked upon
as a kind of temple, a place of refidence of the
Deity, in the compafs of Eight perfons. It comprehended all mankind: which Eight perfons were
thought to be fo highly favoured by heaven, that
they were looked up to by their pofterity with great
reverence; and came at laft to be reputed deities.
Hence in the ancient mythology of Egypt, there
were precifely Eight gods: of thefe the Sun was
the chief, and was faid firft to have reigned. Some
made Hephaiftus the firft king; others Pan;
(v. Herod. l. 2. c. 145.) here is no inconfiftency;
they were titles of the fame deity the Sun: and
when divine honours began to be paid to men, the
Amonians conferred thefe titles upon the great
Patriarch, as well as upon his fon Amon. And as in
the hiftories of their kings, the Egyptians were able
to trace the line of their defcent upwards to thefe
ancient perfonages; the names of the latter were by
thefe means prefixed to thofe lifts; and they were
in

in aftertimes thought to have reigned in that country. This was the celebrated Ogdoas of Egypt, which their posterity held in such high veneration, that they exalted them to the heavens, and made their history the chief subject of their Sphere. II. 233.

OMPHI.

This term is of great antiquity, and denotes an oracular influence, by which people obtained an insight into the secrets of futurity. Hermæus in Plutarch (If. et Ofir.) expresses this term ομφις; and says, that it was the name of an Egyptian deity: he interprets it ευεργέτης. The true rendring was Omphi or Amphi, the oracle of Ham, or Cham, the Sun, or Ofiris. His oracles were stiled both Omphi and Ompi, in consequence of this the mountains, where they were suppofed to be delivered, came to be denominated Har-al-Ompi; which Al-Ompi by the Greeks was changed to Ολυμπος; and the mountain was called ορος Ολυμπου. There were many of this name. They were all looked upon to be prophetic; and suppofed to be the refidence of the chief deity, under whatever denomination he was fpecified, which was generally the god of Light. For thefe oracles no place was of more repute than the hill at Delphi, called Omphi-El, or the oracle of the Sun.

But the Greeks, who changed Al-Omphi into Olympus, perverted thefe terms in a manner ftill more ftrange: for finding them fomewhat fimilar in found to a word in their own language, their caprice immediately led them to think of Ομφαλος, a Navel, which they fubftituted for the original word. This they did uniformly in all parts of the world; and always invented fome ftory to countenance their miftake. Hence, whenever we meet with an idle account of a navel, we may be pretty
sure

fure that there is fome allufion to an oracle.   In
refpect to Delphi, they prefumed that it was the
Umbilicus, or center of the whole world.   The
poets gave into this notion without any difficulty.
Livy (l. 38. c. 47.) does not fcruple to accede to
this notion.   Strabo fpeaks of it with fome hefitation (l. 9. p. 642.)   Varro (de Ling. Lat. l. 6.)
very fenfibly refutes this idle notion.   Epimenides
(Plutarch. περι λιλοιπ. Χρησηρ.) had long before faid
the fame ;

Ουτε γαρ ην γαιης μεσος ομφαλος, ουτε θαλασσης.

But fuppofing·that this name and character had
fome relation to Delphi, how are we to account for
other places being fo called?   They could not all
be umbilical: the earth cannot have different
centers.   Nor could the places thus named be
always fo fituated, as to be central in refpect to the
nation, or the province, in which they were included.   Writers try to make it out this way : yet
they do not feem fatisfied with the procefs.   The
contradictory accounts fhew the abfurdity of the
notion.   It was a term borrowed from Egypt,
which was itfelf an Omphalian region.   What the
Græcians ftiled Omphalus was certainly Ompha-
El, the fame as Al-Ompha; and related to the
oracle of Ham or the Sun : and thefe temples were
Prutaneia, and Puratheia, with a tumulus or high
altar, where the rites of fire were in ancient times
performed.   As a proof of this etymology, moft of
the places ftiled Olympian, or Omphalian, will be
found to have a reference to an Oracle.   Diodorus
(l. 5.) fpeaking of an oracle in Crete, fuppofes that
the true name was ομφαλος; and fays, that it was fo
called (ftrange to tell) becaufe Jupiter, when he
was a child, loft his navel here, which dropped into
the river Triton.   Callimachus in his hymn to
Jupiter dwells upon this circumftance.   Who would
imagine,

imagine, that one of the wifeſt nations that ever
exiſted could reſt ſatisfied with ſuch idle figments?
and how can we account for theſe illuſions, which
overſpread the brighteſt minds? It is however to
be obſerved, that this blindneſs is only in regard to
their religion; and to their mythology, which was
grounded thereon. In all other reſpects they were
the wifeſt of the ſons of men. I. 235.

OMPAI.

The name of the ſacred cakes purchaſed at the
oracular temple of Ampi, Ompi. I. 297.

ON, EON, or AON,

A title of the Sun among the Amonians: hence
it was that Ham, who was worſhiped as the Sun,
got the name of Amon, and Ammon; and was ſtiled
Baal-Hamon. It is ſaid of Solomon, that he *had a
vineyard at Baal-Hamon* (Canticles viii.) a name
probably given to the place by his Egyptian wife,
the daughter of Pharaoh. I. 16.

OPH

Signifies a Serpent, and was pronounced at times,
and expreſſed Ope, Oupis, Opis, Ops; and by
Cicero (de N. Deor. l. 3.) Upis. The Greeks called Apollo himſelf Python, which is the ſame as
Opis, Oupis (Doricè) and Oub. Vulcanus Ægyptiis
Opas dictus eſt, eodem Cicerone teſte (Huet. Dem.
p. 83.) I. 47.

OPHELTES.

Lycurgus (v. Pauſan. l. 2.) is the ſame as Lycus,
Lycaon, Lycoreus, the Sun: and Opheltes his
ſuppoſed ſon, is of the ſame purport. Indeed
Opheltes, or, as it ſhould be expreſſed, Ophel-tin,
is the place; and Ophel the deity, Sol Pytho, whoſe
ſymbol was a Serpent. Opheltin was a Taphos
with

with a τεμενος, or facred inclofure: it was a facred
mound to the Ophite deity. Archemorus, like
Opheltis, was faid to have been left in a garden by
his nurfe, and in her abfence flain by a Serpent.
Each of them had feftivals inftituted, together with
facred games, in memorial of their misfortune.
They are therefore by many fuppofed to be the
fame perfon. But they were places, not perfons.
Opheltin is the place, and altar of the Ophite god;
and Archemorus was undoubtedly the name of the
neighbouring town or city. It is a compound of
Ar-Chemorus; i. e. the city of Cham-Orus, the
fame who is ftiled Ophel. I. 462.

ÓPHIOLATRIA.

It may feem extraordinary, that the worfhip of
the Serpent fhould have ever been introduced into
the world: and it muft appear ftill more remarkable, that it fhould almoft univerfally have prevailed.
As mankind are faid to have been ruined through
the influence of this being, we could little expect
that it would, of all other objects, have been
adopted, as the moft facred and falutary fymbol;
and rendered the chief object of adoration. Yet fo
we find it to have been. In moft of the ancient
rites there is fome allufion to the Serpent. παρα
παντι των νομιζομενων παρ' ύμιν θεων Οφις συμβολον μεγα
και μυστημον αναγραφεlαι. (Juftin. Mart. Apol. l. 1.)
This fymbolic worfhip began among the Magi, who
were the fons of Chus: and by them it was propagated in various parts.

Olympias, the mother of Alexander, was very
fond of thofe Orgies, in which the Serpent was introduced. Plutarch (in Alexandro) mentions, that
rites of this fort were practifed by the Edonian
women near mount Hæmus in Thrace; and carried
on to a degree of madnefs. She copied them
clofely in all their frantic manœuvres. She ufed

I   to

to be followed with many attendants, who had each
a Thyrſus with ſerpents twined round it.   They
had alſo ſnakes in their hair, and in the chaplets
which they wore: ſo that they made a frightful
appearance.   Their cries were very ſhocking: and
the whole was attended with a continual repetition
of the words, Evoe, Saboe, Hues Attes, Attes
Hues, which were titles of the god Dionuſus.

In Egypt was a Serpent named Thermuthis,
which was looked upon as very ſacred; and the natives are ſaid to have made uſe of it as a royal tiara,
with which they ornamented the ſtatues of Iſis.
Diodorus (l. 3.) tells us that the kings of Egypt
wore high bonnets, which terminated in a round
ball; and the whole was ſurrounded with the figures
of Aſps.   The prieſts likewiſe upon their bonnets
had the repreſentations of ſerpents.

It is ſaid that in the ritual of Zoroaſter, the great
expanſe of the heavens, and even nature itſelf, was
deſcribed under the ſymbol of a Serpent.   The like
was mentioned in the Octateuch of Oſtanes: and
moreover, that in Perſis and in other parts of the
Eaſt they erected temples to the ſerpent tribe, and
held feſtivals to their honour, eſteeming them θεους
τους μεγιϛους, και αρχηγους των ὁλων. (Euſeb. P.E. l. 1.)
The worſhip began among the people of Chaldea:
from thence it paſſed into Egypt, where the Serpent deity was called Can-oph, Can-eph, and
C'neph.   There were pillars ſacred to the Pytho
Sol, with curious hieroglyphical inſcriptions, which
alſo had the name of Ob-El: they were very lofty,
and narrow in compariſon of their length; hence
among the Greeks, who copied from the Egyptians,
every thing gradually tapering to a point was ſtiled
Obelos, and Obeliſcus.   Ophel was a name of the
ſame purport.

Hercules was eſteemed the chief god, the ſame
as Chronus; and was ſaid to have produced the
                                        Mundane

Mundane Egg. He was reprefented in the Orphic
Theology under the mixed fymbol of a lion and a
ferpent; and fometimes of a ferpent only. Where-
ever the Cuthites fettled, a notion prevailed that
that place fwarmed with ferpents. They came
under different names, Leleges, and Pelafgi; but
more particularly thofe of Elopians, Europians,
Oropians, Afopians, Inopians, Ophionians, and
Æthiopes; and in moft places where they
refided, there were handed down traditions, which
alluded to their original title of Ophitæ. Among
other places they fettled in Crete; and fo increafed
in numbers, that Minos, by an unfeemly allegory,
was faid οφεις ευρησαι.

The ifland Seriphus was one vaft rock; by the
Romans called faxum feriphium. It is ftiled by
Virgil (in Ceiri) *ferpentifera:* it had this epithet
not on account of any real ferpents, but according
to the Greeks from Medufa's head which was
brought hither by Perfeus, by this is meant the
Serpent deity, whofe worfhip was here introduced
by people called Perefians. What the Greeks
rendered Σεριφος was properly Sar-Iph, and Sar-Iphis,
the fame as Ophis: which fignified Petra Serpentis,
five Pythonis. Egypt is reprefented as having
been of old over-run with ferpents; and almoft de-
populated through their numbers. Diodorus (l.3.)
feems to underftand this literally: but a region,
which was annually overflowed, and that too for fo
long a feafon, could not well be liable to fuch a
calamity. They were ferpents of another nature:
and the hiftory relates to the Cuthites, the original
Ophitæ, who for a long time poffeffed that country.
They paffed from Egypt to Syria, and to the Euphrates: and mention is made of a particular breed
of ferpents upon that river, which were harmlefs to
the natives, but fatal to every body elfe. This
could not be underftood literally. They were

X   Ophite

Ophite priefts, who ufed to fpare their own people, and facrifice ftrangers; a cuftom which prevailed once in moft parts of the world. The Ophite priefts were very learned; and as they were Ophites, whoever had the advantage of their information, was faid to have been inftructed by Serpents. Hence there is a tradition, that Melampus was rendered prophetic from a communication with thefe animals. (Apollodorus, L. 1.) Something fimilar is faid of Tirefias.

As the worfhip of the Serpent was of old fo prevalent, many places and people received from thence their names. There were Opici, or Ophici in Campania; there were places called Opis, Ophis, Ophitæa, Ophionia, Ophioëffa, Ophiodes, and Ophiufa: there were alfo places denominated Oboth, Obona, and reverfed Onoba, from Ob, which was of the fame purport.

It may feem ftrange, that in the firft ages there fhould be fuch an univerfal defection from the truth: and above all things fuch a propenfity to this particular mode of worfhip, this myfterious attachment to the Serpent. What is fcarce credible, it obtained among Chriftians: and one of the moft early herefies in the church was of this fort, introduced by a fect, called by Epiphanius Ophitæ, by Clemens of Alexandria Ophiani. They are particularly defcribed by Tertullian (de Præfcript. Hæret. c. 47.) whofe account of them is well worth our notice. Accefferunt his Hæretici etiam illi, qui Ophitæ nuncupantur: nam ferpentem magnificant in tantum, ut illum etiam ipfi Chrifto præferant, ipfe enim, inquiunt, fcientiæ boni et mali originem dedit. Hujus animadvertens potentiam et majeftatem Moyfes æreum pofuit ferpentem: et quicunque in eum afpexerunt, falutem confecuti funt. Ipfe, aiunt, præterea in Evangelio imitatur ferpentis ipfius facram poteftatem, dicendo,

dicendo, et ficut Moyfes exaltavit ferpentem in deferto, ita exaltari oportet filium hominis. Ipfum introducunt ad benedicendum in Euchariftia fua. In the above we fee plainly the perverfenefs of human wit, which deviates fo induftrioufly; and is ever after employed in finding expedients to countenance error, and render apoftafy plaufible. It would be a noble undertaking, and very edifying in its confequences, if fome perfon of true learning, and a deep infight into antiquity, would go through with the hiftory of the Serpent. I. 473.

OPIUM,

By the Egyptians, was diftinguifhed by the facred name of Ophion. I. 333.

ORCHOMENUS

Is a compound of Or-Chom-Men, three titles, which need no explanation. II. 513.

ORCHOM-OUS,

(v. Plutarc. in Thef. v. 1. p. 13.) like Afterous, Ampelous, Maurous, Amathous, Achorous, fignifies a place facred to Or-Chom. He was the Orchamus of the eaft; and the fame perfonage from whom the cities called Orchomenos had their name. III. 478. n.

ΟΡΕΣΧΩΟΣ.

Strabo (l. 8.) fays, ἐνιοι Κωους μαλλον τα τοιαυτα κοιλωματα λεγισθαι φασιν. Hence he truly explains a paffage in Homer. (Iλ. I. v. 266.) The poet fpeaking of Thefeus, Dryas, Polyphemus, and other heroes of the Mythic age, mentions their encountering with the mountaineers of Theffaly, whom he ftiles φηρις ορισχωοι :

X 2

Καρτιροι

Καρτιτοι δη κεινοι επιχθονιων τραφεν ανδρων,
Καρτιτοι μεν ισαν, και καρτιτοις εμαχοντο
Φηρσιν ορεσχωοισι :

Ορεσχωος fignified a perfon, who lived in a mountain habitation : whofe retreat was a houfe in a
mountain. Co, and Coa, was the name of fuch
houfe. I. 115.

ORGAN.

This river, which ran into the Mæander from
the Campus Hyrcanus, was properly Ur-chan.
I. 210. n.

ORION.

Orion was Nimrod. Homer (Οδ. Λ. v. 571.)
defcribes him as a great hunter; and of an enormous ftature ;

Τον δε μετ' Ωριωνα Πελωριον εισενοησα,
Θηρας ομου ειλευντα κατ' ασφοδελον λημωνα.

The Poet ftiles him Pelorian; which betokens
fomething vaft, and is applicable to any towering
perfonage, but particularly to Orion. For the
term Pelorus is the name, by which the towers of
Orion were called. There was a famous tower
near Zancle, called Pelorus, becaufe it was facred
to Alorus (the firft king of Babylon) the fame perfon as Orion, and Nimrod. Diodorus (l. 4.) informs us that, according to the tradition of the
place, Orion there refided : and that, among other
works, he raifed this very mound and promontory,
together with the temple upon it.

The defcription in Homer (v. Otus) is of a
mixed nature : wherein he retains the ancient tradition of a gigantic perfon; but borrows his ideas
from the towers facred to him. All temples were
of old fuppofed to be oracular; and were by the

Amonians

Amonians called Pator and Patora (q. v.) this
temple was undoubtedly a Pator; to which mariners
reforted to know the event of their voyage, and to
make their offerings to the god; it was therefore
ftiled Tor Pator; which being by the Greeks expreffed Τριπαίωρ, gave rife to the notion, that this
earthborn giant had three fathers. Thefe towers
near the fea were made ufe of to form a judgement
of the weather, and to obferve the heavens; and
thofe, which belonged to cities, were generally in
the acropolis, or higher part of the place. This
by the Amonians was named Bofrah; and the citadel of Carthage, as well as of other cities, is
known to have been fo denominated. But the
Greeks by an unavoidable fatality rendered it
Βυρσα, a *fkin:* and when fome of them fucceeded to
Zancle in Sicily, finding that Orion had fome reference to Ouran or Ouranus, and from the name of
the temple (τριπαίωρ) judging that he muft have had
three fathers, they immediately went to work, in
order to reconcile thefe different ideas. They accordingly changed Ouran to Ουρειν; and thinking
the mifconftrued hide Ѕυρσα no improper utenfil for
their purpofe, they made thefe three fathers co-
operate in a moft wonderful manner for the pro-
duction of this imaginary perfon; inventing the moft
flovenly legend, that ever was devifed (Schol. in
Lycophron. v. 328. Etymol. Magn. v. Ωριων.)
Τρεις (θεοι) του σφαγεντος ѕοος ѕυρση ενουρησαν, και εξ αυτης
Ωριων εγενετο. Tres dei in bovis mactati pelle minx-
erunt, et inde natus eft Orion. I. 413.

ORITAE.

There were many tribes of people, who lay upon
the Indus and the Ganges; and who betrayed their
origin in their name. Of the latter river Dionyfius
(Peri. v. 1096.) thus fpeaks:

X 3

Κεινος τοι πολεων απολιμνεlαι εθνεα φωlων·
Ητοι μεν δυνονlος επι κλισιν ηελιοιο
Ωριlας τ' Αριβας τε, λινοχλαινους τ' Αραχωlας.

See alfo Prifcian. v. 1001. and the Scholiaft upon
Dionyfius more particularly; προς δυσιν του Ινδου
πολαμου Ωριlαι. The titles of Oritæ and Aribes,
like that of Æthiopes, were peculiar to the fons of
Chus. Hence, when mention is made of Scythia
Indica, and when Prifcian (v. 996.) tells us,

Eft Scythiæ tellus auftralis flumen ad Indum;

we may be affured that the country alluded to was
Cuthia. The inland Oritæ in fome degree degenerated from their forefathers, and became in habit
like the natives of the country; but differed from
them in fpeech, and in their rites and cuftoms;
(Arrian. Hift. Ind. p. 340. 338.) fo that we may
be affured, that they were not the original inhabitants, though they came thither very early. One
region of the Gangetic country was named Cathaia,
and the people Cathaians. Arrian fpeaks of them
as a very brave and refpectable people; and fays,
that their chief city was Singala. (Arrian. Exp.
Alex. L. 5.) Cathaia is no other than Cuthaia, as
Aribes is for Arabes; and the latter are rendered by
Arrian Αραβιες; (the country, to the weft of the
Indus, is called Araba at this day,) who fpeaks of
them as refiding upon one of the mouths of the
Indus, near the ifland Crocale. They lived upon
the river Arabis, which ferved as a boundary to
them, and to their brethren the Oreitæ. The chief
city of thefe latter was Ur, like that in Chaldea;
but expreffed by the Greeks Ωρα. They had been
for ages an independent people; but were obliged
to fubmit to the fortunes of Alexander, to whom
they furrendered their city. III. 197.

ORPHEUS.

He went over many regions of the earth; and in all places, whither he came, was efteemed both as a prieft, and a prophet. His fkill in harmony is reprefented as very wonderful. He is mentioned, as having been twice in a ftate of death; which is reprefented as a twofold defcent to the fhades below. There is alfo an obfcure piece of mythology about his wife, and a ferpent; alfo of the Rhoia or Pomegranate: which feems to have been taken from fome fymbolical reprefentation at a time, when the purport was no longer underftood. The Orpheans dealt particularly in fymbols, as we learn from Proclus (in Theol. Platon. L. 1. c. 4.) His character for fcience was very great: and Euripides (Alceft. v. 968.) takes particular notice of fome ancient tablets, containing much falutary knowlege, which were bequeathed by Orpheus to the Thracians. He one while refided in Greece, and particularly at Thebes in Bœotia. Here he introduced the rites of Dionufus, and celebrated his Orgies upon mount Cithæron. He is faid to have been the firft who inftituted thofe rites: and was the author of all myfterious worfhip. He went over a great part of the world. (Paufan. L. 5.)

'Ωϛ ιχομην επι γαιαν απειρέ]ον, ηδε πολναϛ,
Αιγυπ]ω, Λιϭυη τε, ϭρο]οιϛ ανα Ͽεσφα]α φαινων.

Writers differ as to the place of his birth: and there is great uncertainty about his parents. Plato (de Rep. L. 2.) ftiles both Orpheus, and Mufæus, .Σελnnϛ και Μουσων εγγονοι; in which account is contained fome curious mythology. He was not only a poet, and fkilled in harmony, but a great theologift, and prophet; alfo very knowing in medicine, and in the hiftory of the heavens. According to Antipater Sidonius, he was the author of heroic

X 4   verfe:

verfe : and fome go fo far as to afcribe to him the invention of letters; and deduce all knowledge from him.

Many of the things, reported to have been done by Orpheus, are attributed to Eetion, Mufæus, Melampus, Linus, Cadmus, and Philammon. Some of thefe are faid to have had the fame parents. As to his death, the common notion is, that he was torn to pieces by the Thracian women. His name occurs among the Argonauts. But there are who place him eleven generations before the fiege of Troy, confequently ten generations before that expedition. Some fay, that no fuch perfon ever exifted. The truth is, that under the character of Orpheus, we are to underftand a people named Orpheans; who as Voffius rightly intimates, were the fame as the Cadmians. In confequence of this, there will fometimes be found a great fimilarity between the characters of thofe two perfons.

Suidas fays, Ορφευς εςι πολις υπο τη Πιεριη. But the place was originally expreffed Orphi, by which is meant the oracular temple of Orus. From hence, and from the worfhip here inftituted, the people were called Orphites, and Orpheans. They were noted for the Cabiritic myfteries, and for the Dionufiaca, and worfhip of Damater. But the Græcians have comprehended under the character of one perfon the hiftory of a people.

They were much addicted to celibacy; and were in a great meafure reclufes after the mode of Egypt, and Canaan. According to the moft common accounts concerning the death of Orpheus, it was owing to his principles, and manner of life. He was a folitary, and refufed all commerce with womankind : hence the Mænades, and other women of Thrace, rofe upon him, and tore him to pieces. It is faid, that his head and lyre were thrown into the Hebrus; down which they were wafted to Lemnos,

This

This relates to the Orpheans; their temple on mount Hæmus was ruined; probably on account of the cruelties there practised, and their unnatural crimes, to which there are frequent allufions. Thofe who furvived, fled down the Hebrus, to Lefbos; where they either found, or erected a temple; and where the fame worfhip was inftituted. They feem to have named this temple Orphi, and Orphii caput; and it was famous for its oracle. The Babylonians had a great veneration for a temple called Orphi: but this was Ur, în Chaldea, the feat of the ancient Magi, ftiled Urphi, or Orphi, on account of its being the feat of an oracle; it was not a proper name, but an appellative, by which oracular places were in general diftinguifhed. Orphon, of the fame purport with Orpheus, was one of the appellations, by which the Magi were called. In fhort, under the character of Orpheus, we have the hiftory both of the deity, and of his votaries. The head of Orpheus was faid to have been carried to Lemnos, juft as the head of Ofiris ufed to be wafted to Byblus. He went to the fhades below, and returned; thus Ofiris was fuppofed to have been in a ftate of death, and after a time to have come to life. The death of Orpheus (which had fomething myfterious in it) was celebrated with the fame frantic acts of grief, as people practifed in their lamentations for Thamuz and Ofiris, and at the rites of Baal. Orpheus was the fame as Orus of Egypt, whom the Greeks efteemed as Apollo, and Hephaiftus.

Many undertook to write his hiftory; but all feem to have run into that general miftake of forming a new perfonage from a title; and making a deity a native, where he was enfhrined. The writings, tranfmitted under his name, were innumerable. There were fome curious hymns, which ufed of old to be fung in Pieria, and Samothracia; and which

Onomacritus

Onomacritus copied. They contain indeed little more than a lift of titles, by which the deity in different places was addreffed. But thefe titles are of great antiquity: and though the hymns are tranfmitted in a modern garb, the perfon, through whom we receive them, being as late as Pififtratus, yet they deferve our notice. They muft neceffarily be of confequence, as they refer to the worfhip of the firft ages, and afford us a great infight into the theology of the ancients. Thofe fpecimens alfo, which have been preferved by Proclus, in his differtations upon Plato, afford matter of great curiofity. They are all imitations, rather than tranflations of the ancient Orphic poetry, accompanied with a fhort comment. This poetry was in the Amonian language, which grew obfolete among the Helladians, and was no longer intelligible: but was for a long time preferved in Samothracia, and ufed in their facred rites. (Diod. Sic. L. 5.) II. 126.

ORUS,

The god of Light, was often ftiled Az-El. I. 206. He was the fuppofed fon of Ifis, who was an emblem of the Ark, that receptacle which was ftiled the Mother of mankind. He is reprefented as undergoing from the Titans all that Ofiris fuffered from Typhon: and the hiftory at the bottom is the fame. Hence it is faid of Ifis, that fhe had the power of making people immortal; and that, when fhe found her fon Orus in the midft of the waters dead through the malice of the Titans, fhe not only gave him a renewal of life but alfo conferred upon him immortality. II. 327. 330.

Both Orus, and Ofiris, were ftiled Heliadæ; and often reprefented as the Sun himfelf. Hence many have been mifled; and have referred, what has been faid of thefe perfonages, to the luminary. But the
Egyptians

Egyptians in this title did not allude to the Sun, but to a perfon, who had been wonderfully preferved; as appears from their hieroglyphics. 394. Orus is fometimes defcribed erect, but fwathed in bandages, like a perfon embalmed. In his hands he holds fome implements of art: over his fhoulder there feems to be the figure of a ploughfhare; and upon his head the Nymphæa. 400. No mention is made of any conquefts atchieved by him, as he was the fame as Ofiris; but he was more particularly Ofiris in his fecond ftate; and therefore reprefented by the Egyptians as a child. 83.

OSIRIS.

He appears to have been a wonderful traveller and conqueror; and is faid to have been the fon of Rhea: and his chief attendants in his peregrinations were Pan, Anubis, Macedo, with Maro a great planter of vines; alfo Triptolemus much fkilled in hufbandry. Some fay that he was born at Nufa in India; others at Nufa in Arabia; many make him a native of Egypt. He vifited many places upon the ocean: and although at the head of an army, yet he was attended by the Mufes, and the Sciences; his march likewife was conducted with fongs and dances, and the found of every inftrument of mufic. He built cities in various parts; particularly Hecatompolis, which he named Theba, after his mother. He inftructed the people in planting, and fowing, and other ufeful arts.

Primus aratra manu folerti fecit Ofiris,
Et teneram ferro follicitavit humum.

Tibullus, L. 1. El. 8.

He particularly introduced the vine; and taught the ufe of ferment to make barley wine. He was efteemed a great bleffing to the Egyptians, both as

a law-

a lawgiver and king. He firſt built temples to the
gods and was reputed a general benefactor of Mankind. He returned in triumph to Egypt, where
after his death, he was enſhrined as a deity. His
Taphos was ſhewn in many places. (v. Diod. Sic.
L. 1.) What was ſaid to be atchieved by one
perſon, was the work of many. Oſiris was a title
conferred upon more perſons than one; by which
means the hiſtory of the firſt ages has been in ſome
degree confounded.

In an inſcription on a ſacred pillar at Memphis,
he is ſaid to have been the ſon of Cronus. By
Cronus we are to underſtand the ſame perſon as is
alſo repreſented under the name of Sous; by which
is meant the Sun; under which title the Amonians
alluded to their great anceſtor, the father of all; as
by Oſiris they generally meant Ham. In reſpect
to the travels of Oſiris, the poſterity of Ham did
actually traverſe at different times the regions
which he was ſaid to have done; and in many of
them took up their abode. Oſiris is a title often
conferred on the great Patriarch himſelf: and there
is no way to find out the perſon meant but by obſerving the hiſtory, which is ſubjoined. II. 58.

Diodorus (l. 1.) ſays, ſome think that Oſiris is
Serapis; others that he is Dionuſus; others Pluto;
many take him for Zeus, or Jupiter; and many for
Pan. This was an unneceſſary embarraſſment: for
they were all titles of the ſame god. I. 309.

The following paſſage in Plutarch is too remarkable to be omitted. He ſays, that it was to avoid
the fury of Typhon, that Oſiris went into his Ark:
and that it happened on the ſeventeenth day of the
month Athyr, when the Sun was in Scorpio. Now
it is to be obſerved, that there were two feſtivals, at
oppoſite parts of the year, eſtabliſhed by the Egyptians on account of Oſiris being thus incloſed: one
in the month Phamenoth, which they termed
ἐμβασιν

εμζασιν Οσιριδος εις την Σεληνην; the other, was on the
fame account, but in autumn. This was the ceremony, ἡ λεγομενη καθειρξις εις την σορον Οσιριδος, in
memory of his having been in his life time thus
concealed: which Ark they termed Σεληνη, and other
nations Menoa, *the moon* (Μην Σεληνη). Plutarch
deſcribes the ſeaſon very preciſely, when Oſiris was
ſuppoſed to have been thus confined. It was in the
month Athyr, upon the ſeventeenth day of that
month; when the Eteſian winds were paſſed; when
the overflowing of the Nile had ceaſed, and the
country became dry; μηκυνομενης δε νυκτος αυξείαι το
σκότος. It was, in ſhort, upon the ſeventeenth day of the
ſecond month after the autumnal equinox, εν ᾧ τον
Σκορπιον ὁ Ἡλιος διεξεισιν: this, if I miſtake not, was
the preciſe month, and day of the month, on which
Noah entered the Ark. v. Gen. vii. 11. Hence,
I think, there can be no doubt, but in this hiſtory
of Oſiris we have a memorial of the Patriarch, and
the Deluge. As this event happened, according to
the Egyptian traditions, when the Sun was in
Scorpio; that ſign is continually commemorated
in the Diluvian hieroglyphics. II. 336.

Plutarch in de Iſid. et Oſir. endeavours to ſhew
that Bacchus and Oſiris were the ſame deity. One
reaſon, and that a plauſible one, is, that the ſame
plant is ſacred to both: the ivy of Bacchus being
called in the Egyptian language *chenoſiris*; which
he interprets *the plant of Oſiris*. But he makes a
wrong reference of the terms of which the word
conſiſts; and does not give the right interpretation.
The true reading is Chan Oſiris; and in the original,
Cahen or Cohen Sehor, *the lord Sehor* or *Oſiris*. It
is a name given to a vegetable; as among us plants
and flowers have names given them from great perſonages: but it does not originally ſignify a vegetable; being the title of the god to whom it was
conſecrated. *Obſerv.* 166.

OTUS

And Ephialtes: there is reafon to imagine, that
thefe gigantic youths, fo celebrated by the poets,
were two lofty towers. They were buildings to
Alohim, called Aloëus; and were probably thrown
down by an earthquake. (Diod. Sic. l. 5.) They
are fpoken of by Pindar as the fons of Iphimedeia;
and are fuppofed to have been flain by Apollo in
the ifland Naxos. Pyth. Ode 4.

ιν δε Ναξῳ
Φαν]ι Θανειν λιπαρα Ιφιμεδειας παιδας
Ωτον, και σε, τολμαεις Εφιαλ]α αναξ.

They are alfo mentioned by Homer (Οδ. Λ. v. 306.)
who ftiles them γηγενεις; and his defcription is fine.

Και ρ' ιλεκεν δυο παιδε, μινυνθαδιω δε γενεσθην,
Ωτον τ' αν]ιθεον, τηλεκλει]ον τ' Εφιαλ]ην·
'Ους δη μηκιςους Θρεψε ζειδωρος αρουρα,
Και πολυ καλλιςους με]α γε κλυ]ον Ωριωνα.
Εννεωροι γαρ τοιγε, και εννεαπηχεις ησαν
Ευρος, α]αρ μηκος γε γενεσθην εννεοργυιοι.

I. 412.

OURANUS.

The term Ουρανος related properly to the orb of
the Sun; but was afterwards made to comprehend
the whole expanfe of the heavens. It is compounded of Our-Ain, the fountain of Orus. I. 53.
In Cyprus was a temple to Our-ain, ftiled Urania.
92. The Cunocephali are faid to have given to
Hermes the firft hint of dividing the day into twelve
equal parts; δωδεκα]ις ημερας καθ' ικαςην ωραν ΟΥΡΕΙ
Κυνοκεφαλος. Horapollo. L. 1. 16. Thefe Cunocephali were a facred college, whofe members were
perfons of great learning. They were particularly
addicted to aftronomical obfervations; and by con-
templating the heavens, called Ouran, they learned
                                                to

to diftinguifh the feafons, and to divide the day into parts. But the term Ouran the Greeks by a ftrange mifconception changed to ουρειν; and from this abufe of terms the filly figment took its rife. I. 339.

P.

PAEONIA.

A REGION in Thrace fo called; which feems to have been fo called from P'Eon, the god of light (who was alfo called Peor). The natives of thefe parts were ftiled both Peonians, and Pierians; which names equally relate to the Sun, the object of their worfhip. (v. Maxim. Tyr. differt. 8. Strabo. Epitom. l. 7.) I. 207.

PALÆMON

And the Dolphin, and the ftory of Arion, have both the fame reference. Palæmon was the fame as Dionufus; the fame alfo as Hercules. II. 379. 411. Neptune was the fame as Palæmon of Corinth; he was defcribed, as a child expofed upon the feas, and fupported by a Cetus. Sometimes he was reprefented upon the Corinthian Cupfelis or Ark; and behind him there is commonly a pine tree. There were the fame offerings made to Palæmon in Greece, as were exhibited by the Latines to Mania. He is ftiled βρεφοκλονος, on account of the children,

1   which

which were offered at his fhrine. Hence we may plainly fee, that there was a correfpondence in the rites and mythology of thefe different nations; and that they had univerfally a reference to the fame hiftory. 458.

PALÆPHATUS

Wrote early: and feems to have been a ferious, and fenfible perfon; one who faw the abfurdity of the fables, upon which the theology of his country was founded. In the purport of his name is fignified an antiquarian; a perfon who dealt in remote refearches. As he wrote againft the mythology of his country, probably Παλαιφαῖος was an affumed name, which he took for a blind, in order to fcreen himfelf from perfecution; for the nature of his writings made him liable to much ill will. A treatife of his about Orion is quoted verbatim by the Scholiaft upon Homer Il. Σ. v. 486. who gives it to Euphorion. But as many learned men were of that name, it may be difficult to determine which was the author of this treatife. I. 411.

PAN.

He was by fome reprefented as the fovereign deity; and efteemed lord of all the elements.

Πανα καλω, κραῖερον Νομιον, κοσμοιο τε συμπαν,
Ουρανον, ηδε θαλασσαν, ιδε χθονα παμβασιλειαν,
Και πυρ αθαναῖον, ταδε γαρ μελη ιςι τα Πανος.
Κοσμοκραῖωρ, αυξηῖα, φαεσφορε, καρπιμε Παιαν,
Ανῖροχαρις, βαρυμηνις, ΑΛΗΘΗΣ ΖΕΤΣ Ὁ ΚΕΡΑΣ_
ΤΗΣ.

Orphic. H. 10. I. 311.

PAPPAIUS.

PAPPAIUS.

The ancients esteemed the Earth their common parent, and they gave her the name of Apia, as they gave the title of Pappaius to Zeus; whom they looked upon as their father.

Pappa, and Pappus, signified in many languages *a father.* Hence, παππαζουσιν, παπιρα προσαγορευουσιν. Hesych. Nausicaa in Homer (Od. Z. 57.) thus addresses her father;

Παππα φιλ᾽, —— —— Il. 421.

PARAIA.

Philo from Sanchoniathon says that Cronus had three sons in the region of Paraia: this is a variation of P'Ur-aia; and means literally the land of Ur in Chaldea: the region from whence ancient writers began the history of mankind. I. 123.

ΠΑΡΘΕΝΟΣ.

Many of the temples called Prutaneia, were dedicated to the deity under the name of Persephone, or Proserpine, the supposed daughter of Ceres: but they were the same personage. Persephone was stiled Κορα; which the Greeks misinterpreted Παρθενος, *a virgin*, or damsel. How could a person, who according to the received accounts had been ravished by Pluto, and been his consort for ages; who was the reputed queen of hell, be stiled by way of eminence Παρθενος? Κορα, Cora, which they understood was the same as Cura, a foeminine title of the Sun; by which Ceres also was stiled at Cnidos. However mild and gentle Proserpine may have been represented in her virgin state by the Poets; yet her tribunal in many places seems to have been very formidable. In consequence of this we find her with Minos, and Rhadamanthus, condemned to

Y   the

the fhades below, as an infernal inquifitor. Nonnus (l. 44.) fays, Περσεφονη Θωρηξεν Εριννυας. The notion of which Furies arofe from the cruelties practifed in thefe Prutaneia. II. 41.

PEGADÆ.

Cal-Chus, the hill, or place of Chus, was converted to Chalcus, Χαλκος, *brafs*; this being a fecret to Philoftratus has led him into a deal of myfterious error. He fays (Vita Apoll. L. 3.) that Apollonius came to a fettlement of the Oreitæ upon the Indian ocean. He alfo vifited their Pegadæ; he met with a people, whofe very rocks were brazen; their fand was brazen; the rivers conveyed down their ftreams fine filaments of brafs; the natives efteemed their land golden on account of the plenty of brafs. This is a fhameful perverfion of terms. The country whither Apollonius is fuppofed to go, was a province of the Indo-Cuthites, who were to be met with in various parts under the title of Oreitæ. They were worfhippers of fire; and came originally from the land of Ur; and hence had that name. The Pegadæ of the country are what we now call Pagodas. I. 363.

PEGASUS.

Marus Balus (Ælian. V. H. l. 9. c. 16.) an ancient deity of Italy was reprefented under an hieroglyphic, as a perfon with the face of a man before, and of a horfe behind, and was faid to have lived three times. The hiftory of Pegafus, the winged horfe, is probably of the fame purport. Palæphatus (de Belleroph.) a judicious writer, interprets it fo; and fuppofes Pegafus to have been nothing elfe but a fhip: ονομα δ' ην τῳ πλοιῳ Πηγασος. II. 411.

PELASGI.

PELASGI.

The moſt general appellation, under which the colonies from Egypt paſſed before the name of Ionians and Dorians, and that ſtill more univerſal one of Hellenes, was that of Pelaſgi. They are repreſented indeed as a different people, and of a different character: but this difference was not of perſons, but of times. They were very numerous; and ſuppoſed to have been for a long time in a wandering ſtate. Beſides Hellas, they occupied many regions of great extent, where their name was in repute for ages. There were nations, called Leleges, Caucones, and Pelaſgi in Aſia Minor; who are mentioned by Homer (Il. K. v. 429.) among the allies of the Trojans. Strabo ſpeaks of theſe Pelaſgi as a mighty people: and ſays (l. 13. p. 922.) that the whole coaſt of Ionia from Mycale, and all the neighbouring iſlands were once inhabited by them. They poſſeſſed the whole region of Hetruria; nor do we know the ultimate, to which they were extended. (v. Plutarch. in Romulo. p. 17. Strabo. l. 5. p. 339.)

The perſon, from whom this people are ſuppoſed to have been derived, and named, is by ſome repreſented as the ſon of Inachus; by others as the ſon of Poſeidon and Lariſſa. Staphylus Naucratites (Schol. in Apoll. Rhod. l. 1. v. 580.) mentioned him under the name of Pelaſgus; and ſaid, that he was Αργειον το γενος, which I ſhould render, *of Arkite extraction.* Hence it is ſaid of his poſterity, the Argives; και αυτοι οι Αργειοι εκαλουντο Πελασγοι (Schol. ſupra.) They ſettled very early in Theſſaly; to which they gave the name of Aëria, which was the ancient name of Egypt. All the country about Dodona was particularly ſtyled Hellas; and it was at the ſame time called Pelaſgia. The oracle is ſaid by Scymnus Chius to have been of Pelaſgic

original,

original. (Geogr. Vet. vol. 1. p. 26. v. 448.)
The rites of the place were introduced from Egypt;
confequently the people, who founded the temple,
and inftituted thofe rites, were from the fame
country. The deity was there worfhiped under
the title of Zeuth, whom Homer (Il. II. v. 233.)
ftyles Pelafgic:

Ζευ, Ανα, Δωδωναιε, Πελασγικε, τηλοθι ναιων,
Δωδωνης μεδεων δυσχειμερου.

From what Herodotus fays (L. I. c. 56, 57.
VII. c. 95.) we may be affured, that by the Pelafgi are meant the ancient Dores, Iones, and Helladians. In fhort, all thofe Cuthite colonies, and
thofe of their collateral branches, which I include
under the title of Amonians.

As to the Arcadians, they are faid to have been
fo named from Arcas, the fon of Zeuth. Now
Arcas was a title; and by Pelafgus Arcas was meant
Pelafgus the Arkite. When the people of Phrygia
and Hetruria were faid to be αυτικαθεν Αρκαδες.
(Dion. Hal. l. 1. c. 10.) the true purport of the
expreffion was, that they were ab origine Arkites.
Neither Argolis, nor Arcadia, could have fufficed
to have fent out the colonies, which are faid to
have proceeded from them. They are fuppofed to
have filled regions, before theirfelves were conftituted as a people.

This fuppofed perfonage is reprefented (Paufan.
l. 8. p. 604.) as a great benefactor to mankind;
teaching them the ufe of corn, and inftructing
them in weaving, in order to cloath themfelves.
His name was a title of the chief gentile divinity,
like Helius, Ofiris, and Dionufus, &c. Arcas was
fuppofed by his pofterity to have been buried upon
mount Mænalus: now this term is a compound of
Meen El; by which is fignified Lunus Deus, another title of Arcas, the Arkite god, who had been

worfhiped

worſhiped upon that mountain. When it is ſaid, that the Arcades were prior to the Moon, it meana only, that they were conſtituted into a nation, before the worſhip of the Ark prevailed, and before the firſt war (*Titanian*) upon earth commenced.

Similar to the account given of Arcas, is that of Pelaſgus, but accompanied with many additional and remarkable circumſtances. He was equally a benefactor to mankind; he inſtructed them to cloath themſelves, and to build houſes: he improved them in their diet; and ſhewed them what was noxious. He is ſaid to have built the firſt temple to the Deity. Noah was ſaid to have been ανθρωπος γης; this characteriſtic is obſervable in every hiſtory of the primitive perſons; and they are repreſented as νομιοι, αγριοι, and γηγινεις. Pelaſgus accordingly had this title: and it is particularly mentioned of him, that he was the firſt huſbandman. (Æſchyl. Supp. v. 258. Schol. in Eurip. Oreſt. v. 930.) There is a curious ſketch of his ſtory given by the poet Aſius; which is compriſed in two verſes, but points out very plainly, who was meant by Pelaſgus. It repreſents him as a perſon of a noble character, who was wonderfully preſerved for the good of mankind. (Pauſan. l. 8. p. 599.)

Αντιθεον δε Πελασγον εν υψικομοισιν ορεσσι
Γαια μελαιν᾽ ανεδωκεν, ινα θνητων γενος εη.

Γαια, in its original ſenſe, ſignified a *ſacred cavern*; a hollow in the earth; which from its gloom was looked upon as an emblem of the Ark. Hence Gaia, like Heſta, Rhoia, Cybele, is often repreſented as the mother of mankind. (Orph. Hymn. 25.)

Γαια Θεα, Μητερ Μακαρων, θνητων᾽ ανθρωπων.

In like manner Inachus is ſaid after the deluge to have been ſaved upon the top of a high mountain. Inachus, Pelaſgus, and Danaus, are titles of the ſame

perſon,

perfon; though diverfified by the Greeks, and made princes in fucceffion.

Concerning the language of the Pelafgi, there have been many elaborate difquifitions; and we find, that it was matter of debate, even in the time of Herodotus, (l. 1. c. 57.) Yet the queſtion, if rightly ſtated, amounts only to this: What was the language of this variouſly denominated people, before it had undergone thoſe changes, which neceffarily enſue from time? or, How did the Hellenes difcourfe before the birth of Æfchylus or Pindar? As we have no written records, nor any monumental evidences of that date, or near it; the queſtion may at firſt feem not very eafy to be decided. Yet from the names of places, and of men; and from the terms ufed in their rites and worſhip; but more efpecially from the hiſtory of the people themfelves, and of the country from whence they came; we may be affured that it was the Cuthic of Chaldea. This in a long feries of years underwent the fame changes, as all languages undergo. And this alteration arofe partly from words imported; and partly from a mixture with thofe nations, with whom the Hellenes were incorporated. Exclufive of thefe circumftances, there is no language but will of itfelf infenfibly vary: though this variation may be in fome degree retarded, where there is fome ſtandard, by which common fpeech may be determined and controuled. But the Græcians had no fuch affiftance. Letters undoubtedly came to them late; and learning much later. There was no hiſtorian prior to Cadmus Milefius; nor any public infcription, of which we can be certified, before the laws of Draco. The firſt Græcian, who attempted to write in profe, was Pherecydes the philofopher; and he lived as late as Cyrus the Perfian. Hence there is no change in their language, but fuch as

we

we might expect from an interval of this extent, and from a people thus circumftanced. III. 392.

Sometimes expreffed Pleiades, are faid to have been the daughters of Atlas by the nymph Pleione. According to Pherecydes Syrus, they were daughters of Lycurgus, and nurfes of Dionufus. Among mariners the Dove was thought to be particularly aufpicious: who in their voyages ufed to let a dove or pigeon fly from their fhips, in order to judge from its movements of the fuccefs of their voyage. The moft favourable feafon for fetting fail was at the Heliacal rifing of the feven ftars near the head of Taurus: and they are in confequence of it called Peleiadæ, or the Doves. (v. Ovid. Faft. l. 3.) II. 285.

From circumftances ill underftood, people feigned that in thofe places, where the name of the Peleiadæ and Trerones occurred, there had been perfons turned into Doves, or Pigeons. (v. Ovid. Met. l. 7.—13.) Thefe Peleiai and Peleiades were certainly female attendants; propheteffes, by whom the oracles of the deity were promulged. Πιλααι. ϖιριϛιραι· και αι ιν Δωδωνη διϛπιζουϛαι μανΐαις. Hefych. Servius (in Virg. Ecl. 9. v. 13.) fpeaks to the fame purpofe, when he mentions the Chaonian doves of that temple. Herodotus (l. 2.) fpecifies that they were women, *of a dark complexion*, who came originally from Egypt—they gave out the oracles, and adminiftered at the altar; whence they were faid to feed Zeuth. They were called διαχονοι της τροφης των ϑιων, becaufe they offered up cakes and fruits at their fhrines, attended with libations of wine, oil, and honey. And as in many temples the deity was reprefented under the fymbol of a dove, he was fuppofed to have taken the fhape of that bird. Hence it is faid of Zeuth himfelf (Athenæus, l. 9.) that he

Y 4   was

was changed into a pigeon: which notion prevailed in Achaia; and particularly among the people of Ægium. In fhort, the perfons, who adminiftered to the deity, were ftiled Πιλααι, and Πιλιιαδις; which was a tranflation of the Iönah and Iönim, introduced from Egypt and Chaldea. II. 286—292.

PELION.

In Theffaly every place feems to have had a reference to the Arkite Hiftory: two of the chief mountains were Pelion, and Offa; the former fignifies the mountain of the Dove; and the latter of the Oracle. Οσσα, θιια κλnδωr, και φnμn. Schol. in Iliad. B. v. 93.

nι τις οσσα,
Hι τις αγγιλος ορνις.—Apollon. Argon. l. 3. v. 1110.

II. 503.

PERSEUS

Was one of the moft ancient heroes in the mythology of Greece. The merit of whofe fuppofed atchievements the Helladians took to themfelves; and gave out that he was born at Argos. He was a great conqueror and traveller; and fuppofed to have built Tarfus in Cilicia, reputed the moft ancient city in the world; and to have planted the peach tree at Memphis. The Perfians were fuppofed to be his defcendants. Some of his family were in Italy. The hiftory of Perfeus came from Egypt. (Diodor. Sic. l. 1.) Herodotus (l. 6. c. 54.) more truly reprefents him as an Affyrian, i. e. a Babylonian; and agreeably to this he is faid to have married Afterie, the daughter of Belus, the fame as Afhtaroth and Aftarte of Canaan; by whom he had a daughter Hecate. He is faid to have been a great aftronomer, and a perfon of uncommon knowledge. He inftructed mariners to direct their

way

way in the fea by the lights of heaven; and particularly by the polar conftellation. This he firft obferved, and named it Helice. Though he was
reprefented as a Babylonian; yet he refided in
Egypt, and is faid to have reigned at Memphis.
To fay the truth, he was worfhiped there; for
Perfeus was a title of the deity: Περσευς, ὁ Ἡλιος,
the chief god of the Gentile world. On this account he had a temple of great repute at Chemmis,
as well as at Memphis, and in other parts of Egypt.
Upon the Heracleotic branch of the Nile, near the
fea, was a celebrated watch tower, denominated
from him. His true name was Perez, or Parez,
rendered Perefis, Perfes, and Perfeus: and in the
accounts given of this perfonage we have the hiftory
of the Perfians, Parrhafians, and Perezites, in their
feveral peregrinations; who were no other than the
Heliadæ, and Ofirians. It was a mixed hiftory, in
which their forefathers are alluded to; particularly
their great progenitor, the father of mankind. He
was fuppofed to have had a renewal of life: they
therefore defcribed Perfeus as inclofed in an Ark,
and expofed in a ftate of childhood upon the waters,
after having been conceived in a fhower of gold.
P'aras, P'arez, and P'erez, however diverfified,
fignify the Sun; and are of the fame analogy as
P'ur, P'urrhos, P'orus which betoken fire. As
every animal, appropriated to fome deity, was called
by fome facred title; hence P'arez fignified an
horfe. It was at firft only a mark of reference, and
betokened a folar animal, fpecifying the particular
deity to whom it was facred. There were many
nations, which were diftinguifhed in the fame
manner; fome of whom the Greeks ftiled Parrhafians.

The Poets defcribed the conftellation of Helice
or the Bear by the title of Parrhafis, Arctos, and
Parrhafis Urfa. This afterifm was confeffedly firft

taken

taken notice of by Perez or Perseus, by which is
meant the Persians. Herodotus (l. 7. c. 150.)
makes Xerxes claim kindred with the Argives of
Greece, as being equally of the posterity of Perses,
the same as Perseus, the Sun; under which character
the Persians described the Patriarch, from whom
they were descended. II. 62. Perseus was the same
as Osiris, the same as Helius. 330. 507. And the
same as Mithras, whose sacred cavern was stiled
Perseum. II. 68.

PERSIANS

Venerated fountains, &c. after the Cuthites.
Most of their temples were caverns in rocks, either
formed by nature, or artificially produced. They
had likewise Puratheia, or open temples, for the
celebration of the rites of fire. In the ancient province of Chusistan, called afterwards Persis, there
are to be seen at this day many curious monuments
of antiquity which have a reference to that worship.
These grottos are supposed by the learned Hyde
(de Rel. V. P, c. 23.) to have been palaces or
tombs. See Kæmpfer, Mondesloe, Chardin, Le
Bruyn, Thevenot, and Herbert. But they were
certainly temples. Nothing was more common
among the Persians, than to have their temples
formed out of rocks. Porphyry assures us, that the
deity had always a rock, or cavern for his temple:
that people, in all places, where the name of Mithras was known, paid their worship at a cavern.
It is natural for persons to imagine, that they were
places for burial, who knew not the ancient worship of the people. What have been supposed to
be stone coffins, were cisterns for water, which the
Persians used for their nocturnal lustrations. The
uncommon noises, which were heard by persons
who passed by, undoubtedly proceeded from the
priests at their midnight worship; whose voices at
that

that feafon were reverberated by the mountains, and were accompanied with a reverential awe in thofe who heard them. I. 222.

Was an Amonian term of honour; and was found in many Egyptian names; e. g. Petiphra, Peti-phera, Petifonius, Petofiris, Petarbemis, Petubaftus the Tanite, and Petefuccus builder of the Laby-rinth. Petes, called Peteos in Homer, the father of Mneftheus the Athenian, is of the fame original. (Diodor. Sic. l. 1.) All the great officers of the Babylonians and Perfians took their names from fome facred title of the Sun. Herodotus (l.3. c.61.) mentions Petazithes Magus, and (l. 7. c. 40.) Patiramphes, i. e. Pata-Ramphan, the prieft of the god Ramphan; the Ramphas of the Greeks: he was brother to Smerdis, and a Magus; which was a prieft of the Sun. This term is fometimes fub-joined, as in Atropatia, a province in Media; and in Aorpata, is the fame as Petah Or, the prieft of Orus; or in a more lax fenfe, the votaries of that god. One of the Egyptian deities was named Neith; and her priefts were ftiled Pataneit. It is remarkable that the worfhipers of Wifhnou or Viftnou in India are now called Petacares, and are diftinguifhed by three red lines on their foreheads. The priefts of Brama have the fame title, Petac Arez, the priefts of Arez, or the Sun. I. 43.

The Pateræ, which Q. Curtius (l. 4. c. 7.) copying from the Greeks, has converted into *Silver Bafons*, were the priefts, who in the facred proceffions carried the fhrine of the oracle of Ham, and fupported both the image, and the boat; they were eighty in number. (Diod. Sic. l. 17.) Thefe perfons, who thus officiated, were probably the fame as the Petipharæ of the ancient Egyptians, but were called Pateræ by the Greeks. It was a name, and

and office, by which the prieſt of Delphi, and of many other places beſides thoſe in Egypt, were diſtinguiſhed : and the term always related to ora‑ cular interpretation.

Pator, or Petor, was an Egyptian word ; and Moſes ſpeaking of Joſeph, and the dreams of Pha‑ raoh, more than once makes uſe of it in the ſenſe above. It manifeſtly alludes to an interpretation of that divine intercourſe, which the Egyptians ſtiled Omphi. This was communicated to Pha‑ raoh by a dream : for the Omphi was eſteemed not only a verbal reſponſe, but alſo an intimation by dreams. Theſe Omphean viſions were explained by Joſeph ; wherefore the title of Pator is reckoned by the Rabbins among the names of Joſeph. There is thought to be the ſame alluſion to divine inter‑ pretation in the name of the apoſtle Peter : Πέἷρος, ὁ ἐπιλυων, ὁ ἐπιγνωσκων. Heſych. Hence we learn that the prieſt was ſtiled Petor, and Pator ; the place was called Patora. The coloſſal ſtatue of Memnon in the Thebaïs was a Patora, or oracular image. There was a Patera in Lycia ; a Petra in Achaia, of the like import. Pethor and Pethora was the place where the falſe Prophet Balaam reſided. It ſeems to have been the celebrated place in Arabia, famous in aftertimes for the worſhip of Alilat, and called by the Romans Petra. 247.

Παἷηρ, Pater, when uſed in the religious addreſſes of the Greeks and Romans, meant not a Father, or Parent ; but related to the divine influence of the deity, called Pator. Not only the gods, but the hierophantæ in moſt temples ; and thoſe prieſts in particular, who were occupied in the celebration of myſteries were ſtiled Patres : ſo that it was undoubt‑ edly a religious term imported from Egypt. As the true name of the Amonian prieſts was Petor, or Pator ; ſo the inſtruments, which they held in their hands, was ſtiled Petaurum.

The

The Patora, and Petora, oracular temples of the Sun, in aftertimes called Petra, were afcribed to other gods. Many of them for the fake of mariners were erected upon rocks, and eminences near the fea: hence the term Πέΐρα, Petra, came at length to. fignify any rock or ftone, and to be in a.manner confined to that meaning. But in the firft ages it was ever taken in a religious fenfe; and related to the fhrines of Ofiris, or the Sun, and to the oracles which were fuppofed to be there exhibited. Thus Olympus near Pifa, though only a large mound, or hill, was of old termed Petra, as relating to oracular influence. It is induftrioufly introduced by writers when they fpeak of facred and oracular places. (v. Lycophron. v. 159. Pind. Olymp. Ode 6.)

Ceres is faid, after her wanderings, to have re-pofed herfelf upon a Stone at Eleufis. At Delphi was fhewn the Petra, upon which the Sibyl Hero-phile fat down upon her firft arrival. In fhort, there is in the hiftory of every oracular temple fome legend about a ftone; fome reference to the word Petra. When the worfhip of the Sun was almoft univerfal, this was one name of that deity even among the Greeks. They called him Petor, and Petros; and his temple was ftiled Petra. This they oftentimes changed to λιθος; fo little did they under-ftand their own mythology. The loaves and cakes which were offered were called Πίΐυρα. I. 283.

ΠΕΤΡΑΙ ΑΜΒΡΟΣΙΑΙ.

The mighty works, which the Cuthite colonies carried on, and the edifices, which they erected, wherever they fettled, were truly wonderful. They formed vaft lakes, and canals; they opened roads over hills; (witnefs the paffage through the Alpes Cottiæ, or the Cuthean Alps) and through forefts, which were before impaffable. (v. Strabo. l. 16.

Pocock's

Pocock's Egypt. v. 1. p. 132. Greaves. v. 1.
p. 94, &c. Pocock. v. 2. p. 110.)

The Egyptians looked upon rude bare rocks with
a degree of veneration: and fome of them they left,
as they found them, with perhaps only an hieroglyphic. (Norden. plate 122, 123.) Others they
fhaped with tools, and formed into various devices.
This practice of fhewing a reverential regard to
fragments of rocks, which were particularly uncouth
and horrid, prevailed alfo in many other countries.

It was ufual with much labour to place one vaft
ftone upon another for a religious memorial. The
ftones thus placed, they oftentimes poized fo equa-
bly, that they were affected with the leaft external
force: nay a breath of wind would fometimes make
them vibrate. We have many inftances in our own
country; and they are to be found in other parts of
the world: and wherever they occur we may efteem
them of the higheft antiquity. All fuch works we
generally refer to the Celts, and Druids; under the
fanction of which names we fhelter ourfelves, whenever we are ignorant, and bewildered. But they
were the operations of a very remote age; probably before the time, when the Druids, or Celtæ,
were firft known. I queftion, whether there be in
the world a monument, which is much prior to the
celebrated *Stone-Henge*. There is reafon to think,
that it was erected by a foreign colony; one of the
firft, which came into the ifland. Here is extant
at this day, one of thofe rocking ftones, of which I
have been fpeaking.

The ancients diftinguifhed ftones erected with a
religious view by the name of *Amber*; by which was
fignified any thing folar and divine. The Græcians
called them Πέτραι Αμβροσιαι; and there are reprefentations of fuch upon coins. (Vaill. de num.
Col. v. 2. p.69.148.218.) *Stone-Henge* is compofed
of thefe Amber-ftones: hence the next town is de-

nominated *Ambros-bury*: not from a Roman Am-
brofius; for no fuch perfon exifted; but from the
Ambrofia Petræ, in whofe vicinity it ftands. Some
of thefe were rocking ftones: and there was a
wonderful monument of this fort near Penzance in
Cornwall. It ftill retains the name of Main-
·Amber, by which is fignified the *facred ftones*.
Norden's Cornw. p. 48. who mentions alfo another
called Pendre-Stone, p. 74. [*See likewife Dr. Bor-
lafe's Ant. of Cornwall, l. 3. and particularly c. 4.
concerning the Logan, or Rocking Stones.*] Such a
one is mentioned by Apollonius Rhodius, which
was fuppofed to have been raifed in the time of the
Argonautæ. It ftood in the ifland Tenos, and was
the monument of Calaïs and Zetes, the two winged
fons of Boreas. They are faid to have been flain
by Hercules; and though the hiftory be a fable,
yet they undoubtedly exifted in that ifland, as the
poet defcribes.

Ptolemy Hephæftion (ap. Photium. p. 475.)
mentions a large ftone upon the borders of the
ocean, probably near Gades in Bætica, which he
calls Petra Gigonia: and fays, that it could be
moved with a blade of grafs. Γιγων, from whence
came the term Gigonia, was, according to Hefychius, a name of the Egyptian Hercules. From
hence we may infer, that both the ftone here, and
that alfo in Tenos, were facred to this deity. By
Petra Gigonia was fignified an Herculean monument, not raifed by him, but to his honour: and it
was undoubtedly erected by people of thofe colonies,
who came both from Tyre and Egypt. One of
thefe moving ftones is to be met with in the ifland
Amoy, belonging to the Chinefe empire. It may
be afked, might not thefe ftones have been fettled
in this manner at the Deluge? It is certain that at
the Deluge many vaft ftones were left bare upon the
retreat of the waters. But thofe, which are fo
equally poifed, and fo regularly placed upon others,

muft

muſt have been thus adapted by the contrivance and induſtry of man. For their ſituation is too nice and critical, and they occur too often, to be the effect of chance.

It was ſaid above that the rocking ſtone, near Penzance, is called Main-Amber. Now Main (from whence came *moenia*,) ſignified, in the primitive language, a *ſtone*, or *ſtones*, and alſo a building: *Amber*, any thing ſacred. The word Mineret is of the ſame etymology, from Meen, and Main, *a ſtone*. III. 532.

PHACAT.

Some of the openings and branches of the Nile were formed by the violence of the inundations: there were others, which ſeem to have been the work of art; and were called by the Egyptians Phacat, and by the Greeks διωρυγες. The Phacnammonis is the Phacat No Ammon, *the dike of* No Ammon. Phaccuſa, though ſaid to be the capital of a province as well as a village, is originally the *dike* or *canal* of Cuſa. For a preciſe account of this very famous canal, ſee Herodotus. (l. 2. c. 158.) *Obſerv.* 117.

PHAETON.

The ſtory of Phaeton, who was ſuppoſed to have fallen into the Eridanus, is manifeſtly of Egyptian original. He is by ſome repreſented as the firſt king, who reigned in Chaonia, and Epirus. He was in reality the ſame as Oſiris, the Sun; whoſe worſhip was introduced there very early, as well as upon the Padus. The names of the deities in every country are generally prefixed to the liſts of kings, and miſtaken accordingly. II. 171.

Many of the poets repreſent him as the offspring of the Sun; but this miſtake is found chiefly among the Roman poets: it was a title of Apollo, as the
god

god of Light. Homer (Οδ. Λ. v. 15.) ufes it in this acceptation:

— — — ουδεποτ' αυτους
Ηελιος Φαεθων επιδερκεται ακτινεσσιν.

The ancient mythologifts of Greece univerfally allowed him to be the Sun: Orpheus (de Lapid. v. 90.)

Ηελιον Φαεθοντα εφ' αρμασι πωλοι αγουσι.

He was the fame as Phanes; and is reprefented as the firft born of heaven. I. 369. The name of this much miftaken perfonage, was an ancient title of the Sun, a compound of Phi-Ath-On. I. 123.

PHANES,

The fame with Hanes with the prefix, Ph'anes; and the deity fo called was by the early theologifts thought to have been of the higheft antiquity. They efteemed him the fame as Ouranus, and Dionufus: and went 'fo far as to give him a creative power, and to deduce all things from him. The Græcians from Phanes formed Φαναιος, which they gave as a title both to Zeus, and Apollo. In this there was nothing extraordinary, for they were both the fame god. I. 200.

PHARBETH

Was an abbreviation of Pharabeth, or the houfe of Pharaoth: fo Phainubeth in Egypt is only Phai-nabeth varied, and fignifies the place facred to Phanes. I. 97.

PHAROS.

Orpheus alludes to a Pharos, and to the paintings and furniture of it in his defcription of the Robe, with which Apollo, or Dionufus is invefted. He

Z   fpeaks

ſpeaks of them as the ſame deity. (ex Macrob. Sat.
l. 1. c. 18.)

Ταυ]α δε παν]α τελειν ιερα σκευη πυκασαν]α,
Σωμα θεου πλατ]ειν εριαυγους Ηελιοιο.
Πρω]α μεν αργυφεαις εναλιγκιον ακ]ινεσσι
Πεπλον φοινικεον, πυρι εικελον, αμφιϐαλεσθαι.
Αυ]αρ υπερθε νεϐροιο παναιολου ευρυ καθαψαι
Δερμα πολυςιχ]ον θηρος κα]α δεξιον ωμον,
Αςρων δαιδαλεων μιμημ', ιερου τε πολοιο.
Ει]α δ' υπερθε νεϐρης χρυσεον ζωςηρα ϐαλεσθαι,
Παμφανοων]α, περιξ ςερνων φορεειν, μεγα σημα.
Ευθυς οτ' εκ περα]ων γαιης Φαεθων ανορουσων
Χρυσειαις ακ]ισι ϐαλη ροον Ωκεανοιο.
Αυγη δ' αςπι]ος η, ανα δε δροσω αμφιμιγεισα,
Μαρμαιρη δινησιν ελισσομενη κα]α κυκλον
Προσθε θεου, ζωνη δ' αρ' ιπο ςερνων αμειρη]ων
Φαινε]' αρ' ωκεανου κυκλος, μεγα θαυμ' ισιδεσθαι.

When the poet has thus adorned the deity, we find
towards the concluſion, that theſe imaginary robes
never ſhew to ſuch advantage, as in the morning.
To explain this; obſerve that the whole was depo-
ſited in a Pharos upon the ſea-ſhore, upon which
the Sun at his riſing darted his early rays; and whoſe
turrets glittered with the dew : from the upper ſtory
of the tower, which was of unmeaſurable height,
there was an unlimited view of the ocean.   This
vaſt element ſurrounded the edifice like a zone; and
afforded a wonderful phænomenon.

In the verſes from Nonnus (ſee Art. Harmonia)
we may ſee the method of deviation.   Pharos *a
tower* is taken for Pharos *a garment*; and this altered
to Χι]ων; yet after all, the genuine hiſtory is diſ-
cernable.   The author ſays, that at the bottom
ευκλυςοιο Χι]ωνος, *of the well-woven garment*, flowed
the Ocean, which ſurrounded the world.   This is
certainly a miſinterpretation of the term Φαρος: and
in the original writings, the hiſtory related to a
tower:

tower: and it was at the foot Φαρου Ευκλωςοιο that the ocean beat, by which the earth was encircled.

In the Orphic verfes above, Δερμα—Θηρος; obferve that Maps, and Books alfo, when writing was introduced, were made of fkins, called διφθεραι. (Herod. l. 5. c. 58.) I. 396.

PHASELIS,

A city in Lycia, upon the mountain Chimæra; which mountain had the fame name, and was facred to the god of Fire. Phafelis is a compound of Phi, and Azel (Az-El) and fignifies Os Vulcani, five apertura ignis, a chafm of fire. I. 206.

PHI,

Signifies a Mouth; alfo Language, and Speech. It is ufed by the Amonians particularly for the voice and oracle of any god; and fubjoined to the name of that deity. Hence the terms Amphi, Omphi, Alphi, Elphi, Orphi, Urphi. In Gen. xlv. 51. it fignifies the voice, or command of Pharaoh. Hence, in this acceptation, Φημι, Φημη, Φημυς, Φασκω, Φαλις, Fama, Fari, &c.

Perhaps Pharaoh is a compound of Phi-Ourah, Vox Ori, five Dei. The ancients ufed to call the voice of their prince the voice of god. Phi is alfo ufed for any Opening or Cavity; hence the head of a fountain is often denominated from it; at leaft the place, whence the fountain iffued forth, or where it loft itfelf. As all ftreams were facred, and all cavities in the earth were looked upon with religious horror, the Amonians called them Phi-El, Phi-Amon, Phi-Anes; hence Græce Phiale, Phænon, Phanes, Phaneas, Paneas. The Nile is faid to be loft underground near its fountains; the place was called Phiala. (Plin. l. 5. c. 9.) Sometimes this term occurs without the afpirate, as in Pella, a city of Paleftin, named doubtlefs from its fountains:

Pliny (l. 5. c. 28.) calls it Pellam aquis divitem. I. 88.

Bacchus was called Phi-Anac by the Myfians, rendered by the poets Phanac and Phanaces. Hanes was a title of the fame deity, equally reverenced of old, and compounded Ph'-Hanes; the fountain of light: hence φαινω, φαντις, φανερος: and from Ph'ain-on, Fanum. I. 124.

PHIBESETH.

. There may not poffibly at firft fight appear any great fimilitude between this term and *Bubaftus:* but they were the fame place. The *mouth* or opening of a river or canal was called by the Hebrews *Pi* or *Phi.* Hence Phi Haroth (Exod. xiv. 2.) is tranflated by the LXX κατα ςομα Ειρωθ, over againft the mouth or opening of Haaroth. The Egyptians feem to have ufed it alfo for the mouth of a canal: and it often occurs for the canal itfelf, or branch of a river. Thus Pithom was properly the canal of Thom: Phi Nepthim the canal of Nepthim. In thefe two inftances the word is exactly conformable to the Hebrew pronunciation: but it feems in general to have been pronounced with a B inftead of a P; which letters are in moft languages convertible, and often fubftituted the one for the other. Hence the Bifehor was the canal of the Sehor or Nile proper, which the Greeks called Bufiris: Bicalig was the mouth of the calig or canal, which they termed Bucolicum; and Bi Bifeth the river of Bifeth, the Phibefeth of the Scriptures, changed by the Greeks to Bibefitus, and contracted *Bubaftus.* The Greeks changed it to Bo and Bou. The Boryfthenes feems to be Bo Ruthen, the mouth of the river Ruthen, called fo from the Rutheni. Bithynia is of the fame compofition.

Thyni

Thyni Thraces erant, quæ nunc Bithynia fertur.

Claudian.

Sometimes it was fubjoined to the name of the place which was fpoken of; as Cnoufbi, or Canoufbi, the canal or mouth of the Cnouf, which the Greeks changed to Canoubicum: Athribis, or, as Stephanus reads it, Atharrhabis, the mouth or canal of Athrib. *Obferv.* 114.

PHOENIX. PHOENICES.

Phoinic, or Poinic, were Egyptian, and Canaan-itifh terms of honour; hence Φοινιξ, Φοινιχες, Φοινι-χοεις of the Greeks; Phoinic, Poinicus, Poinicius of the Romans; afterwards changed to Phœnix, Punicus, Puniceus. It was originally a title, which the Greeks made ufe of as a provincial name: but it was never admitted as fuch by the people, till the Greeks were in poffeffion of the country: and then but partially, for the natives were called Sidonians, Tyrians, and Canaanites as late as the days of the Apoftles.

Phœnix was an honorary term, compounded of Anac with the Egyptian prefix. It fignified a lord, or prince; and was particularly affumed by the fons of Chus and Canaan. The Myfians called their god Dionufus, Ph'anac. It was alfo conferred upon many things, which were efteemed princely and noble. Hence the red, or fcarlet, a colour appropriated to great and honourable perfonages, was ftiled Phoinic. The Palm was likewife fo ftiled; and the ancients fpeak of it as a ftately and noble tree. It was efteemed an emblem of honour, and ufed as a reward of victory. We find from Apuleius (l. 2.) that Mercury, the Hermes of Egypt, was reprefented with a Palmbrance in his hand: and his priefts at Hermopolis ufed to have them ftuck in their fandals, on the outfide. The

Z 3 goddefs

goddefs Ifis was thus reprefented: and we may infer that Hermes had the like ornaments; which the Greeks miftook for feathers, and have in confequence of it added wings to his feet. The Jews ufed to carry Palm boughs at fome of their feftivals; and particularly at the celebration of their nuptials: and they were thought to have an influence at the birth. (v. Eurip. in Ione. v. 920.)

The ancients had an opinion, that the Palm was immortal: at leaft, if it did die, it recovered again, and obtained a fecond life by renewal. Hence the ftory of the bird, ftiled the Phœnix, is thought to have been borrowed from hence.

The title of Phoinic feems at firft to have been given to perfons of great ftature: but in procefs of time it was conferred upon people of power, and eminence, like αναξ and αναχίες among the Greeks. The Cuthites in Egypt were ftiled Royal Shepherds, Βασιλεις Ποιμενες, and had therefore the title of Phœnices. A colony of them went from thence to Tyre and Syria; hence it is faid by many that Phœnix came from Egypt to Tyre. Phœnicia, which the Greeks called Φοινιχη, was but a fmall part of Canaan. It was properly a flip of feacoaft, which lay within the jurifdiction of the Tyrians and Sidonians, and fignifies Ora Regia; or, according to the language of the country, the coaft of the Anakim. It was a lordly title; and derived from a ftately and auguft people. All the natives of Canaan feem to have affumed to themfelves great honour. Ezek. xxvi. 16. Ifaiah xxiii. 8. The Scripture term by which they are diftinguifhed is שרים, Sarim: but the title which they affumed to themfelves was Ph'anac or Ph'oinac, the Phœnix of the Greeks and Romans. As it was a mere title, the facred writers of the Old Teftament never ufe it, to diftinguifh either the people or country. This part of Canaan is never by them called Phœnicia:

yet

yet others did call it fo; and the people were called
Phœnices before the birth of Homer. But this was
through miftake: for it was never ufed by the natives as a provincial appellation. It was a title,
or mark of rank and pre-eminence: on this account
it was affumed by other people; and conferred on
other places. For this reafon it is never mentioned
by any of the facred writers before the captivity, in
order to avoid ambiguity. The gentile writers
made ufe of it; and we fee what miftakes have enfued. There were Phœnicians of various countries.
This title was introduced at Sidon, and the coaft
adjoining, by people from Egypt; who the people
were, we learn particularly from Eufebius. (Chron.
p. 27.) Φοινιξ και Καδμος, απο Θηβων των Αιγυπλιων
εξελθονλες ως την Συριαν, Τυρου και Σιδωνος εβασιλευον.

Belus is faid to have carried a colony to the fame
parts. Βηλος απ' Ευφρηλαω κ τ λ. Nonnus. Belus
and Phœnix feem to have been the fame; not perfonages but titles: and under the charaƈters of thefe
two perfonages, Colonies, named Belidæ and Phœnices, went abroad, and fettled in differe ı. parts.
Their hiftory and appellation may be traced from
Babylonia to Arabia and Egypt: and from thence
to Canaan, and to the regions in the Weft. I. 319.

PHORONEUS.

The Patriarch, under whatever title he may
come, is generally reprefented as the father of gods,
and men: but in the charaƈter of Phoroneus (for in
this he is plainly alluded to) he feems to be defcribed merely as the firft of mortals. Hence by
an ancient poet, quoted by Clemens of Alexandria,
(Strom. L. 1.) he is ftiled Φορωνευς, παληρ θνηλων ανθρωπων. Mythologifts vary greatly concerning his
genealogy; but he is generally fuppofed to have
been the fon of Inachus and Niobe. The outlines
of his hiftory are fo ftrongly marked, that we cannot

Z 4   miftake

miftake to whom the mythology relates. He lived
in the time of the flood; he firft built an altar; he
firft collected men together, and formed them into
communities; he firft gave laws, and diftributed
juftice; he divided mankind by their families and
nations over the face of the earth. Nonnus ftiles
him Αρχεγονος, which may fignify either Πρωῖογονος,
or Θηβαιγενης. Anticlides (Plin. l. 7. c. 56.)
efteemed him the moft ancient king in Greece; but
Acufilaus (Clem. Alex. Strom. l. 1.) more truly
looked upon him as the father of mankind. In fhort
he was the ultimate, to which the Græcian hiftory
referred.   Indeed Phoroneus, Apis, Inachus,
Zeuth, Deucalion, Prometheus, were all one perfon.
Some made him the fon of Niobe, fome of Archia,
others of Meliffa; but they like Rhea, Cybele, and
Damater are mere titles, by which a female perfonage was denoted, who was fuppofed to have
been the genius of the Ark, and the mother of
mankind. II. 266.

PI.

This article was in ufe among the ancient
Egyptians and Cuthites, as well as other nations in
the Eaft.   The natives of India were all worfhipers of the Sun; and ufed to call themfelves by fome
of his titles.

Porus, with whom Alexander engaged upon the
Indus, was named from the chief object of his
worfhip אור, Pi-Or, and P'Or; rendered Πωρος.

Pacorus the Parthian, was a compound of
P'Achorus, the Achor of Egypt: fo was alfo the
city Pacoria in Mefopotamia.

Πυρ was of Egyptian or Chaldaic original; and of
the fame compofition (P'Ur) as the words above:
for Plato (in Cratylo) informs us, that πυρ, ὑδωρ,
κυνες, were efteemed terms of foreign importation.
The natives continued the ufe of this prefix, even
after

after the Greeks were poffeffed of Egypt; as did
other nations, which were incorporated with them.
Hence we often find Πιζευς, Πιμαρτυρ, Πιμαθηλης, ϖι-
σωμα, ϖιλαος, Pidux, Picurator, Pitribunus; alfo
names of perfons, as, Piterus, Piturio, Pionius the
martyr, alfo Pior, Piammon, Piambo; all mentioned by ecclefiaftical writers.

Pi is often changed into Pa, as in Pacomius, &c.
There were particular rites, ftiled Pamylia facra,
from Pamyles, an ancient Egyptian deity.   Paamyles is an affemblage of common titles, Am-El-
Eees with the prefix.   Hence the Greeks formed
Meliffa, a facred name.   As of Ham-El-Ait, they
formed Melitta, the name of a foreign deity, more
known in Ionia than in Hellas.

Hades, and Pi-Ades was a common title of the
Sun: the latter in early times was current in
Greece, where the Amonians fettled.   He was
termed Melech Pi-Adon, and Anac-Pi-Adon: but
the Greeks out of Pi-Adon formed Παιδων: for it is
inconceivable, how very ignorant they were of their
ancient theology.   Hence we read of ϖαιδων Ληλους,
ϖαιδων Ζηνος, ϖαιδων Απολλωνος; and legends of ϖαιδων
αθαναλων; and of ϖαιδων, who were mere foundlings:
whofe fathers could never be afcertained, though
divine honours were paid to the children.   This
often puzzled the mythologifts, who could not account for this fpurious race. (v. Plutar. Quæft.
Græ.)   There was a certain myfterious rite performed by the natives of Amphiffa in Phocis.   The
particular gods, to whom it was performed, were
ftiled Αναχλες ϖαιδες.   Who thefe were, neither
Paufanias (l. 10.) nor the priefts could tell: οίλιψς
δι Θεων εισιν όι Αναχλες Παιδες, ου καλα τ᾽ αυλα εςιν ειρημε-
νον.   Many more inftances may be found of this
nature; where divine honours are paid to the unknown children of fathers equally unknown.

Pi

346   P I

Pi is often expreſſed with an aſperate Phi, which
ſignifying *a mouth*, and in a more extenſive ſignification, *ſpeech* and *language*; it may ſometimes cauſe
a little uncertainty about the meaning. However,
in moſt places it is ſufficiently plain. I. 118.

ΠΙΟΝΕΣ,

Πλακουνῖις. Heſych. The name of the cakes,
ſacred to Peon, the god of light. Pi-On, Pi-Or,
and Pe-Or, were Amonian names of the Sun.
I. 297. n.

PIRENE.

In Campania was a fountain Virena; a compound
of Vir-En, ignis fons, from being dedicated to the
deity of Fire: it was a medicinal ſpring, and of a
ſtrong vitriolic nature. (Vitruv. Archit. l. 8.)
The Corinthians had in their Acropolis a Pirene, of
the ſame purport as Virena (indeed they are the
ſame name) it was a beautiful fountain ſacred to
Apollo, whoſe image was at the head of the water
within a ſacred incloſure. I. 193.

PIROMIS.

Herodotus (l. 2. c. 143.) from the account given
to him by the prieſts of Thebes about the kings,
who had reigned in Egypt; ſays " after the fabulous accounts, there had been an uninterrupted
ſucceſſion of Piromis after Piromis: and the
Egyptians referred none of theſe to the dynaſties of
either gods or heroes, who were ſuppoſed to have
firſt poſſeſſed the country." Hence it ſeems plain
that Pi-romis ſignifies *a man*. It has this ſignification in the Coptic: and in the Prodromus Cop-
ticus of Kircher, Πιρωμι, is *a man*; and ſeems to
imply a native. Pirem Racot is an Alexandrine,
or more properly a native of Racotis, called Raſ-
chid,

chid, and Rofetta. Pirem Romi are Romans.
I. 122.

Befides Ob, &c. a ferpent was alfo named Pitan,
or Patan. Many places in different parts were
denominated from this term: and probably had
Dracontia, where were figures and devices relative
to the religion, which prevailed. Ovid (Metam.
l. 7.) defcribing Medea as flying through the air
from Attica to Colchis, fays,

> Æoliam Pitanem læva de parte relinquit,
> Factáque de faxo longi fimulacra *Draconis.*

The Opici, who are faid to be denominated from
ferpents, had alfo the name of Pitanatæ; at leaft
one part of that family were fo called (Hefych.) A
brigade, or portion of infantry, was among fome of
the Greeks named Pitanates; (Hefych.) and the
foldiers in confequence of it muft have been termed
Pitanatæ : undoubtedly, becaufe they had the Pitan,
or Serpent, for their ftandard. Analogous to this
there were foldiers called Draconarii. Probably
in moft countries the military ftandard was an emblem of the deity there worfhiped. I. 487.

Were often fubftituted for the deity, and made
an object of worfhip. I. 92. They had as many
names as the deity worfhiped had titles. 103.

The Græcians were fo prepoffeffed with a notion
of their own excellence and antiquity, that they
fuppofed every ancient tradition to have proceeded
from themfelves. Hence their mythology is
founded upon the groffeft miftakes: as all extraneous hiftory, and every foreign term, is fuppofed
                                                    by

by them to have been of Græcian original.
Plato (with others) faw the fallacy of their claim :
yet in this article no one was more infatuated.
His Cratylus is made up of a moſt abſurd fyſtem of
etymology. Herodotus expreſly fays, (l. 2. c. 4.
and c. 52.) that the gods of Greece came in great
meaſure from Egypt. Yet Socrates is by Plato in
this treatiſe made to derive Artemis from το αρlεμες,
integritas; Poſeidon from ωοσι δεσμον, fetters to the
feet; Heſtia from ουσια, fubftance and effence; Demeter from διδουσα ως μηlηρ, diftributing as a mother;
Pallas from παλλιν, to vibrate, or dance: Arez,
Mars, from αρριν, mafculum, et virile; and Theos,
God, undoubtedly the Theuth of Egypt, from θειιν,
to run. Innumerable derivations of this nature are
to be found in other Greek writers. I. 130.

PLUTO,

Among the beſt theologiſts, was eſteemed the
fame as Jupiter; and indeed the fame as every other
deity. I. 310. Hermeſianax;

Πλουlων, Περσεφονη, Δημηlηρ, Κυπρις, Ερωlες,
Τριlωνες, Νηρευς, Τηθυς και Κυανοχαιlης,
'Ερμης ϑ', 'Ηφαιςος τε κλυlος, Παν, Ζευς τε, και 'Ηρη,
Αρlεμις, ηδ' 'Εκαεργος Απολλων, εις Θεος εςιν.

POETS.

The firſt writers were the Poets; and the miſ-
chief began with them: for they firſt infected tradition; and mixed it with allegory and fable.
" The greateſt abuſes (fays Anaxagoras, Legat.)
of true knowledge came from them. I infiſt that
we owe to Orpheus, Homer, and Heſiod, the fictitious names and genealogies of the Pagan dæmons,
whom they are pleaſed to call gods: and I can produce Herodotus to witneſs what I aſſert. He informs us (l. 2. c. 53.) that Homer and Heſiod
were

were about 400 years before himfelf; and not more. Thefe, fays he, were the perfons who firft framed the theogony of the Greeks; and gave appellations to their deities; and diftinguifhed them according to their feveral ranks and departments. They at the fame time defcribed them under different appearances.: for till their time there was not in Greece any reprefentation of the gods, either in fculpture or painting; nor any fpecimen of the ftatuaries art exhibited: no fuch fubftitutes were in thofe times thought of." I. 160.

P'OMPHI,

Ham was the Hermes of the Egyptians, and his oracle was ftiled Omphi: and when particularly fpoken of as *the oracle*, it was expreffed P'omphi, and P'ompi, the πομπη of the Greeks. Hence Hermes had the name of Πομπαιος, which was mifinterpreted the *meffenger*, and *conductor*; and the deity was in confequence of it made the fervant of the gods, and attendant upon the dead. But πομπαιος related properly to divine influence; and πομπη was an oracle. An ox or cow, was by the Amonians efteemed very facred, and oracular: Cadmus was accordingly faid to have been directed πομπη βοος. Many places were from the oracle ftiled P'ompean: and fuppofed by the Romans to have been fo named from Pompeius Magnus; but they were too numerous, and too remote to have been denominated from him, or any other Roman. There were alfo pillars ftiled Pompean; which by many have been referred to the fame perfon. But they could not have been built by him, nor were they erected to his memory, as may be learned from their hiftory. I. 259.

POSEIDON,

POSEIDON,

God of the fea; his prieft was ftiled a P'urcon, which is ignis vel lucis dominus: and we may know the department of the god from the name of the prieft. He was no other than the fupreme deity, the Sun; from whom all were fuppofed to be derived. He is therefore, like Zeus, ftiled, in the Orphic verfes, the father of gods and men. He was exprefsly ftiled Cun-Ades, being the fame as Apollo. Κυναδης Ποσειδων Αθηνησιν ελιμαλο. (Hefych.) 351. The Patriarch was alfo commemorated by the name of Pofeidon. Hence in the Orphic verfes (Hymn 16.) he is thus addreffed:

Κλυθι Ποσειδαον, Ζηνος παι πρεσβυγενεθλε,
Ουρανιων, Μακαρων τε Θεων παλερ, ηδε και Ανδρων,
Ειρηνην υγιειαν αγων, ηδ' ολβον αμεμφη.

(Zeus is generally made the brother of Pofeidon, but is here fpoken of as his father: which fhews how little we can depend upon the theogony of the Greeks, when they treat of genealogies.)

As Noah was the Pofeidon of the Greeks, we need not wonder at the epithets beftowed upon that deity; fuch as Παληρ, Ασφαλιος, Γενεσιος, Γενεθλος, Φυλαλμος, or Sativus. In Arcadia was a temple of Ποσειδων Εποπλης, *Neptune looking out.* None of thefe titles have the leaft reference to the Pagan Pofeidon, as god of the fea: but to the hiftory of the Patriarch they have a wonderful relation, and are particularly applicable. II. 268.

PRIAPUS.

Polytheifm originally vile, and unwarrantable, was rendered ten times more bafe by coming through the hands of the Greeks and Romans. Among all the dæmon herd, what one is there of a form, and character, fo odious, and contemptible as Priapus?

Priapus? an obfcure, ill-formed deity, who was ridiculed and difhonoured by his very votaries.

Yet this contemptible god, this fcarecrow in a garden, was held in high repute at Lampfacus, and efteemed the fame as Dionufus. The Egyptians reverenced him as the principal god; no other than the Chaldaic Aur, the fame as Orus and Apis. Hence the Priapus of Greece is only a compound of Peor-Apis among the Egyptians: fometimes called Peor fingly; fometimes Baal Peor; the fame with whofe rites the Ifraelites are fo often upbraided: his temples were ftiled Beth Peor. In fhort, this wretched divinity of the Romans was looked upon by others as the foul of the world; the firft prin-ciple, which brought all things into light, and being. There is an ancient infcription in Gruter (V. 1. p. xcv. n. 1.) PRIEPO PANTHEO. Phurnutus (de Nat. Deor. c. 17.) fuppofes Priapus to have been the fame as Pan, the fhepherd god; who was equally degraded, and mifreprefented on the one hand, and as highly reverenced on the other. των αρχαιων δ' ειςι δαιμονων. Yet the one was degraded to a filthy monfter; and of the other they made a fcarecrow. I. 141.

PRIESTS.

The priefts of old were almoft univerfally deno-minated from the god whom they ferved, or from his temple. I. 15. And they were oftentimes called the fons of the deity, whom they ferved. II. 466. The Egyptian priefts feem to have been from their complexion denominated Crows, or Ravens. Strabo (l. 17.) fays, that Alexander upon his expedition to the temple of Ammon, was con-ducted by two crows. Curtius (l. 4. c. 7.) fays that a good number went out to meet him, *modico volatu*, &c. Thefe crows were certainly the priefts of the place. II. 291.

PROMETHEUS.

8

PROMETHEUS.

Eufebius tells us, ἑρμηνευουσι Νουν τον Δια· Προμηθεα δε Νουν ελεγον· διο και μυθυονται τους ανθρωπους μεταπεπλασθαι. (v. Eufeb. Hift. Synag.) If we take the hiftory without his comment, it will be found for the moft part true. The original account was, that not only Zeus, or Zeuth, but alfo Prometheus, *qui genus hominum refinxit*, was Noos, or Noah. Prometheus raifed the firft altar to the gods;—he conftructed the firft fhip; Æfchyl. Prometh.

Θαλασσοπλαγκια δ᾽ ουτις αλλος αντ᾽ εμου
Λινοπτερ᾽ ευρε ναυτιλων οχηματα.

And tranfmitted to pofterity many ufeful inventions:

παντα συλληβδην μαθε,
Πασαι τεχναι βροτοισιν εκ Προμηθεως.   Id.

He was fuppofed to have lived in the time of the deluge; and to have been guardian of Egypt at that feafon. His influence was limited to that region; becaufe the Egyptians, like the people of Phocis, Argos, Theffaly, and Dodona, confined the deluge to the boundaries of their own country. Hence we may plainly fee the perfon who is alluded to under the character of Prometheus. He was the fame as Ofiris; the fame alfo as Dionufus, the great hufbandman, the planter of the vine, and inventor of the plough. II. 273.

PROTEUS

Was a title of the Patriarch. Homer reprefents him as an ancient prophet; a perfon of great truth. (Οδ. Δ.) γερων αλιος, νημερτης, αθανατος Πρωτευς. In his departments he was the fame as Pofeidon. II. 270.

ΠΡΟΘΥΡΑΙΑ.

ΠΡΟΘΥΡΑΙΑ.

Noah and all of the animal creation with him, had been for a long time inclofed in a ftate of obfcurity. On this account the Genius of the Ark, under the character of Rhea and Cybele, is by Lucretius ftiled (l. 2. v. 598.) Magna deûm mater, materque *ferarum*. The opening the door of their prifon houfe, and their enlargement was efteemed a fecond iffuing to life. Hence as the ancients formed a genius or dæmon from every circumftance in mythology, they fuppofed the Genius of the Ark to prefide over the birth, under the name of Lucina, Diana, Juno, and of a goddefs particularly ftiled Προθυραια. II. 364. v. Orphic. Hymn 1.

PROTOGONUS,

The firft man upon earth, was certainly defigned to reprefent the great Patriarch. Orphic. Hymn 5.

Πρωΐογονον καλεω, διφυη, μεγαν αιθεροπλαγχΙην,
Ωογενη, χρυσεαισιν αγαλλομενον πΙερυγεσσιν.

I invoke Protogonus, the firft of men: him who was of a twofold ftate, or nature: who wandered at large under the whole heavens; inclofed in an ovicular machine, (whence he was termed Ωογενης, Ovo genitus,) *who was alfo,* hieroglyphically, *depicted with golden wings.*

Γενεσιν Μακαρων, ΘνηΙωνΙ' ανθρωπων.

The fame was the father of the Macares (ftiled Heroes, Αθαναλοι, Ἡλιαδαι, the Demigods, and Dæmons) *the parent alfo of all mankind.*

Ὁσσων ὁς σκόΙοεσσαν απημαυρωσιν ὁμιχλην.

Who difpelled the mift and darknefs, with which every thing had been obfcured. The golden wings were undoubtedly taken from the tints of the Iris:

A a . and

and thefe defcriptions are borrowed from ancient
hieroglyphical pictures; where the fame emblem
was differently appropriated; yet ftill related to the
fame hiftorical event. Eros was alfo ftiled διφυη.
(Orphic. Hymn 57.) II. 353.

PSUCHE.

, The moft pleafing emblem among the Egyptians
was exhibited under the character of Pfuche,
Ψυχη. This was originally no other than the
Aurelia or butterfly; but in aftertimes was reprefented as a lovely female child with the beautiful
wings of that infect. The circumftance of a fecond
birth, or iffuing into life, after a confinement, is
continually defcribed under the character of Pfuche.
And as the whole (the prefervation in the Ark, &c.)
was owing to divine Love, of which Eros was an
emblem, we find this perfon often introduced as a
concomitant of Pfuche. They are generally defcribed as accidentally meeting, and enjoying a
pleafing interview; which is attended with em-
braces and falutes; and every mark of reconciliation
and favour.

From this union of divine Love, and the Soul,
the ancients dated the inftitution of marriage. And
as the renewal of mankind commenced from their
iffuing out of the Ark, and from the gracious promife of increafe made by the Deity upon that occafion; they thought proper to affign to Iönah, or
Juno, the emblem of Divine Providence, the office
of prefiding at that ceremony. II. 388.

PUR,

Pir, Phur, Vir: all fignify Fire. I. 194. n.

PURAMOUN

(Expreffed by the latter Greeks Πυραμουϛ, a
facred *Cake*) fo denominated from Pur-Ham, and
Pur-Amon. I. 297.

PURATHEIA,

PURATHEIA,

From P'ur-Aith. At Cumana in Cappadocia, ſtood one of the nobleſt Puratheia's in Aſia. The deity worſhiped was repreſented as a feminine, and ſtiled Anait, and Anais. She was well known alſo in Perſes, Meſopotamia, and at Egbatana in Media. I. 202.

ΠΥΡΓΟΣ,

Purgos; this ancient term was properly Pur-Go, and ſignified a light houſe, or temple of fire, from the Chaldaic Pur. I. 117.

P'UR.

This was the ancient name of Latian Jupiter; the term by length of time was changed to Puer. He was the deity of fire; and his miniſters were ſtiled Pueri: and becauſe many of them were handſome youths ſelected for that office, Puer came at length to ſignify any young perſon. Some of the Romans would explain this away, as if it referred to Jupiter's childhood: but the hiſtory of the place will ſhew that it had no ſuch relation. It was a proper name, and retained particularly among the people of Præneſte, who had been addicted to the rites of fire. (Virg. Æn. l. 7. v. 679.) They called their chief god Pur: and dealt particularly in divination by lots, termed of old *Purim*. (Cic. de Divinat. l. 2.) This manner of divination was of Chaldaic original, and brought from Babylonia to Præneſte. (v. Eſther iii. 9.) In Gruter there are inſcriptions Iovi Puero, and Fortunæ Primigeniæ Iovis Pueri. That this word Puer was originally Pur may be proved from a well known paſſage in Lucretius. (L. 4. v. 1020.)

Puri ſæpe lacum propter ac dolia curva, &c.

It was a name originally given to the prieſts of the

A a 2   deity,

deity, who were named from the Chaldaic אור, Ur:
and by the ancient Latins, P'uri. I. 125.

P'UR-TAN,

Hence came Πρυ]ανεις and Πρυ]ανεα among the
Greeks of Hellas.

P'UR-TOR.

This term in aftertimes was rendered Prætorium:
and the chief perfons, who officiated, Prætores.
They were originally priefts of fire; and for that
reafon were called Aphetæ: and every Prætor had
a brazier of live coals carried before him, as a badge
of his office. I. 62.

PYRRHA.

Near Pagafæ and Iolchus was a promontory fo
named; and near it two iflands, named the iflands
of Pyrrha and Deucalion. This and other circumftances are wonderful evidence of the Arkites,
and their rites, which were introduced there.
II. 504.

PYRRIC DANCE,

Which the Amonian priefts danced round a large
fire in honour of the Sun, whofe orbit they affected
to defcribe. At the fame time they exhibited other
feats of activity, to amufe their votaries, who reforted to their temples. This dance was fometimes performed in armour, efpecially in Crete:
and being called Pyrric was fuppofed to have been
fo named from Pyrrhus, the fon of Achilles: but
long before his time it was faid to have been practifed by the Argonautic Heroes. It was a religious
dance, denominated from fire, with which it was
accompanied. (v. Betarmus.) There is reafon to
think that the circular dances of the Dervifes all
over the Eaft are remains of thefe ancient cuftoms.

In

In the first ages this exercise was esteemed a religious rite, and performed by people of the temple where it was exhibited: but in aftertimes the same feats were imitated by ropedancers, and vagrants, called Petauriftæ, and Petauriftarii; who made use of a kind of pole, called Petaurum. Juvenal. Sat. 14.

> An magis oblectant animum jactata *petauro*
> Corpora, quique folent rectum defcendere funem?

Manilius. L. 5.

> Ad numeros etiam ille ciet cognata per artem
> Corpora, quæ valido faliunt excuffa petauro:
> Membraque *per flammas orbefque* emiffa flagrantes,
> Delphinûmque fuo per inane imitantia motu,
> Et viduata volant pennis, et in aere ludunt.

In thefe verfes of Manilius fome remains of the original inftitution may be obferved. I. 285.

R.

RAB

SIGNIFIES *great*, and being doubled, Rabrab, *very great*. I. 24. Rabfhekah fignifies the great prince; Rabfares, the chief eunuch; Rabmag, the chief of the Magi. 74.

A a 3

RAM,

RAM, RAMA, RAMAS, RAMIS,

Signified fomething high, and noble, and great. It occurs in the Vedam at this day; and in moft of the mythological writings, which are tranfmitted from India. It was a title not unknown among the Greeks; Ραμας, ὁ Ὑψιϛος Θεος. Hefych. Ραμαιθας (the city Laodicea) αφ᾽ ὑψους ὁ Θεος· Ραμαν γαρ εγχωριον το ὑψος· Ἀλαν δε ὁ Θεος. Euftath. in Dionyf. Perieg. v. 915. Stephanus renders the name Ramanthan; and gives this interpretation; Ραμαν γαρ το ὑψος, *Raman relates to height.* Ram makes a part in Rameffes, and Rameffomenes; and in the name of the Egyptian deity Remphan, which fignifies the great Phanes. Rhamnufia, the deity of Juftice, is a compound of Rham-Nous; and is a feminine title of that juft man Noah, ftiled Nus, Nous, and Noufios. II. 304. Ραμνους, δημος Ατλιχης, ɯθα τη Νεμεσι ὁ Ζευς συνεκαθευδησεν, ἡτις ἡλκεν Ωον. (Schol. in Callim. H. in Dian. v. 232.) Ram Nous is ὁ μεγας Νοος, or Noas, from whom the diftrict was named. 361.

RAMTXANDER.

Many of the ancient ftupendous ftructures, which are met with in the farther parts of India, have been attributed to Ram-Scander, or Alexander the Great: but there is nothing among thefe ftately edifices, which in the leaft favours of Græcian workmanfhip; nor had that monarch, nor any of the princes after him, opportunity to perform works of this nature. We have not the leaft reafon to think, that they ever poffeffed the country: for they were called off from their attention this way by feuds, and engagements nearer home. There is no tradition of this country having been ever conquered, except by the fabulous armies of Hercules and Dionufus. (Strabo, l. 15.) What has led people
to

to think, that thefe works were the operations of Alexander, is the fimilitude of the name Ramtxander. To this perfon, they have fometimes been attributed. But Ramtxander was a deity, the fuppofed fon of Bal; and he is introduced among the perfonages, who were concerned in the incarnations of Vifhnou. (Kircher's China. p. 158.)

Thevenot (Travels into India. Part 3. c. 4.) having defcribed the pagod of Elora, near Aurangeabed, in the province of Balagate; concludes with faying, that he made diligent inquiry among the natives, about the origin of thefe wonderful buildings; and the conftant tradition was, " That all thefe pagodas, great and fmall, with all their works and ornaments, were made by Giants: but in what age they could not tell." (See Perron's Zend-Avefta. Vol. 1. p. 234.) III. 567.

RAVEN.

This bird Noah fent out of the Ark, by way of experiment; it difappointed him, and never returned. This bird is however depicted in the Sphere; and a tradition is mentioned, that the Raven was once fent out upon a meffage by Apollo; but deceived him; and did not return, when he was expected. It may feem ftrange that the Dove, the meffenger of good tidings, fhould not be found in the Sphere. I make no doubt but it was to be found in the Chaldaic and Egyptian fpheres: but in that of Greece, there is, in the fouthern hemifphere, a vaft interval of unformed ftars; which were omitted by the aftronomers of that country, as being either feldom feen, or elfe totally obfcured from their view. II. 236.

The Raven, which never returned, was for the moft part efteemed a bird of ill omen: and yet it was confidered as an augural bird; and is faid to have preceded, and directed the colony, which

A a 4   Battus

Battus led to Cyrene. (Callim. H. in Apoll. v. 66.)
284. And though its very croaking would put a
ftop in the procefs of matrimony, yet we are
affured, that there were times, when it was otherwife
efteemed. Ælian (de Animal. l. 3.) tells us, εν ταις
γαμοις μεtα του 'Υμεναιον Κορωνην καλειν, There was a
fong (Horapollo. l. 1. c. 8.) Εκκοριι, Κορα, Κορωνην.
The treat confifted of figs; και τη Κορωνη παρθενος
φερει συκα. (Athenæus. l. 8.) This ceremony was
doubtlefs owing to a tradition, that the Raven upon
a time was fent by Apollo upon a meffage; but
difappointed him; and inftead of fulfilling his
orders he perched upon a fig-tree, and waited till
the fruit was ripe. (Ovid. Faft. l. 2. 243, &c.)
The mythologifts out of every circumftance and
title formed a perfonage. Hence Paufanias (l. 2.)
fpeaks of the Raven as an ancient hero, and mentions his family: Κορωνου δε γινονlαι Κοραξ, και Λα-
μεδων. 392.

RELIGION.

When there was a change made in Religion,
people converted the heathenifh temples to fanc-
tuaries of another nature: and out of the ancient
names of places they formed faints, and holy men.
Hence we meet with St. Agnes, St. Allan, St. Earth,
St. Enador, St. Herm, St. Levan, St. Ith, St. San-
crete, in Cornwal: and from the Caledonian
Columba, there has been made a St. Columbus.
_ II. 474.

RHINOCOLURA.

The name of an ancient frontier town of Egypt;
which the Greeks unnaturally derived from ρις,
ρινος, a nofe; and fuppofed that fome people's nofes
were cut off here. I. 169. n.

RHOIA.

RHOIA.

As the Ark was looked upon as the mother of mankind, and ſtiled Da Mater: ſo it was figured under the ſemblance of the Ῥοια, *Pomegranate*; ſince abounding with ſeeds, it was thought no improper emblem of the Ark, which contained the rudiments of the future world. Hence the deity of the Ark was named Rhoia, and was the Rhea of the Greeks. The ancient Perſians uſed to have a pomegranate carved upon the top of their walking-ſticks and ſceptres: undoubtedly on account of its being a ſacred emblem. What is alluded to under the character of the goddeſs Rhoia, or Rhea, is very plain from her imputed attributes, Orphic. Fragm. 34. p. 395.

> Ῥιιη, τοι ΝΟΕΡΩΝ ΜΑΚΑΡΩΝ πηγη τι, ῥοη τι·
> Παντων γαρ πρωτη δυναμιι κολποισιν αφραςοις
> Διξαμινη γινιαν ιπι παν προχιιι τροχιουςαν.

Orphic. H. 13.

> Πολνα Ῥια, θυγατηρ πολυμορφου Πρωτογινοιο,
> Μητηρ μιν τι θιων, ηδι θνητων ανθρωπων,
> Ελθι, μακαιρα θια, σωτηριος.——

The Pomegranate was alſo called Rimmon; uhder which name it was worſhiped in Syria; and was held ſacred in Egypt. In an ancient temple at Peluſium, there was a ſtatue of Zeus Caſius, having this myſterious fruit in his hand. (Achill. Tatius. l. 3.) The god Rimmon (2 Kings v.) was probably repreſented in the like manner. Peter Texeira (Travels, c.9.) mentions two round mounts not far from Ana upon the Euphrates; called by the natives Rumanhen; which, he ſays, ſignified the two pomegranates.

Another name for the Pomegranate was Side; of which name there was a city in Pamphylia: and

another

another in Bœotia; which was faid to have been
built by Side, the daughter of Danaus; which
hiftory may be in great meafure true: for by a
daughter of Danaus is meant a prieftefs of Da
Naus, the Ark, the fame as Da Mater. II. 380.

S.

SABACON

Of Ethiopia, was Saba-Con, or king of Saba.
I. 41. n.

SAID-ON,

Dagon was fo called, and likewife Sidon; a
name precifely of the fame purport. Philo Biblius, fuppofing the latter to relate to corn, terms
it Σιίων; as if it were of Græcian etymology.
Herein we may fee the futility of thofe tranflators,
who would reduce every thing to their own language. What he renders Siton, and derives from
σῖτος, corn, was in the original Sidon, or Saidon; and
Sanchoniathon, from whom he copied, intended to
fhew that Said-On, and Dag-On were equivalent
terms; and that both referred to one perfon worfhiped under the character of a fifh: both Dag and
Said, fignifying, in the language of Syria and Palæftine, a fifh. II. 300.

SAITÆ.

SAITÆ.

They founded Athens; alfo Thebes in Bœotia.
They were of Egypt, but came laft from Sidon.
(Eufeb. Chron. p. 14.) I. 184.

SALEM.

John baptized in Ænon near to Salim, &c. (John
iii. 23.) Ænon, Ain-On, fons Solis. Salem is not
from Salem, *peace,* but from Sal, *the Sun.* Salim,
Aquæ Solis; alfo Aquæ falfæ. I. 51.

SALENTINI,

According to Pliny (l. 2. c. 110.) boafted of
having a facred and fpontaneous appearance of fire
in their temple. Hence undoubtedly came the
name of Salentum, which is a compound of Sal-
En, Solis fons, (Sal, the Sun; hence Sol of the
Latines. I. 51. n.) and arofe from this facred fire
to which the Salentini pretended. They were
Amonians, who fettled here, and who came laft from
Crete. Strabo (l. 6.) τους δε Σαλευ]ινους Κρη]ων αποι-
κους φασι. The ancient Salentini worfhiped the Sun
under the title of Man-zan, or Manzana; by which
is meant Menes, Sol. Feftus in v. Octobris.
I. 203.

SAMA-CON

Is rendered Samicon by Strabo, l. 8. Sama-Con
is, fignum cœlefte, five fignum Dei. Strabo fuppofes that Samos and Samicon were fo named from
Sama, *high.* And it certainly had that meaning;
but here Sama fignifies fignum; fimilar to σαμα and
σημα, which were derived from it. II. 513.

SAMARITANS.

SAMARITANS.

A colony of Cuthites settled in Samaria, and brought with them the infignia of their country; and fhewed great veneration for the Dove. On this account they were reproached by the Jews, as worfhipers of the Dove. (v. Bochart. v. 3. c. 1. Selden. de diis Syr. Synt. 2.) That they were in great meafure Cuthites is plain from the hiftory which they gave of themfelves to Jofephus. (Antiq. l. 9. c. 14. l. 11. c. 4.) Σαλμαναζαρης ὁ των Αϲ-ϲυριων βασιλευς εκ της ΧΟΥΘΙΑΣ ἡμας μέ]ηγαγε, και Μηδιας. II. 303.

SAN, SON, ZAN, ZAAN,

The moft common name for the Sun was San, and Son; expreffed alfo Zan, Zon, and Zaan. Zeus of Crete, who was fuppofed to have been buried in that ifland, is faid to have had the following infcription on his tomb. (Cyril. c. Julian. l. 10.)

Ωδε μεγας κει]αι Ζαν, ὁν Δια κικλησκουσι.

The Ionians expreffed it Ζην, and Ζηνα. The Sun was called Σαως by the Babylonians. Hefych. As the Græcians in foreign words omitted the final nu, fubftituting a figma: the true name was undoubtedly Σαων, oftentimes expreffed Σωαν.

Ham, and others of his family were collectively called the Baalim: analogous to this they were likewife called the Zaanim, and Zaananim. And a temple was erected to them by the ancient Canaanites, called Beth-Zaananim. In the fame country was a place called Sanim, rendered by Eufebius Σωναμ; undoubtedly fo named in honour of the fame perfons: for their pofterity looked up to them, as the Heliadæ, or defcendants of the Sun, and denominated them from that luminary. It was a title,

title, of old-not unknown in Greece: Ζανιδες, Ἡγεμονες. Hefych.

Beth-San is the temple of the Sun. (1 Sam. xxxi.) This term feems fometimes to have been ufed with a re-duplication; as there was a city Sanfanah in Canaan; by which is fignified a place facred to the moft illuftrious Orb of day. There were fome ancient ftatues near mount Cronius in Elis; καλουνlαι δε ὑπο των επιχωριων Ζανες. Paufan. l. 5. fuppofed to have been of Zeus: but Zan was the Sun; and they were ftatues of perfons, who were denominated from him. One of thefe perfons, ftiled Zanes, and Zanim was Chus; whofe pofterity fent out large colonies to various parts of the earth. Some of them fettled upon the coaft of Aufonia, afterwards called Italy, where they worfhiped their great anceftor under the name of San-Chus. Sabini *San-cum* colunt. Lactant. de F. R. l. 1. He was not unknown at Rome (the name was not of Roman original, but far prior to Rome.) εν ἱερῳ Διος Πιςιου, ὁν Ῥωμαιοι Σαγχον καλουσι. Dion. Hal. A. R. l. 4. There are in Gruter infcriptions to him, wherein he is ftiled Semon (Sem-On, cœleftis Sol) and Sanctus:

SANCTO. SANCO.
SEMONI. DEO. FIDIO.
SACRUM.

Vol. 1. p. 96. n. 6. 5. 7. 8.

Some of the ancients thought that the foul of man was a divine emanation; a portion of light from the Sun: hence probably it was called Zoan. Macrob. Sat. l. 3. c. 8. From San came the Latine terms Sanus, Sano, Sanctus, Sancire: and hence perhaps came Ζωειν and Ζην *to live*; and Ζωον, *anima!*: alfo the title of Apollo Ζηνοδοτηρ. I. 35.

SAR, ZAR,

A rock, alfo *a promontory.* As temples were particularly erected upon fuch places, thefe emi-nences

nences were often denominated Sar-On, from the deity to whom the temples were facred.

Sar was oftentimes ufed as a mark of high honor (often in the Pfalms) and without a metaphor, for a title of refpect; but it feems then to have been differently expreffed. Thus the lordly people of Sidon and Tyre, were called Sarim. (Ifai. xxiii. 8.) The name of Sarah was given to the wife of Abraham by way of eminence; and fignifies, a lady, or princefs.

It is continually to be found in the compofition of names, which relate to places, or perfons, efteemed facred by the Amonians, e. g. Serapis, Serapion, Serapammon; alfo, Sarchon, and Sardon (for Sar-Adon) Sarchedonus (Tobit i. 22.) the fame name as the former, but with the eaftern afpirate. The Sarim in Efther (i. 16.) are taken notice of as perfons of high honour; it was rendered Sarna, or Sarana among the Philiftim: hence the Tyrian word Sarranus for any thing noble and fplendid. Sarfechim in Jeremiah (xxxix. 3.) is a plural, compounded of Sar, and Sech, or Shec, a prince, or governor: Sar-Sechim fignifies the chief of the princes and rulers. Many places in Syria and Canaan have the Sar in compofition, viz. Sarabetha, Sariphæa, Sareptha. Sardis the capital of Crœfus, was the city of Sar-Ades, the fame as Atis, the deity of the country.

High groves, or rather hills with ancient woods of Oaks, were named Saron; being facred to the deity fo called. Pliny (l. 4. c. 8.) Portus Cœnitis, Sinus Saronicus olim querno nemore redimitus; unde nomen. The oaks and the place were denominated from the deity Sar-On, and Chan-Ait, rendered by the Greeks Σαρων, and Κοινειλις; titles nearly of the fame purport. Saron was without doubt an ancient god of Greece. Lilius Gyraldus (Syntag. 4.) ftiles him deus marinus; but he was

properly

properly the Sun. Diana is named Saronia.
Hefych. At Troezen there were Saronia facra,
with a feſtival; here Orus (the fame as Sar-On, the
lord of light) was ſuppoſed to have been born.
Pauſan. l. 2.

Rocks were called Saronides (Hefych.) from
having temples and towers facred to this deity.
Callimachus (H. in Del.) calls the iſland Aſterie
κακον σαρον. This by the Scholiaſt is interpreted
καλυνſρον· but it certainly means a rock.

As oaks were ſtiled Saronides, ſo likewiſe were
the ancient Druids, by whom the Oak was held ſo
facred. Hence Diodorus Siculus, (l. 5.) ſpeaking
of the prieſts of Gaul, ſtiles them φιλοσοφοι, θεολογοι
—περιτιως τιμωμενοι, ους ΣΑΡΩΝΙΔΑΣ ονομαζουσι. This
is one proof among many how far the Amonian
religion was extended: and how little we know of
Druidical worſhip, either in reſpect to its eſſence or
its origin. I. 73.

SATURN.

The Romans made a diſtinction between Janus
and Saturn; they were two titles of the fame perſon. Saturn is repreſented as a man of great piety
and juſtice; under whom there was an age of feli-
city; when as yet there were no laws, no ſervitude,
no ſeparate property. (v. Juſtin. l. 43. c. 1.)
When the earth produced every thing ſpontaneouſly
for the good of man. He was however ſometimes
deſcribed with the fickle in his hand; and repreſented as going over the whole earth, teaching to
plant, and to ſow. Plato ſuppoſed him to be the
ſon of Oceanus: others of Cœlus. Like Janus he
is faid (Diod. Sic. l. 5.) to have brought mankind from their foul and favage way of feeding to
a more mild and rational diet: like him he had keys
in his hand; and his coins had the figure of a ſhip.
He was looked upon as the author of time; and often
9   held

held a ferpent in his hand, whofe tail was in his
mouth, and formed a circle; by this emblem they
denoted the renovation of the year. He was reprefented as of an uncommon age; and yet there
was a notion, that he could return to fecond childhood. Martial's addrefs to him, though fhort, has
in it fomething remarkable; for he fpeaks of him
as a native of the former world.

Antiqui Rex magne poli, mundique prioris,
   Sub quo prima quies, nec labor ullus erat.

To other gods the Romans facrificed, with their
heads veiled; but in thofe to Saturn the veil was
taken away. He had the name of Septimianus;
and the Saturnalia, which were days fet apart for
his rites in December, were in number feven.
Thefe rites are faid to have been of great antiquity;
far prior to the foundation of Rome. The poet
Accius (Macrob. Sat. l. 1.) looked upon them as
the fame as thofe which the Græcians ftiled
Κρονια :

  Maxima pars Graiûm Saturno, et maxime Athenæ,
  Conficiunt facra, quæ Cronia effe iterantur ab illis.
  Eumque diem celebrant per agros, urbefque fere
    omnes
  Exercent epulis læti; famulofque procurant
  Quifque fuos; noftrique itidem : et mos traditus
    illinc
  Ifte, ut eum dominis famuli epulantur ibidem.

Among the Romans Saturn feems to have been
held in a ftate of confinement for the greater part
of the year. When the Saturnalia began, there was
a myfterious ceremony of taking off thefe bonds.
This, though a fecret to the ancients, is plain to
thofe, who confider the various perfonages under
which the Patriarch was reprefented.

Saturn

Saturn was ftiled Sator by the Romans; making
ufe of a term in their own language, which was not
inapplicable to his hiftory. Yet perhaps this was
not a title of Roman original, but imported from
Egypt and Syria by the Pelafgi; and. adopted by
the people of Italy. It feems to be a compound of
Sait-Our, which among the eaftern nations fignified
Oliva Ori, five Dei; or Oliva cœleftis. All the
upper part of Egypt was named Sait, and the people Saïtæ.

Saturn was not unknown to the ancient Germans; among whom he was worfhiped by the
name of Seatur. He is defcribed by Verftegan
(p. 78.) as ftanding upon a fifh with a wheel in
one hand, and in the other a veffel of water filled
with fruits and flowers. Schedius (de diis Germ.
Synt. 4. c. 2.) mentions him by the name of Crodo;
and fays that he was the fame as Saturn of the
Romans. II. 260.

The ancients had a notion, that when Saturn
devoured his own children, his wife Ops deceived
him by fubftituting a large ftone in lieu of one of
his fons, which ftone was called Abadir. But Ops,
and Opis, reprefented here as a feminine, was the
ferpent deity, and Abadir is the fame perfonage
under a different denomination. One of thefe
ftones, which Saturn was fuppofed to have fwallowed (καταπινειν) inftead of a child, ftood according to Paufanias (l. 10.) at Delphi. It was efteemed
very facred, and ufed to have libations of wine
poured upon it daily; and upon feftivals was otherwife honoured. The purport of the above hiftory
feems to have been this: It was for a long time a
cuftom to offer children at the altar of Saturn; but
in procefs of time they removed it, and in its room
erected a ςυλος, or ftone pillar; before which they
made their vows, and offered facrifices of another
nature. The ftone which they thus fubftituted,

B b   was

was called Ab-Adar from the deity reprefented by
it. I. 476.

SCANDINAVIANS.

It is wonderful, how far the Amonian religion
and cuftoms were carried in the firft ages. The
ancient Germans and Scandinavians, were led by
the fame principles; and founded their temples in
fituations of the fame nature, as theirs were. Above
all others they chofe thofe places, where were any
nitrous, or faline waters. (v. Tacit. Annal. l. 13.
c. 57.) I. 34.

SCYLLA

Was a perfonage of the fame fort with the Sirens.
Callimachus (Fragm. 184.) gives a fhort, but a
moft perfect, defcription of her character.

Σκυλλα, γυνη καλακασα, και ου ψυθος ουνομ᾽ εχουσα.

The learned Hemfterhufius thus juftly remarks:
Καλακασα cur latine vertatur *malefica* non video.
Si Grammaticis obtemperes, *meretricem* interpreta-
bere: erat enim revera Νησιωτης καλη εταιρα, ut He-
raclitus περι απις: c. 2. Scylla then, the chief
prieftefs of the place, was no other than a hand-
fome ifland ftrumpet. She was, like the Sibyl of
Campania, faid by Stefichorus (v. Schol. Apollon.
l. 4. v. 828.) to have been the daughter of Lamia.
She is faid alfo to have been the daughter of
Hecate and Phorcun. Phor-Cun fignifies Ignis
Dominus, the fame as Hephaftus. The daughter
of a deity means the prieftefs. II. 20.

SCYPHUS.

There feem to have been facred cups in the form
of boats, called Cymbia, and Scyphi, Κυμβια, και
Σκυφοι, of which a religious ufe was made. They
were alfo introduced at feftivals, and upon other
folemn

folemn occafions. Perfeus is faid to have introduced in Perfis the deteftable rites of the Scyphus.
(Chron. Pafch. p. 40.) The author fays, that they
were firft eftablifhed by Zeus, who was called Pecus.
(p. 38.) The Scyphus which Hercules is faid to
have ufed, was made of wood; and well fecured with
pitch, to preferve it from decay. There were
many cups formed in imitation of this ancient
veffel; which were efteemed facred, and ufed only
upon particular occafions. (v. Athenæum. l. 11,
12. 15.)

The rites of the Scyphus undoubtedly confifted
in a commemoration of the Ark, accompanied
with all the circumftances of the Deluge. Helius
is alfo faid to have traverfed the ocean in a cup.
There are fome remarkable verfes of Stefichorus
upon this fubject, preferved by Athenæus. (l. 11.)

'Αλιος δ' Υπεριονιδας
Δεπας ες καλεβαινε χρυσεον,
Οφρα δ' ωκεανοιο περασας
Αφικηθ' ιερας ποτι βενθεα νυκτος ερεμνας,
Ποτι ματερα, κουριδιαντ αλοχον,
Παιδας τε φιλους· οδ' ες αλσος ιβα
Δαφναισι καλασκιον
Ποσσι Παις Διος.

II. 403.

SCYTHIA.

As the hiftory of this country has been long involved in obfcurity, the accounts given of it are
very unfatisfactory. There was a province in
Egypt, and another in Syria, called Scythia. There
was one alfo in Afia Minor, upon the Thermodon
above Galatia; the country about Colchis, and
Iberia; a great part of Thrace, and Mœfia, and all
the Tauric Cherfonefus, were ftyled Scythic.
Laftly, there was a country of this name far in the

eaft, of which little notice has been hitherto taken. It was fituated upon the great Indic ocean; and confifted of a widely-extended region, called Scythia Limyrica. But the Scythia fpoken of by the ancient Greeks, and after them by the Romans, confifted of thofe countries, which lay upon the coaft of the Euxine; and efpecially of thofe upon the north, and north-eaftern parts of that fea. In fhort, it was the region of Colchis, and all that country at the foot of mount Caucafus, as well as that upon the Palus Mæotis, and the Borifthenes, which was of old efteemed Scythia. However unknown they had lain for ages, there was a time, when the natives rendered themfelves very refpect-able. For they carried on an extenfive commerce; and were fuperior in fcience to all the nations near them. But this was long before the dawn of learning in Greece: even before the conftitution of many principalities, into which the Hellenic ftate was divided. They went under the name of Col-chians, Iberians, Cimmerians, Hyperboreans, Alani. They got footing in Paphlagonia; where they were called Amazonians, and Alazonians; alfo in Pieria, and Sithonia, near mount Hæmus in Thrace. Thefe were proper Scythic nations: however widely extended they might be, yet the Greek writers went too far. (Strabo, l. 11. p. 774.)

To me it appears manifeft, that what was termed by the Greeks Σκυθα, Σκυθια, Σκυθικα, was originally Cutha, Cuthia, Cuthica; and related to the family of Chus. He was called by the Babylonians and Chaldeans Cuth; and his pofterity Cuthites and Cutheans. The countries where they at times fettled, were uniformly denominated from them. (Jofeph. Ant. l. 9. c. 14.) But what was pro-perly ftyled Cutha, the Greeks expreffed with a Sigma prefixed: which, however trifling it may appear, has been attended with fatal confequences.

Whence

Whence this mode of expreſſion aroſe, is uncertain: it has univerſally obtained; and has very much confounded the hiſtory of ancient times, and of this people in particular. Epiphanius (adv. Hæres. l. 1. p. 6.) who has tranſmitted to us a moſt curious epitome of the whole Scythic hiſtory, ſpeaks to the following purport: " Thoſe nations, which " reach ſouthward from that part of the world, " where the two great continents of Europe and " Aſia incline to each other, and are connected, " were univerſally ſtyled Scythæ, according to an " appellation of long ſtanding. Theſe were of " that family, who erected of old the great tower, " and who built the city Babylon." From hence we learn preciſely, that the Scythians were the Cuthians, and came from Babylonia. They were the ſame as the Chaldaic Iōnim under a different name.

The ſame author in another place ſays, Σκυθισμος απο του καlακλυσμου αχρι του Πυργου; *from the deluge to the erecting of the tower* (of Babel) *Scuthiſm prevailed.* This notation is perhaps carried too far back; but the meaning is plain; and what he alludes to, is certainly Κυθισμος. The purport of the paſſage teaches, that from the time of the Deluge to the conſtruction of the tower was eſteemed the Cuthic age. It was for the moſt part a period of uſurpation and tyranny under the ſons of Chus, which was in a great degree put a ſtop to at the diſperſion: at leaſt the intention of keeping mankind together, and conſtituting one great empire was prevented: for this ſeems to have been the deſign of the Cuthians and their leader. III. 143.

SEIRA.

The Ark was deſcribed under various ſymbols: and there is a fragment of the Orphic poetry,

quoted

quoted by Natalis Comes (l. 6.) where it is spoken
of as an Hive, Seira, or the Hive of Venus.

Ὑμνεομεν Σειρην πολυωνυμον Αφρογενιας,
Και πηγην μεγαλην βασιληϊον, ἡς απο παντες
Αθανατοι, πτεροεντες, ανεβλαστησαν Ερωτες.

Some interpret σειρα, *a chain*; and many of the ancients allude to this history under a mysterious notion of a chain.   But the context in these verses
shews that it cannot be understood so here.   Seira,
among other interpretations, signified Melitta, *a
bee*, also *an hive*, or *house of Melitta*. Hesych.
Such is the sense of it in this passage: and the Ark
was thus represented in the ancient mythology, as
being the receptacle, from whence issued that
swarm, by which the world was peopled.   It was
therefore truly stiled Πηγη, *the fountain, from which
the Loves*, Ερωτες (i. e. the Iönim) were again produced; all the supposed sons of Eros and Iönah,
who had been in a state of death.   The Seira is the
same in purport as Baris, Theba, Cibotus, Aren,
Larnax, Bœotus; and hence stiled Σειρα πολυωνυμος,
or *Seira with many names.* II. 373.

As the Melittæ, and Melissæ, were priestesses of
Melitta; the Cupselides of the Cupselis; so doubt-
less were the Seirenes priestesses of the Seira, called
Seiren: and all these terms related to the Ark.
The Σειρηνες were celebrated for their songs; because
they were of the same order as the Melissæ, who
were greatly famed for their harmony. 379.

The coast of Campania, was as much dreaded by
mariners, as that of Rhegium, and Sicily.   Here
the Sirens inhabited, who are represented, as the
bane of all, who navigated those seas.   Homer
(Oð. M.) gives a most affecting account:

Σειρηνας μεν πρωτον αφιξεαι, αἱ ῥα τε πανίας
Ανθρωπους θελγουσιν, ὁτις σφεας εισαφικανει·
Ὁςις αϊδρειη πελασει, και φθογγον ακουσει
Σειρηνων, τῳ δ᾽ ουτι γυνη, και νηπια τεκνα
Οικαδε νοςησανίι παριςαίαι, ουδε γανυνίαι·
Αλλα τε Σειρηνες λιγυρη θελγουσιν αοιδη,
Ἡμενοι εν λειμωνι· πολυς τ᾽ αμφ᾽ οςεοφιν θις
Ανδρων πυθομενων, περι δε ῥινοι φθινυθουσιν.

They like the Lamii were Cuthite, and Canaani-
tiſh prieſts. They were much addicted to the
cruel cuſtom of enticing ſtrangers into the purlieus
of their temples, and then putting them to death:
ſo that the ſhores are deſcribed as covered with the
bones of men deſtroyed by their artifice;—multo-
rumque oſſibus albos. (Virg. Æn. l. 5. 873.) II. 17.
See Temple Rites.

SEMELE,

The ſuppoſed mother of Niobe, was Sama-El,
the token of God. Semele, Ino and Hermione are
different names for the ſame emblem. Her hiſtory,
as well as that of Dionuſus, was brought from Ur
in Chaldea: whence it was fabled that he was born
in fire; and that Semele was conſumed in the ſame
element. It is moreover ſaid of her, that ſhe was
confined in the ſhades below; but recalled to light
by Dionuſus. This circumſtance is alluded to in
the Orphic hymn (H. 43.) to Semele.

Τιμας τευξαμενη παρ᾽ αγαυης Περσεφονης
Εν θνηίοισι ϐροίοισι—— II. 311.

SEMIRAMIS.

The wonderful actions of Ninus and Semiramis
may be read in divers hiſtorians, Herodotus, Strabo,
Diodorus Siculus, Cteſias, &c. The accounts are
inconſiſtent and incredible: and indeed what credit

can be given to the hiſtory of a perſon, Semiramis, the time of whoſe life cannot be aſcertained within 1535 years? for ſo great is the difference of the extremes of the following numbers.

Years.

According to Syncellus ſhe lived before Chriſt 2177
         Patavius makes the term   -   2060
         Helvicus   -   -   2248
         Euſebius   -   -   1984
         Mr. Jackſon   -   -   1964
         Abp. Uſher   -   -   1215
         Philo Biblius fromSanchoniathon 1200
         Herodotus about   -   713

The hiſtory of Ninus and Semiramis is in great meaſure founded upon terms, which have been miſconſtrued; and fictions have been invented in conſequence of theſe miſtakes. Under the character of Semiramis we are certainly to underſtand a people called Semarim, a title aſſumed by the ancient Babylonians. They were called Semarim from their inſigne, which was a dove, expreſſed Semaramas. It was uſed as an object of worſhip; and eſteemed the ſame as Rhea, the mother of the gods: Σεμιραμιν και την Ρεαν καλουμενην παρ' Ασσυριοις. (Chron. Paſch. p. 36.) It was a common mode of expreſſion to call a tribe or family by the name of its founder: and a nation by the head of the line. People are often ſpoken of collectively in the ſingular under ſuch a patronymic. Hence we read in Scripture, that Iſrael abode in tents; that Judah was put to the worſt in battle; &c. When it was ſaid, that the Ninevite performed any great action, it has been aſcribed to a perſon called Ninus, the ſuppoſed founder of Nineveh. But we may be aſſured, that under the character of Ninus, and Ninyas, we are to underſtand the Ninevites; as by Semiramis is meant a people called Samarim: and the-

the great actions of thefe two nations are in the
hiftories of thefe perfonages recorded. But writers
have rendered the account inconfiftent, by limit-
ing, what was an hiftorical feries of many ages, to
the life of a fingle perfon.

The Ninevites and Samarim did perform all that
is attributed to Semiramis, and Ninus. They did
conquer the Medes and Bactrians; and largely extended their dominions. But thefe events were
many ages after the foundation of the two kingdoms. They began under Pul of Nineve; and
were carried on by Affur Adon, Salmanaffur, Sen-
nacherib, and others of his fucceffors. Nineve was
at laft ruined, and the kingdom of Affyria was
united to that of Babylon. This is probably alluded to in the fuppofed marriage of Semiramis
and Ninus. Then it was, that the Samarim performed the great works attributed to them. For
exclufive of what was done at Babylon (which they
built; which was faid by Eupolemus to have been
built by Belus, and the Giants. Eufeb. Præp. l. 9.)
There are, fays Strabo, l. 16. *almoft over the face of
the whole earth, vaft mounds of earth* (thefe were
high altars, on which they facrificed to the Sun)
*and walls, and ramparts, attributed to Semiramis; and
in thefe are fubterraneous paffages of communication,
and tanks for water, and ftaircafes of ftone. There
are alfo vaft canals to divert the courfe of rivers, and
lakes to receive them; together with highways and
bridges of a wonderful ftructure.* They built the
famous terraces at Babylon; and thofe beautiful
gardens at Egbatana, after that city had fallen into
their hands. To them was owing that cruel device
of emafculating their flaves, that their numerous
wives, and concubines might be more fecurely
guarded. They found out the art of weaving
cotton; which difcovery has been given to thofe of
their family, who went into Egypt: for there were

Samarim

Samarim here too. The Samarim of Egypt and Babylonia, were of the fame family, the fons of Chus. They came and fettled among the Mizraim, under the name of the Shepherds. II. 99.

Although fome hiftorians have reprefented Semiramis as a woman, and a great princefs who reigned in Babylon: yet others, of better intelligence, have mentioned her as a deity. *She was, fays* Athenagoras (Legatio. p. 307.) *efteemed the daughter of Dercetus, and the fame as the Suria dea,* which was dea Solaris, the fame both as Rhea, and Dercetus, called alfo Atargatus. Hence many make Rhea, Ifis, Aftarte, Atargatus and Semiramis, one deity: and Lucian (de Sur. dea) tells us, that they were fo efteemed by the Syrians of Hierapolis; and the fame may be collected from other writers. They were all different fymbols relating to the fame object. Semiramis was faid to have been changed into a dove; becaufe they found her always depicted and worfhiped under that form. A notion likewife prevailed, that fhe had an unnatural love for a horfe: which arofe from the ancients not underftanding their own hieroglyphics. So Europa and Pafiphäe (who was worfhiped in Crete, and Meffenia) were in love with bulls; Saturn with a mare; Ifis with a fifh: the Bull, Hippa, and Cetus, being emblems of the fame purport, and relating to the fame hiftory. Of thefe the Dove was particularly held in veneration. διο και τους Ασσυριους την περιστεραν τιμαν ως θεαν. Hence it feems plain that Semiramis was an emblem; and that the name was a compound of Sama-Ramas, or Ramis. It fignified the *divine token,* the type of Providence: as a military enfign, it may with fome latitude be interpreted *the ftandard of the moft high.* It confifted of the figure of a Dove; which was probably incircled with the Iris, as thofe two emblems were often reprefented together. All who went under that

that ftandard, or worfhiped that emblem, were ftiled Semarim, and Samorim.

One of the gates of Babylon was called the gate of Semiramis; undoubtedly from having the facred emblem of Sama Ramis, or the Dove, engraved over it. Probably the lofty obelifk of Semiramis mentioned by Diodorus (l. 2.) was named from the fame hieroglyphic. The title Samarim, or Semiramis, did not relate to one perfon, but to many: and it feems particularly to have been ufurped by princes. The Cuthites fettled about Cochin, and Madura, in India; and the great kings of Calecut were ftiled Samarim even in later times: when thofe countries were vifited by the Portuguefe and Englifh.

The image of the Suria dea was richly habited, and upon its head was a golden Dove. What is very remarkable, the image was by the people called Σημηϊον. Lucian takes pains to inform us, that this was not a Græcian, but a Syriac word; a term made ufe of by the natives. He writes in the Ionic dialeçt: and what he calls Σημηϊον, was by the people exprefled Sema-Ion, or Sama-Ion, *the token of the Dove*; *the emblem of the Arkite Ïonah.*

According to Hefychius, and others, by Semiramis was particularly fignified a wild pigeon: and there is reafon to think, that this intelligence was derived from fome ancient tradition; and that Noah did fend out of the Ark a Dove of the wild fpecies, for a tame one would have returned upon the leaft difficulty, perhaps of choice. A wild one would not, but through neceffity. Such a return plainly indicated that the earth was not yet habitable; and afforded the intelligence required.

It is faid of this ideal perfonage, that fhe was expofed among rocks; but delivered, and preferved by Σιμμα, a Shepherd; and was afterwards married to one Menon: fhe is likewife faid to have con-

ftructed

ſtructed the firſt ſhip. Now Simma is a perſonage made out of Sema, or Sama, *the divine token.* Menon is the deus Lunus, under which type the Ark was reverenced in many regions: and as it was the firſt ſhip conſtructed, with which the hiſtory of the Dove was cloſely connected, they have given to Semiramis the merit of building it. 305.

SESOSTRIS.

, Among the Writers, who have written concerning this extraordinary perſonage, Diodorus Siculus is the moſt uniform and full: ſee his firſt book. The detail given of him is very plain and precifeﾐ and we proceed very regularly and minutely in a geographical ſeries from one conqueſt to another; ſo that the ſtory is rendered in ſome degree plauſible. But we may learn from Diodorus himſelf, that little credit is to be paid to this narration, after all the pains he may have taken to win upon our credulity. He ingenuouſly owns, that not only the Græcian writers, but even the prieſts of Egypt, and the bards of the ſame country, varied in the account, which they gave of this hero; and were guilty of great inconſiſtence: and concludes with an ingenuous confeſſion, that little could be obtained that was preciſely true. The hiſtory however of this perſonage has been admitted as credible by the moſt learned writers and chronologiſts; though they cannot determine the æra of his reign within a thouſand years. Notice has been taken under ſeveral articles of the ſuppoſed conquerors of the earth: and among them the reputed deities of Egypt, under the names of Oſiris, Perſeus, &c. Theſe are ſuppoſed, if they ever exiſted, to have lived in the firſt ages of the world, when Egypt was in its infant ſtate: and Seſoſtris is made one of the number. He is by ſome placed before Orus; and by ſome after. He is alſo repreſented under the

different

different names of Sethos, Sethofis, Sefoothis, Seconthofis, and Sefoftris. The author of the Chronicon Pafchale, after relating all his great conquefts, gives us this further information, that this prince was the firft of the line of Ham, who reigned in Egypt: in other words, he was the firft king of the country. Hence it appears, that if fuch a perfon as Sefoftris ever exifted, his reign muft have been of the earlieft date.

Ofiris is faid to have conquered the whole earth; then Zeus, then Perfeus, then Hercules, all nearly of the fame degree of antiquity; if we may believe the beft mythologifts. Myrina comes in for a fhare of conqueft in the time of Orus. After her Thoules fubdues the whole from the eaftern ocean, to the great Atlantic: and as if nothing had been performed before, Sefoftris fucceeds, and conquers it over again. By comparing the hiftories of ancient perfonages together, we may perceive that they bear a manifeft fimilitude to one another; though they are attributed to different perfons. They contain accounts of great atchievements in the firft ages: in effecting which thefe ancient heroes are reprefented as traverfing immenfe regions; and carrying their arms to the very limits of the known world. Some of them feem to have been of the fame age; and to have carried on thefe conquefts at nearly the fame time: and thofe, whofe æra may poffibly differ, have this in common with the others; that they vifit the fame countries, march for the moft part by the fame rout; and are often joined by the fame allies, and are followed by the fame attendants. They are in general efteemed benefactors, wherever they go; and carry the fciences with them, as well as their religious rites, in which they inftruct the natives in different parts of the world. Thefe are certainly noble occurrences; which however could not poffibly have happened,

as

as they are reprefented. It is not to be fuppofed, that any perfon in thofe early ages, or in any age, could go over fuch a tract of country; much lefs that he fhould fubdue it. It is ftill more impro- bable, that fuch extenfive conquefts fhould be fo immediately repeated; and that they fhould in fome inftances be carried on by different perfons at nearly the fame time. To fay the truth, the very per- fonages are ideal, and have been formed out of the titles of the Deity: and the hiftory, with which they are attended, related not to conqueft, but to peregrinations of another nature; to Colonies, who went abroad, and fpread themfelves almoft every where. The Ancients were wont to give to a perfon, what in reality belonged to a people. If we make this fmall allowance, the feveral hiftories will be found in great meafure to be true. II. 85.

Sefoftris is faid to have conftructed a fhip (Diod. Sic. 1. 1.) two hundred and eighty cubits in length. It was of cedar, plated without with gold, and inlaid with filver: and it was, when finifhed, dedicated to Ofiris at Thebes. It is not credible that there fhould have been a fhip of this fize, efpecially in an inland diftrict, the moft remote of any in Egypt. It was certainly a temple, and a fhrine. The former was framed upon this large fcale; and it was the latter, on which the gold and filver was fo lavifhly expended; the whole was probably intended in its outlines to be the exact reprefentation of the Ark, in commemoration of which it was certainly built. It was a temple facred to Ofiris at Theba; or, to fay the truth, it was itfelf called Theba: and both the city, faid to be one of the moft ancient in Egypt, as well as the province, was undoubtedly denominated from it. το αρχαιον ἡ Αιγυπτος Θηβαι καλουμενη. (Ariftot. Meteor. 1. 1.) Now Theba, תבה, is the very word ufed for the Ark by the facred writer (Gen. vi. 15.)

vi. 15.) fo that we may be affured of the prototype, after which this temple was fafhioned. It was an idolatrous temple; faid to have been built by Sefoftris in honour of Ofiris. The ignorance of the Greeks, in refpect to ancient titles; and their mifapplication of terms in many inftances is noto-rious; efpecially in their fuppofing temples to have been erected by perfons, to whom in reality they were facred. Sefoftris was Ofiris; the fame as Dio-nufus, Menes, and Noah. He is called Seifithrus by Abydenus, Xixouthros by Berofus and Apollo-dorus; and is reprefented by them as a prince, in whofe time the Deluge happened. He was called Zuth, Xuth, and Zeus: and certainly had divine honours paid to him. 221.

SHEM, SHAMEN, SHAMESH.

Sham, and Shamefh, are terms, which relate to the heavens, and to the Sun, fimilar to שום, שמים שמש, of the Hebrews. Many places of reputed fanctity, fuch as Same, Samos, Samothrace, Sa-morna, were denominated from it. Philo Biblius (ap. Eufeb. P. E. l. 1.) informs us, that the Syri-ans, and Canaanites, lifted up their hands to Baal-Samen, the lord of heaven, under which title they honoured the Sun. Ephefus was a place of great fanctity: its original name was Samorna; which feems a compound of Sam-Oran, cœleftis Sol, fons lucis. We read of Samicon in Elis (Paufan. l. 5.) with a facred cavern; and of a town Samia, which lay above it. The word Σεμνος was a contraction of Semanos, from Sema-On; and properly fignified divine and celeftial. Hence Σεμναι Θεαι, Σεμνη Κορα. Ancient Syria was particularly devoted to the wor-fhip of the Sun, and of the Heavens; and it was by the natives called Shems and Shams: which undoubtedly means the land of Shemefh, from the worfhip there followed. It retains the name to
this

this day. Abulfeda fuppofes, that Syria is called
Scham, quafi finiftra. It was called Sham for the
fame reafon that it was called Syria. Συρος γαρ ὁ
Ἡλιος, the fame as Σειριος. Perfæ Συρα Deum vocant. (Lill. Gerald. Syntag. 1.) Συρια Θεα, i. e.
dea cœleftis. Syria is called at this day Souriftan.
Souris from Sehor, Sol, Σειριος of Greece. In Canaan there was a town and temple, called Beth-
Shemefh. What fome expreffed Shem and Sham,
the Lubim feem to have pronounced Zam: hence
the capital of Numidia was named Zama, and
Zamana, from Shamen, cœleftis. This we may
learn from an infcription in Reineccius. (Syntag.
Claff. 6. cxxii.)

> JULIO. PROCULO.
> PRÆF. URB. PATRONO.
> COL. BYZACENÆ. ET. PA
> TRONO. COLON. ÆLIÆ.
> ZAMANÆ. REGIÆ.

El-Samen was probably the name of the chief
temple at Zama: and comprifed the titles of the
deity, whom the Numidians worfhiped. El Samen
fignifies deus cœleftis, or cœlorum: which El
Samen was changed by the Romans to Ælia
Zamana. From Sam, and Samen, came Summus: and
Hercules Summanus; Samabethi, Samanæi, Sa-
monacodoma. I. 64.

SHEPHERDS.

Herodotus (l. 2. c. 109.) mentions determinately, that the knowlege of the heavens, and every
thing relating to the diftribution of time, was imported from Babylonia. As thefe Babylonians,
fons of Urius, manifeftly came to Greece by the
way of Egypt, it appears pretty evident, that they
were the fons of Chus, of the Shepherd race, who

fo

fo long held the fovereignty in that kingdom.
Hence it is, that throughout the whole mythology
of the Græcians there are continual allufions to
Shepherds: a title, which was peculiar to the
Auritæ of Egypt. II. 181.

*The following further account concerning the Shep-
herds, is extracted from Mr.* BRYANT's *Obfervations
upon the Ancient Hiftory of Egypt.* p. 140.

We are told by Syncellus (Chronogr. edit. Paris.
p. 51.) that Egypt had been in fubjection to a threefold race of kings; who are termed the Auritæ, the
Meftræi, and the Egyptian. Syncellus places the
Auritæ firft, becaufe he thought they were firft in
time. The Meftræi were undoubtedly the genuine
defcendants of Mizraim, who firft gave name to the
country: the traces of which are not yet effaced;
Al Cahira, and, indeed, the whole of Egypt being
called Mezrè at this day. The Auritæ were the
Arabian Shepherds, and their kings; who reigned
here a confiderable time, maintaining themfelves
by force; till, after many ftruggles, they were
finally expelled by the natives.

After this, there occurs at fome interval a piece
of hiftory relating to another fet of people, who
were fojourners in Egypt in the reign of Ameno-
phis. (Jofeph. c. Appion. l. 1. §. 14.) They were
in fubjection to the prince of the country, and
treated by him as flaves, becaufe they were infected
with the leprofy. As they increafed in numbers to
a great amount, he employed them in the ftone
quarries that were on the eaft fide of the Nile, in
company with fome of the Egyptians. It is faid of
this prince, that he longed much to be admitted to
the prefence of the gods, as Orus, a former king,
had been. But it was told him that his wifh would
never be accomplifhed, till he purged his land of
the diftempered people. He fent them therefore
to the Arabian quarries: and, as they laboured

C c   under

under great inconveniences in that place, upon a
remonftrance made to him, he granted them for a
retreat the city Abaris, where the former Shepherds
had refided, which now lay defolate.

Jofephus (ibid. §. 26.) again quotes from Ma-
hetho; but it is too long to be here tranfcribed.
Let it fuffice that this people " chofe themfelves a
" leader; one who was a prieft of Heliopolis, and
" whofe name was Ofarfiph. He enjoined them
" to pay no regard to the gods of the country, nor
" to the animals which were held facred by the
" Egyptians; but to facrifice and feed indiffer-
" ently: and not to have any connections out of
" their own community.—In fhort, this prieft of
" Heliopolis was the founder of their republic, and
" their lawgiver: and after he had lifted himfelf
" with this body of men, he changed his name to
" Mofes."

From hence we learn that there was a twofold race of people, who fojourned in Egypt: and,
however their hiftory may be in fome refpects confufed, yet much light may be obtained from it.
They were each of them efteemed Shepherds: the
firft were lords and conquerors; the others were
fervants; and had the very city given them to in-
habit, which the firft had evacuated. Thefe latter
are manifeftly a feparate and diftinct people: and
though they may have fome circumftances blended
and mifplaced; yet from the name of their leader
and lawgiver, it is plain that they were *Ifraelites*.
As to the firft, they are fuppofed to have been Arabians; and are faid to have come from the Eaft; i.e.
from a country fituated eaftward, in refpect to that
to which they came. They were undoubtedly the
Auritæ: and the city they founded was Auris,
called by the Græcians Αυαρις, and fometimes Αβαρις
(Avaris and Abaris) by an eafy and natural inflection. The city Avaris is no other than the city
                                        Ur,

Ur, or Aur, אור, which fignifies light and fire; of which element the Auritæ muft have been wor- fhipers, as all the Arabians were. Their chief god was Alorus: fuppofed to be the Hephæftus of the Greeks, and the Mulciber or Vulcan of the Latines, and by fome efteemed Bacchus; but anfwering nearly to their Ouranus and Ourania, which were derived from it.

The meaning of Alorus is the god of fire. It is originally a Babylonifh god and hero. As a god it reprefents the Sun, the fuppofed god of light and fire: when it betokens a Man, it feems to refer both to Chus and Nimbrod; but more particularly to the latter, who was the firft monarch upon earth, and the firft deified hero. The Shepherds were called Auritæ from the chief objed of their wor- fhip.; and their kings were ftiled priefts of Alorus; according to the Greeks, the priefts of Vulcan; which title often occurs in the ancient annals of Egypt. Hence we may infer that they came from Babylonia, which lay due eaft from Egypt, and which was the original feat of the genuine Arabians, and the true fource whence their religion flowed. The two principal cities of that country were Ur, or, as it is otherwife written, Aur, and Babylon. In memory of which they built two of the fame name in Egypt. The place of refidence, where their kings held their courts, was Memphis: but the provinces, of which they were particularly feifed, where Phaccufa and Heliopolis. In all thefe places they introduced the Tzeba Schamaim, or Zabian worfhip, together with the worfhip of fire. Hence we learn from Herodotus, that Vulcan was particularly honoured at Heliopolis and Memphis. Both thefe places they are faid to have built: and to the latter they gave the name of Ain Shems, or Shemifh, i. e. *the fountain of the Sun*; which the Egyptians feem to have pronounced On, and

fome-

fometimes Aven. The temple was called Beth-fhemefh: and they are both frequently alluded to by the prophets, and facred writers, together with the neighbouring province Bubaftus. (Ezek. xxx. 17. Jerem. xliii. 13.) Thefe names given to the places, and the worfhip introduced there, befpeak them of Arabian original: and Pliny tells us (Nat. H. l. 6. c. 29.) that Juba in his hiftory particularly maintained that Heliopolis was built by Arabians. And Diodorus (l. 1.) alludes to the fame circumftance, when he fays, that Uchoreus, or the prince Orus, was the founder of Memphis. For Orus is a name of Chaldean original; by which their chief deity was fignified: as well as fome of their kings, who affumed the name to themfelves, or had it beftowed upon them by their fubjects. The worfhip of Orus was brought into Egypt by the Arabians, and fuperadded to the religion of the country. And as the Græcians called the city Aur in Egypt Avaris and Aouaris; fo they liquidated and changed the name of Orus, whom they called Aoueris, by the fame inflexion: whofe hiftory is epitomized in Plutarch de Ifid. et Os. Where the reading Apovηρις fhould be corrected.

The Greeks and Romans called thefe people Arabians: but their true name was Cufhan or Cufeans; the fame which they gave to the province where they fettled. This is evident from the etymology of Phaccufa, which is compounded of פחת ברעש, Phacat Cufan, or the canal of Cufhan: being called from the canal that it was bounded by, as many places in Egypt were. Cufh and Cufhan in Scripture almoft always relate to Arabia.

Thefe ftrangers therefore who fettled in Egypt were no other than the Cufeans; and have been ftiled Arabian Shepherds: for all the primitive Arabians were *Nomades* or Shepherds.

We

We are informed by Manetho, that the Shepherds who came firſt into Egypt were called Ύκσως, Hycſos; the firſt ſyllable, in the ſacred dialect, ſignifying a lord or prince; and the latter, in the national common tongue, a Shepherd. This is not ſatisfactory; though taken, as Joſephus aſſures us, from Manetho. There are few inſtances of words compounded from two different languages. Beſides, the etymology was probably to be looked for in the language of the people who were called ſo. Euſebius (Pr. Ev. l. 10. c. 13.) has given us this title ſomewhat different, and deduces it from one language only : εκαλειτο δε το συμπαν αυ]ων εθνος Ύκουσσως· τουΊο δε εςι, βασιλεις ποιμενες. το γαρ Ύκ, καθ' ιεραν γλωσσαν, βασιλεα σημαινει· το δε ΟΥΣΣΩΣ, ποιμην εςι. Euſebius ſeems to have taken ſome pains, to give us a more genuine reading than that which is found in Joſephus: and from the light which he affords us, we may poſſibly arrive at the true meaning of the word, though contrary to his determination. The Græcians were very unfortunate in their etymologies; and bad copiers of every thing from the Orientals: ſo much ſo, that there is ſcarce an inſtance of their repreſenting things truly. Manetho his ſelf was an Egyptian greciſed: and the miſtake may be originally in him; as he was as little acquainted with the ſacred language as a foreigner; the language being in his time loſt. The Cuſeans were certainly Shepherds, and were generally termed ſo by the Egyptians. But this muſt not be eſteemed their gentile name: for they were denominated from their country, and diſtinguiſhed by the name of their fathers. The name was Cuſh and Cuſhan; which the Greeks expreſſed by Χους and Χουσος. This Euſebius has preſerved; but has not tranſmitted the name entirely pure. Uc or Ouc certainly ſignifies lord or prince, ſomething great or noble. It is a Babyloniſh word; and was adopted by the

Egyptians,

Egyptians, and occurs often in the name of their
kings. The original which Jofephus copied was
Ύκκους, or with the Greek termination, Ύκκουσος;
i. e. the great Cuſh, or lord Cuſean. It is true,
Ύκκουσος, or as it had better be written, Ύκχουσος,
relates to a people who were Shepherds ; but that
profeſſion is not neceſſarily nor originally included
in the name. Jofephus having faid that Σως fignified a ſhepherd, induced Euſebius to retain it, and
to write the word Ύκκουσως; a miſtake that is eaſily
remedied. The term then Ύκκουσως, which ſhould
have been Ύκχουσσος or Ουκχουσσος, fignifies the lord
Cuſean : and it might eaſily have been miſtaken
for a Shepherd. For, as the Egyptians hated the
memory of the fons of Chus, who were of that profeſſion ; it was natural for them to call every Shepherd a Cuſean : fo that a Cuſean and a Shepherd
might have been taken for fynonymous terms: but
the true meaning is as I have repreſented it.

SIGMA, or S.

This letter was often prefixed to words. E. g.
ύλη was by the Latines rendered *fylva*; ἑπλα,
feptem; ἑρπω, *ferpo*; and from ἁλς, ἁλος of Greece
was formed *fal*, and *falum*. The river Indus was
often called Sindus ; Ur of Chaldæa was ſtyled
Sur, Σουρ ; the Elli, prieſts of the Sun at Dodona,
were called Selli; the Alpes Cottiæ are by Procopius ſtyled Σκουλιαι ; and Lycophron (v. 1361.)
fpeaking of the Alps in general, inſtead of Αλπια
φη, calls them Σαλπια.

This letter is uſed by the Welſh as an aſpirate;
and it has undoubtedly been introduced by many
nations for the fame purpoſe. III. 146. n.

SILENUS.

This name, however varied by the Græcians,
was originally the maſculine of Selene. The Roman

man poets defcribe him merety as a beftial drunken
vagrant, fupported by a favage crew of Sileni and
Satyrs.   But the ancient mythologifts held him in
a different eftimation.   It is faid of him, that he
had three fons, who are ftiled by Catullus Nufigenæ
(Pel. et-Thetis. v. 253.)   He is reprefented as a
man of the earth (Nonnus. l. 29.) who came into
life, αυλολοχευλος, by his own means, without the
affiftance of his parent.   He was efteemed, like
Proteus and Nereus, a great prophet; one, who
tranfmitted an hiftory of the world, and its origin.
He is alfo faid to have difcourfed with Midas of
Phrygia about another world. (Tertullian adver.
Hermog.) Theopompus (Ælian. V. H. l. 3.
c. 18.) defcribed him as a Dæmon; one who was
inferior to the Deity; but fuperior to man, and
exempted from the common condition of mortality.
In fhort, Silenus and Dionufus were the fame.
II. 450.

SIN NOO, SIN NUM.

As the hiftory of China is fuppofed to extend
upwards to an amazing height; it may be worth
while to confider the firft æras in the Chinefe annals, as they are reprefented in the writings of
Japan. For the Japanefe have preferved hiftories
of China. Such a comparifon, which has not
hitherto been made, may lead to the difcovery of
fome important truths.
    In the hiftories of this country, the firft monarch
of China is named Foki (v. Kæmpfer. l. 2. p. 145,
&c.) the fame, whom the Chinefe call Fohi, and
place at the head of their lift. This prince had,
according to fome the body, according to others
the head, of a ferpent. If we may believe the
Japanefe hiftorians, he began his reign above
twenty-one thoufand years before Chrift. The
fecond Chinefe emperor was Sin Noo; by the people

of China called Sin Num : and many begin the chronology of the country with him. He is fuppofed to have lived about three thoufand years before Chrift : confequently there is an interval of near eighteen thoufand years between the firft emperor and the fecond : a circumftance not to be credited. The third, who immediately fucceeded to Sin Noo, was Hoam Ti.

In this account we may, I think, perceive, that the Chinefe have acted like the people of Greece, and other regions. The hiftories, which were imported, they have prefixed to the annals of their nation ; and adopted the firft perfonages of antiquity, and made them monarchs in their own country. Whom can we fuppofe Fohi, with the head of a ferpent, to have been, but the great founder of all kingdoms, the Father of mankind ? They have placed him at an immenfe diftance, not knowing his true æra. And I think, we may be affured, that under the character of Sin Num, and Sin Noo, we have the hiftory of Noah : and Hoam Ti was no other than Ham.

[Sin Num, or Sin Noum, is very fimilar to Noamus ; by which name the Patriarch was fometimes called. Num in fome degree correfponds with the Nun of Irenæus, and Epiphanius ; who is alfo mentioned by Lilius Gyraldus. Fuit etiam Nun, quem ad Jaadal Baoth natum prodiderunt. Synt. 1. p. 72.]

According to Kæmpfer Sin Noo was of exactly the fame character as Serapis of Egypt. *He was an hufbandman, and taught mankind agriculture; and thofe arts, which relate to the immediate fupport of life. He alfo difcovered the virtues of many plants: and he was reprefented with the head of an ox; and fometimes only with two horns. His picture is held in high efteem by the Chinefe.* Such is the hiftory of this fuppofed monarch, according to Kæmpfer:
and

and he might well think, that in Sin Noo he faw the character of Serapis; for this perfonage was no other than * Sar-Apis, the great Father of mankind; the fame as Men-Neuas of Egypt; the fame alfo as Dionufus, and Ofiris. By Du Halde (V. 1. p. 272. 8vo.) He is called Ching Nong, and made the next monarch after Fohi.

The Chinefe accounts afford the fame hiftory, as has been given above. They mention him *as a perfon very knowing in agriculture, who firft made the earth fupply the wants of his people. He invented the neceffary implements of hufbandry; and taught mankind to fow five forts of grain. From hence he was called Chin-Nong, the Divine hufbandman.* Whether the etymology be true I much doubt: the hiftory however is very curious, and correfponds with the Japanefe account in all the principal articles.

As the family of Noah confifted of eight perfons inclufive, there have been writers, who have placed fome of them in fucceffion; and fuppofed, that there were three or four perfons, who reigned between Sin Noo, and Hoam. But Du Halde fays, that in the true hiftories of the country the three firft monarchs were Fohi, Chin Nong, and Hoam, whom he ftyles Hoang Ti. To thefe, he fays, the arts and fciences owe their invention and progrefs. Thus we find, that thofe, who were heads of families, have been raifed to be princes: and their names have been prefixed to the lift of kings; and their hiftory fuperadded to the annals of the country. It is further obfervable, in the accounts given of thefe fuppofed kings, that their term of life, for the firft five or fix generations, correfponds with that of the Patriarchs after the flood; and

* This was the true name of the Deity. Sar-Apis fignifies Dominus, vel Magnus Pater; alfo Pater Taurinus.

decreafes

decreases in much the same proportion. III. 582.
v. *China*.

SOCRATES.

The Græcians tell us, that the Egyptians stiled
Hermes *a dog*; but they seem to have been aware, that
they were guilty of an undue reprefentation. Hence
Plutarch (Is. et Os.) tries to soften what is mentioned, by saying, ου γαρ κυριως τον Ἑρμην ΚΥΝΑ λεγουσιν
(οἱ Αιγυπ]ιοι): by which this learned writer would insinuate, that it was not so much the name of a dog,
as the qualities of that animal, to which the Egyptians alluded. But the truth is, that the Egyptians
neither bestowed it nominally; nor alluded to it
in any degree. The title, which they gave to
Hermes, was the same, that they bestowed upon
Hercules: they expreffed it Cahen, and Cohen;
and it was very properly reprefented by the Greek
term Χων, *Chon*.

It is said of Socrates, that he sometimes made
use of an uncommon oath, μα τον κυνα, και την χηνα,
by the dog and the goofe: which at first does not
feem confiftent with the gravity of his character.
But we are informed by Porphyry (de Abstinentia.
l. 3.) that this was not done by way of ridicule: for
Socrates esteemed it a very serious and religious
mode of atteftation; and under these terms made a
folemn appeal to the son of Zeus. The purport of
the words is obvious: and whatever hidden meaning there may have been, the oath was made ridiculous by the abfurdity of the terms. Befides,
what poffible connection could there have fubfifted
between a dog and a deity; a goofe and the son of
Jove? There was certainly none: yet Socrates,
like the reft of his fraternity, having an antipathy
to foreign terms, chofe to reprefent his ideas
through this falfe medium; by which means the
very effence of his invocation was loft. The fon of
Zeus,

Zeus, to whom he appealed, was the Egyptian Cahen; but this facred title was idly changed to κυνα και χηνα, *a dog and a goofe*, from a fimilitude in found. That he referred to the Egyptian deity is manifeft from Plato, (in Georgia,) who acknowledges, that he fwore, μα τον κυνα τον Αιγυπτιων Θεον. By which we are to underftand a Cahen of Egypt. Porphyry (l. 3.) exprefsly fays, that it was the god Hermes the fon of Zeus and Maia: κατα τον του Διος και Μαιας παιδα εποιειτο τον όρκον. I. 344.

SOL,

The Sun. From hence the priefts of the Sun were called Soli and Solimi in Cilicia, Selli in Epirus, Salii at Rome, all originally priefts of Fire. As fuch they are defcribed by Virgil:

Tum Salii ad cantus incenfa altaria circum.

In like manner the Silaceni of the Babylonians were worfhipers of the fame deity, and given to the rites of Fire, which accompanied the worfhip of the Sun.

The chief city of Silacena was Sile or Sele, where were eruptions of fire. Sele is the place or city of the Sun. Whenever therefore Sal, or Sel, or the fame reverfed, occur in the compofition of any place's name, we may be pretty certain that the place is remarkable either for its rites or fituation. I. 32.

SONCHIN

Signifies a prieft of the Sun: for Son, San, Zan, are of the fame fignification; and Son-Chin is Ζανος ιερευς. Proclus fays, that it was the title of the priefts; and particularly of him, who prefided in the college of Neith at Saïs. I. 45.

ΣΠΑΡΤΟΙ

ΣΠΑΡΤΟΙ.

The Cadmians, and people of other colonies, who came into Greece, were called Σπαρτοι. The natives of Bœotia had this appellation. Lacedæmon was peculiarly called Sparta. Traditions of this fort prevailed in Attica, and at Colchis: and a notion prevailed, that the people in those parts took their rife from fomething which was *fown*. Hence the twofold perfonage Cecrops is faid to have originally fprung from the teeth of a ferpent fcattered in the ground. The term Sparti was foreign to Greece, and manifeftly imported. Timagoras (Steph. Byz.) informs us, that Sparta received its name from people, who had *wandered* from their own country, and who fettled here.

, They were denominated Sparti from an ancient word analogous to Parad of the Hebrews, and Σπαρατω of the later Greeks; by which was fignified, *to part, fever*, and *difperfe*. (hence *partior, difpertior, partitio*.) Their feparation and flight from Babel was continually commemorated under the notion of the flight of Bacchus, and Ofiris, and the fcattering abroad of their limbs. Androtion (ap. Sch. in Lycoph. v. 1206.) fpeaks of the Sparti as Σποραδες; by which term he does not mean people *fown*: but the purport of his words is, that *Cadmus came to Thebes with fome people of the Difperfion.* As to thofe, who gave name to Sparta, Euftathius (in Hom. Il. B.) tells us τους πρωτους συνοικησαντας την πολιν Λελεγας ΔΙΕΣΠΑΡΜΕΝΟΥΣ εις ταυτην συνελθειν. In their hiftory we have continual allufions to the Flood; and to their diffipation afterwards. Hence Lycophron (v. 1206.) ftyles them natives, of Thebes. Ωγυγου Σπαρτος λεως; (Og, Ogus, and Ogugus, fignify the fea, or ocean. From Ogua came Aqua, *water*.) And Æfchylus (Sept. ad Th. v. 418.)

Σπαρτων

Σπαρίων δ' απ' ανδρων, ὡν Αρης εφεισαῖο.

They were the fame as the Titanians: hence the Cecropians, who came into Attica, were ftiled Γηγινεις (which was a title of the Titans); and their country Titanis.

The great object of the Cuthites in erecting the tower of Babel was, that they might not be dif- perfed. (Gen. xi. 4.) They were however won- derfully diffipated : and this circumftance of their difperfion is to be found commemorated in all their hiftories.

Perfeus, Cadmus, and other leaders of colonies, were ftyled Αληῖαι, or *wanderers*. ὁι και Αληῖαι και Τῖανες καλουνῖαι. (Sanchon. ap. Eufeb. P. E. l. 1. c. 10.) Pindar (Olymp. Od. 13. v. 17.) calls the Corinthians the children of the Aletæ. By the Gentile accounts given of this people, it appears, that they were not only exiled, and difperfed; but alfo doomed to wander for ages, before they could get a place of reft. This is the hiftory given of the Leleges, and Pelafgi, and other wandring tribes. Orpheus, in the Argonautica, v. 98, &c. gives an account to Jafon of his peregrinations; and that at laft he had obtained a fettlement, in the room of that which he had loft. As by Aletes (mentioned by the Scholiaft in Pind. fup. citat. as the leader of the colony) we are not to underftand a perfon, but the colonifts themfelves who founded Corinth : fo here, under the character of Orpheus, we are to underftand thofe of the Orphitæ who fettled in Thrace. Saturnus, ex Creta fugiens, in Italia a Spartanis abfconditur. (Jul. Firmicus, p. 27.) By this flight was fignified the difperfion of a people, called Saturnians; who, after many wanderings, fettled in that country, and introduced there the rites of this god. The Titans, or Giants, were Aletæ: and Athenagoras (p. 303.) goes fo far as

to

to say, that even after their death they had no rest: των Γιγανίων ψυχαι, δι ωιρι τον κοσμον ιισι ωλανωμινοι Δαιμονες.

The Sparti were supposed to be Heliadæ, or offspring of the Sun: and at the same time Ophitæ, worshiping that deity under the figure of a serpent. They called the Sun, Zan, San, and Shan. Now Shan, שן, signified also *a tooth*. Hence the Græcians, instead of saying, that the Sparti had their origin from the Serpent deity the Sun, made them take their rise from the teeth of a serpent. And as they were Sporades, by which term is meant any thing, that is either scattered abroad, or sowed in the ground; they took it in the latter sense; and supposed, that these teeth had been sowed in the earth, and produced an army of men. III. 409.

SPARTO-HEBRÆI.

Ιουδαια· Αλιξανδρος ο Πολυιςωρ απο ωαιδων Σιμιραμιδος, Ιουδα και Ιδουμαια· ως δι Κλαυδιος Ιολαος απο Ιουδαιου Σπαρίωνος, ικ Θηβης μία Διονυσου ρραίιυοιίος. Steph. Byz.

In the first part of the above, we find that the children of Edom and Judah are represented as the sons of Semiramis. This at first may appear foreign to the truth; yet, it is very consonant to the history of those nations. For their forefathers were natives of Chaldea, and Babylonia: and Abraham came from thence to Canaan. Hence they might easily by the eastern nations be looked upon as of the race of the Semarim, or Babylonians. In consequence of which their posterity are by this writer styled the sons of Semiramis. According to Cl. Iölaus they were descended from Judæus Sparton. By this is meant, that they were of the family styled Sparti; from the people, who were dispersed. This naturally follows from their being esteemed of the line of the Semarim:

and

and we have reafon to think, that there is great truth in this hiftory. For though Terah and Abraham, who refided in Chaldea, were not of that number; yet we may infer, that many of the fons of Heber were. For they muft have been pretty numerous at this time; and feem to have been all idolaters; and to have refided upon forbidden ground in the vicinity of Babel.

It is added, that *Judæus Sparton went with Dionufus from Thebes, and attended him in his warlike expeditions.* It is to be obferved, that thofe nations, who preferved any traditions of their forefathers having been preferved in the Deluge, came in procefs of time to think, that the hiftory related to their family alone: at leaft they confined it to thofe, who had the beft memorials of that event. Among thefe were the people of Judea, who were efteemed a branch of the Semarim. Hence it is mentioned as peculiarly characteriftic, that Sparton, by whom is meant the head of the family, which was difperfed, came with Dionufus, εκ Θηβης; by which is meant, not from Thebes, but *out of the Ark:* and it is added, that he attended him in his wars. Thefe are two hiftories; and fhould be accordingly diftinguifhed. The Græcians continually confounded Dionufus and Bacchus, and often fpeak of them as one perfon. But they were two diftinct characters: and the firft of thefe hiftories belongs to the one, and the fecond to the other. The coming out (εκ Θηβης) *from the Ark* relates to Dionufus: the warlike expedition to Bacchus, and to his fons the Cuthites.

[Note. Dionufus was the Patriarch, the head of all. By Bacchus is fometimes meant Zeus Pachus, ftyled Πηχος by the Ionian writers, who was Chus. At other times, the title relates to Nimrod, who, as Bochart very truly fuppofes, was named Bar-Chus,
the

the fon of Chus. The names of two perfonages, from fimilitude, have been blended into one.]

As to the Hebrews, and Ifraelites, whom C. Iölaus deduces from Judæus Sparton, they were, according to the Scriptural account, the fons of Heber. This name is by interpretation περάτης, *one who paſſes over*. The names of the Patriarchs were moſt of them prophetically given; and had a reference to fome future contingency. The name Ham, or Cham, was prognoſtic both of the worſhip, and complexion of his poſterity: and thus Heber had a name given him, which fignified περάτης, and was prophetic. Abraham was the fixth in defcent from Heber, on which account the fons of Heber muſt have been very numerous in his time. Yet many have imagined, that the name of Abraham was a compound of Aber, *to paſs over*: than which notion there can be nothing more idle. It is notorious, that Abraham is called the Hebrew; which would be unneceſſary, and redundant, if his original name had that fignification. He is not ſtyled Heber, but like his poſterity, an Hebrew. This ſhews, that he did not give, but receive the name. It was a patronymic: a name, by which his fathers had before him been diſtinguiſhed. The authors of the Greek verſion are therefore guilty of a miſtake by tranſlating it περάτης, inſtead of Ἑβραῖος. (Gen. xiv. 15.) For they introduce it as referring to an uncertain piece of hiſtory, about the *paſſage of a river*; when it is in reality an *hereditary* title.

As to thofe, who have imagined that the name of Abraham is a compound of Aber, *to paſs*; their notion is founded upon a notorious miſtake in etymology. The Patriarch had two names, which were both given prophetically, and were of high confequence; relating to great events, which in the fulnefs of time were to be accompliſhed. He was called both Abram (Ab-Ram) and Abraham; which

names

names are faid to fignify *Pater illuftris*, and *Pater multitudinis*. They were both given before he had a child, and when there was little profpect of his having fuch a progeny.

The perfon alluded to under the name of Περαιης was Heber: he was the father of the Hebrews; and they are fpoken of as his pofterity by Mofes. (Numb. xxiv. 24. Gen. x. 25.) The name of Heber, like the names of moft of the Patriarchs, was prophetically given; and it did not relate to the paffing of a river, but to a trefpafs of his pofterity. They *paffed* over from the ftock of their fathers; and dwelt upon forbidden ground, among the fons of Ham, and Chus, in Shinar, and Chaldea, where they ferved other gods. Doubtlefs the true meaning of the name Heber, was not fo much περαιης, *the paffer over*, as παραβαιης, *the tranfgreffor*; and related to this apoftafy of his family.

They were the defcendants of Shem; but refided among the enemies of the truth, to whom they had gone over. From this land Abraham was called; and brought with him his father Terah, and others of his family, who refided afterwards at Haran. (See Jofhua xxiv. 2.) As they had refided fo long in a foreign land, the facred writer feems to have been apprehenfive, that their true line might one day be miftaken; and that they might be adjudged to a wrong family. Hence he ftrongly inculcates, that Shem was *the father of all the children of Heber.* (Gen. x. 21.) Nor was this caution unneceffary; as we may perceive from their being ftyled the fons of the Semarim, and of the Chaldeans. The word Σπαρτων therefore fhould not be reprefented as a proper name; for by Σπαρτων is meant Σπεραδων; and by the hiftory we are to underftand, that they were reputed of the family of thofe perfons, who were of old *difperfed* abroad. III. 416.

SPHERE.

The Egyptians made the history of the celebrated Ogdoas the chief subject of the Sphere. This will appear very manifest in their symbolical reprefen- tation of their folar fyftem; of which Martianus Capella (Satyric. l. 2.) has tranfmitted to us a very curious fpecimen. *Ibi (in fyftemate folari) quan- dam navem totius naturæ curfibus diverfa cupidi- tate moderantem, cunctáque flammarum congefti- one pleniffimam, et beatis circumactam mercibus confpicimus: cui nautæ* septem, germani tamen fuique fimiles, *præfidebant. In eadem vero rate fons quidam lucis æthereæ, arcanifque fluoribus manans, in totius mundi lumina fundebatur.* Thus we find that they efteemed the Ark an emblem of the fyftem of the heavens. And when they began to diftinguifh the ftars in the firmament, and to reduce them to particular conftellations; there is reafon to think, that moft of the afterifms were formed with the like reference. For although the delineations of the Sphere have by the Greeks, through whom we receive them, been greatly abufed; yet there ftill remains fufficient evidence to fhew that fuch reference fubfifted. The watery fign Aquarius, and the great effufion of that ele- ment, as it is depicted in the Sphere, undoubtedly related to this hiftory. Some faid, that the perfon meant in the character of Aquarius was Ganymede. Hegefionax (Hygin. Poet. Aftron. c. 29.) main- tained that it was Deucalion, and related to the Deluge. *Eubulus autem Cecropem demonftrat effe; antiquitatem generis demonftrans, et often- dens, antequam vinum traditum fit hominibus, aqua in facrificiis deorum ufos effe: et* ante *Cecropem regnaffe, quam vinum fit inventum.* The reader may here judge, whether Cecrops, the celebrated king of Attica, who lived before the

5   plantation

plantation of the vine, and was figured under the character of Aquarius, like Deucalion, be any other than Deucalion himself, the Noah of the East.

Noah was reprefented, as we may infer from Berofus (Eufeb. Chron. p. 6.) under the femblance of a fifh by the Babylonians: and thofe reprefentations of fifhes in the fphere probably related to him and his fons. The reafons given for their being placed there were, that Venus, when fhe fled from Typhon, took the form of a fifh; and that the fifh, ftiled Notius, faved Ifis in great extremity; pro quo beneficio fimulacrum Pifcis et *ejus filiorum,* inter aftra conftituit. By this we may perceive, that Hyginus fpeaks of thefe afterifms as reprefentations of perfons: and he mentions from Eratofthenes, that the fifh Notius was the father of mankind; ex eo pifce natos homines. II. 234.

STREAMS.

All falutary ones were confecrated to the Sun. There were fome waters of this nature near Carthage, which were named Aquæ Perfianæ. They were fo named from Perez, the Sun, to whom they were facred. II. 66. n.

SUN.

The deity which the fons of Ham originally worfhiped, was the Sun. But they foon conferred his titles upon fome of their anceftors: whence arofe a mixed worfhip. They particularly deified the great Patriarch, who was the head of their line; and worfhiped him as the fountain of Light; making the Sun only an emblem of his influence and power. I. 2.

The Sun in the Perfic language is Hama. 3. n. He was worfhiped all over Syria; and one large province was hence named Curefta, and Cureftica, from Κυρ 'Εςος, Sol Heftius. I. 229.

The

The worship of the Sun was once almost uni-verfal. Examples may be found even in the great Pacific ocean, among thofe nations, with whom we have fo lately opened a communication. We are accordingly told by one of thofe, who were fent to make difcoveries in the Southern parts of the globe; that in an ifland, called Eafter ifland by the Dutch, lat. 27° S. long. from London 106° 30″ W. were found Indians of a religious caft, who worfhiped the Sun. They proftrated themfelves before two immenfe ftones, one of which was flat, and very broad; the other was erect, about ten feet high, and feven fathoms round. It was carved at the top with a man's head, and a garland; which was of mofaic, or inlaid work, and not ill performed. The name of one ftone was Dago; of the other Taurico. II. 442.

T.

TANTALUS.

Some fay, that he was fet up to his chin in water, with every kind of fruit within reach: yet hungry and thirfty as he was, he could never attain to what he wanted. But from what is faid by Pindar (Ifthm. Ode 8.) Alcæus, Alcman (Sch. in Pind. Olym. Ode 1. p. 8.) and other writers, his punifh-ment confifted in having a ftone hanging over his head; which kept him in perpetual fear. What is
                                                            called

called λιθος, was doubtlefs originally Petros; which has been mifinterpreted *a ftone.* Tantalus is termed by Euripides αχολαςος την γλωσσαν, a man of an ungovernable tongue: and his hiftory at bottom relates to a perfon, who revealed the myfteries, in which he had been initiated. The Scholiaft upon Lycophron (v. 152.) defcribes him in this light; and mentions him as a prieft, who out of good nature divulged fome fecrets of his cloifter; and was upon that account ejected from the fociety. The myfteries, which he revealed, were thofe of Ofiris, the Sun: the Petor, and Petora of Egypt. He never afterwards could behold the Sun in its meridian, but it put him in mind of his crime: and he was afraid that the vengeance of the god would overwhelm him. This deity, the Petor, and Petora of the Amonians, being by the later Greeks exprelled Petros, and Petra, gave rife to the fable about the ftone of Tantalus. To this folution the fame Scholiaft upon Pindar bears witnefs, by informing us, that the Sun was of old called *a ftone:* and that fome writers underftood the ftory of Tantalus in this light: intimating that it was the Sun, which hung over his head to his perpetual terror. I. 292.

TAPH, TUPH, TAPHOS, TOPH,

Names among the Amonians, by which they called their λοφοι, or high places. Lower Egypt being a flat, and annually overflowed, the natives were forced to raife the foil, on which they built their principal edifices, in order to fecure them from the inundation: and many of their facred towers were erected upon conical mounds of earth. But there were often hills of the fame form conftructed for religious purpofes, upon which there was no building. Thefe were very common in Egypt. Hence we read of Taphanis, or Taph-Hanes,

Taph-

Taph-Ofiris, &c. all of this country. In other parts were Taphioufa, Tape, Taphura, Tapori, Taphus, Taphofus, Taphitis. All thefe names relate to high altars, upon which they ufed often-times to offer human facrifices. Typhon was one; a compound of Tuph-On, which fignifies the hill or altar of the Sun. Tophet, where the Ifraelites made children pafs through fire to Moloch, was a mount of this form. (2 Kings, xxiii. 10. 2 Chron. xxviii. 3. See Jerem. vii. 31. xix. 5.) There was a mount named Tophel (Toph-El) near Paran upon the Red Sea. (Deut. i. 1.) Thefe cruel operations were generally performed upon mounts of this fort; which from their conical figure were named Tuph, and Tupha.

It feems to have been a name current in many countries. The high Perfian bonnet had the fame name from its fhape: and Bede (Hift. Angliæ. l. 2. c. 16.) mentions a particular kind of ftandard in his time; which was made of plumes in a globular fhape, and called in like manner, Tupha. Philo Judæus (de legibus fpecial.) fays, that the calf, worfhiped by the Ifraelites, was exhibited after the model of an Egyptian Tuphos; Αιγυπλιακου μιμημα Τυφου. This feems not to have been a Græcian word (for *fumus* or *faftus*, will not here make fenfe) but the name of a facred orbicular mount, analogous to the Touphas in Perfis.

The Amonians, when they fettled in Greece, raifed many of thefe Tupha, or Tapha in different parts. Thefe, befide their original name, were ftill farther denominated from fome title of the deity, to whofe honour they were erected. But as it was ufual in ancient times to bury perfons of diftinction under heaps of earth formed in this fafhion; thefe Tapha came to fignify tombs: and almoft all the facred mounds, raifed for religious purpofes, were looked upon as monuments of deceafed

ceafed heroes. Hence Taph-Ofiris was rendered
ταφος, or the burying place of Ofiris : and as there
were many fuch places in Egypt and Arabia, facred
to Ofiris and Dionufus, they were all by the Greeks
efteemed places of Sepulture. Through this
miftake many different nations had the honour
attributed to them of thefe deities being interred in
their country. The *tumulus* of the Latines was
miftaken in the fame manner. It was originally a
facred hillock; and was often raifed before temples,
as an altar; fuch as before defcribed. It is reprefented in this light by Virgil. (Æn. L. 2.)

Eft urbe egreffis tumulus, templumque vetuftum
Defertæ Cerevis; juxtaque antiqua cupreffus.

In procefs of time the word *tumulus* was generally
looked upon as a tomb; and *tumulo* fignified *to
bury*. The Greeks fpeak of numberlefs fepulchral
monuments, which they have thus mifinterpreted.

It does not feem credible, however blind idolatry
may have been, that people fhould enfhrine
perfons as immortal, where they had the plaineft
evidences of their mortality. If divine honours
were paid, they were the effects of time, and conferred at fome diftance ; not upon the fpot, at the
veftibule of the charnel houfe. Befides it is evident,
that moft of the deified perfonages never had ex-
iftence ; but were mere titles of the deity, the Sun;
as has been in great meafure proved by Macrobius.
Nor was there any thing of fuch detriment to ancient hiftory, as the fuppofing that the gods of the
gentile world had been natives of the countries,
where they were worfhiped. They have by thefe
means been admitted into the annals of times : and
it has been the chief ftudy of the learned to regifter
the legendary ftories concerning them; to conciliate
abfurdities, and to arrange the whole in a chronological feries. A fruitlefs labour, and inexplicable!

D d 4   for

for there are in all thefe fables fuch inconfiftences, and contradictions, as no art, nor induftry, can remedy. Hence all, who have expended their learning to this purpofe, are in oppofition to one another; and often at variance with themfelves. The greateft part of the Græcian theology arofe from mifconceptions and blunders: and the ftories concerning their gods and heroes were founded on terms mifinterpreted and abufed. Thus from the word ταφος, which they adopted in a limited fenfe, they formed a notion of their gods having been buried in every place, where there was a *tumulus* to their honour. I. 449.

Nonnus (l. 18.) makes Jupiter kill Campe: but Diodorus gives the honour to Dionufus; who is fuppofed to have flain this monfter at Zaborna in Lybia; and to have raifed over him, χωμα παμμεγεθις, *a vaft mound of earth*. This heap of foil was in reality a high place or altar; which in after times was taken for a place of burial. Thefe inclofures grew by degrees into difrepute; and the hiftory of them obfolete. In confequence of which the ταφοι, or mounds, were fuppofed to be tombs of heroes. The Græcians, who took every hiftory to themfelves, imagined that their Jupiter and Dionufus, and their Hercules had flain thefe heroes. But what they took for tombs of enemies were in reality altars to thefe very gods; who were not confined to Greece, nor were they of Græcian original. II. 54.

TARTARUS. EREBUS.

It was the prevailing opinion, that the Titans, after their war againft heaven, were banifhed to Tartarus, at the extremities of the earth. The ancient Græcians knew very little of the weftern parts of the world. They therefore reprefent the
Titans,

Titans, as in a ſtate of darkneſs; and Tartarus as an infernal region.

Theſe fictions took their riſe from true hiſtory. A large body of Titanians, after the diſperſion, ſettled in Mauritania, which is the region ſtyled Tartarus. Diodorus Siculus (l. 5. p. 334.) mentions the coming of Cronus into theſe parts; he mentions the names of ſeveral; Atlas was one of them, from whom they were named Atlantians. (l. 3. p. 189.) They were looked upon as the offspring of heaven. However the poets may have repreſented the country, he ſpeaks of it as a happy region; χωραν ευδαιμονα. The mythologiſts adjudged the Titans to the realms of night; and conſequently to a moſt uncomfortable climate; merely from not attending to the purport of the term ζοφος.

Ενθα θεοι Τιτηνες υπο Ζοφῳ ηεροεντι
Κεκρυφαται·——Heſiod. Theog. v. 729.

It is to be obſerved, that this word had two ſignifications. Firſt, it denoted the *weſt*, or place of the ſetting ſun. Hence Ulyſſes, being in a ſtate of uncertainty, ſays (Od. K. v. 190.) ου γαρ τ' ιδμεν, οπη ζοφος, ουδ' οπη ηως· *we cannot determine, which is the weſt, or which is the eaſt.* It ſignified alſo *darkneſs:* and from this ſecondary acceptation the Titans of the weſt were conſigned to the realms of night: being ſituated in reſpect to Greece towards the regions of the ſetting ſun. The vaſt unfathomable abyſs, ſpoken of by the poets, is the great Atlantic ocean; upon the borders of which Homer places the gloomy manſions, where the Titans reſided.

The ancients had a notion, that the earth was a widely-extended plain; which terminated abruptly, in a vaſt cliff of immeaſurable deſcent. At the bottom was a chaotic pool, or ocean; which was ſo far ſunk beneath the confines of the world, that, to
expreſs

exprefs the depth and diftance, they imagined, an
anvil of iron toffed from the top would not reach
it under ten days. But this mighty pool was the
ocean above-mentioned; and thefe extreme parts of
the earth were Mauritania, and Iberia: for in each
of thefe countries the Titans refided. They were
fuppofed to live (being banifhed thither) in a ftate
of darknefs beyond the limits of the known world.

— — πρσθεν δε, θεων εκλοσθεν απανλων,
Τιλνες γαιουσι περην χαεος ζοφεροιο.

(Hefiod. Theog. v. 813.) By χαος ζοφερον we muft
certainly underftand *the weftern ocean*; upon the
borders of which, and not beyond it, thefe Titanians dwelt. By the Nubian Geographer (p. 4.
p. 6. p. 156.) the Atlantic is uniformly called
according to the prefent verfion *Mare Tenebrarum.*
Aggreffi funt mare tenebrarum, quid in eo effet,
exploraturi.

Another name for Tartarus, to which the poets
condemned the Titans and Giants, was Erebus.
This, like ζοφος, was a term of twofold meaning.
For *Ereb* fignified both the *weft*, and alfo *darknefs*:
and this ferved to confirm the notion, that the
Titans were configned to the regions of night.
But gloomy as the country is defcribed, and horrid,
we may be affured from Diodorus (l. 3. p. 189.)
that it was quite the reverfe; and we have reafon to
think, that it was much reforted to; and that the
natives for a long time kept up a correfpondence
with other branches of their family. Homer (Il.
Θ. v. 477.) affords fome authority for this opinion:
and in the Ion of Euripides (v. 796.) Creufa, being in great diftrefs, wifhes, that fhe could fly
away to the people of the weftern world, which fhe
alludes to as a place of fecurity.

Αιθ' υγρον αν πλαιην αιθερα
Προσω γαιας Ἑλλανιας
Αστρας Ἑσπριους·
Ὁιον ὁιον αλγος επαθον.

From the words in Homer, and thefe of Creufa, we
may infer, that in the firft ages it was not uncommon for people in diftrefs to retire to thefe fettlements. Probably famine, ficknefs, and oppreffion,
as well as the inroads of a powerful enemy, might
oblige the Iönim to migrate. And however the
Atlantic Titanians may have been like the Cimmerians, defcribed as a people devoted to darknefs;
yet we find them otherwife defcribed by Creufa,
who ftyles them Αστρας Ἑσπριους, *the ftars of the
weftern world.* They were fo denominated from
being the offspring of the original Iönim, or Peleiadæ, of Babylonia; in memory of whom there was
a conftellation formed in the heavens. Thefe
Peleiadæ are generally fuppofed to have been the
daughters of Atlas, and by their names the ftars in
this conftellation are diftinguifhed. III. 56.

TAR, TOR, TARIT.

The firft navigators, when they traverfed unknown feas, and were liable to be entangled
among rocks and fhelves, muft have laboured under
great apprehenfions. To obviate thefe difficulties,
and to render the coaft lefs dangerous; they built
upon every hill, and promontory, where they had
either commerce or fettlement, obelifks, and towers,
which they confecrated to fome deity. Thefe
ferved in a twofold capacity; as feamarks by day,
and for beacons by night. As people then made
only coafting voyages, they continually went on
fhore with offerings, to obtain the affiftance of the
god, whoever there prefided. Thefe towers were
temples; built fometimes on artificial mounds;
but

but generally on natural eminences, that they might be the better seen. They were called by the Amonians, who first erected them, Tar, and Tor; the same as the תור of the Chaldees, which signified both a hill and a tower.

Tor-Is signifies a fire tower: hence the *turris* of the Romans; and τυρις, τυῤῥις, τυρσις, τυρσος of the Greeks: who, when the word Tor occurred in ancient history, often changed it to ταυρος, *a bull*; and invented many idle stories in consequence of this change. Tor-Ophel, or Oph-El was a temple sacred to the Ophite god Osiris; this term the Greeks rendered Ταυρσπολις. Strabo (l. 16.) says, Νησον Ικαριον, και ιερον Απολλωνος εν αυλη, και μαντειον Ταυροπολου. Here, instead of Osiris, or Mithras, the serpent deity, the author presents us with Apollo, the manager of bulls.

Gades was a principal, and most ancient settlement of the Amonians: here Geryon was supposed to have reigned. The fine harbour had many Tor, or Towers to direct shipping. As it was usual to imagine the deity to whom the temple was erected, to have been the builder, this temple was said to have been built by Hercules. The Greeks, taking every thing to themselves, attributed the whole to the hero of Thebes: and as he was supposed to conquer wherever he came, they made him subdue Geryon; and changing the Tor, or Towers, into so many head of cattle, they describe him as carrying them off in triumph.

The bulls of Colchis with which Jason was supposed to have engaged, were probably of the same nature and original. The people were Amonians; and, for the security of their trade, they erected towers at the entrance of the Phasis. These were both light-houses and temples; and were sacred to Adorus: and were called Tynador, whence the Greeks formed Tyndarus, Tyndaris, and Tyndaridæ.

They

They were built after fome, which ftood near the city Parætonium of Egypt. (v. Dionys. Per. v. 688.)

There are however fome facred towers, which were really denominated Tauri from the worfhip of the myftic bull, the fame as the Apis, and Mneuis of Egypt. Such was probably the temple of Minotaurus in Crete, where the deity was reprefented under an emblematical figure; which confifted of the body of a man with the head of a bull. In Sicily is a promontory Taurus, called alfo Tauromenium: this latter was an ancient compound, and no part of it of Græcian original. It is the fame as Menotaurium reverfed: and the figure of the deity was varied exactly in the fame manner; as is apparent from the coins and engravings which have been found in Sicily. (v. Parut. Sicil.)

Among the Hetrurians this term (Tor) feems to have been taken in a more enlarged fenfe; and to have fignified a city, or town fortified.

Lycophron (v. 1248.) mentions Ταρχων τε, και Τυρσηνος, αιθωπες λυκοι. From Tarchon there was a city and diftrict named Tarcunia; from whence came the family of Tarquins, or Tarquinii, fo well known in the Roman hiftory. The Amonians efteemed every emanation of light a fountain; and ftiled it Ain, and Aines: and as they built lighthoufes upon every ifland and infular promontory, they were in confequence of it called Aines, Agnes, Inis, Inefos, Nefos, Nees: and this will be found to obtain in many different languages and countries.

Another name for buildings of this nature was Turit, or Tirit; which fignified a tower or turret.

Torone in Macedonia fignifies litterally the Tower of the Sun: but the poets (who miftook temples for deities, and places for perfons) have formed out of it a female perfonage, and fuppofed

her

her to be the wife of Proteus. So Amphi-Tirit is merely an oracular tower: but they changed it to a female Amphitrite, and made her the wife of Neptune. Triton is a contraction of Tirit-On, the tower of the Sun: the poets have formed a deity from it, compounded of a man and a fish; this could be no other than a reprefentation of Atargatis and Dagon. Paufanias (l. 9.) mentions a tradition of a Triton near Tanagra, who ufed to moleft women, when they were bathing in the fea; and who was guilty of other acts of violence. He was at laft found upon the beach overpowered with wine; and there flain. This Triton was properly a Tritonian prieft (of a Tritonian temple; and fuch were efteemed oracular) they appear to have been very brutal, and great tyrants. This perfon had ufed the natives ill; who took advantage of him, when overpowered with liquor, and put him to death.

The term Tor in different parts of the world occurs fometimes a little varied. Whether this happened through miftake, or was introduced for facility of utterance, is uncertain. The temple of the Sun, Tor-Heres, in Phœnicia, was rendered Τριηρης; the promontory Tor-Ope-On in Caria, Triopon; Tor-Hamath in Cyprus, Trimathus; Tor-Hanes in India, Trinefia; Tor-Chom, or Chomus, in Paleftine, Tricomis. In ancient times the title of Anac was often conferred upon the deities, and their temples were ftiled Tor-Anac, and Anac-Tor; hence Anactoria, and Αναχτοϱον.

From Tor-Anac Sicily was denominated Trinacis and Trinacia; (Homer, Od. λ.) which at laft was changed to Trinacria, from a miftaken reference to the triangular fhape of the ifland; for Rhodes was called Trinacia, which was not triangular.

The

The city Τραχιν in Greece was properly Tor-Chun, turris facra vel regia, like Tarchon in Hetruria. Chun and Chon were titles, faid peculiarly to belong to Hercules: and Trachin was called Heraclea. (Hefych.)

Both the towers, and the beacons on the fea-coafts, had the name of Tor-Ain. This the Græcians changed to Τριαινα, and fuppofed it to have been a three-pronged fork. The beacon or Toraiŋ confifted of an iron or brazen frame, wherein were three or four tines, which ftood up upon a circular bafis of the fame metal. They were bound with a hoop; and had either the figures of dolphins, or elfe foliage in the intervals between them. They were thus made capable of holding combuftible matter. This inftrument was put upon a high pole, and hung floping fea-ward over the battlements of the tower, or from the ftern of a fhip; with this they could maintain either a fmoke by day, or a blaze by night. There was a place in Argos named Triaina; which was fuppofed to have been fo called from the *Trident* of Neptune; to whom it does not appear to have had any relation. It was undoubtedly a tower, called Tor-ain. It ftood near a fountain, where arofe the waters of Amumone. I. 399.

Tar, fignifying a hill or tower, is found in the compofition of many names of places; as Tarcunia, Taracena, Tarracon in Spain; Tarne (Tar-Ain) which gave name to a fountain in Lydia; Taron (Tar-On) in Mauritania.

Towers of old were either Prutaneia, or light-houfes, and were ftiled Tor-Is: thefe terms were fometimes reverfed, and the tower was called Aftur. Such a one was near fome hot fprings, not far from Cicero's Villa. The river too was called Aftura. I. 94.

TELCHINES

TELCHINES

Were fuppofed to have made their firft appearance at the time of a Deluge, which Diodorus
would confine to Rhodes; (l. 5.) and Nonnus,
(l. 24.) from fome emblematical reprefentation,
has defcribed them, as wafted over the ocean upon
feahorfes.   They are faid, under the character of
Heliadæ, to have been very famous for navigation:
and through them many ufeful arts were tranfmitted to mankind: τεχνων ευρέίας, και των εις τον βιον
χρησιμων. (Diod. l. 5.)   They were likewife the firft
introducers of idolatry; and deeply fkilled in
Magia: and we may infer from Diodorus, that
they were of the Anakim, or gigantic race, for fuch
are faid to have been the firft inhabitants of
Rhodes.

Great confufion has arifen from not confidering,
that the deity and prieft were named alike; and
that the people were often comprehended under
the fame title.   Helius was called by the Egyptians
and other people Talchan: for Tal, the Talus of
the Greeks (Suid.) fignified the Sun.   The term
Tal-chan, which the Greeks rendered Telchin,
fignified Sol Rex: and under this title he was worfhiped at Lindus in Rhodes.   His priefts alfo and
votaries were denominated in the fame manner.
Talus by Apollodorus (l. 1.) is faid to have been
the fame as Taurus.

The Telchinian, and Cabaritic rites confifted in
Arkite memorials.   They paffed from Egypt and
Syria to Phrygia and Pontus: from thence into
Thrace, and the cities of Greece.   They were
carried into Hetruria, and into the regions of the
Celtæ; and traces of them are to be obferved as
high up as the Suevi. (Tacit. de Mor. Germ.)
II. 471.

The following obſervation muſt be conſtantly remembered; that it was common among the Greeks, not only out of the titles of the deities, but out of the names of towers, and other edifices, to form perſonages, and then to invent hiſtories, to ſupport what they had done. When they had created a number of ſuch ideal beings, they tried to find out ſome relation: and thence proceeded to determine the parentage, and filiation of each, juſt as fancy directed. The truth and neceſſity of this obſervation appear under divers articles.

Some colonies from Egypt and Canaan ſettled in Thrace; and it was their cuſtom in all their ſettlements to form Puratheia; and to introduce the rites of fire, and the worſhip of the Sun. The Proteus of Egypt was a fire tower. The words Purathus and Puratheia, were in the language of Egypt Pur-Ath, and Por-Ait, formed from two titles of the god of fire. Of theſe the Græcians made a perſonage, Πρωίος, whoſe daughters, or rather prieſteſſes, were the Prætidæ; and as they held, following the Egyptians, a Cow ſacred, they were ſuppoſed to have been changed into cows. Torone was a Pharos, and ſtiled φλεγραια Τορωνη; the country was called Φλεγρα. Proteus is ſaid to have married Torone. Lycophron, v. 115.

φλεγραιας ποσις
Στυγνος Τορωνης, ᾧ γελως απεχθῆλαι,
Και δακρυ.

The epithet στυγνος implies a bad character, which aroſe from the cruel rites practiſed in theſe places. In all theſe temples, they made it a rule to ſacrifice ſtrangers, whom fortune brought in their way. Torone ſtood near Pallene, which was ſtiled

E e   Γηγενων

Γηγινων τροφος. (Lycoph. v. 127.) Under this character both the fons of Chus, and the Anakim of Egypt are included. Lycophron (124.) acquits Proteus, and makes his fons only (by whom are meant the priefts) guilty of murdering ftrangers.

These places were courts of juftice, where the priefts feem to have practifed a ftrict inquifition; and where pains and penalties were very fevere. The notion of the Furies was taken from hence. Furia is from Ph'ur, ignis, and fignifies a prieft of fire. It was on account of the cruelties here practifed, that moft of the ancient judges are reprefented as inexorable; and are therefore made judges in hell. (v. Virg. Æn. l. 6. v. 556.)

The temple at Phlegya in Bœotia was probably one of thefe courts; where juftice was partially adminiftered, and great cruelties were practifed by the priefts. Phlegyas (who was made a perfonage, Vir. Æn. l. 6. v. 618.) was in reality the Sun: fo denominated by the Æthiopes, or Cuthites; the fame as Mithras of Perfis. They confidered him as their great benefactor, and lawgiver: and introduced his worfhip among the natives of Greece.

Minos indeed is fpoken of as an upright judge: and the perfon alluded to under that character was eminently diftinguifhed for his piety, and juftice. But his priefts were efteemed far otherwife, for they were guilty of great cruelty. Minos was looked upon as a judge of hell, and ftiled Quæfitor Minos. He was in reality a deity, the fame as Menes, and Menon of Egypt; and as Manes of other countries. There was a temple in Crete called Men-Tor, the tower of Men, or Menes. The deity, from a particular hieroglyphic, was ftiled Minotaurus. To this temple the Athenians were obliged annually to fend fome of their prime youth to be facrificed; juft as the people of Carthage

thage ufed to fend their children to be victims at Tyre. (Diodor. Sic. l. 20.)

The places moft infamous for thefe cuftoms: were thofe, which were fituated upon the fea-coaft : and efpecially thofe dangerous paffes, where failors were obliged to go on fhore for affiftance, to be directed in their way. Scylla upon the coaft of Rhegium was one of thefe : and appears to have been particularly dreaded by mariners. (Homer, Od. M. 222.) There was a rock of that name, but attended with no fuch peril. (Plin. Ep. 79.) There was a temple on that eminence, and the cuftoms which prevailed therein, made it fo detefted. This temple was a Petra. Homer calls it Σκυλλη Πιlραιη; and the *Dogs*, which are faid to have furrounded her, were Cahen, or priefts.

As there was a Men-Tor in Crete, fo there was in Sicily (reverfed) a Tor-Men, and Tauromenium. There is reafon to think, that the fame cruel practices prevailed here. It ftood upon the river On-Baal, which the Greeks rendered Onoballus. From hence we may conclude, that it was one of the Cyclopian buildings.

Silenus is by Euripides (Cyclops. v. 126.) made to fay, that the moft agreeable repaft to the Cyclops was the flefh of ftrangers : no one came within his reach, upon whom he did not feed.

Γλυκυlαlα, φησι, τα κρεα τους ξενους φιφειν·
Ουδεις μολων δευρ', όςις ου καlεσφαγη.

From thefe accounts fome have been led to think, that the priefts in thefe temples did really feed upon the flefh of the perfons facrificed : and that thefe ftories did allude to a fhocking depravity ; to fuch, as one would hope, human nature could not be brought. Nothing can be more horrid, than the cruel procefs of the Cyclops, as it is reprefented by Homer. (Od. I. 389.) And though it be

veiled

veiled under the fhades of poetry, we may ftill learn the deteftation, in which thefe places were held.

One would not be very forward to ftrengthen an imputation, which difgraces human nature: yet there muft certainly have been fomething highly brutal and depraved in the character of this people, to have given rife to this defcription of foul and unnatural feeding. What muft not be concealed, Euhemerus, an ancient writer, who was a native of thefe parts, of Zancle, and whofe evidence muft neceffarily have weight, did aver, that this beftial practice once prevailed. Saturn's devouring his own children is fuppofed to allude to this cuftom. And we learn from this writer (v. Lactant. Div. Inftit. v. 1. c. 13.) that not only Saturn, but Ops, and the reft of mankind in their days, ufed to feed upon human flefh. He fpeaks of Saturn, and Ops, as of perfons, who once lived in the world, and were thus guilty. But the priefts of their temples were the people to be really accufed: the Cyclopians, Lamiæ, and Leftrygons.

It is faid of Orpheus by Horace, Cædibus, et victu fædo deterruit. But this could not be true of him; fince he enjoined the very thing, which he is fuppofed to have prohibited. See Clement. Cohort. (p. 11.) In the ifland of Chios it was a religious cuftom to tear a man limb from limb by way of facrifice to Dionufus. The fame obtained at Tenedos. Porphyry (περι αποχης. l. 2.) who was a ftaunch pagan, gives the account, and his evidence muft be of confequence. Hence we may learn one fad truth, that there is fcarce any thing fo impious and unnatural, as not at times to have prevailed.

The moft cruel rites alfo prevailed in Cyprus, which had in great meafure been peopled by per-fons of the collateral branches of Chus, and Ca-naan.

naan. One of their principal cities was Curium, from Curos (Κυρος) the Sun, to whom it was facred. Strangers, whether fhipwrecked, or otherwife dif-treffed, ufed to fly to the altar of the chief deity, Θεου φιλιου, και ξενιου, for protection. But thefe were deftroyed under an appearance of a religious rite. Whoever laid their hands upon the altar of Apollo, were caft down the precipice, upon which it ftood. (Strabo, l. 14.) A like cuftom prevailed at the Tauric Cherfonefe. (Herod. l. 4. c. 103.)

Cacus has been reprefented as a fhepherd, and the fon of Vulcan. Many ancient divinities, whofe rites and hiftory had any relation to Ur in Chaldea, are faid to have been the children of Vulcan; nay oftentimes to have been born in fire. There ftood a temple of old upon the Aventine mount in La-tium, which was the terror of the neighbourhood. The cruelties of the priefts, and their continual depredations, may be inferred from the hiftory of Cacus. Virg. Æn. l. 8.

> Hic fpelunca fuit, vafto fubmota receffu,
> Semi hominis Caci, facies quam dira tegebat,
> Solis inacceffum radiis: femperque recenti
> Cæde tepebat humus; foribufque affixa fuperbis
> Ora virûm trifti pendebant pallida tabo.
> Huic monftro Vulcanus erat pater.

As there were Lamii, and Lamiæ, fo we read of a Cacus, and a Caca. Under the character of Cacus, we have the hiftory of Cacufian priefts; a fet of people devoted to rapine and murder.

Cocytus was a temple in Egypt, called Co-Cutus; we fuppofe it to have been a river: for rivers were generally denominated from fome town, or temple near which they ran. It was the temple, or houfe of Chus; a place of inquifition, where great cruelties were exercifed. Hence the river was efteemed a river of hell; and was fuppofed to have

continual

continual cries, and lamentations refounding upon
its waters. Claudian (de Rapt. Profer. l. 1.) defcribed it as the river of tears:

> ———— preffo lacrymarum fonte refedit
> Cocytus————————. II. 1.

For a further account of Human Sacrifices, fee Mr.
BRYANT's *Obfervations upon the Ancient Hiftory of
Egypt.* p. 267.

TERAMBUS,

The deity of Egypt; who was called the Shepherd Terambus, is a compound of Tor-Ambus, or
Tor-Ambi, the oracular tower of Ham. He is
faid to have been the fon of Eufires, Ευσιρου τευ
Ποσιιδωνος, and to have come over, and fettled in
Theffaly near mount Othrys. He is alfo faid to
have been very rich in flocks; a great mufician,
and inventor of the pipe. It is fabled of him, that
he was at laft turned into a bird called Cerambis,
or Cerambix: Cerambis is Cer-Ambi, the oracular
tower of the Sun. I. 445.

THABION.

The fymbolical hiftories of the Eaftern countries
were firft compofed by a perfon ftiled the fon of
Thabion. Priefts were called the fons of the deity,
whom they ferved. He was no other than the
prieft of Theba-Iön, the Arkite Dove. II. 466.

THALASSIUS.

Among the Romans it was ufual to fcatter nuts,
and to invoke a deity, called Thalaffius. (Catull.
Epithal. Liviæ. v. 132. Livius. l. 1. c. 9.) The
Romans did not know the purport of this obfolete
name. Thalaffius was the god of the fea, the fame
as Pofeidon; the fame as Belus, and Zeus. Thalah,
according to Berofus (Eufeb. Chron. p. 6.) was
among

among the ancient Chaldeans the name of the sea. From hence came Thalatta, and Thalaffa of the Greeks; and the god Thalaffius of the Romans. II. 391.

THEBA

In Egypt was a most ancient Arkite temple : but this must be spoken with a reference to Chaldea, and Babylonia; for from that quarter the Arkite rites originally proceeded. And the principal place where they were first instituted, was probably Erech, said to be the first city founded in the world. II. 522. Theba was also one name of the Ark.

THEBOTHA.

Homer (Od. N. v. 106.) speaking of a mysterious grotto, (it stood in the harbour sacred to Phorcum) sacred to the nymphs of Ithaca, by which was meant an ancient Arkite Petra, among other cir‑ cumstances mentions,

—— ενθα δ᾽ επειτα Τιθαι Βωσσουσι Μελισσαι.

These words the commentators apply literally to *bees*. But the whole is a mystery, which probably Homer did not understand. ΘηΒωθα, from whence the strange word τιθαι Βωσσουσαι is formed, signifies the Ark. (Clem. Alex. Strom. l. 5. perhaps an old Chaldaic term.) The words relate to a temple, where the Melifsæ of Damater sang hymns in memory of the Ark Theba, called also Thebotha. II. 377.

ΘΕΟΙ ΠΑΤΡΩΟΙ.

Every oracular temple was a Petra, and Petora. Hence it proceeded that so many gods were called Θεοι Πετραιοι, and Πατρωοι· we read of Παι Ποσειδωνος Πατραιου (Pindar) Αρτεμις Πατρωα, Apollo, Bacchus, Zeus Patröus, and Vesta Patroa, &c.

The

The Greeks, whenever they met with this term, even in regions the moſt remote, always gave it an interpretation according to their own preconceptions; and explained Θεοι Πατρωοι, the oracular deities, by dii Patrii, gods of the country. Thus in the Palmyrene inſcription (Gruter. Inſcrip. lxxxiv.) two Syrian deities are characterized by this title.

ΑΓΛΙΒΩΛΩ ΚΑΙ ΜΑΛΑΧΒΗΛΩ
ΠΑΤΡΩΟΙΣ ΘΕΟΙΣ.

Cyrus in his expedition againſt the Medes made vows Εϛια Πατρωα, και Διι Πατρωω, και τοις αλλοις Θεοις. But the Perſians could not mean dii Patrii; for it would be unneceſſary to ſay of a Perſic prince, that he made vows to Perſic deities. This muſt be taken for granted, unleſs there be evidence to the contrary. His vows were made to Mithras, who was ſtiled by the eaſtern nations Pator: his temples were Patra, and Petra, and his feſtivals Patrica. I. 296.

THERMÆ.

Mount Pyrene was ſo called from being a fountain of fire: ſuch mountains often have hot ſtreams in their vicinity, which are generally of great utility. Such were in Aquitania at the foot of this mountain; they were called Thermæ Oneſæ. Oneſa ſignifies ſolis ignis, analogous to Hanes. I. 201.

THETIS.

The garment of Thetis, which the poets mention as given her upon her ſuppoſed marriage with Peleus, was a Pharos. We may learn from Catullus (Epithalam. v. 47.) who copied the ſtory, that the whole alluded to an hiſtorical picture preſerved in ſome tower: and that it referred to matters of great antiquity: though applied by the Greeks to later times, and aſcribed to people of their own nation,

nation, it contained a particular account of the Apotheofis of Ariadne: who is defcribed, whatever may be the meaning of it, as carried by Bacchus to heaven. I. 394.

THEUTH,

Thoth, Taut, Taautes, are the fame title diverfified; and belong to the chief god of Egypt. Eufebius fpeaks of him as the fame as Hermes. From Theuth the Greeks formed ΘΕΟΣ; which was their moft general name of the Deity. Plato (in Phædro) calls him Θευθ. He was looked upon as a great benefactor, and the firft cultivator of the vine. Anthologia. l. 1.

Πρωΐος Θωθ εδαη δρεπανην επι βοΐρυν αγειρειν.

He is alfo fuppofed to have found out letters; which was alfo given to Hermes. Suidas fays, that he was the fame as Arez, ftiled by the Arabians Theus Arez, Θευσαρης, and fo worfhiped at Petra. Inftead of a ftatue there was λιθος μελας, τεΐραγωνος, αΐυπωΐος. It was the fame deity, which the Germans and Celtæ worfhiped under the name of Theut-Ait, or Theutates; whofe facrifices were very cruel: Lucan. (l. 1. v. 444.)

Et quibus immitis placatur fanguine diro
Theutates.――― I. 11.

TIN

Seems to have fignified a facred place for facrifice; a kind of high altar. The Greeks generally exprefled it in compofition, Τις· hence we read of Opheltis, Altis, Baaltis, Abantis, Abfyrtis. It was in ufe among the ancient Hetrurians and other nations: hence Aventinus, Palatinus, Numantinus, &c. It feems to be the fame as Tan in the Eaft, which occurs continually in compofition, as in Indoftan,

Indoftan, Mogoliftan, Chufiftan, Pharfiftan. So
Tan-agra, Tan-is, Tyndaris. Palæftine in Canaan.
Tin in fome languages fignified *mud*, or *foil*.
I. 94.

TIRESIAS,

That ancient prophet, was no other than an
oracular tower; a compound of Tor-Ees, and Tor-
Afis; from whence the Greeks formed the name.
He was efteemed a diviner, to whom people ap-
plied for advice; but it was to the temple they
applied, and to the deity, who was there fuppofed
to refide. He is faid to have lived nine ages; till
he was at laft taken by the Epigoni, when he died.
The truth is, there was a tower of this name at
Thebes, built by the Amonians, facred to Orus.
It ftood fo long, and was then demolifhed.
Apollodorus calls him the fon of Eures (doricè
Euares) Hyginus of Eurimus; and in another
place Eurii filius, Paftor. Eurius, Eurimus,
Euarez (Uc Arez) are all names of the Sun, or
places facred to him. Tirefias is called Paftor,
becaufe all the Amonian deities, as well as their
princes, were called Shepherds: and thofe, who
came originally from Chaldea, were ftiled the
children of Ur, or Urius. I. 444.

TIT and TITH.

When towers were fituated upon eminences
fafhioned very round, they were by the Amonians
called Tith; which anfwers to τίθη, and τίθος in
Greek. They were fo denominated from their
refemblance to a woman's breaft: and were particularly facred to Orus, and Ofiris, the deities of
light, who by the Græcians were reprefented under
the title of Apollo. Hence the fummit of Parnaffus was named Tithorea from Tith-Or. Mounds
of

of this nature are often .by Paufanias, and Strabo, termed from their refemblance μαϛοειδεις.

Tithonus, is Tith-On, μαϛος ηλιου, a Pharos facred to the Sun. Tethys, the ancient goddefs of the fea, was an old tower upon a mount; it is Tith-Is, μαϛος πυρος. Thetis feems a tranfpofition of the fame name; and was probably a Pharos, or Fire-tower near the fea. I. 417.

TITÆA. TITHANA.

The·Giants, whom Abydenus makes the builders of Babel, are by other writers reprefented as the Titans. They are faid to have received their name from their mother Titæa. (Dio. Sic. l. 3. p. 190.) By which we are to underftand, that they were all denominated from their religion and place of wor-fhip. Ancient altars, which confifted of a conical hill of earth, were oftentimes ftyled λοφος μαϛοειδης, Titæa, Τιταια, was one of thefe. It is a term com-pounded of Tit-Aia; and fignifies literally *a breaft of earth*, analogous to τιθος αιας of the Greeks. Thefe altars were alfo called Tit-an, and Tit-anis, from the great fountain of light, ftyled An, and Anis. Hence many places were called Titanis and Titana, where the worfhip of the Sun prevailed. Titana was fometimes expreffed Tithana, by the Ionians Tithena: and as Titæa was fuppofed to have been the mother of the Titans; fo Tithena was faid to be their nurfe. But they were all uniformly of the fame nature, altars raifed of foil. That Tith-ana was a facred, mound of earth, is plain from Nonnus (Dionus. l. 40. p. 1048.) who mentions an altar of this fort in the vicinity of Tyre; and fays, that it was erected by thofe earth-born· people, the Giants.

.Note. Tit is analogous to Tid, of the Chaldeans. There were places named Titarefus from Tit-Ares,

8 · the

the fame as Tit-Orus. Orus was the Apollo of Greece. III. 48.

TITANS,

Τῖlανῖς, were properly Titanians; a people fo denominated from their worfhip, and from the place, where it was celebrated. They are, like Orion and the Cyclopians, reprefented as gigantic perfons; and they were of the fame race, the children of Anac. The Titanian temples were ftately edifices, erected in Chaldea, as well as in lower Egypt, upon mounds of earth, λοφοι μαροειδῖς, and facred to Hanes. Τῖlανῖς, and Τῖlανῖς, are compounds of Tit-Hanes; and fignify literally μαρος ἡλιου, the conical hill of Orus. They were by their fituation ftrong, and probably made otherwife defenfible. I. 423.

TITANIAN WAR.

The firft war of the Titans confifted in acts of apoftafy, and rebellion againft heaven: but there was another war, in which they were engaged with a different enemy, being oppofed by men; and at laft totally difcomfited after a long and bitter contention. There were two memorable occurrences, though confidered by moft writers as one fingle event: I mean, the migration of families to their feveral places of allotment; and the difperfion of the Cuthites afterwards. This war is to be diftinguifhed from both; being of ftill later date, yet not far removed from the difperfion. It was no other than the war mentioned by Mofes, which was carried on by four kings of the family of Shem, againft the fons of Ham and Chus; to avenge themfelves of thofe bitter enemies, by whom they had been greatly aggrieved. Upon the expulfion of this people from Senaar it was, that the fons of Shem got poffeffion of that city, and region: and after this fuccefs, they proceeded farther, and attacked

the

the Titanians in all their quarters. Their purpofe
was either to drive them away from the countries
which they had ufurped; or to fubdue them totally,
and reduce them to a ftate of vaffalage. They accordingly fet out with a puiffant army; and after a
difpute of fome time, they made them tributaries.
But upon their rifing in rebellion after the fpace of
thirteen years, the confederates made a frefh inroad
into their countries, *where they fmote the Rephaims
in Aflaroth Karnaïm*, who were no other than the
Titans. (See Gen. xiv. 5. 2 Sam. v. 18. Judith
xvi. 8. in the LXX. Procop. Gaz. ad l. 2. Regum.
c. 5. Mof. Chæron. l. 1. c. 5. p. 17.) Cedrenus
affures us, that there were records in Egypt, which
confirmed the account given by Mofes, concerning
thefe perfonages of fo extraordinary ftature; and
that they particularly flourifhed about the times of
Abraham and Ifaac.

The moft full account of the Titans and their
defeat, is to be found in fome of the Sibylline
poetry. The Sibyls were Amonian priefteffes; and
were poffeffed of ancient memorials, which had
been for a long time depofited in the temples
where they prefided. A great part of thofe com-
pofitions, which go under their name, is not worth
being mentioned. But there are fome things
curious; and among thefe is part of an hiftorical
poem, to which I allude. It is undoubtedly a
tranflation of an ancient record, found by fome
Græcian in an Egyptian temple; and though the
whole is not uniform, nor perhaps by the fame
hand, yet we may fee in it fome fragments of very
curious hiftory.

Αλλ' ὁποίαν μεγαλοιο Θεου τελιωνιαι απειλαι, &c.

" But when the judgments of th' almighty God
Were ripe for execution; when the Tower
Rofe to the fkies upon Affyria's plain,

And

And all mankind one language only knew:
A dread commiſſion from on high was given
To the fell whirlwinds, which with dire alarm
Beat on the Tower, and to its loweſt baſe
Shook it convuls'd.   And now all intercourſe,
By ſome occult, and overruling power,
Ceas'd among men : by utterance they ſtrove
Perplex'd and anxious to diſcloſe their mind;
But their lip fail'd them; and in lieu of words
Produc'd a painful babbling ſound : the place
Was hence call'd Babel; by th' apoſtate crew
Nam'd from th' event.   Then ſever'd far away
They ſped uncertain into realms unknown :
Thus kingdoms roſe; and the glad world was
       fill'd.
     " 'Twas the tenth age ſucceſſive, ſince the
          Flood
Ruin'd the former world; when foremoſt far
Amid the tribes of their deſcendants ſtood
Cronus, and Titan, and Jäpetus*,
Offspring of Heaven and Earth : hence in return
For their ſuperior excellence they ſhar'd
High titles, taken both from Earth and Heaven.
For they were ſurely far ſupreme; and each
Rul'd o'er his portion of the vaſſal world,
Into three parts divided : for the earth
Into three parts had been by Heaven's decree
Sever'd ; each his portion held by lot.
No feuds as yet, no deadly fray aroſe;

---

* From a common notion that Jäpetus was Japhet, this name is
aſſigned to one of the three brothers : and the two others are diſtinguiſhed by the names of Cronus, and Titan.   But they are all three
indeterminate titles.   Jäpetus was a Titanian ; and is mentioned as
ſuch by Diodorus. (l. 5.)   He was one of the brood, which was
baniſhed to Tartarus, and condemned to darkneſs. (See Homer II.
Θ. 478.)   He is alſo mentioned as an earth-born Giant; one of the
prime apoſtates in Virgil. (Georg. l. 1. 270.)   The hiſtory of
Jäpetus had no relation to Japhet.   Ιαπιλος ιις των Γιγανλων. Sch. in
Hom. ſupra,   Jäpetus was one of the Giants.

For

For the good fire with providential care
Had bound them by an oath: and each well knew
That all was done in equity, and truth.
But foon the Man of Juftice left the world,
Matur'd by time, and full of years. He died:
And his three fons, the barrier now remov'd,
Rife in defiance of all human ties,
Nor heed their plighted faith. To arms they fly,
Eager and fierce: and now their bands compleat,
Cronus and Titan join in horrid fray;
Rule the great object, and the world the prize.
  " This was the firft fad overture to blood ;
When war difclos'd its horrid front; and men
Inur'd their hands to flaughter. From that hour
The gods wrought evil to the Titan race;
They never profpered."

This Sibylline hiftory is of confequence. It has
been borrowed by fome Helleniftic Jew, or Gnoftic,
and inferted amid a deal of trafh of his own
compofing. The fuperior antiquity of the above
is plain, from its being mentioned by Jofephus.
(Antiq. l. 1. c. 4. See alfo Athenagoras. Leg.
p. 307. Thophil. ad Antol. l. 2. p. 371.) The
verfes contain a very interefting hiftory ; and are
tolerably precife, if we confider the remotenefs of
the times fpoken of. We have an accurate account
of the confufion of fpeech, the demolition of the
tower of Babel, and of the Titanian war which
enfued. And we are moreover told, that the war
commenced in the tenth generation after the
Deluge; and that it lafted ten years; and that it
was the firft war, in which mankind were engaged.
The author, whoever he may have been, feems to
allude to two quarrels. The one was with the
head of the family, and proceeded from a jealoufy
and fear, left he fhould have any more children: as
that would be a detriment in poffeffion to thofe,
whom

whom he already had. (See Sibyll. verfes. l. 3. p. 227.) Something of this nature runs through the whole of the Pagan mythology. The other quarrel began through ambition, and a defire of rule among the Titans; and terminated in their ruin. Abydenus (Eufeb. P. E. l. 19. c. 14. p. 416. See alfo Athenag. Leg. p. 315.) conformably to the account above given, mentions, that foon after the demolition of the tower commenced the war between Cronus and Titan : and that it was carried on by people of uncommon ftrength and ftature. Eupolemus alfo calls them Giants; (Eufeb. P. E. l. 9. c. 17. p. 418.) and fays, that they were fcattered over the face of the earth.

The facred writings take notice of the conclufion of the war, which ended almoft in the extirpation of fome families; efpecially of thofe, which were properly Titanian. And that this was the fame war which happened in the time of Abraham, is manifeft from its being in the tenth generation from the Deluge: for Abraham was tenth in defcent from Noah; and confequently from the Deluge. In Mofes indeed we read only of the conclufion: but the Gentile writers give a detail of the whole procedure from the beginning of the quarrel. We accordingly find, that there were three brothers, and three families; one of which was the Titanian: that they had early great jealoufies, which their father, a juft man, forefaw, would, if not prevented, become fatal. He therefore appointed to each a particular portion in the earth; and made them fwear, that they would not invade each other's right. This kept them during his lifetime in order: but after his demife, the Titans commenced hoftilities, and entered into an affociation againft the family of Shem. When they firft formed themfelves into this confederacy, they are faid to have raifed an altar: and upon this they fwore

never

never to abandon the league nor to give up their pretenfions. This altar was the work of the Cyclopians, a people who feem to have been wonderfully ingenious: and it is thought that the Chaldeans in memorial of this tranfaction inferted an altar in their ancient fphere. (Eratofthenes. After. Θυσιαςηριον. p. 14.) Some however think, that it was placed there upon another account; in memorial of the firft altar raifed after the Flood.

From the facred hiftorian we may infer, that there were two periods of this war. Hefiod (Theog. v. 629. 636.) takes notice of both. In the fecond engagement the poet informs us, that the Titans were quite difcomfited, and ruined: and, according to the mythology of the Greeks, they were condemned to refide in Tartarus, at the extremities of the known world. III. 71.

TITIUS

Is by the poets reprefented as a ftupendous being, an earth-born giant; Virg. Æn. l. 6. 595.

Terræ omniparentis alumnum,
— per tota novem cui jugera corpus
Porrigitur.

By which is meant, that he was a tower, erected upon a conical mount of earth, which ftood in an enclofure of nine acres. He is faid to have a vulture (Homer fays two) preying upon his heart, or liver. Prometheus is fabled to have had an eagle preying upon his heart. Thefe ftrange hiftories are undoubtedly taken from the fymbols and devices, which were carved upon the front of the ancient Amonian temples: and efpecially thofe of Egypt. Prometheus was worfhiped by the Colchians as a deity; and had a temple and high place, called Πέιρα Τυφαονια, upon mount Caucafus: and the device upon the portal was Egyptian, an

eagle over a heart. The magnitude of thofe perfonages was taken from the extent of the temple
inclofures. I. 425.

TORTOISE

Was admitted into the Egyptian fymbolical defcriptions: and was reprefented as the fupport of
the world. The Brahmins of India at this day
have a notion that the earth refts upon the horns of
an Ox, or Cow; which ftands upon the back of a
Tortoife. The Egyptians ufed to put this emblem
upon the fhrines of Venus. The fame goddefs was
defcribed by the people of Elis with her foot upon
the back of this animal, to denote her relation to
the Sea. II. 398.

TOURS,

A city in Gaul, called Ταυρους by Stephanus, was
the capital of the ancient Turones. It is faid to
have been named from Taurus, *a bull*, which was
an emblem of a fhip: though they fuppofe it to
have been the παρασημα of that fhip, by which the
firft colony was brought. There was a curious
piece of ancient fculpture in the fame country, of
which the Abbe Banier (Mythol. Vol. 3. B. 6.) has
given a fhort account. It was placed upon the
gate of the Hotel Dieu of Clermont, and reprefented
a Celtic divinity. It was the figure of a woman's
head with wings difplayed above; and two large
fcales arifing out of the fide of the head near the
ear. This head was encompaffed with two ferpents whofe tails were hidden beneath two wings.
Some took the head, which was fet off with a beautiful countenance, to have been that of Medufa:
others, certainly nearer the truth, of Dagon, or
Derceto. The name of the perfonage reprefented
by this hieroglyphic is faid to have been Onuava.
II. 441.

ΤΡΑΧΩΝ,

ΤΡΑΧΩΝ,

Trachon, (corrupted for Tarchon.) There were two hills of this denomination near Damafcus; from whence undoubtedly the Regio Traconitis received its name. Thefe were hills with towers; beautiful to behold. This term feems to have been ftill farther fophifticated by the Greeks, and expreffed Δρακων: from whence in great meafure arofe the notion of virgins, and treafures being guarded by fleeplefs Dragons. When the Greeks underflood that in thefe temples people worfhiped a ferpent deity, they concluded that Trachon was a ferpent; and hençe came the name of Draco to be appropriated to fuch an animal. For the Draco was an imaginary being. All the poetical accounts of heroes engaging with dragons, have arifen from a mifconception about thefe towers and temples; which thefe perfons either founded, or elfe took in war. Or if they were deities, of whom the ftory is told; thefe temples were erected to their honour. But the Greeks made no diftinction: they were fond of heroifm: and no Colony could fettle any where, and build an Ophite temple, but there was fuppofed to have been a contention between a hero and a dragon. I. 421.

TRIAD.

Cronus was certainly Noah; and Proclus gives us this covert hiftory of him; Βασιλευς Κρονος ὑποσ-αlης—της ἐσι αμηλιχlου Τριαδος. (in Plat. Timæum. l. 5. c. 10.) What fome by miftake ufed to render μηλιχος, and μηλιχιος, he has expreffed αμηλιχlος. This is a Græcian word formed from the ancient terms Melech, and Melechat, to which it had no relation. The purport of the mythology, which he copied, may be eafily made out. It fignified that Cronus, or Noah, was the founder of the Royal

F f 2   Triad.

Triad. Proclus fays, that Cronus had the title of Κορονονους; which we may be affured was originally Κοιρανος Νους. By this is fignified the *great Ruler*, the head of all; in other words the *Patriarch Noah*. As all mankind proceeded from the three great families, of which the Patriarch was the head; we find this circumftance continually alluded to by the ancient mythologifts. And the three perfons, who firft conftituted thofe families, were looked upon both as deities, and kings: fo that we may be pretty certain, that the Αμειλιχίος Τριας, however fophifticated, meant originally the *Royal Triad*.

Some very learned perfons have thought that they difcovered an allufion to a myfterious truth of another nature in the Triad of Plato, and of his followers. But if we collate, what thefe writers have added by way of explanation, we fhall, I believe, find that they had no idea of any fuch myftery; and that the whole of what they have faid is a refinement upon an ancient piece of hiftory.

Hefiod (O. et D. v. 111.) fpecifies more particularly who thefe three perfons were, and when they lived. Ὁι μεν ὑπο Κρονου ησαν: in whofe reign was the golden age, when the life of man was at its greateft extent.

Αὐίαρ επει κεν τουίο γενος καία γαια καλυψεν,
Ὁι μεν Δαιμονες εισι——
Εσθλοι, επιχθονιοι, φυλακες θνηίων ανθρωπων.

Thefe were the Βασιλεις, or Royal perfonages, of Orpheus and Plato: out of which was conftituted the αμειλιχίος Τριας of Proclus. II. 278.

TRIPOS.

Apollo, who is fuppofed by moft to have been victor in his conflict with the Pytho, is by Porphyry faid to have been flain by that ferpent. Pythagoras affirmed, that he faw his tomb at Tripos in Delphi, (Porphyr. vita Pythagoræ.) and wrote there an epitaph to his honour. The name of ·Tripos is faid to have been given to the place, becaufe the daughters of Triopus ufed to lament there the fate of Apollo. But Apollo and the Python were the fame; and Tripus and Triopus, was a variation for Tor-Opus, the Serpent-hill, or temple, where they were both worfhiped, being one and the fame deity. The daughters were the prieftefses of the temple, who chaunted hymns in memory of the Serpent. What is very remarkable, the feftival was originally held upon the feventh day. I. 464.

TROPHONIUS

Was a facred tower; being compounded of Tor-Oph-On. It was an oracular temple, fituated near a vaft cavern; and the refponfes were given by dreams. I. 444.

TYPHON.

The fable of the Mundane Egg, and of Typhon, feems to be of the fame original and purport: for Typhon fignified a Deluge. The overflowing of the Nile was called by the Egyptians Typhon. When Venus was faid to have taken the form of *a fifh*; it was in order to fly from Typhon, whom fhe is fuppofed to have efcaped, by plunging into the waters of Babylonia. (Manilii Aftron. l. 4. Ovid. Faft. l. 2.)

There was a Typhon, which fignified a high altar: but the Typhon of the prefent article fignified a mighty whirlwind and inundation; and it oftentimes denoted the Ocean; and particularly the Ocean in a ferment. For as Plutarch obferves (Is. et Os.) by Typhon was underftood any thing violent and unruly. Both were derived from Tuph; which feems here to have been the Suph of the

Hebrews.

Hebrews. (S and T are often convertible, as
Θαλασσα, θαλατ]α ; &c.) By this they denoted a
whirlwind. Euripides (Phœnissæ. v. 1170.) expresses it Tuphos :

Αταλαν]ης γονος
Τυφως συλαισιν ὡς τις εμπεσων.
τυφων, ανεμος μεγας. Hesych.

The history of Typhon is attended with some
obscurity. The Græcians have comprehended
several characters under one term, which the
Egyptians undoubtedly distinguished. The term
was used for a title, as well as a name : and several
of those personages, which had a relation to the
Deluge, were styled Typhonian, or Diluvian. The
real Deity, by whom the Deluge was brought upon
the earth, had the appellation of Typhonian ; by
which was meant Diluvii Deus. It is well known
that the Ark was constructed by a divine commis-
sion : in which God inclosed the Patriarch and his
family. Hence it is said, that Typhon made an
Ark of curious workmanship, that he might dispose
of the body of Osiris. Into which Osiris entered,
and was shut up by Typhon. (Plut. Is. et Os.) The
stay in the Ark was esteemed a state of death, and
of regeneration. The passage to life was through
the door of the Ark, which was formed in its side.
Through this the Patriarch made his descent : and
at this point was the commencement of time. This
history is obscurely alluded to in the account of
Typhon : of whom it is said, that, without any
regard to time or place, he forced a passage ; and
burst into light through the sides of his mother (the
Ark was spoken of as the Mother of mankind.) This
return to light was described as a revival from the
grave. II. 321.

U.

U CH,

EXPRESSED alfo Ach, Och, Oχα, was a term of honour among the Babylonians, and the reft of the progeny of Chus : and occurs continually in the names of men and places, which have any connection with their hiftory. The name of Ofiris feems to have been Uc-Sehor, and Uc-Sehoris. Ifiris, Ufiris, and Ofiris feem to be all Uc-Sehoris foftened, and accommodated to the ears of Greece. El-Uc, the Λυκος of the Greeks, was the name of the Sun : hence, wherever this term occurs in compofition, there will be commonly found fome reference to that deity, or to his fubftitute Apollo. e. g. Perfons, Lycorus, Lycomedes; places, Leuce, Leuca, Λυκια, Leucas, Leucate. (v. Delphi.) Near Parnaffus was a town called Lycorea, facred to the god of Light. From Lucos in this fenfe came Lux, Luceo, Lucidus, and Jupiter Lucetius, of the Latines : and Λυχνος, Λυχνια, Λυχνευω, of the Greeks : alfo Λυκαβας, and Αμφιλυκος. Hence infcriptions DEO LEUCANIÆ : which term feems to denote, Sol-Fons. Λυκοφρων, which fome would derive from Λυκος, *a wolf,* fignifies a perfon of an enlightened mind. Groves were held very facred : hence lucus, which fome would abfurdly derive a *non lucendo,* was fo named from the deity there worfhiped.

F f 4   This

This term Υκ was obsolete, and scarce known in the times when Greece most flourished. The only person who seems knowingly to have retained this word, and to have used it out of composition, is Homer. He had been in Egypt; and was an admirer of the theology of that nation. He adhered to ancient terms with a degree of enthusiasm; and introduced them at all hazards, though he many times did not know their meaning. This word he has preserved, and makes use of it adverbially in its proper sense, when he describes any one superlatively great, and excellent. It always precedes the same word, αρισος; a word borrowed from Egypt and Chaldea. (v. Comparison.)

Orpheus indeed makes use of it in the hymns ascribed to him; but they are of later date, and manifest imitations of Homer. Euripides has retained it under the term Οχος. Suppl. v. 131.

From Uc and Uch came Euge: also Ευχη, Ευχομαι, Ευχωλη.

From Uc-El came Euclea sacra; and Ευκλος Ζευς. Ευκλεια, Αρτεμις. I. 76,

VENUS.

When the Cuthite Shepherds came into Egypt, they made Memphis the seat of royal residence: and hard by was the nome of Aphrodite, and the Arabian nome, which they particularly possessed: and which in consequence of it were both stiled the regions of the Cuthim. Hence came the title of Aphrodite Chruse: this is plainly the Cuthite Venus; the deity of the Cuthim. I. 362.

A bearded Apollo was uncommon; but a Venus Barbata must have been very extraordinary: yet she is said to have been thus exhibited in Cyprus, under the name of Aphroditus. (Hesych. Servius in Virg. Æn. l. 2. v. 632.) Calvus speaks of her as masculine: pollentemque *deum* Venerem. (v.

Macrob.

Macrob. Sat. l. 3. c. 8.) ·She was looked upon as prior to Zeus, and to moſt other of the gods. I. 313.

As Venus was no other than the ancient Iönah, we ſhall find in her hiſtory numberleſs circumſtances relating to the Noachite Dove, and to the Deluge. Thus Dione or Venus is ſaid to have riſen from the ſea; to preſide over waters; to appeaſe the troubled ocean; to cauſe by her preſence an univerſal calm; that to her were owing the fruits of the earth; and that the flowers of the fields were renewed by her influence. She was the Οιναϛ of the Greeks; whence came the Venus of the Latines. The addreſs of Lucretius (l. 1. v. 1.) to this goddeſs is founded on traditions, which manifeſtly allude to the hiſtory of the Arkite Dove, and afford wonderful evidence in its favour.

Æneadum genetrix, hominum divûmque voluptas,
Alma Venus ——— ——— ——— ——— ———
Quæ mare navigerum, quæ terras frugiferentes
Concelebras; per te quoniam genus omne ani‑
     mantûm
Concipitur, viſitque exortum lumina Solis;
Te, dea, te fugiunt venti; te nubila cœli,
Adventumque tuum: tibi ſuaves dædala tellus
Submittit flores: tibi *rident æquora ponti*;
· *Pacatum*que nitet diffuſo lumine *cælum.* II. 317.

There was a city Arca in mount Libanus; from which undoubtedly Venus Architis had her name; and upon which mount ſhe had a temple. 335.

She was called Diónæa, a compound of De Iöne. 340.

She was the ſame deity as Juno under a different title. Hence in Laconia there was an ancient ſtatue ſtiled Venus Junonia. 344.

There are ſome verſes in Nonnus (l. 41.) which contain an addreſs to Venus Cuthereia, who roſe
from

from the fea; and have many allufions to the
Noachic Dove, to the new birth of the world, and
the renovation of time and feafons.

'Ριζα ϭιου Κυθερεια, φυ⁷οσπορε, μαια γενεθλης,
Ελπις ολου χοσμοιο, τεης ὑπα νευμαῖι ϭουλης,
Απλανεες κλωθουσι ϖαλυῖροπα νημαῖα Μοιραι·
Ειρομενη θεσπιζε, και ὡς ϭιοῖοιο τιθηνη,
'Ως τροφες Αθαναῖων, ὡς συγχρονος ἡλιχι χασμῳ,
Ειπε, χ. τ. λ.

We find that the thread of life had been interrupted;
but from the appearance of Venus, the Dove, it
was renewed by the Fates, and carried on as before.
370.

She was alfo called Πονῖια, Επιπονῖια, Λιμενια, Πελαγια, Αναδυομενη; alfo Ουρανια, Genetrix, Mater
Deûm, Genelillis. 318. n.

URANIA

Is derived from Ur-Ain, and fignified the Fountain of Light. I. 57.

URIA

And Oraia, however differently expreffed, fignify
literally the land of Ur. II. 178.

VULCAN.

Some writers, among whom is Gale, think him
to be Tubalcain, mentioned Gen. iv. 22. Philo
Biblius (ap. Eufebium P. E. l. 1. c. 10.) fpeaking
of Chrufor, a perfon of great antiquity, and who is
faid firft to have manufactured iron, fuppofes him
to have been Vulcan. Bochart (Geogr. Sac. l. 2.
c. 2.) derives his name from Chores Ur, an artificer in fire. Thefe learned men do not confider,
that though the name, to which they refer, be ancient, and oriental, yet the character, and attributes,
are comparatively modern, having been introduced
from

from another quarter. Vulcan the blackfmith, the mafter of the Cyclops, and who forged iron in mount Ætna, was a character familiar to the Greeks and Romans. But this deity among the Egyptians, and Babylonians, had nothing fimilar to this defcription. They efteemed Vulcan as the chief of the gods, the fame as the Sun: and his name is a facred title, compounded of Baal-Cahen, Belus fanctus, vel princeps: equivalent to Orus, or Ofiris. If the name were of a different original, yet it would be idle to feek for an etymology founded on later conceptions, and deduced from properties not originally inherent in the perfonage. According to Hermapion (Marcellinus. l. 22. c. 15.) he was looked upon as the fource of all divinity, and in confequence of it the infcription upon the portal of the temple at Heliopolis was Ἡφαιϛῳ τῳ Θεων Παℸρι. In fhort, they who firft appropriated the name of Vulcan to their deity, had no notion of his being an artificer in brafs or iron: or an artificer in any degree. Hence we muft be cautious in forming ideas of the ancient theology from the current notions of the Greeks, and Romans: and more efpecially from the defcriptions of their poets. I. 139.

The fable of Vulcan, who was thrown down from heaven, and caft into the fea, is founded upon the ftory of the overthrow of Babel, and the fuppofed perifhing of Nimrod therein.

He is faid to have been the fon of Juno, and detefted by his mother, who threw him down with her own hands. (Homer H. to Apollo. v. 317. It related probably to the abolition of Fire-worfhip at the deftruction of Babel.)

Many writers fpeak of him as being thrown off from the battlements of a high tower by Jupiter: and there is a paffage to this purpofe in Homer (Il, A. 591.) which has embarraffed commentators;

though

though I do not think it very obfcure, if we confider the hiftory to whom it relates.

Ριψε ποδος τιλαγων απο Βηλου Θεσπεσιοιο.

The poet, who was a zealous copier of ancient
mythology, mentions, that Vulcan was caft down
by Jupiter from an eminence.   He fays, that he
was thrown απο Βηλου; which muft certainly fignify
απο πυργου Βηλου, or αφ' ιερου Βηλου; for the fentence is
manifeftly elliptical.

He feiz'd him by the foot, and headlong threw
From the high tower of Belus.

This is the purport of the paffage; and it is confonant to all hiftory. III. 47.

W.

WRITERS SACRED.

THEY feem to have laid down an excellent rule,
which would have been attended with excellent
utility, had it been univerfally followed : this was,
of exhibiting every name, as it was expreffed at the
time when they wrote, and by the people, to whom
they addreffed themfelves.   If this people through
length of time did not keep up to the original etymology in their own pronunciation, it was not neceffary for the facred Penmen to maintain it in their
writings.   They wrote to be underftood : but they
would have defeated their own purpofe, if they had
called things by names, which no longer exifted.
If length of time had introduced any variations, to
thofe

thofe changes they attended, e. g. What was called Shechem by Mofes (Gen. xxxiv. 4.) is termed Σιχαρ, or Συχαρ by the Apoftle. (John iv. 5.) Quirinus, or Quirinius is Curenius, Luke ii. 2. Bethbara, Judges vii. 24. is Bethabara, John i. 28. Almug, 1 Kings x. 11. is Algum, 2 Chron. ii. 8. Ram, 1 Chron. ii. 10. is Matth. i. 5. Aram, &c. I. 58.

Z.

————————

ZODIAC.

MANY of the Conftellations are apparently of Egyptian original; and were defigned as emblems of their gods, and memorials of their rites and mythology. The Zodiac, which Sir Ifaac Newton fuppofed to relate to the Argonautic expedition, was an affemblage of Egyptian hieroglyphics. Aries, which he refers to the golden fleece, was a reprefentation of Amon; Taurus of Apis; Leo of Arez, the fame as Mithras, and Ofiris; Virgo with the fpike of corn was Ifis. They called the Zodiac the grand affembly, or fenate, of the twelve gods, εν δωδεκαλομορια Θεοι Βουλαιοι. The planets were efteemed Ῥαβδοφοροι, lictors and attendants, who waited upon the chief deity, the Sun. Thefe (the Egyptians) were the people who firft obferved the influences of the ftars; and diftinguifhed them by names: and from them they came to Greece. (Schol. in Apollon. Argon. l. 4. v. 261.) II. 483.

ZOROASTER.

ZOROASTER.

By Zoroaſter was denoted both the deity, and alſo his prieſt. It was a name conferred upon many perſonages.

Of men, ſtiled Zoroaſter, the firſt was a deified perſonage, reverenced by ſome of his poſterity, whoſe worſhip was ſtiled Magia, and the profeſſors of it Magi. His hiſtory is therefore to be looked for among the accounts tranſmitted by the ancient Babylonians, and Chaldeans. They were the firſt people ſtiled Magi; and the inſtitutors of thoſe rites, which related to Zoroaſter. From them this worſhip was imparted to the Perſians, who like-wiſe had their Magi. The Perſians were originally named Pereſians, from the deity Perez, or Parez the Sun; whom they alſo worſhiped under the title of Zor-After.

It may be worth while to conſider the primitive character, as given by different writers. He was eſteemed the firſt obſerver of the heavens; and it is ſaid that the ancient Babylonians received their knowledge of Aſtronomy from him. He was looked upon as the head of all thoſe, who are ſup-poſed to follow his inſtitutes; conſequently he muſt have been prior to the Magi, and Magia, the prieſts, and worſhip, which were derived from him. Of what antiquity they were may be learned from Ariſtotle. (Diog. Laert. procem.) *They were prior even to the Egyptians.* In his childhood he is ſaid to have been under the care of Azonaces; in proceſs of time he was greatly enriched in knowledge, and became in high repute for his piety and juſtice. He firſt ſacrificed to the gods, and taught men to do the ſame. He likewiſe inſtructed them in ſcience; and was the firſt who gave them laws. The Babylo-nians ſeem to have referred to him every thing, which by the Egyptians was attributed to Thoth
and

and Hermes. He had the title of Zarades, ·i. e. the lord of light, and is equivalent to Orus, Oromanes, and Ofiris. It was fometimes expreffed Zar-Atis, the lord of fire, and fuppofed to belong to a feminine deity of the Perfians. Mofes Chorenenfis (l. 1. c. 5.) ftiles him Zarovanus, and fpeaks of him as the father of the gods. It is faid of him that he had a renewal of life : and that whilft he was in the intermediate ftate of death, he was inftructed by the gods. Some fpeak (D. Chryfoft. Orat. Boryfth.) of his retiring to a mountain of Armenia, where he had an intercourfe with the deity : and when the mountain burned with fire, he was preferved unhurt. The place to which he retired, according to the Perfic writers, was in the region called Adarbain ; where was the greateft Puratheion in Afia. This region was in Armenia. To him has been attributed the invention of magic ; which notion has arifen from a mifapplication of terms. The Magi were priefts, and they called religion in general Magia. They, and their rites, grew into difrepute; in confequence of which they were by the Greeks called απαΐιωντς φαρμακευΐαι : but the Perfians of old, efteemed them very highly. By Zoroafter being the author of the Magia, is meant, that he was the firft promoter of religious rites, and the inftructer of men in their duty to God.

The war between Ninus and Zoroafter of Bactria relates probably to fome hoftilities carried on between the Ninivites, and the Bactrians, who had embraced the Zoroaftrian rites. Their priefts, or prince, for they were of old the fame, was named Oxuartes (Diod. Sic. l. 2.) but from his office had the title of Zoroafter; which was properly the name of the Sun, whom he adored. This religion began in Chaldea ; and it is exprefsly faid of this Bactrian king, that he borrowed the knowledge of

it

it from that country, and added to it largely; when the Perſians gained the empire in Aſia, they renewed theſe rites, and doctrines. Theſe rites were idolatrous; yet not ſo totally depraved, and groſs, as thoſe of other nations. They were introduced by Chus; at leaſt by the Cuthites; a branch of whom were the · Pereſians, or Perſians. The Cuthites of Chaldea were the original Magi, and they gave to Chus the title of Zoroaſter Magus, as being the firſt of the order. But titles were not always determinately appropriated: nor was Chus the original perſon, who was called Zoroaſter. There was another beyond him, who was the firſt deified mortal, and the *Prototype* in this worſhip.

The purport of the term Zoroaſter is by ſome ſaid to be *the living ſtar*; as if of Græcian etymology, from ζωον, and αςηρ. The latter among many nations did ſignify *a ſtar*. But by Zoro-Aſter was certainly meant Sol Aſterius. Zor, Sor, Sur, Sehor, among the Amonians always related to the Sun. In conſequence of this, we find that his temple is often called Beth-Sur, and Beth-Sura. It was alſo called Beth-Sor, and Beth-Soron.

That Suria was not a provincial title is plain from the Dea Suria being worſhiped at Eryx in Sicily; and from an inſcription to her at Rome. She was worſhiped under this title in Britain, as we may infer from an inſcription at Sir Robert Cotton's, Cambridgeſhire.

DEÆ SURIÆ
SUB CALPURNIO
LEG. AUG. &c.

The Græcians therefore were wrong in their etymology. The origin of the miſtake is eaſily traced. When they were told that Zor-Aſter was the ſame as Zoan-Aſter, they by an uniform mode

of

of miftake expreffed the latter Ζωον; and interpreted Zoroafter Αςερα Ζωον. But Zoan fignified
the Sun. Both Zor-After, and Zoan-After, fignified Sol Afterius. The Meno-Taur, and Taur-
Men, were fometimes called fimply Taurus; which
was alfo called After, and Afterius. ὁ Αςηριος ὁυίος
ςιν ὁ και Μινοίαυρος. (Lycoph. Schol. v. 1301.)
This Taur-After is exactly analogous to Zor-After.
It was the fame emblem as the Mneuis, or facred
bull of Egypt; which was defcribed with a ftar
between his horns. II. 128.

Gg   INDEX.

INDEX.

A.

AB. 1.
  Abad. 73.
Ab-Adar. 370.
Abaddir, Abadir. 1. 369.
Abaddon. 1.
Abaris. 386.
Abafa. 107.
Abilera. 1.
Abderus. 1. 155.
Ab-El. 1.
Ab-El-Eon. 1.
Abelion. 39.
Aber-Men-Ai. 287.
Abis. 2.
Ab-On, Ab-Or. 1.
Abor, Aborus, Aborras. 2.
Abraham. 88. 398. 432.
Abyla. 2. 219.
Ac-Ach. 2.
Acadamus, Academus. 3. 84.
Ac-Caph-El, Αχεφαλοι. 2.
Ach. 2.
Achad, Achon. 3. 84.
Achæans. 247.
Achar. 3.
Achar-Ain. 145.
Acharon. 4.
Αχαιμενης, Achamin. 3.
Achancherez. 5. 105.
Acharez. 5. 105.

Acheron. 3.
Acherufia. 141. 221.
Achilles. 5. 112.
Achor, Achur. 4. 145.
Achorez. 4.
Achorus. 135.
Acmon. 5. 142.
Acon. 3.
Acrifius. 6.
Acurana. 4. 145.
Ad, Ada. 6. 245.
Adad. 6. 53. 281.
Adam. 7. 101. 147.
Adama, Adamafec. 7. 147.
Adas. 6.
Adir, Addir, Adorus. 1. 2.
Ad-Ees, Adis. 7.
Adefa. 7. 168.
Ad-Ham. 7. 101. 147.
Adiona. 7. 245.
Adon. 6, 7. 117. 184. 220.
Adonians. 26.
Adonis. 6, 7. 117. 135. 184.
Ador. 182.
Adorians. 160.
Adorus. 6. 412.
Ador-San—Sol. 164.
Æacus, Æaceum. 8. 163.
Æetes. 8. 47.
Ægeon. 9.
Ægeus. 60.
Ægina. 13. 299.

Ælia

Ælia Zamana. 384.
Ænon. 9. 12. 363.
Æon. 9.
Æputus. 16.
Aeria. 61. 323.
Æsculapius. 113.
Æson. 239.
Æthiopes. 272.
Ætna. 9.
Aεθλος. 11.
Aελια. 12. 14. 177.
Æther. 10.
Agamedes. 19.
Agamemnon. 10.
Agathodæmon. 217.
Age Golden. 10.
Ager Pisanus. 41.
Agn, Αγνος. 171.
Αγων. 11.
Ai, Aia. 8. 11. 125.
Aia-Olcas. 243.
Ai-Ata, Ai-ete. 12.
Ai-Gupt. 12. 14.
Αιγυπλιοι ιθαγενεες. 162.
Ai-Mon. 12.
Aimonia. 52.
Αιμος. 12.
An, Ain. 12. 175.
Ain-Ades. 13.
Ain-Aptha 13. 38.
Ain-Ees. 9.
Aineius. 13.
Ain-El-Sham. 13. 242.
Ainesius. 13.
Aineas. 13.
Ain Moth. 214.
Ain-Omphe. 13. 197. 296.
Ain-On. 9. 171. 299.
Ain-Opus. 243.
Ain-Shemesh. 175. 387.
Air. 14.
Ait, Aith. 6.14.165.177.256.
Aith-Ain. 13.
Aithalia. 61.
Αιβαλοεν. 14.

Aith-El. 14.
Aith-On. 14.
Αιθοψ. 14. 136.
Αιθιοπες θεουδεες. 188.
Αιθωνα. 14.
Aithraia. 61.
Aithyia. 15.
Aituna. 9.
Ai-Tur. 12.
Al-As, Αλς, Αλας, Αλος. 15.
Al, El. 15. 179.
Al-Achor. 15.
Al-Al. 179.
Αλ-Αρχαιος. 53.
Alazones. 21.
Alba, Albani. 15.
Al-Cuon. 272.
Alector. 16.
Alesa, Alesium, Alesian. 16. 53.
Αλπλαι. 397.
Alexander the Great. 16. 178. 358.
Αλλαλα, Αλαλαζει, &c. 17.
Al-Laban. 15.
Allane. 213.
Almon. 17.
Al-Ompha. 18.
Al-Ompi. 300.
Alorus. 18. 179. 278. 289. 308. 387.
Al-Ourah. 18.
Alpes Cottiæ. 131. 390.
Alpes Tridentini. 236.
Alpha. 18.
Alpheus. 19.
Alphi. 18. 339.
Alphira. 19.
Alphita. 19.
Amad. 7.
Amathus. 144. 209.
Amazonians. 19. 231.
Amber, Ambrosbury. 334.
Am-Ees-Ain. 24.
Αμειλιχλος. 24. 435.

Ameleck,

Ameleck. 268.
Amida. 7. 111.
Αμιλλα. 11.
Αμμα. 240.
Ammon. 24.
Ammonites. 24.
A ron. 24. 201. 267.
Amonians. 6. 24. 103. 106.
   140. 202.
Amora. 30. 230.
Ampel. 30.
Amphi. 18. 31. 300. 339.
Amphilochus. 119.
Amphi-On. 31.
Amphictuons. 31.
Amphiprumnais. 33.
Amphi-Tirit, Amphitrite.
   32. 414.
Ampycus. 31. 40.
Amumone. 33.
Amunus. 276.
Amyclæ, Amycus. 33.
An-Ait. 13. 33. 355.
Anac. 34. 341.
Anac-Pi-Adon. 345.
Anakim. 34.
Anachus. 34. 241.
Αναγωγια. 187.
Αναχεια. 34.
Αναχίες. 34. 85.
Αναχίορια. 34. 85.
Αναχίοίελεςαι. 129.
Anaia, Anais. 188. 250. 355.
Anath. 59.
Anathoth. 84.
Anaxagoras. 34.
Anazzo. 171.
Ancients. 35.
And-Erech. 183.
Ανδροχίονοι. 20.
Andromeda. 35.
Anelon. 36. 126.
Ανεσιος. 57.
Animal. 36.
Annachus. 292.
Anopians. 36.

Anopus. 56.
Antediluvian. 36. 279.
Antiochæa. 37. 246.
Anubis, Anuphis. 119.
Aorpata. 20. 37. 331.
Apæfantus. 37.
Apamea. 37. 115.
Apaturia. 38. 57.
Ape. 37.
Apha-Aftus. 57.
Aphetæ. 356.
Αφρηίωρ. 57.
Aphrodite Chrufe. 440.
Apia. 38. 321.
Apis. 39. 44. 77. 153. 278.
Αποβαίηριον. 39.
Αποβαθμος. 39.
Apollo. 32. 38. 39. 67. 71. 80.
   110. 118. 122. 156. 208.
   217. 220. 247. 336. 426. 436.
——— Ifmenius. 80. 250.
——— Cunnius. 118.
——— Φαναιος. 337.
Apollonius Rhodius. 40.
Αποῤῥοιαι. 178.
Apha, Aphtha, Aphthas. 37.
Αφείηριοι. 38.
Aqua, whence. 396.
Aquæ { Perfianæ. } 40. 403.
     { Pifanæ. }
Aqua Perenna. 86.
Aquarius. 41. 402.
Ar. 14. 41.
Ara. 14.
Arabia. 102. 175.
Aracca. 182.
Arachna. 183.
Arachnaon. 41.
Ararat. 54. 69. 254.
Arbela. 41. 198.
Arbelus. 41.
Arca. 41. 438.
Arcades. 42. 52.
Arcadians. 42. 324.
Αρχαιοι. 52.
Arcalus.

INDEX.

Arcalus. 111.

Arcas. 6. 41. 183. 324.

Arcas-Ionah. 6.

Arcasius 6.

Archæus. 51.

Archaia. 41.

Αρχαια, Αρχαιοι, Αρχαιος, Αρχη. 52.

Αρχηγειαι. 40. 42.

Archel. 219.

Archemagoras. 42. 219.

Archemorus. 303.

Archia. 146. 344.

Archon. 62.

Arcles. 219.

Arclus. 130.

Ar-Chota. 106.

Ardeo, *whence*. 63.

Ard-Erech. 183.

Arech. 69.

Areimanius. 42.

Αρειη Αθηνη. 200.

Arelate. 53.

Aren, Arene. 43.

Arez. 43. 105. 445.

Arez-Ain. 54.

Αρης Ιππιος. 43.

Argaius. 43.

Argæi. 42.

Argeiphontai. 44.

Argo. 43.

Argoi. 52.

Argonautæ. 52. 177. 275.

Argonautic Expedition. 45.

Argos. 44. 239. 269.

Argos Hippium. 149.

Argus. 41. 44. 110.

Aribes. 310.

Aries. 445.

Arimaspians. 50. 231.

Arion. 50. 319.

Ark. 41. 50. 69. 71. 111. 280. 283. 299. 374. 382. 399. 402. 440.

Arkite deity. 51. 257.

Arkite Moon. 254.

—— rites. 183. 423.

Arkites. 52. 177. 269. 275.

Arles. 53.

Armenia. 53.

Arpe. 86.

Arpi. 54. 212.

Αρπυιαι. 54. 212.

Arsinoe. 54.

Artemis. 54. 176.

Arx. 55.

As. 55.

Asclepius. 56. 82.

As-El. 15.

Asia Proper. 56.

Asiatic { Coins. 21. 56. { Greeks. 56.

Asso, Assare, *whence*. 53.

Asopians. 56.

Asorus. 53. 188.

Assyrii. 21.

Ast, Asta. 57. 189.

Astabeni. 57. 235.

Astacana, Astacene. 58.

Astachan. 57.

Astaroth. 58. 251.

Astarte. 58. 193. 247. 251. 378.

Aster, Asterie, Asterion. 58. 328.

Αστερας Εσπεριους. 411.

Astræa. 11.

Astrachar. 144.

Astro-Caer. 58.

Astronomy, *first inventor of*. 248.

Astu. 57. 189.

Astur. 415.

Astus. Astes, 57, 189.

Atar. 59.

Atarbeck, Atarbechis, 59.

Atargatis, Atargatus. 98. 153. 378.

Atesh, Atesh-Perest. 59.

Ath, Ath-Ain. 59.

Athamas.

Athamas. 288.
Αθαν. 59.
Αθαναλοι. 59. 132. 150.
Athar. 59.
Ath-El, Αθηλα. 59.
Athemanes. 60.
Αθεμιςος. 57.
Ath-En. 60.
Αθηνα. 13. 59.
Athenians. 60. 203. 247. 272.
Athens. 57. 60.
Ath-Herm. 59.
Ath-Man, Ath-Manes. 60.
Athon. 201.
Ath-Ope, —— Opis. 190.
Athoth. 84.
Athrib. 341.
Athribites. 59.
Athyr. 61. 316.
Atis. 6. 74. 286.
Atlantians. 62.
Atlantic ocean. 409.
Atlas. 61.
Attes Hues. 304.
Attica. 62.
Αυαρις. 386.
Aub. 1. 297.
Aven. 175. 388.
Aur. 63. 351. 387.
Aurelia. 63.
Auritæ. 63. 85. 137. 176.
  217. 385.
Aza-Bel. 240.
Az-El. 314. 339.
Azaz, Aziz. 53.
Azizus. 287.
Αζομαι, Αζω, &c. whence. 53.
Azonaces. 64.
Azones. 21.
Azoni. 64.
Azon-Nakis. 64.
Azor, Azur. 53.
Azora. 64.

B.

Baal Cahen. 443.
Baaltis. 65. 92.
Baba. 133.
Babel, Babylon. 65.
Bacca. 278.
Bacchus. 66. 122. 156. 340.
  396. 399.
Bad. 73.
Badius. 67.
Bai. 67.
Baiæ. 68.
Βαιη. 67.
Βαιλυλια. 241.
Bal, Baal. 68. 285.
Baalim. 68. 132. 150. 257.
Baal-Berith. 68.
—— Hamon. 302.
—— Hermon. 211.
—— Maon. 250. 280.
—— Sameh. 69. 383.
—— Shamaim. 70.
—— Zebub. 4.
Bal-Aln. 68.
— Athis. 74.
— Bec. 68.
— Beth. 68.
Balenæ. 68.
Balnea, whence. 68.
Balsam. 69.
Bar-Chus. 399.
Baris, Barit, Barith. 50. 69.
  254. 283.
Barsanes. 69.
Barsippa. 69. 183.
Βασιλεις Ποιμανες. 342.
Bat. 73.
Battus. 70. 78. 111.
Bay. 67.
Beans eating of, why forbidden.
  195.
Bees. 70.
Bel. 70. 220.

Bela.

INDEX.

Bela. 133.

Bel-Adon, Bel-Hamon, Bel-On, Bel-Orus. 70.

Bellona. (*whence.* 70.) 251.

Belial, Beliar. 70.

Belidæ. 71. 343.

Belin. 71.

Belochus. 70.

Belus. 71. 137. 167. 289. 343.

Bendis. 71.

Berith. 69.

Beröe. 9. 69. 71.

Beroea. 73.

Berytus. 69. 71.

Befa. 81.

Befhet. 176.

Befus. 241.

Βηλαγων. 74.

Betarmus. 73.

Βἑλης. 74.

Beth. 73.

—— Anath. 13. 74.

—— Arbel. 74.

—— Aur-Eel. 74.

—— Baal-Berith. 68. 74.

—— Befa. 81.

—— Meon. 280.

—— Shemefh. 388.

Βἑλης. 74.

Bicalig, Bifehor, Bi Bifeth, Bithynia. 340.

Bochus, Bocchus. 66. 269.

Bod. 110.

Βοες Λαρινοι. 74.

Bœotus. 43. 70. 78. 111.

Bœotians. 78.

Bolathes. 74.

Boryfthenes. 149. 340.

Bofporus. 116.

Βου, Βους, Boun. 75. 76.

Βουκενlαυροι. 144.

Βουν Μνευην. 280.

Bou-Sehor. 75.

Bouta. 111.

Boutus, Boutoi. 70. 78.

Bozrah, Bofrah. 76. 169. 309.

Brenner. 76.

Βρεφοκlονος, 76.

Britain. 26. 76. 209.

Bubaftus. 340.

Bucentaur. 77.

Budha. 110.

Budo. 78. 110.

Budfo. 110.

Bulls. 76, 77. 412.

Bufiris. 75. 78.

Βυθος. 199.

Buto. 78.

Butus. 111.

Butzan. 79.

C.

Caanthus. 80. 250.

Ca-Afta-Bala, Ca-Aftor. 92.

Caballion, Caballis. 80.

Cabarni. 82.

Cabafa. 81.

Cabeira, Cabiri. 56. 81.

Ca-Cnas. 143.

Cacus. 80. 151. 421.

Ca-Cuta. 125.

Cadmaia. 116.

Cadmians. 22. 34. 61. 105. 137. 312. 390.

Cadmilus. 84.

Cadmus. 3. 80. 83. 181. 211.

Caen. 90.

Caer. 116.

Caer-Alter. 58.

Cahen. 118. 221. 284.

Cahen-Ades. 95.

Cahen-Caph-El. 120.

Cahen-On, C. Oura. 122. 121.

—— Sehor. 121. 317.

Cai,

INDEX.

Cahen-Taur. 112.
Cai, Χαι, Caia, Caias. 79.
Καιαδας. 79.
Cai-Atis. 129.
Caieta. 79. 256.
Caimin. 132.
Cait, Caiatio. 256.
Cal-Chus. 322.
Cala *in compofition.* 125.
Calcutta. 115.
Calecut. 115. 125.
Callimachus. 85.
Calpe. 85. 219.
Calypfo. 29.
Camarina. 85. 102. 140.
Cambaiar. 100.
Cam-El. 198.
Camera. 103.
Camefe, Cam-ees-ain. 86.
Cami. 109.
Cam-Il. 87.
Camillus, Camulus. 87.
  103. 179.
Caminus. 103.
Camœnæ. 86.
Campanians. 87. 106.
Campe. 86. 408.
Camphire. 87.
Campi, Campigeni. 86.
Campfa. 87.
Can-Oph, Can-Eph, C'neph.
  304.
Canaan. 87. 117. 143.
Canah. 120.
Canebro. 90.
Canis. 119. 221.
Canis Sirius. 121.
Canobus. 46.
Can-Opia. 117.
Canopus. 91.
Canothoth. 84.
Ca-Noubi. 296.
Canoubis. 81. 90.
Canoufbi. 341.
Canouphis, Canuphis. 119.

Cantharus. 120.
Can-Thoth. 80. 118.
Canufi. 110.
Ca-Ouran. 93.
Cap, Caph. 91. 120.
Capella, Capellanus. 121.
Cap-Eon. 91.
Caph-Ait,Caph-Arez,Caph-
  Aur, Caph-El. 91. 120.
Caphifus. 92. 267.
Caph-Is,Caph-Tor. 91. 276.
Capis, Ceipis. 37.
Cappadocia. 92.
Capthorim. 246. 255. 276.
Car-Chadon. 116.
Carina. 53.
Carnas. 96.
Carnëus. 40. 96.
Cartha, Carthada, Carthago.
  116. 169.
Caryftus. 144. 180.
Cafius. 114.
Caftabala. 92.
Caftor. 34. 38. 92.
Cafus. 114. 137. 241.
Καλαχασα. 370.
Catacombe. 103.
Καλαγωγια. 187.
Cathaia. 107. 310.
Cava, Cavea, Cavus. 79.
Caverns. 61. 63. 276.
Ca, Cau, Co, Coa. 198. 308.
Caucafus. 93.
Cau-Come. 136.
Caucon. 118. 162.
Καυμα, *whence.* 103.
Cauones. 93.
Cecropia Minerva. 251.
Cecrops. 61. 94. 396. 402.
Celane. 115.
Celeus. 124.
Celts. 334. 416.
Celtus. 140.
Centaurus. 51. 77. 94. 112.
Cephale, Κεφαλη. 120.
                       Cephas.

Cephas. 91.
Cephifus. 92.
Cerambis. 422.
Ceramus, Ceramicus. 94.
Ceranëus. 40.
Κερας. 96.
Ceraftis. 144.
Cerberus. 95.
Cercetus. 95.
Cercofura. 95.
Cercyon. 97.
Keren. 2. 96.
Ceres. 66. 96. 104. 129.
    146. 251. 227. 321.
Cer-Ham. 95.
Κηlωεσσα, f. Καιelωεσσα. 128.
Ceffius. 114.
Cetæans, Cetonians. 99.
Ceto. 228.
Ceuta. 114.
Ceylon. 100.
Chabar. 83.
Cha-Baren. 101.
Chabor. 53.
Χαινων. 122.
Χαλκιον. 125.
Chaldæa. 21. 101. 136.
Chalybes. 21.
Cham. 53. 103. 108.
Chamma. 103.
Chambalu. 108.
Chamus, Chumus. 102.
Chamin, Chaminim, Cham-
    marim. 103.
Chamis. 109.
Cham-Orus. 303.
Champfa. 132.
Cham-Ur. 106.
Chan. 108. 118.
Chan-Abor. 115.
——— Adon. 121.
——— Ait. 122.
——— Amon. 115.
——— Arez. 115.

Chan-Or. 115.
——— Ofiris. 317.
Chaon, Chaonia. 156.
Chaos. 199.
——— ζοφερον. 410.
Cha.Our. 81.
Χαρχηδων. 116.
Χαρις, Charis. 50. 104.
Charifius. 129.
Charmion. 179. 221.
Charon. 103. 129. 261.
Charonium. 104.
Charops, Χαροποι. 104. 261.
Charopus. 56.
Cha-Zene. 198.
Chemia. 174.
Chemmis. 105.
Chenofiris. 317.
Cheres. 105.
Chefs. 27.
Chimæra. 106.
Chin Nong. 393.
Chingis Chan. 90.
China. 19. 26. 106.
Chiniladanus. 90.
Kir-Abor. 95.
Chiron. 94. 112. 129.
Κιρρα. 135.
Χιlων. 338.
Χνα. 117. 147.
Cho, Choa. 113.
Χοιχος. 113.
Cholcians. 265.
Chom, Chum. 102. 134.
    262.
Χωμα. 408.
Chon. 394.
Chon-Or. 62.
Chonuphis. 239.
Cotha. 114.
Χρυσειοι χυνες. 122.
Χρυσος, χρυσωρ, Chrufaor,
    Chrufor. 113. 442.
Chumah. 262.

Chus.

INDEX.

Chus. 10. 102. 113. 118. 136. 448.

Χυσος. 113.

Chufiftan. 100. 114.

Kiakiack. 109.

Χιϐωλος, Cibotus. 51. 115. 195.

Cimmerians. 231. 233.

Cinaras. 115.

Cinnabar. 115.

Cinnamon. 115.

Cinnor. 115.

Κιονες κοσμου. 62.

Cippi. 116.

Circe. 29.

Kir. 116.

Kiriath. 116.

Kironia. 117.

Kiroon. 103.

Kir-Upis. 207.

Ciffia. 114.

Clufius. 238.

Cnaan. 117. 143.

Cneph. 119. 217.

Cnopia. 31. 117.

Cnoufbi. 341.

Cnuphis. 117. 119.

Kobotus. 112.

Cocutus, Cocytus. 118. 421.

Coel. 61. 123.

Cœla. 123.

Cœlus. 5. 10. 61. 123. 139.

Cohen. 90. 118.

Cohinus. 122.

Χοιλα, Coilus. 123.

Κοινος — Ἑρμης. 122.

Κοινοι Βωμοι, — Θεοι. 122.

Coins. 124. 133. 237.

Col, Cal, Calah, Calach. 125.

Colchis. 106. 125.

Col-On. 116. 125.

Colonies. 83. 382.

Colophon. 126.

Columba. 179.

Columbkil. 126.

Coma. 108. 127. 262.

Comana. 134.

Comar. 100.

Comatas. 70. 127.

Comparifons Greek, whence. 127.

Con. 90. 118.

Conah. 101. 118. 127.

Conchares. 105.

Conteft Sacred. 127.

Copti. 12.

Κορα. 321.

Corinth. 129.

Corn. 129.

Coronis. 129.

Coros. 135.

Κορονονους. 436.

Κορωνος. 360.

Corybantes. 129.

Corycian cave. 152.

Cos. 271.

Cofet. 130.

Cothon. 130.

Cothopolis. 106.

Κοθος. 130.

Cotys. 131.

Cottius. 131.

Cou-El, Covella. 123.

Couli Chan. 90.

Cow. 77. 84. 111. 278.

Crane. 2.

Cranëus. 40. 96.

Crocodile. 132.

Crodo. 269. 369.

Cronia. 368.

Κρονιδαι. 132.

Cronus. 5. 58. 129. 132. 179. 293. 316. 435.

Crows. 178. 351.

Chrufe. 95.

Cuamites. 133.

Cuamon. 133. 195.

Cubeba. 133.

Cubela, Cubele. 133. 215.

Cu-Cnaos. 143.

INDEX.

Cu-Cœl-Ops. 141.

Κυκνος. 142.

Cum. 108.

Cuma. 134.

Cun, Cunius. 39. 118. 218.

Cun-Ades. 122. 350.

Κυνες. 344.

Κυννιδαι, Κυνοδων, Κυνοδον/ες. 118. 121.

Κυνειν, *whence.* 118.

Κυνοκεφαλος, *Cunocephali.* 120. 318.

Cunofoura. 121.

Κυων. 119. 284.

Cunæthus, Cunthus. 80.

Cupher. 144.

Cupris, Cupra. 134.

Cupfelis. 134. 374.

Κυρ, Cur. 135.

Cura. 135. 321.

Kur Ain. 145.

Cur-Ait. 136.

Κυρβεις. 266.

Κυρβιας 'Αρμονιας. 210.

Curefta. 403.

Curetes. 135.

Κυρις. 135.

Curium. 421.

Curnus. 80.

Κυρος, Κυρρα, Κυρραιος. 135.

Cufcha. 80. 136.

Cufeans. 102. 114. 136. 176.

Cufhan. 136. 388:

Cufhet, Cufhitæ. 138.

Cuth, Cutha. 113, 114. 372.

Cuthaia. 107. 114. 310.

Cuthia Indica. v. *Ceylon.*

Cuthites. 100. 114. 136. 213. 231. 372.

Κυθισμος. 373.

Cybele. 133. 146. 165. 344. 353.

Κυκλωψ, Cyclopians, 26. 36. 138. 200. 221. 287. 420.

Cycnus. 142.

Cymbia. 370.

Cyprus. 144.

Cyrene. 145.

D.

Da, *Chaldaic particle.* 145.

Dabys. 110.

Δαιμονες, Dæmons. 132. 150. 257.

Dag, Dago, Dagon. 149. 252. 362. 404. 434.

Dagun. 109.

Dai, Daibod, Dai Maogin, Dainitz No. 107. 110.

Da-Jonia. 149.

Dama, Damafcus, Damafea 147.

Damater. 82. 133. 145. 215. 280. 344. 361.

Danaper. 149.

Danaus. 39. 147. 325. 362.

Danae. 6. 147.

Danaidæ. 147.

Danube. 148.

Daunia. 149.

Decani. 149.

Deified perfons. 407.

Deity. 151. (*Deities miftaken for Kings.* 336.) *fatal miftakes of the Greeks.* 417.

Delos. 151.

Delphi. 152.

Deluge. 151. 199.

Dercetidæ. 246.

Dercetis, Dercetus. 98. 153. 194. 378. 434.

Dervifes, dance of. 356.

Deucalion.

Deucalion. 153. 162. 163. 216. 292. 295.
Devices *on the front of temples.* 433.
Deus Lunus. 132. 154.
Di. 154.
Diana. 155. 353.
——— *agrestis.* 176.
——— *Erunome.* 194.
——— *Orthia.* 256.
Dictynna. 251.
Dido. 180.
Diespater. 155.
Diluvii Deus. 438.
Diodorus. 159.
Diomedes. 155.
Dione. 7. 65. 155. 441.
Dionusus. 66. 81. 109. 111. 131. 155, 156. 186. 219. 253. 326. 337. 341. 351. 391. 393. 399. 403.
Dionusia. 158. 172.
Dios. 156.
Dioscorides. 159.
Diospolis. 114.
Dis. 114. 154.
Disarez. 154.
Dithyrambic-bus. 209.
Diu. 154. 158.
Diva, Dive. 158.
Diu-Medes. 155.
Divine Wisdom. 200. 267.
Divi Potes. 154.
Dodona. 159. 216.
Dogs. (v. *Cohen.*) 212.
Door, *of the Ark.* 51. (*goddess of.* 353.) 438.
Dorians. 160. 247.
Dorsanes. 164. 218.
Dove. 134. 159. 178. 200. 245. 327. 364. 378. 441.
Dous. 154.
Draco, Dragon. 164. 435.
Δραχων. 60. 435.
Dracontia. 164. 347.

Druids. 209. 280. 334. 367.
Dura. 165.
Dus. 154.
Dusarez. 154.
Dyndamena. 134. 165.
Dyndyma. 1. 165.

E.

Eagle. 14. 165.
Eanus. 165.
Earth, *partition of.* 88. 166.
——— the ancient's notion of. 409.
Easter Island. 404.
Ebro. 170.
Exas, Exalos, Exelos. 40. 168.
Ekron. 4.
Εγχειρογαστη. 58.
Edessa. 168.
Edomites. 169.
Edonians. 131.
Ees. 170.
Ees-Ain. 171.
Eesel. 179. 275.
Egbatana. 171.
Egg Mundane. 111. 172.
Egnatia. 171.
Egypt, Egyptians. 14. 173. 177. 301. 382. 385.
Eight. 299.
Ειλειθυια επι γονασι. 240.
Eiras. 178.
El. 18. 179.
El-Ain, Elana. 213.
Ελανισμος. 214.
El-Aphas. 179.
Ελαφηβολος. 179.
El Bars. 69.
Elees. 170. 179. 180. 275.
El-Eon.

El-Eon. 261.
Ελελευ. 179.
El-Ham. 255.
Eli, Elion. 179.
ΗλιϹαλος. 180.
Ἡλιος, Ἡελιος. 114. 179.
Elis Cœla. 180.
Elifa. 116. 180.
Elizabeth. 73. 180.
Elli. 216.
Ellopia, Ellopians, Ellopis. 36. 56. 180. 183.
Elorus. 139. 179.
Elphi. 18. 339.
El-Samen. 384.
El-Uc, El-Uc-Or, El-Uc-Aon. 181. 439.
Elyſian Plain. 181.
Emblems. 282.
Emeſa. 181.
Empuria. 57.
En. v. Ain.
Encheliæ. 181.
Endor. 182.
Enneſia. 9.
Επαξιος. 40.
Eph, Epha. 193.
Epheſus. 383.
Ephialtes. 318.
Ἡρα. 210. 218.
Ereb, Erebus. v. Tartarus.
Erech. 69. 182.
Erectheus. 182. 272.
Ericthonius. 182.
Eridanus. 7. 184.
Ἑρμης. 59.
Eros. 184. 199. 354.
Erythea. 137. 169.
Erythreans. 187. 272.
Erythria. 188.
Eryx. 187.
Eſorus. 188.
Eſta, Eſtas, Eſtus, &c. 57. 188.
Eſtachar. 188. 250.
Eſtes. 189.

Ἑσια. 57. 189.
Ηθειος. 189.
Ethemon. 59. 189.
Ethiopia. 61. 136.
Ethiopians. 190.
Ethopians. 190.
Ηθος, Ηθιχα, whence. 189.
Etymology, rules concerning. 190.
Eva, Evan. 193.
Euarez. 426.
Eubœa. 137. 193.
Eudoxus. 193.
Euge, Ευχομαι, &c. whence. 440.
Euhemerus. 420.
Eumolpidæ. 193.
Eunuchs, when firſt made. 377.
Ευοι ΣαϹοι. 131. 304.
Eurimus, Eurius. 426.
Europa. 84. 193. 378.
Europians. 36.
Europus. 56. 193.
Eurunome. 194.
Ευρυοπα, whence. 194.
Eye. 26. 104.

F.

Faba Ægyptiaca. 110. 195.
Fama, Fari, whence. 339.
Fanum, whence. 195. 340.
Faraglioni. 141.
Fathers, the. 195.
Ferentum. 196.
Feriæ Latinæ, whence. 196.
Feronia. 92. 196.
Fiſhes. 403.

Fleſh,

INDEX.

Flesh, *raw eating of.* 36, 279.
Foki, Fohi. 391.
Formiæ. 256.
Fortification, *art of, introduced.* 221.
Fountains. 197.
Furies. 96. 197. 418.
Fusing of metals, *whence.* 142.

Grannus. 40.
Græcians. 121. 202. 247. 273. 290. 345. 347. 383.
Grotto. 206.
Groves. 439.
Γρυπες, Gryphons, *whence the notion of.* 207.
Gupher *wood.* 144.
Gupti. 12.

G.

Gades. 412.
Gaia. 325.
Galatæ. 140.
Games *Delian,* — *Iſthmian,* — *Nemæan,* — *Olympian.* 98.
Γαοίροχειρ. 58.
Gatus. 98.
Gau, Go. 198.
Gaugamela. 41. 198.
Gauzan, Gauzanitis. 198.
Gaza. 199. 246.
Gehon. 267.
Gentile. 199.
Γεραιςος. 200.
Γερανος. 2. 96.
Γερηνιος. 200.
Geryon. 412.
Gib, Gibeon, Gibethon. 201.
Gibel-Tar, Gibraltar. 85.
Gierat Eddahib. 95.
Giezere te. 100.
Gigonia. 335.
Giwon. 201.
Go-Carene. 53.
Gods. 201.
Gofan. 198. 242.
Goſhen. 242.
Graces. 104.

H.

Hagnes. 171.
Hagnon. 171. 208.
Haleſus. 126.
Ham. 7. 18. 30. 35. 84. 102. 114. 164. 166. 174. 208. 276. 278. 293. 302. 316. 349. 364. 400.
—— Melech. 268.
Hama. 403.
Hamad. 7.
Hamalel. 101.
Hamath. 209.
Ham-Ees. 182.
Hameles. 268.
Ham-Ourah. 285.
Hamon. 7.
Hanes. 53. 171. 188. 209. 274. 337. 340.
Har, Hara, Hor. 43. 210.
Har-al-Ompi. 300.
Haren. 89.
Hares. 104.
Harmonia. 84. 210.
Harpies. 211.
Heart. 15. 177.
Heber. 399.
Hebrew *language.* 212.
Hecate. 251. 328.

Heer,

INDEX.

Heer, Herus, Heren. 218.
Heliadæ. 64. 329.
Helice. 329.
Heliopolis. 175. 242.
Helius. 130. 136. 214. 217.
320. 371.
Hellas. 202. 212.
Hellen, Hellenus. 161. 216.
Hellenifmus. 213.
Hephaiftus, Hephaftus. 57.
299.
Hera. 217.
Heraclidæ. 161. 272.
Hercules. 5. 48. 98. 104.
218. 269. 272. 284. 304.
371. 412.
——— Summanus. 384.
Herculeans. 62.
Herm-Athena. 60.
Hermes. 73. 72. 84. 87. 209.
219, 220. 252. 341. 349.
395. 425. 447.
Hermione. 181. 221.
Hermon. 210.
Heftia. 189.
Hetruria. 12. 221.
Hierapolis. 222.
Hieroglyphics. 223.
High Places. 225.
Hippa. 157. 226.
Hipparene. 228.
Hippius. 226.
Hippocrene. 227.
Hippos. 127. 227, 228.
Hirpi. 197. 211. 229.
Hiftory. 229.
Hive. 374.
Hivites. 45. 84. 229.
Hoam Ti. 392.
Homer. 229.
Homoura. 230.
Hor. 210.
Hora, whence. 63.
Horn, 230. 261.

Horfe White. 112.
Horfes, miftakes about. 155.
226.
Hues Attes, Hyas Atis. 157.
304.
Hupereia. 85.
Hyades. 157.
Hymen. 230.
Hyperboreans. 231.
Hyrcani, Hyrcania, Hyrci-
nian foreft. 235.

J.

Jacchus. 110.
Iäch-Iäch, Jachufi. 109.
Jaboc. 236.
Jämus. 208.
Jambi, Jamphi. 208.
Ιαμϐος, whence. 208.
Jäna. 155.
Janua, whence. 238.
Januarius, whence. 238.
Janus. 151. 165. 236. 367.
Jaolcus. 243.
Ιαονες. 248.
Japan. 19. 26. 106. 225.
Japetus. 430.
Japhet. 166.
Jäs. 249.
Jafius. 235.
Jafon. 238.
Javan. 202. 248. 273.
Iberia. 170.
Ibis. 2.
Iconuphy. 239.
Idal-Baoth. 286.
Idæi Dactyli. 142.
Ideonus. 131.

Idione.

4

INDEX.

Idione. 7.
Idithyia. 15.
Idmon. 239.
Idolatry. 248.
Iënis. 242.
Ἱερον, &c. whence. 63.
Ἱερος. 41.
Jethro. 214.
Jews. 137.
Jezebel. 240.
Ignetes. 240.
Ignis. 171.
Ilithya, Ilithyia. 15. 240, 241.
Illyrius. 140.
Images. 241. 255.
Inachia. 251.
Inachus. 153. 241. 325.
Ind. 12.
Indi. 137.
Indo-Cuthites. 27. 106. 272.
Ineſſus. 9. 242.
Inis, Inys. 242.
Inneſa. 10. 242.
Ino. 221. 243.
Inopians. 36.
Inopus. 243.
Jo. 243, 246.
Jo Bacchus. 236.
Ἰωαννης. 245.
Iolcus. 243.
Iön. 217. 244. 247.
Iona. 199. 243.
Jonah, Jonas. 7. 159. 165. 244. 328. 354. 441.
Iönes. 216.
Ioneus. 157.
Ionians. 247.
Ionichus. 248.
Iönim. 21. 162. 177. 216. 246. 328. 411.
Joſeph. 90. 332.
Ἱπποβοτος, 128.
Ἱππος. (Hippos.) 127.
—— Ἀρααν. 50.

Irac. 69.
Ireland. 26. 76.
Iris. 178. 184. 251. 265.
Iſiris. 117. 249. 439.
Iſis. 146. 240. 247. 249. 251. 257. 280. 293. 314. 378. 403.
Iſlands, newly diſcovered. 26. 404.
Iſmenius. 250.
Iſraelites. 386.
Iſtachar. 188. 250.
Judæus Sparton. 398.
Juno. 123. 134. 217. 251. 353. 354.
—— Argiva. 251.
Jupiter. 208. 252. 355.
—— Lucetius. 253. 439.
—— Μειλιχιος. 268.
Ivy of Bacchus. 317.

L.

Laban. 254.
Labana, Labar, Labara. 250. 254. 260.
Lacedæmonians. 255.
Lama, Lamas. 108.
Lamiæ. 255. 420.
Language. 256. 271. 273. 326.
Laodicea. 257.
Laomedon. 48.
Lar, Laranda, Laren. 74. 257.
Lares. 150.
Larina. 257.
Laris, Lariſſa, Larinæum. 44. 257.
Λαρναξ, Larnaſſus. 51. 257.
Larunda. 257. 265.

H h   Latona.

Latona. 250.
Laurus. 258.
Leda. 173.
Lehabim. 277.
Leïtus. 258.
Leleges. 162.
Lenæ. 130.
Leo. 445.
Lesbos. 137.
Lestrygons. 420.
Letters, *when first used.* 258.
Libanus. 260.
Liber. 66. 260.
Λινοχλαινοι, Linen. 106.
Linus. 232.
Lion. 43. 261.
Λιθος. 405.
Logan, or Rocking Stones. 335.
Λοφοι. 405.
—— μασοειδεις. 261. 427.
Lotos, Lotus. 108. 215. 297.
Loves *the.* 374.
Love *divine.* 354.
Luban, Lubar. 254.
Lubentia. 255.
Lubim. 190. 277.
Λυκαβας, *whence.* 439.
Λυκαων. 181.
Lucian, *his account of the Deluge.* 294.
Lucina Ingenicula. 240.
Λυκοφρων, *whence.* 439.
Λυκος, Λυκωρευς, Lucus. 181. 439.
Λευχνος, &c. *whence.* 439.
Lud. 12.
Luna. 51. 151. 251. 263.
Lunette. 51. 111. 124. 254. 260. 270.
Lunus Architis. 254.
—— Cupido. 186.
—— Deus. 260.
Lux, Luceo, &c. *whence.* 439.
Lybia *proper.* 277.

Lycaon, Lycaones. 129.
Lycoreus, Lycorians. 152. 302.
Lycurgus. 302.
Lympha, Lymphati. 18.

M.

Ma, Mas. 263.
Macar. 263.
Macaria, Μακαρες, Μακαρονες. 264.
Macon. 263.
Macra, Macrai, Macris. 264.
Mænades. 130.
Mænalus. 324.
Magi, Magia. 264. 303. 446.
Magic. 114.
Magnetes. 115. 270.
Magog. 107. 222. 265.
Magus. 107. 264. 276. 331.
Main-Amber. 335.
Malech, Malaga. 268.
Malchom. 268.
Man. 51. 132. 265.
Mana. 275.
Maneros. 186.
Manes. 51. 150. 257. 265. 270. 418.
Maneth. 275.
Mania. 274. 319.
Man-Zan. 172. 363.
Maon. 134. 165.
Maps. 265.
Mare tenebrarum. 410.
Marriage, *institution of.* 354.
Mars. 19.
Marti Ciradino. 117.
Marus Balus. 322.
Masis. 54.
Materea. 242.

Mather,

Mather, Mathuer. 145.275.
Matutinus. 237.
Mauri. 21. 272.
Maximus Tyrius, *corrected.* 188.
Medea. 28.
Medusa. 267. 305.
Meed, Meet, Mꝏtis. 252. 267. 274.
Meen. 51. 275. 279.
Meen-Hippa. 110.
Μειλιχιος. 24. 268.
Melampus. 306.
Melas, Meles. 268.
Melech. 24. 268. 435.
Melech Pi-Adon. 345.
Melia. 80.
Melibochi. 269.
Melicartus. 269.
Melissa, Melissæ, Melitta. 70. 146. 269. 344, 345. 374.
Memphis. 269.
Mnv. 270.
Menas. 132.
Menes. 51. 172. 263. 270. 275. 279. 418.
Menæi. 275.
Meneiadæ. 270.
Menelaus. 10. 270.
Menippe. 110.
Menith. 275.
Men-Mneuas. 154.279.393.
Menoa. 317.
Menon. 270. 379 418.
Meno-Taurus. 270.
Mentor. 271. 418.
Mercury. 341.
———— *pedisſequus.* 220.
Meropes. 271.
Meſtra, Meſtræ, Meſtraia. 177. 276.
Meſtræi. 385.
Meth, Methanæ. 274.
Metroa. 131.
Mezrè. 385.

Metzor. 276.
Migdol. 276.
Mineret. 336.
Minerva. 15. 274.
Mines. 274.
Minnæi. 275.
Minoa. 199.
Minos. 279. 418.
Minotaur. 279. 413.
Minua. 17. 274.
Minyæ. 21. 42. 49. 275.
Miſor. 276.
Miſora. 174.
Mithras. 179.275.330.418. 424.
Mither. 275.
Mithur, Mithyr. 145.
Mizraim. 117. 174. 276.
Mneuis. 154. 278.
Moloch. 268.
Mœonians. 263.
Mon, Moon. 134. 165.270. 280.
Mona. 280, 281.
Monia. 274.
Monimus. 281.
Monks. 281.
Mopſus. 119.
Moſes. 214. 282. 386.
Mounds, *ſacred.* 261. 377. 405.
Mulciber. 387.
Mundane Egg. 111. 305.
Mur, Mar, Mor. 163.
Mur-Medon, Myrmidons. 163. *ſee Dorians.*
Murex. 283.
Muſagetes. 219.
Μυσαρα. 276.
Myrina. 284.
Myrrh. 285.
Myſians. 100.
Myſor. 276.
Myſteries Gentile. v. *Gentile.*

N. .

N *final.* 15. 76. 249. 257.
Nachi, Nacchi. 34.
Nahor. 89.
Naiku. 110.
Naiades. 13.
Nana. 286.
Nannachus. 241. 292.
Naos. 147. 287.
Naptha. 38.
Navel. 300.
Navis biprora. 33.
Nauplians. 287.
Naus, Nauſai. 148.287.291.
Naxos. 158.
Νεϐρος, Νεϐρωδ. 289.
Nebridæ. 287.
Necho, Necus. 34.
Nees. 413.
Negus. 34.
Neith. 287.
Νεφαλη, Nephelim. 288.
Neptune. 228. 258. 319.
Nereus. 288.
Neſos. 413.
Nnus. 148.
Nigritæ. 278.
Nieper, Nieſter. 149.
Nile, Nilus. 139. 174. 184.
  267.
Nimrod. 18. 102. 167. 289.
  308.
Ninivites. 376.
Ninus, Ninyas. 375.
Niobe. 7. 146. 290. 344.
Noa. 275.
Noachus. 241. 293.

Noah. 39. 51. 61. 77. 82.
  109. 147. 148. 150. 153.
  157. 199. 241. 245. 236.
  270. 278. 286, 287, 288.
  290. 325. 350. 352. 358.
  383. 392. 403. 435.
Noas. 291.
Noë Agathodæmon. 217.
Νομευς. 40.
Notius. 403.
Noubi. 290. 296.
Nous, Nouſis, Noor. 35.291.
  352.
Nun. 286.
Nus, Nuſa, Nuſus, Nuſos.
  157.
Nuſigenæ. 391.
Nympha. 14. 296.
Nymphæa. 297.
Nymphæum. 296.

O.

Oan, Oannes. 245. 258.
Ob. 1. 182. 297.
Obeliſk, *whence ſo called.* 304.
Obion. 298.
Oceanus, *whence.* 80. 262.
  298.
Och. Οχα. 439.
Oc-Gehon. 9. 267.
Ochuras. 4.
Οχλω. 299.
Ωδακων. 149.
Oenone. 13. 299.
Oenuphis. 239.
Og. 396.
Ogdoas. 299. 402.
Ogenus. 267.
Ogua. 396.

Ogus

Ogus. 80. 396.
Ogyges. 80.
Οιχλιςης. 40.
Oinas. 244.
Οινιαξ, Οιωνος, &c. whence. 244.
Ολκας. 243.
Olen. 204. 232.
Oliva Ori. 369.
Ολυμπος, Olympus. 300. 333.
Olympias. 303.
Omoritæ. 230.
Ompai. 302.
Ομφαλος. 300.
Omphel. 30.
Omphi, Ompi. 18. 209. 300. 332. 339.
On, Aon, Eon. 175. 242. 252. 302.
Onefa. 424.
Onium. 434.
On-Ob. 298.
Onoballus. 419.
Onuava. 434.
Ωογενης. 353.
Opas. 194. 302.
Oph. 297. 302.
Opha. 193.
Opheltes, Ophel-tin. 302.
Ophiolatria. 303.
Ophion. 307.
Ophitæ. 84. 138. 229. 305.
Ophiufa, Ophiodes. 144. 229.
Ops, Opis. 40. 50. 194. 302. 369. 420.
Opici. 347.
Opium. 307.
Opus. 194.
Or. 18.
Ora Regia. 342.
Orchomenus. 307.
Orchom-Ous. 307.
Orchon. 62.

Ωρια, Ουρεα, Ορμοι. 126.
Ορεοχωος. 307.
Organ. 308.
Oria. 442.
Orion. 289. 308.
Oritæ. 64. 309. 322.
Oro, whence. 63.
Oromanes. 446.
Oromafdes. 172.
Oropus. 56. 193.
Oropians. 36.
Orpheus. 281. 311. 420. 440.
Orphi. 18. 212. 312. 339.
Orphon. 313.
Orus. 1. 18. 63. 110. 201. 214. 250. 313, 314. 388. 426. 443. 446.
—— Adonis. 184.
Ofarfiph. 386.
Ofirians. 329.
Ofiris. 5. 8. 63. 70. 77. 84. 139. 149. 154. 156. 177. 179. 194. 215. 217. 219. 249. 252. 285. 297. 299. 313. 315. 330. 333. 336. 352. 383. 393. 396. 405. 412. 426. 438, 439. 443. 446.
Ossa. 328.
Ostracifmus. see Letters.
Oub. 40. 182. 193.
Ουθος. 297.
Ouc Cahen Cheres. 105.
———— Ouph. 239.
Oupis. 41. 302.
Our-Ain. 117. 318.
Ouran. 309.
Ουρανιωνες. 62.
Ουρανος, Ouranus. 318. 337. 387.
Ουρειν. 309. 319.
Our-chol. 219.
Ox. 278. 349.

INDEX.

P.

Pa, Paamyles. 345.
Pacorus. 344.
Pæonia. 131. 319.
Pagoda. 322.
Παιδων. 345.
Palæmon. 319.
Palæphatus. 320.
Palæſimunda. 100.
Palæſtin. 277.
Palatinus *mons.* 232.
Palm tree. 341.
Pamyles, Pamylia ſacra. 345.
Pan. 299. 320. 351.
Pappa, Pappaius, Pappus. 321.
Paraia. 321.
Parez. 329.
Parnaſſus. 257.
Partior, &c. *whence.* 396.
Parrhaſians. 42. 329.
Paſiphae. 378.
Παρθενος. 321.
Patan, Pitan. 347.
Pataneit. 287.
Pata-Ramphan. 331.
Πατηρ, Patres. 332.
Pateræ *of Q. Curtius explained.* 331.
Pator, Patora. 332. 423.
Patriarchs, *their names prophetic.* 400.
Patulcius. 237.
Πατρωοι Θεοι. 423.
Peacock. 251.
Πηχος. 399.
Pegadæ. 322.
Pegaſus. 228. 322.
Pelaſgi. 323.
Peleg. 75.

Peleiades, Peleiadæ. 7. 23. 327.
Πελειαι. 159.
Pelias. 52.
Pelion. 328.
Pella. 339.
Pelorus. 18. 138. 308.
Penates. 258.
P'Eon, Peor. 319.
Peor Apis. 351.
Περατης. 400.
Perez. 40. 329. 403. 446.
Perizites. 329.
Perſephone. 146. 321.
Perſes. 330.
Perſeus. 285. 328.
Perſians, Pereſians. 330. 446.
Peſſinuntia. 251.
Petacares. 331.
Petah. 331.
Petaliſmus. 260.
Petauriſtæ, Petauriſtarii. 357.
Petaurum. 332.
Peter, *Apoſtle.* 332.
Petiphra, Petiphera, Petiſonius, Petoſiris, Petarbemis, Petazithes Magus, Petes, Petubaſtus, Peteſuccus. 331.
Petor. 35. 405.
Petra. 138. 180. 182. 333.
Πετραι Αμβροσιαι. 333.
—— Gigonia. 335.
—— Τυφαονια. 433.
Petroma. 146.
Πετρος. 405.
Phacat, Phaccuſa. 336.
Phæmonoe. 159.
Phænon. 339.
Phaeton. 142. 336.
Φαινω, &c. 340.
Phainubeth. 337.
Φαναιοι. 337.
Phanac, Phanaces. 340.
Phanes. 186. 199. 230. 337.
Φανησια.

INDEX.

Φατσια. 274.

Pharbeth. 73. 337.

Pharoah. 339.

Pharos. 5. 211. 218. 337.

Phaſelis. 339.

Phenicia. 169.

Φημι, Φασκω, &c. whence. 339.

Phi, — Amon, — Anac, — Anes, —El, —Haroth, — Nepthim, — Ourah. 339.

Phiala. 339.

Phi-Ath-On. 337.

Phibeſeth. 340.

Philiſtim. 277.

Phinon. 274.

Phlegyas. 418.

Phœnices. 141. 341.

Phœnix. 71.

Phont. 44.

Phooley. 102.

Phor-Cun. 370.

Phoroneus. 153. 343.

Phratriai. 57.

Φρυξ. 288.

Phrygians. 273.

Ph'ur. 418.

Phut. 190. 277.

Pi, Πιζευς, &c. Pidux, &c. 344.

Pi-Ades. 345.

Pierians. 29. 131.

Pionians. 23. 346.

Pi-Or, P'Or. 344.

Pir, Phur. 354.

Pirates. 99.

Piromis, Piram Racot, Pirem Romi. 346.

Pirom-Thoth. 182.

Pireae. 346.

Pithom. 340.

Pitanates. 279.

Places, miſtaken for perſons. 103. 133. 347. 413.

Planets. 445.

Plato. 347.

Pleg, Peleg. v. Boo.

Pleione. 7. 155. 327.

Pluto. 348.

Plutonium. 104.

Poets. 348.

Ποιμνιος. 40.

Poinic. 341.

Pollux. 34. 92. 98.

Polyphemus. 139.

Polytheiſm. 350.

Pomegranate. ſee Rhoia.

Πομπη, Πομπαιος, P'ompean, P'omphi, P'ompi. 209. 349.

Πονίου Λειψανα. 82.

Poppy. 263.

Por-Ait. 417.

P'orus. 329. 344.

Poſeidon. 111. 183. 263. 350.

Præſtites. 258.

Prætidæ. 417.

Prætores. 356.

Priapus. 350.

Prieſts. 351.

Procyon. 121.

Πρωίτος. 58. 417.

Prometheus. 35. 81. 136. 153. 182. 216. 352. 433.

Proſerpina. 251. 321.

Proteus. 81. 352.

Προθυραια. 353.

Protogeneia. 216.

Protogonus. 353.

Pſuche. 354.

Puer, whence. 355.

Pul. 377.

Punicus, Puniceus. 341.

P'ur. 252. 355.

Πυρ. 344.

P'Ur-aia. 321.

Purait. 58.

Puramoun. 354.

Puratheia. 57. 355. 417.

P'urcahen. 121.

P'Urchon. 204. 350.

Πυργος. 355.

Purim.

INDEX.

Purim. 355.
Πυρου ταμειον. 97.
Purrhos, 329.
Pur-tain, P'ur-Tan. 97. 356.
P'ur-tor. 38. 356.
Pyracmon. 142.
Pyrene. 424.
Pyrrha. 51, 52. 356.
Pyrric Dance. 356.
Pythagoras. 232.
Python. 40.
Pytho Ops. 36. 436.

Q.

Quan, Quano. 108.
Quirites, whence so named. 136.

R.

Rab, Rabrab. 357.
Rainbow 178.
Ram, Rama, Ramas, Ramis. 124. 257. 358.
Ramæthan. 257.
Ram-Scander, Ramtxander. 358.
Ravens. 351. 359.
Religion. 360.
Remphan. 358.
Rephaims. 429.
Rham-Nous, Rhamnusia. 251. 358.
Rhea. 133, 134. 146. 165. 193. 215. 250. 260. 344. 353. 361. 376. 378.
Rhinocolura. 360.
Rhoia. 129. 133. 361.
Rimmon. 361.

Robe. 337.
Rocks, bare, uncouth, held sacred. 334.
Rumanhen. 361.
Rupes Ægyptiaca. 220.
Rutherforth, Dr. cited. v. Argonauts Expedition.

S.

S, prefixed. 390.
S, final. 124.
Saba. 131.
Sabacon. 90. 362.
Sabazia. 131.
Sabos. 131.
Sacæ, Sacaia. 107.
Sacrifice, human. 113. 406. see Temple Rites.
Sadyc. 81. 276.
Saidon. 362.
Saints, places dedicated to, who never existed. 360.
Sais. 248.
Saitæ. 247. 274. 363. 369.
Sal. 15. 363. 390.
Salem. 363.
Salentini. 171. 363.
Salii. 395.
Sama, Sama-Con, Sama-El. 363. 375.
Samarim. 376.
Samaritans. 364.
Sama-Sema-Ion. 379.
Samorna. 383.
Samothrace. 137.
San, Son, Zan, Zaan. 364.
San-Chus. 365.
Sancire, Sanctus, whence. 365.
Sardis, Sardes. 218.
Sanim. 364.
Sanfannah. 365.
Sanus, &c. whence. 365.
Σααν,

Σαων, Σαως. 364.

Sar, Zar, Sarah. 365.

Sar-Adon. 366.

Sar-Ait. 155.

Sar-Apis. 393.

Sardis. 366.

Sarim. 342. 366.

Sar-Iph. 305.

Sarna. 366.

Sar-On. 366.

Saronia. 155. 367,

Saronides. 367.

Satanaki. 34.

Sat-Ur, Sator. 158. 369.

Saturn. 367. 420.

Saturnalia. 368.

Satyri. 130.

Sauromatæ. 231.

Scandinavians. 370.

Scham. 384.

Scorpio. 316.

Scin. 109.

Scuphius. 128. 228.

Scyphus. 370.

Scylla. 370. 419.

Scythia. 371.

Scythæ. 100. 131. 138. 188. 265.

Σκυθισμος. 166. 373.

Seatur. 369.

Seira, Seirenes. 269. 373.

Σειριος. 384.

Selene, Σεληνη. 51. 71. 111. 124. 146. 215. 251. 254. 260. 317.

Σεληνιλαι. 42.

Selli. 216. 390.

Σημα. 363.

Samaritans. 364.

Semaramus, Semarim, Semiramis. 246. 375. 398.

Semele. 157. 375.

Σεμνος, Σεμναι Θεαι, Semon. 383.

Seran-dive. 100.

Serapis. 296. 392.

Seres. 106.

Seriphus. 305.

Septimianus. 368.

Serpent. 190. (lifting up of in the wilderneſs. 282.) 297.

—— (worſhip of. 303.)

Serpo, whence. 390.

Serpentigenæ. 60.

Scruch. 213.

Serugh. 254.

Sefoſtris. 266. 380.

Sethos, Sethofis, Sethoufis, Seconthofis. 381.

Seventh day. 437.

Sexes, not to be regarded in the Pagan deities. 92. 151.

Shaman. 54.

Shan. 398.

Shem, Shamen, Shamefh. 166. 383. 387.

Shem, Sham. 208. 428.

Shepherds. 27. 40. 63. 137. 384. 426.

Sibyls. 429.

Sibylla Cumana. 134.

Side. 361.

Sidon. 362.

Silaceni. 395.

Sileni. 130.

Silenus. 390. 419.

Σιμμα. 379.

Sindi. 107.

Sindus. 390.

Sinæ. 107.

Sin Noo, Sin Num. 391.

Siſtrum. 21.

Sifuthros. 258.

Sithonians. 131.

Σιλων. 362.

Socotra, inſula. 159.

Socrates, oath of. 394.

Sol, Sal, Salum. 15. 363, 395.

Sol Aſterius. 448.

Sol

INDEX.

Sol Hestius. 403.
Soli. 395.
Sol Pytho. 298. 302.
Solymi. 395.
Sonchin. 395.
Souchus. 132.
Souristan. 384.
Σως. 390.
Söus. 316.
Σπαρατίω. 396.
Σπαρίοι. 396.
Sparto-Hebræi. 398.
Spes Divina. 146.
Sphere. 46. 300. 359. 402. 433.
Spider. 183.
Σποραδες. 396.
Standard military. 347.
Stone Henge. 334.
Stones conical. 116. 241.
Strangers, cruel treatment of. 20. 33. 97. 101. 138. 155. 305. 375. see Temple Rites.
Streams. 403.
Στυλοι. 62. 124.
Συμβωμοι. 19.
Summus, whence. 384.
Sun. 40. 43. 93. 104. 201. 209. 220. 275. 297. 299. 321. 329. 333. 337. 344. 350. 364. 383. 403. 405. 447.
Suph. 437.
Sur. 390.
Suria dea. 378. 448.
Susiana. 100.
Swan. 14. 142. 281.
Sylva, whence. 390.
Symbols. 282.
Syn Mu. 111.
Syri. 21.
Syria, Syrian. 109. 123. 383.

T.

Talus. 416.
Talchan. 416.
Tan. 425.
Tantalus, story of, explained. 404.
Taph, Taphos, Toph, Tuph, Tapha. 127. 405. 407.
Taprobane. 101.
Tar, Tor, Tirit. 411.
Tarchon. 262. 435.
Tarquin. 413.
Tartarus. 408.
Tartarian nations. 107.
Taur-After. 449.
Taurico. 404.
Taurini. 131.
Tauro-Men. 279. 413.
Ταυροπολις, Taurus. 412. 445. 449.
Taut, Taautes. 211. 425.
Telchines. 240. 416.
Telegonus. 241.
Temples. 308.
Temples, mistaken for deities. 413.
Temple Rites. 417.
Tensio Dai Sin. 110.
Terah. 89. 254. 399.
Terambus. 422.
Τεθαιβωσσουσι, explained. 423.
Tethys. 427.
Tha, Thas. 37.
Thabion. 422.
Θαλασσα, whence. 423.
Thalassius. 422.
Thamamin. 54.
Thamus. 8. 186.
Thaumas, Θαυμαζω, &c. 185.
Theba, 110. 159. 382. 423.
Thebes. 399.

Thebotha,

INDEX.

Thebotha. 423.

Themiscir, Themiscura. 54.

Θεμισαι. 57.

Θεος, whence. 154.

—— Απομυιος. 3.

—— Γενεθλιος. 298.

—— Γενεσιος. 298.

—— Μυιαγρος. 3.

—— Προπυλαιος. 5.

—— Σωτηρ. 296.

—— Φυλαλμιος. 298.

Θεοι Δυναλοι, Μεγαλοι, Χρη-
σοι. 82. 154.

—— Βουλαιοι. 445.

—— Παλρωοι. 423.

Thermæ, Θερμαι, Θερμος,
Θερμαινω, whence. 59. 424.

Thermuthis. 117. 304.

Thessaly. 51.

Thetis. 424. 427.

Theuth, —— Arez, Theut-
Ait. 43. 348. 425.

Thon. 183.

Thonos Concoleros. 90.

Thoth. 211. 425. 446.

Thoules. 381.

Thrace. 26.

Θριαμβος. 209.

Thyades. 130. 157.

Thyone. 157.

Tibareni. 101.

Tid. 427.

Time. 229.

Tin. 425.

Tiresias. 306. 426.

Tirit, Turit. 413.

Tiryns. 58.

Tit, Tith. 426.

Titæa. 427.

Titanis. 397. 427.

Titans. 29. 88. 272. 397.
408. 427, 428.

—— War. 428.

Titaresus. 427.

Tithana. 427.

Tiθη, Tiθθος. 426.

Tithonus. 427.

Tithorea. 426.

Tithrambo. 209.

Tit-Ur. 158.

Tityri. 130.

Tityus. 433.

Tongues, confusion of, 65.

Tophel, Tophet. 406.

Tor, Tar. 411.

Tor-Ain. 33. 222. 415.

— Ambus. 422.

— Anac. 414.

— Asis. 426.

— Chom. 414.

— Caph-El. 95.

— Chares. 104.

— Chum. 415.

— Keren. 95.

— Ees. 426.

— Hamath. 414.

— Hanes. 414.

— Heres. 414.

— Is. 412.

— On.   See Torone.

— Ophel. 412.

— Ope-On. 414.

— Oph-On. 437.

— Opus. 437.

— Pator. 309.

Torone. 413. 417.

Tortoise. 434.

Tours. 434.

Τοξος. 130.

Τραχιν. 415.

Τραχων. 435.

Τρηρωνες. 159.

Triaina. 33. 415.

Triad Royal. 150. 435.

Tricomis. 414.

Trident, whence. 415.

Τρηπης. 414.

Τριχαρηνος. 95.

Τριχεφαλος. 95.

Trimathus. 414.

Trinacis,

INDEX.

Trinacis, Trinacia, Trina-
cria. 414.
Trinesia. 414.
Triopus. 437.
Τριπαΐωρ. 309.
Tripos. 436.
Triton. 222. 414.
Triumphus, *whence.* 209.
Troglodytæ. 277.
Trojans. 48. 273.
Trophonius. 10. 437.
Tshamanim. 54.
Tubalcain. 442.
Tupha, Tuphos. 406.
Τυφω, *whence.* 407.
Turditani. 30.
Turris, *whence.* Τυρις, Τυῤῥις,
Τυρσις, Τυρσος. 412.
Turones. 434.
Turzenia. 221.
Tynador. 412.
Tyndaris. 412.
Typhon. 262. 406. 437.
Tzeba Schamaim. 387.

U.

Υας. 157.
Υκ, Uch. 143. 439.
Uc-Cnas, Uc-Cnaus. 143.
Uchoreus. 4. 388.
Uch-Sehor. 78. 439.
Υκκους, Υκκουσος, Υκχουσος,
Υκσως. 389.
Uch-Ur. 135.
Υδριαι. 148.
Υδωρ. 344.
Veneti. 77.
Venus. 153. 243. 246. 403.
434. 440.
——— *Architis.* 255. 260. 441.
——— *Barbata.* 252. 440.

Venus *Cytherea.* 440.
——— *Dionæa.* 7. 155. 441.
——— *Genetilla.* 241.
——— *Junonia.* 251. 441.
——— *Lubentina.* 255.
——— *Lunaris.* 255.
——— *Paphia.* 251.
Πονⱡια, Επιπονⱡια, Λιμενια,
Πελαγια, Αναδυομενη, Ου-
ρανια, Genetrix, Mater
deûm, Genetillis. 442.
Vesta. 57. 146. 215.
——— Patroa. 423.
Vir. 354.
Virene. 346.
Virgo. 445.
Vishnou. 109.
Umbelicus. 301.
Upis. 302.
Ur. 27. 102. 168.
Ur-Adon. 184.
Urania. 117. 442.
Urchani. 63. 101.
Urchöe, Urhöe. 168.
Uria. 442.
Urius. 27. 384.
Uro, *whence.* 63.
Urphi. 18. 339.
Usiris. 439.
Vulcan. 66. 104. 297. 302.
421. 442.
Vulture. 14.

W.

Water. 298.
Wine. 27.
Wistnou. 109.
Wolf. 181.
Writers Sacred, *their excellent
rule.* 444.
Writing, *when first known.*
278.
Xixouthros.

X.

Xixouthros. 383.
Xuth. 216. 247. 383.

Z.

Zaanim. 364.
Zabians. 179.
Zam, Zama, Zamana. 384.
Zan, Zeen. 221. 242. 266.
  364. 398.
Ζαωδες. 365.
Zar. *see* Sar.
Zar-Ades, Zar-Atis. 446.
Zarovanus. 446.
Zas. 266:
Ζαψ. 240.
Zela. 33.
Ζην, Ζηνα. 364.
Zeus. 10. 24. 139. 183. 194.
  208. 220. 293. 351. 383.
—— Αιγιαιος. 209.
—— Bœotius. 79.

Zeus Casius.
—— Ευκλος. 440.
—— Ομβριος. 157.
—— Pachus. 399.
—— Pappius. 321.
—— Patrous. 423.
—— Pecus. 371.
—— Φαναιος. 337.
—— Sebazius. 131.
—— Σωτηρ. 158.
—— { Αγριος, Αροτριος, Νομιος. } 452.
Zeuth. 35. 81. 153. 159.
  216. 252.
Zoan. 87. 242. 365.
Zoan-Aster. 448.
Zodiac. 445.
Ζωειν, Ζην, Ζωον; *whence.*
  365.
Zon. 22. 64. 242.
Zona. 22. 64.
Zoni. 64.
Ζοφος. 409.
Zor, Sor, Sur, Sehor. 448.
Zoroaster, Zor-Aster. 64.
  446.
Ζωτηρ. 22.
Zuth. 28. 383.

F I N I S.

ERRATUM.

Page 257, line 18, *after* προσενιχθναι, *insert*, Larnaffus seems to be a compound of Laren-Nafos. Nees, νσος, νασος, signified of old, not only an ifland, but any hill or promontory. The Aeropolis at Thebes in Boeotia was called νσος.

.iE'

under no circur
‘om the Bn

www.ingramcontent.com/pod-product-compliance
Lightning Source LLC
LaVergne TN
LVHW012208040326
832903LV00003B/183